PAULINE FREDERICK REPORTING

PAULINE FREDERICK REPORTING

A Pioneering Broadcaster
Covers the Cold War

MARILYN S. GREENWALD

Foreword by Marlene Sanders

 POTOMAC BOOKS | *An imprint of the University of Nebraska Press*

© 2014 by Marilyn S. Greenwald

All rights reserved. Potomac
Books is an imprint of the
University of Nebraska Press.
Manufactured in the United
States of America.

Library of Congress Cataloging-
in-Publication Data

Greenwald, Marilyn S.
Pauline Frederick reporting: a
pioneering broadcaster covers the
Cold War / Marilyn S. Greenwald;
foreword by Marlene Sanders.

pages   cm

Includes bibliographical
references and index.
ISBN 978-1-61234-677-9 (cloth: alk. paper)
ISBN 978-1-61234-678-6 (pdf)
1. Frederick, Pauline. 2. Women
journalists—United States—
Biography. 3. Cold War—Press
coverage—United States. I. Title.

PN4874.F636G74 2014
070.92—dc23
2014032930

Set in Lyon by Lindsey Auten.
Designed by N. Putens.

For Tim

The pursuit of peace and progress cannot end in a few years in either victory or defeat. The pursuit of peace and progress, with its trials and its errors, its successes and its setbacks, can never be relaxed and never abandoned.

DAG HAMMARSKJÖLD

CONTENTS

PHOTOGRAPHS

FOREWORD

Marlene Sanders

Those of us who entered network news in the 1960s have been called pioneers in broadcasting. While we were few, one person was decades ahead of us: Pauline Frederick was the true groundbreaker, and she did it alone in the 1940s and 1950s.

When I started in local news in the mid-1950s, I was only dimly aware of Pauline. She reported mostly from the United Nations, and most often her voice was not heard. The men who ran the radio and television networks felt that a woman's voice was not authoritative and would not be believed. She would do the interviews, but she herself was edited out. So, her work went mostly unnoticed by people like me at that time.

Her beat, while working for ABC and later NBC, was the United Nations, not a coveted post by most reporters. It generated little news that the main media outlets considered important. There would be occasional reports on radio, but if something major happened at the UN, the main evening news anchors would "bigfoot" the beat reporter and take over the story. Pauline cared enough about international news not to worry about the lack of visibility in that job.

The cult of personality and the publicity machinery for TV anchors and correspondents came later and was too late for Pauline. Besides, she was not a flashy performer; she was serious, attractive in a conventional way, and she generated little press. The more glamorous posts of White House correspondent or anchor got the publicity. Some of us managed to enter network news in the early 1960s. But it was not until the 1970s that women began to be hired in numbers by broadcasting organizations. This was no accident. It was in direct response to those of us who organized within our news organizations as the women's movement emerged. We had been covering protests by feminist groups but had not focused on our own shops. The time had come, and women at the newspapers, magazines, and television networks organized. We wanted more women hired on air and behind the scenes, and we wanted equal pay with our male colleagues. Most of that took place in 1975—the epicenter of our activism. Pauline was not a participant in our network groups. She was by then in her sixties and nearing compulsory retirement at NBC. She was older and far removed from what her younger colleagues were up to. Twenty years earlier she had fought her own lonely battle to get where she was. Her reputation was sterling, and one would have thought that the respect she had from network executives would have spilled over and taught them that women could do the job. But this did not happen. Those of us who came after her had to fight the same battles all over again. Despite her forced retirement, her passion for international news and her talent had not diminished, and she joined National Public Radio and continued to report from the UN. And finally, Pauline was not exclusively married to her work. She actually did get married in 1969, at the age of sixty-one.

Possibly her career would have been nonexistent if she had married early in her professional life. At that time potential employers would have been even more resistant to hiring a married woman than someone young and totally devoted to the job. Even today many female reporters have chosen to remain single or, if married, childless in order to bypass the conflicts over family and work.

By the 1980s cable news had come on the scene. CNN recognized the impact of the women's movement, and its anchor hires were teams of men and women. All across broadcasting the numbers improved, but women are still a minority in the media.

Many of today's newswomen do not know about Pauline Frederick, who broke ground for the women journalists who followed her. Those of us who knew her are fortunate to have met a compassionate, charming woman as well as a superb reporter. She paved the way slowly and steadily, fighting a lonely battle, with intelligence, determination, and grace. I am grateful that her story is now being told.

ACKNOWLEDGMENTS

After several years of examining the life of Pauline Frederick, I learned a few lessons from her. One of the most important is that fulfilling any long-term commitment takes a combination of perseverance, luck, and, perhaps most important, the assistance of others. I was fortunate enough to get the help and support of many people who made it possible for me to persevere and complete this biography—librarians, archivists, friends, colleagues, and those who knew Frederick. I could not have told her story without them.

I am especially grateful to Joe Bernt, who read an old *Saturday Evening Post* profile of Frederick and forwarded it to me, suggesting that her life story could make an interesting biography. I am particularly indebted to Robert Astle and Elizabeth Demers, both of whom saw the value of Frederick's story and who, literally, made the book possible.

I also want to recognize the continual support of my friends and colleagues Doug Daniel, Tom Mascaro, and Pat Washburn, who offered guidance about organizing the vast amount of material available to me; and Fred Heintz and Nancy Lewis, longtime friends who shared my excitement about this project. I am also indebted to Bob Stewart and other colleagues at the E. W. Scripps School of Journalism for their encouragement and to my research assistants, Audrey Bonfig and Nick Hirshon, for their help with the sometimes tedious work that is a part of a project such as this one. Financial support from the Ohio University Research Committee made it possible for me to visit the archives that housed material associated with this biography.

Because Pauline Frederick has been gone for nearly twenty-five years, having access to the papers she and others left behind was crucial in telling her story. I offer thanks to the many librarians and archivists with whom I worked. The archivists at the Sophia Smith Collection at Smith College—Amy Hague, Karen Kukil, and others—were enormously hospitable and helpful to me during many visits there. Also, Michael Henry at the Library of American Broadcasting at the University of Maryland went out of his way to help me gather and sort original materials related to the history of women in broadcasting. Thank you, too, to the staff at the Library of Congress in Washington DC, which houses the NBC History files; to the United Nations staff that compiled the extensive communications website of that organization; and to librarians at American University, Frederick's alma mater.

But documents cannot tell the whole story. I am very grateful to Frederick's only surviving relatives: her niece Catharine Cole and Catharine's husband, Dan. They spoke candidly to me about Frederick and recalled in great detail important events and interesting anecdotes that painted for me a true picture of Frederick. They opened up their home to me and put no restrictions on the use of any material. I very much appreciate their generosity and their insights.

Similarly, Frederick's husband's son and former daughter-in-law, Dick Robbins and Ann Stevens, were very open in sharing their recollections as well as photos of Frederick's "extended" family.

Thank you, too, to Marlene Sanders, another pioneering broadcaster, for sharing with me her thoughts about Frederick and reflecting on the struggles and rewards of being a trailblazer. Her book, *Waiting for Primetime*, written with Marcia Rock, was pivotal to me in understanding broadcasting history and women's role in that history.

For me to "know" Frederick, I attempted to get an idea of the environment in which she worked. Her former colleagues Robert Asman, Charles Coates, Brian Urquhart, Garrick Utley, Richard Valeriani, and Bob Zelnick assisted me greatly in that task, and I thank them for their time and candor.

And to my husband (and editor), Tim Doulin, who remained cheerful as he shared a home for a long time with me and Pauline Frederick. Thank you for many years of love, support, and encouragement.

INTRODUCTION

In the early 1960s, during what many consider the golden age of network news, portraits of NBC's most respected and high-profile correspondents lined the hallway of the fifth floor of 30 Rockefeller Center. A small but distinguished fraternity that included David Brinkley, John Chancellor, Chet Huntley, and Edwin Newman, these were the gatekeepers who delivered the news to a worried nation—correspondents for the top-rated network whom the public relied on to ferret out details of the pivotal events of the era. Known as "Murderers' Row" by NBC producers, this distinguished group was assigned to report and interpret the news; they were indirectly charged with informing citizens about what they should and should not fear in an era when Americans first began to realize that nuclear war was a real possibility. The public trusted them to translate and explain events that could affect their very existence.

To many viewers these correspondents were celebrities and household names. They received fan letters, lecture invitations, and even gifts. It is likely, however, that only one member of Murderers' Row received what one grateful citizen considered a thoughtful yet practical present: a pair of panty hose.

To Pauline Frederick, longtime Murderers' Row member, the gift was taken with a grain of salt. The only female network correspondent for more than ten years, she was accustomed to being the only woman in the room—whether that room was the NBC newsroom, the United Nations General Assembly hall, or the tiny quarters of a troop ship. Despite an increasing emphasis in society on equality of the sexes in the mid-twentieth century, she was still the only network correspondent who had to make sure the curlers were out of her hair before she dashed off to deliver a special news report. Still, the fact that Frederick was the first female network reporter does not necessarily mean that she merits special attention; what is noteworthy, however, is that she was the only full-time network reporter for so long—she began reporting full-time in the late 1940s, but it was a decade before another woman reporter, Nancy Dickerson, joined a news network and even longer before another small group that included Marlene Sanders, Liz Trotta, and a few others joined them.

Her role as the only woman in a male-dominated field meant that Pauline Frederick had to tread lightly, and she had to tread lightly for a very long time. If she used a heavy hand, she could lose her job as well as jeopardize the hiring of other women who hoped to follow her. So, Frederick had to engage in a series of balancing acts. She had to look attractive and well put together but refrain from being too glamorous or sexy because that could intimidate her bosses and viewers; she had to stand up for herself and defend criticism leveled against her, but she could not be seen as too shrill or argumentative; and she had to promote her achievements and abilities while refraining from behavior that could be perceived as pushy or aggressive. And while on the job, she had to be willing to question authority and shaky information without appearing cynical or bitter.

It was quite a task for a girl from Gallitzin, Pennsylvania, who was the daughter of a postmaster and a homemaker. But even in the early 1920s, when she was growing up, Frederick straddled two worlds: she was an overachieving student, a debate champion, and a teenager who loved talking with her father about politics and history. Yet as she and her sister grew up, it was assumed that they would become wives and mothers whose main purpose was to provide a stable environment for their families. And the bright and hardworking Frederick was fine with that; it was, indeed, what she hoped to do—that is, until a life-changing tragedy struck.

Most lives are informed by a series of experiences, people, and happenstance. Frederick's life was no different. But two events deeply affected the direction her life took and her world outlook. Both, in their ways, were tragic, and one was deeply personal. When she was in high school and in her mid-teens, she suffered severe abdominal pain, which doctors believed was a symptom of uterine cysts. During what was initially expected to be a minor operation, surgeons determined that she had a more serious condition and performed a hysterectomy. Frederick was shattered by the result. And she soon came to believe that if having children was out of the question, so was marriage. She vowed to concentrate on her career.

After college Frederick, who had become a freelance print journalist, joined a team of correspondents that covered the immediate aftermath of World War II in Western Europe (she persevered despite a rejection letter from legendary CBS correspondent Edward R. Murrow, who said he could not call her manner "distinguished"). The death and destruction she witnessed overseas—particularly the sight of countless dead, maimed, and homeless children—would haunt her for the rest of her life and trigger in her a visceral hatred of war. Her experiences in Europe horrified her, yet they also instilled in her a type of idealism—she became thrilled by the idea of a newly formed organization whose mission was to establish a new world order that could keep peace worldwide through diplomacy and reasoned discussion rather than armed conflict. As this organization— the United Nations (UN)—was born, so was Pauline Frederick's hope that neither she nor any other reporter would ever again have to cover a major war. And because of her journalistic ability and her passionate support of the organization, she would ultimately become one of the most respected United Nations reporters in the world.

And so Pauline Frederick's balancing act continued: this time it was as the stealth idealist who masqueraded as the objective reporter. And indeed, for more than twenty years Frederick and NBC provided extensive, fair, and objective reporting of the UN and what would become known as the Cold War. But in her heart she believed in the mission of the United Nations and was devastated when she realized that the organization's overriding goal would never be realized.

Frederick always kept Murrow's rejection letter—perhaps as an incentive to prove him wrong—and as she became well-known, she often spoke of it. But even Edward R. Murrow would probably admit that Frederick did not do too badly. She met and knew many of the top newsmakers of the twentieth century, she received just about every national broadcasting award ever given—and was usually the first female recipient—and she collected literally dozens of honorary college degrees. Many of the female journalists who followed her called her a role model and credited

CHRONOLOGY

1908 February 13, born in Gallitzin PA

1926 Graduated from Central High School, Harrisburg PA

1930 Graduated from American University with a bachelor's degree in political science

1931 Graduated from American University with a master's degree in international law

1931–39 Freelance correspondent for *United States News, Uncle Sam's Diary*, and the North American News Alliance

1938 Began working as an assistant for correspondent H. R. Baukhage, NBC "Blue" Radio network

1945–46 Toured China and Burma, covered post–World War II as a freelance correspondent, and covered the Nuremberg trials

1946 Joined ABC Radio as a freelance correspondent

1949 Hired full-time by ABC

1953 Joined NBC News as United Nations correspondent

1954 Received Alfred I. duPont Award

1955 Received Peabody Award

1959 Elected president of United Nations Correspondents Association

1967 Published *Ten First Ladies of the World*

1969 March 31, married Charles Robbins

1974 Retired from NBC

1975 Joined National Public Radio as international correspondent

1976 Moderated second Ford-Carter presidential debate

1980 Received Paul White Award

1990 Died May 9, Lake Forest IL

PAULINE FREDERICK REPORTING

1 *A Quirk of Fate*

> The difficulties Pauline Frederick experienced making her mark
> in broadcasting so much resembled a soap opera that her story
> could be called "The Perils of Pauline."
>
> DAVID H. HOSLEY and GAYLE K. YAMADA, *Hard News*, 1987

Shortly before six o'clock on the morning of Monday, September 18, 1961, the shrill ring of her telephone awoke NBC-TV United Nations correspondent Pauline Frederick. Eight years earlier, as a jack-of-all trades commentator and only female reporter for ABC Radio, she had usually arrived at work by five or five thirty for a live morning broadcast and returned home more than twelve hours later after an early evening broadcast. Now, at the National Broadcasting Company, she occasionally had to be at work by seven or so for a live broadcast on the *Today* show. Her hours were so long that she had secured an apartment at Thirty-Ninth Street and Park Avenue, not far from the marble-and-glass United Nations complex on the East River. It was so close, in fact, that she could see the structure from the terrace of her sixteenth-floor apartment.

At this point in her career the fifty-three-year-old Frederick had nearly seen it all—she had covered such stories as the Berlin airlift, the Nuremberg trials, and the formation of the new international peacekeeping body, the United Nations. She had traveled on airplanes and ships with troops and had interviewed families in Europe who had lived in the bombed-out shells of their former homes.

By 1961 little surprised or alarmed the veteran correspondent. On this cool dawn in late summer, however, Frederick heard news unlike any she had ever received as a reporter. The DC-6B aircraft carrying UN secretary-general Dag Hammarskjöld and fifteen other passengers, all on a peacekeeping mission, was missing on a flight from New York to war-torn Katanga in the Congo.

Frederick quickly dressed and dashed to UN headquarters, arriving there even before Andrew Cordier, Hammarskjöld's assistant, and others of the UN staff. She was torn between her personal distress at the news and her obligation as a reporter to broadcast the latest developments to millions of viewers, many of whom had just tuned in the previous night to an NBC special report about the upcoming opening that week of the Sixteenth UN General Assembly. The activities of the UN and the latest crisis involving a possible military takeover by Belgium of its former African colony, the Republic of the Congo, had so consumed the American public that the network had aired a special broadcast.

Eerily, Frederick had predicted in that broadcast that Hammarskjöld, whom she described as the "peacemaker," would be "sacrificed." Indeed, her words in that special program, when heard the next day, were chilling. She had meant he would be ruined politically, predicting he would not serve a third five-year term as secretary-general because he had incurred the wrath of Soviet Union officials, who had demanded his resignation the previous year. Even more unnerving, Frederick noted later, was the fact that Hammarskjöld's plane probably crashed close to the time the television special aired.

Frederick's words the evening before Hammarskjöld's death are direct yet eloquent as she issued a warning of sorts that failure of the UN and its member nations to work together could have tragic consequences for the world:

> The United Nations has only one idea: that the conference table should be substituted for the battlefield. It becomes reality only if the Members so choose. Instead, they have chosen to make it a banner under which to fight the cold wars, big and little. Defeating a political enemy has been more important than defeating the common enemy: war.
> Hammarskjöld's greatest fault is his dedication to finding the answer to what he believes is man's greatest prayer, which asks not for victory but for peace. In a day when victory is still the goal, even though there

can be no victory, this peacemaker will be sacrificed. And so will the United Nations, on the altar of military might, until there is acceptance by all that salvation in the nuclear age lies on the conference table, not on the battlefield.

After nearly five hours of waiting for some word about the fate of the plane and Hammarskjöld, she recalled, everyone's worst fears were realized around noon, when they learned that the plane had crashed in what was then Northern Rhodesia, killing Hammarskjöld and the other fifteen passengers.

Frederick was shaken by the news—which rocked the world—but she could not afford to be distracted. That day she and a team of correspondents, which included veteran broadcasters Herb Kaplowe and Frank McGee, scrambled to produce still another hour-long special related to the UN. This one focused on the life and death of Hammarskjöld, the brilliant and quietly charismatic Swedish diplomat who had captured the hearts of the American public with his single-minded devotion to negotiation and peace at a time when the Cold War was raging and, for the first time, nuclear war had become a real possibility. Hammarskjöld was recognized worldwide as a problem solver and a man of conviction—someone who did what he thought was right rather than what was popular.

Dag Hammarskjöld was one of two men whose world outlook and opinion would ultimately had a dramatic effect on Frederick's thinking and activities. She met Hammarskjöld when she was middle-aged and a seasoned news reporter but also at a time when the world was changing dramatically with the advent of nuclear power and other technological advancements.

She had met the other influential man in her life when she was in college. It was her onetime government professor at American University, Arthur Flemming, who served as an intellectual role model and who persuaded her to seek a graduate degree in international relations, telling her that she could ultimately contribute more to society by being a journalist or diplomat rather than an attorney. (Flemming ultimately went on to serve as a college president and advisor to every president from Franklin Roosevelt to Bill Clinton.) In interviews throughout her life Frederick recalled the difficulty of reporting on the death of Dag Hammarskjöld. She admired him more than anyone she had ever covered as a reporter and possibly more than anyone in her personal life. And although she never stated it in words, she probably loved him, in part because the two of them were so similar. Both were idealists who believed one person can make a difference in the world, and both believed, against all evidence, that human beings could live together peacefully. Both were smart and accomplished, and both were elegant, concise communicators. Both enjoyed the finer things in life—music, art, and literature—and both had a lifelong interest in and passion for international events. Even more important, both were spiritual and even religious, though in unconventional ways. According to Dan Cole, the husband of Catharine Crowding Cole, Frederick's niece, Hammarskjöld and Frederick's idealism is what drew them together. "They shared a common dream," Cole said. "That was at the heart of her relationship with Dag Hammarskjöld."

Frederick and Hammarskjöld were close in age. He was fifty-six at the time of the crash; she was fifty-three. Neither had married. But Frederick laughed off speculation by some people years later that they had had a romantic relationship, and there is no evidence of that. They always addressed each other formally, never by first name, although as head of the United Nations Correspondents Association, she talked to him one on one more than any of the other UN correspondents. And when she received the prestigious Peabody Award for excellence in broadcasting in 1955, he was one of the first to send her a message of congratulations—and Frederick said that the praise from Hammarskjöld was nearly as important to her as the award itself. Her respect and admiration for him endured for the rest of her life, and for decades she could recall in detail the terrible twenty-four hours following the plane crash.

Twenty-five years after Hammarskjöld's death, when Frederick was asked to describe the second secretary-general of the United Nations, her comments centered on his humility: "He was diffident . . . he did not make an effort to place himself in front . . . He said when he first came to the United Nations, 'In my new official capacity, the private man should disappear and the international civil servant take his place.' He . . . never sought publicity." The same can be said of Frederick, despite her high-profile perch for thirty-five years as a reporter and commentator for some of the largest and most prestigious media outlets in the world. Frederick, like Hammarskjöld, shunned the spotlight, which in many ways was thrust upon her. A former newspaper and syndicate reporter who was "drafted" into broadcasting in the early days of radio and then television, she always questioned why the job required looking good for the camera. Still, she acquiesced and agreed to look the part. Television was so new when Frederick entered the field that no one even knew how to do makeup for the camera—she learned by trial and error and initially did her own makeup *and* that of her subjects.

On May 10, 1990, the day after she died, NBC *Nightly News* anchorman Tom Brokaw devoted the last few minutes of his 6:30 p.m. broadcast to Frederick, noting that she was a radio anchorwoman before the term *anchorwoman* even existed. Ironically, the woman who drew kudos from Brokaw in front of millions of viewers—"we lost a friend," he said—had been rejected decades earlier by legendary television broadcaster Edward R. Murrow. After he heard her audition tape in 1946, Murrow wrote: "Her voice is pleasing, but I would not call her material or manner particularly distinguished." Many women applied for jobs in broadcasting, he added, but very few would get those jobs because the network found it had "little opportunity" to use them on the air. Frederick did not let that rejection get her down, but she did keep the note from Murrow and referred to it occasionally throughout her life.

A print reporter when she first began in the business in the early 1930s, Frederick took a chance in the mid-1940s and applied for a press junket with the army air force to cover nineteen countries in Asia and Africa. She then obtained press credentials to travel to Europe, Asia, and Africa to cover the aftermath of World War II as a stringer for two syndicated news services and for ABC Radio. In some ways she was very successful— her stories as a news syndicate freelancer were published in newspapers all over the country, including the *New York Times*. And when radio news began to come of age in the mid-1940s, she, like many print reporters, transformed herself into a broadcast journalist, filing radio reports from such locations as China and Germany, where she covered the Nuremberg trials. Still, Pauline Frederick faced a catch-22 situation in the early and mid-1940s: her competence may have actually held her back. The news syndicates for which she worked were able to distribute her stories to news outlets without hiring her full-time. And when radio news blossomed, her written reports were good enough to be used regularly on the air—but a male voice had to deliver them because women's voices were not considered authoritative. While Frederick obviously did not have the requisite male voice to get her hired, her voice was low and melodious, and this quality, combined with her tall and willowy physique, may have contributed to her early success as a woman broadcaster, according to veteran television broadcaster and producer Marlene Sanders, who knew her. While she was not physically striking or provocative, she always appeared elegant—she usually dressed in simple A-line dresses or classic suits, wore a few pieces of classic jewelry, and styled her hair in a basic curly bob. The look, Sanders believes, was not intimidating or threatening to men but conveyed intelligence and competence. Frederick was finally hired full-time in 1948, when ABC gave her a one-year contract. She was forty years old.

Thus, by 1961 Pauline Frederick had grown accustomed to her role as the only woman in a room full of men. She learned early in her long career as a news reporter how to navigate and succeed in a male-dominated industry and world. She learned that thriving in such an environment took tact and diplomacy, talent, and, most of all, perseverance.

Frederick was the only female correspondent on NBC's hour-long special broadcast the night of September 18, 1961, nearly twenty-four hours after Hammarskjöld's plane had crashed. Both viewers and television critics considered the broadcast a reflection of excellent and sensitive journalism. Several television critics made reference to its poignancy, accuracy, and news value, and Frederick and others received many laudatory letters from viewers. With less than twelve hours to prepare, it was full of information and gracefully written. Frederick's piece, in particular, was eloquent and sensitive: "'It was dawn on the East River—a time that Dag Hammarskjöld had seen so often while trying to save the world from war—when word first came to the UN that his plane was missing,' Frederick said on the broadcast. 'Each hour brought increasing anxiety until the stunning confirmation just before noon. There was no longer the respite for hope. New hard facts must be faced.'"

Frederick's final comments during her portion of the news special were particularly moving and spoke to her admiration for Hammarskjöld: "As so many looked to Dag Hammarskjöld for inspiration in life, so there is comfort in remembering what he stood for now that he is no longer here. Dag Hammarskjöld was known for courage. His brother said he walked fearlessly along dangerous precipices. He himself once said, 'It's when we all play safe that fatality will lead us to our doom. It is in the dark shade of courage alone that the spell can be broken.' Many people tonight are trying to remember most of all the courage of Dag Hammarskjöld for the perilous days ahead."

Frederick's viewers knew she spoke from the heart, and many sensed the grief she felt. Viewers seemed to know that one man could make a difference, and a week after the plane crash President John F. Kennedy noted that Hammarskjöld's death was "not the death of one man" but a tragedy that affected the international community. Within a week of that Monday evening special broadcast, hundreds of letters, sympathy cards, and notes from viewers inundated Frederick and NBC News officials. The outpouring also showed that viewers depended on Frederick and trusted her to let them know what was happening in the world and, more important, to humanize and decipher the news coming out of the United Nations. With the advent of the Cold War and the feeling for the first time among U.S. citizens that the world could be destroyed by nuclear war, Frederick, through her calm demeanor and clear interpretation of UN events, may have given some viewers hope for survival.

Frederick received nearly one hundred condolence cards and letters, some praising her work covering the secretary-general's death and some complimenting her work overall for NBC News; many viewers noted they felt they could always trust her. Some of the notes were typed neatly, and others were handwritten in sympathy cards: "'Mr. Raab and I were deeply touched with your words and it brought tears to our eyes,' wrote Manda Raab of Fort Lauderdale. 'Your dear sweet face reflects a sadness and a great spiritual understanding. Mr. Raab and I admired and loved Mr. Hammarskjöld. He was a man of peace.'" Edith McDowell of Penney

Farms, Florida, wrote: "You always seem to me like a fine, unseen friend as across the air waves you endeavor to interpret to us some of the great events and people of these tremendous times . . . I was deeply touched by the intimate picture you gave us of Dag Hammarskjöld's richness and 'things of the spirit.'" "Seldom am I moved to letter writing for a cause," wrote Mrs. Thomas Pringle of Akron, Ohio. "Since the untimely death of Dag Hammarskjöld, there has been a depression, suppressed in the daily tasks of caring for my husband and three children, but still present. But for TV and news reports we might never have known Dag Hammarskjöld. The loss seems personal . . . P.S. This is not an afterthought; we think you are the correspondent who is the most outstanding in our news media today."

Some writers were so moved that they asked her for a transcript of Frederick's comments on the special broadcast: Requesting a transcript, Allan R. Brown of San Mateo, California, wrote: "For me, and for many others, I am sure, your remarks were deeply moving and truly inspiring . . . as a concerned citizen, I would like to express my appreciation to the National Broadcasting Company for making it possible for the American public to sit in the television presence of such insight, perspective, and wisdom as yours . . . In times such as these, it is reassuring to know that there are decision makers in the television industry with such a high sense of public duty and responsibility."

Some viewers said that they appreciated the fact that a woman could excel in a male-dominated profession. From Nathan Benson of Cleveland:

> It gives me distinct pleasure to convey to you the live admiration I have for you. Before listening to your newscasts . . . I felt that women had no place in the broadcasting field, however, you have convinced me that not only do they have a place, but are a tangible part of the Industry. To try to describe the elegance you implemented in your tribute to Dag Hammarskjöld, man of peace, would only be repeating a Platitude you know so well. It was indeed a moving experience and I don't mind admitting that I had a difficult time fighting back tears.

Pauline Annabel Frederick was born on February 13, 1908. The middle child of Susan Catharine Stanley, a homemaker, and Matthew Philip Frederick, a postmaster and later state worker, she was born in the central

Pennsylvania coal mining town of Gallitzin (named after a Russian prince who was sent to the United States to convert the heathen) and raised in nearby Harrisburg. Frederick's father, whose paternal grandfather was born in Ireland, was a career civil servant. In Gallitzin he was postmaster and ran a small dry goods store with his brother-in-law. When President Woodrow Wilson came to power, patronage jobs went to the Democrats, so the Republican Frederick lost his job and moved the family to Tyrone, Pennsylvania, where they lived briefly, and then to Harrisburg, where he was a labor negotiator for the state's Department of Labor and Industry and later held jobs with the Pennsylvania Bureau of Mediation and Arbitration and the Bureau of Bedding and Upholstery.

According to friends and relatives, the dark-haired, brown-eyed Pauline was tall and gawky—she grew to become five foot, nine inches—and, as she herself described it later in her life, bucktoothed; as a result, she was self-conscious about her appearance. Although neither of her parents attended college, Pauline—or Polly, as she was known as a girl—was a self-described bookworm who always worked hard and excelled at school in Harrisburg, where her family moved when she was a little girl. (Indeed, copies of grade cards found among her personal papers bear out her academic prowess; throughout her junior high and high school years she received grades of 90 and 95 percent in nearly all her subjects, including nonacademic subjects such as sewing, drawing, and "physical training." The highest grades were in reading, spelling, geography, and history. Her only grades of B were in civics and science during two grading periods.)

The timing of Frederick's birth and adulthood—between two world wars and during a period of great social and cultural change—had a dramatic effect on her thinking. She and her two siblings—older sister Catharine, known as Kitty, who was four years older than she, and younger brother Stanley—grew up with the fear of war and were particularly worried that their father would be drafted to serve. (Another Frederick daughter, Amelia, died of scarlet fever at age two, when Kitty was a year old.) This apprehension was instilled in them by their parents, who themselves developed the preoccupation as young adults during World War I. Frederick was a young woman during the political upheaval that would eventually lead to World War II, so that conflict and its potentially disastrous consequences were also very much on her mind during her formative years. And the 1920s, when Frederick was a teenager, were a time of changing social values and economic problems that ultimately led to the rise of labor unions and, of course, Prohibition, certainly heady times for such a bright and motivated girl as Polly Frederick. In some ways this accident of timing was lucky for her, she said decades later. This historic period cultivated in her an interest in international affairs and, consequently, journalism: "I had always been interested in international affairs from the point of view of fearing and dreading war," she said. "From the time I was a little girl, there was always the fear of my father being called into the draft of the first world war . . . And so as a consequence, I had always had this uppermost in my mind. And as a result, I always gravitated toward covering news that had to do with international relations."

While earning excellent grades and undertaking many extracurricular activities—including serving as president of her sophomore class and stints reporting on her school newspapers as well as the three local newspapers, the *Telegraph*, the *Patriot*, and the *Evening News*—Pauline Frederick was also very much a product of the culture in which she lived. She came from a family of devout Methodists ("I grew up in a family that was very churchy," she once recalled) and attended Sunday school, church services, and Wednesday night prayer meetings as a child. Nevertheless, she got conflicting messages from her parents about her devotion to home, religion, and school. Girls could excel in school, of course, but it was an unspoken assumption that their role in life would ultimately be as wife and mother. And Frederick had no problem with this expectation, even though her self-described "gawky" looks made her feel insecure personally. (Her niece Catharine Cole said that Pauline's looks came from the Frederick side of the family—she was taller and bigger than her sister, Kitty, who had the delicate features and slender body type of the Stanleys. The two sisters looked nothing alike.) Although neither one of her parents attended college, her father was an avid reader who had a great interest in politics and world affairs, interests he shared with Pauline and which his daughter seemed to care about quite deeply; she told an interviewer later in her career that her mother once caught her crying in her bedroom "over the ascendancy of Hindenburg to power in Germany." In fact, it was her father and not her mother with whom she most identified; Polly never had an interest in the domestic arts, even when she lived at home. But she was not a rebel either.

Her focus on academics while still keeping an eye on marriage as a goal was reflected in the inscription written about her under her photograph in the Central High School yearbook, the *Argus*: "This is Polly—the queen of our hearts, literary talent, debating fire, executive ability, and all round good sportsmanship—how's that for a president? By the way, do you know why the Evening News is such a good paper? Polly's the reporter! No kiddin', honey, we expect to see your name in headlines as a brilliant journalist, and will be disappointed if we don't—unless someone realizes your worth and gives you a diamond!"

The yearbook description was prescient in more ways than one. Polly Frederick was a brilliant and popular student who demonstrated even at a young age that she had the drive and talent to excel at whatever interested her. The bright and motivated Polly may have indeed given up her career aspirations if someone had given her a diamond, but she said much later that, sadly, she was never given the choice of choosing between a career and a husband. Fate intervened when she was still a teenager.

Certainly, Pauline Frederick could not have achieved what she had as a student if she were not content. But she was plagued by some chronic physical ailments as a child and young woman, including severe allergies, headaches, and gynecological problems. Frederick's niece Catharine Cole said that Frederick was self-conscious about her appearance, and Frederick mentioned this later in her life in interviews, explaining that she was particularly self-conscious about her height—she towered over many of her male classmates. Polly felt like the ugly duckling compared to Kitty, who was always known as the prettier of the two girls. Although Pauline grew up to become a willowy and attractive woman, this initial insecurity about her appearance may have shaped her strong feelings later about the unfairness of women in television news receiving intense scrutiny regarding their physical appearance.

But a turning point in her life came when she was eighteen or nineteen, according to Cole. She had experienced abdominal pain, which doctors diagnosed as uterine cysts or polyps. But when doctors operated to remove the seemingly benign cysts, they found what they considered cancerous tissue. They immediately sought approval from the Fredericks to perform a hysterectomy. The news that she could never have children left Pauline devastated, and she was furious at her parents for allowing the operation to be performed. Her anger led to an uncharacteristic act of rebellion: she chopped off her hair to spite her parents, and photos of her during her first year in college show a long-legged, tall, thin girl with short hair. To her niece the hysterectomy was nothing short of a "calamity" for her. "It really affected her life tremendously," she said. "There were several things in her life that were calamities as her life went on and affected her. That was the big one."

Whether she would have given up her professional ambitions to lead a conventional life of wife and mother will of course never be known. Her activities in public school and in college certainly indicate that she was leaning toward a career in either diplomacy or journalism. Nevertheless, it was not until she was in graduate school at American University in Washington DC that a series of circumstances and luck led to a pivotal event in her life: the publication of one of her stories in the respected *Washington Star*. Pauline Frederick realized one thing when she saw her name in print in a major newspaper in the nation's capital: she was hooked on journalism.

2 *Polly the Prizewinner*

This Week [Sunday newspaper supplement] has now established
a policy of no controversial articles. In general, the attitude of the
American public and the editors is that the war is over, let's forget it.

FAUSTINA ORNER, January 4, 1946

If the people back home could look once in a while beyond their
own . . . shores, they'd know that the war is far from won . . . We
haven't succeeded in bringing democracy, or much of anything
else to our poor benighted neighbors on this side of the water.

PAULINE FREDERICK, reporting from Nuremberg, Germany, in
a letter to her editor, Farnham Dudgeon, January 7, 1946

In the fall of 1926 Pauline Frederick, a small-town girl born in the coal mining town of Gallitzin, Pennsylvania, population about two thousand, and
raised in nearby Harrisburg, was exhilarated to find herself in Washington
DC. She knew she would love the city, having read for years about the
place where presidents lived, laws took shape, and congressional leaders
hashed out intricate deals that affected the lives of millions of people. At
Edison Junior High and Central High she was a big fish in a little pond.
Now, as a freshman at American University, just outside the District, she
found herself a nobody in the big city. She did not mind.

The influence of her father, the volatility of the times in which she grew
up, and an inborn curiosity about the world all cultivated in Frederick an
interest in politics and world events. But she also demonstrated a natural
ability to write and to express herself. Clippings from local newspapers in
her archival papers at Smith College include numerous front-page stories

about Frederick winning writing contests and honors. She won a contest at age eight for an essay on "Safety First"; she won a Kiwanis Club historical essay contest when she was in high school; at Edison Junior High she was one of three students who won awards for overall "excellence"; and she was first in "Highest Scholastic Standing" in junior high. She was so adept at competition that she became known in school as "Polly the Prizewinner," a nickname she hated. Despite her disdain for the label, however, she acknowledged that the prizes were important to her. And her collection of awards expanded throughout her college and professional life.

In high school, according to the *Argus*, the Central High School yearbook, she was president of her "midyear" (probably sophomore) class; president of the Debating Club; associate editor of the yearbook; a member of the junior Civics Club; general chairman of the Crossword Puzzle Bazaar; and a member of the honor roll. Throughout these years of achievement she freelanced for the local Harrisburg newspapers—the *Telegraph*, the *Patriot*, and the *Evening News*.

She wrote for both her junior and senior high school newspapers and edited the midyear *Buzz*, an apparently ad hoc newspaper published by the midyear Edison class of 1924. Like most talented writers, she was versatile: she wrote fiction as well as nonfiction, as evidenced by a lighthearted story she wrote in junior high school for the *Buzz*, a story in which she could "see" what her classmates would be doing as adults in the future, à la *A Christmas Carol* by Charles Dickens. The short article twists and turns, beginning with a dark tone but ending up humorous and light.

Frederick's piece initially creates an ominous mood in which, as an adult, she is walking at night to her childhood home: "The evening shadows were slowly falling as I wended my homeward way. My heart yearned for even a look upon some of my old friends who had attended Edison when I did . . . Going up the walk that led to the home I noticed the house looked very dark and mother had been suddenly called away." Then a ghost appears and leads her down the street "and to the leading college of our country," where she sees many of her high school friends. From there she sees other friends at full-time jobs that reflect their activities and desires as high school students—for instance: "The spirit led me to a courtroom. There stood Fred Lumb as a lawyer pleading hard for the life of a cat, who had walked across a cranky neighbor's back fence in an effort to reach the street from the home of its mistress."

Despite her versatility as a writer—and a clear love of writing—Frederick as a girl had mixed feelings about "journalism" (which, she noted decades later, was a pretentious term in the 1920s, when most people called it simply "reporting"). She recalled in many interviews that her first experience working in newspaper journalism on a full-time basis was not a positive one and soured her on journalism. She worked as society reporter for the *Harrisburg Evening News* the summer before she went to college and substituted for a few weeks when the society editor went on vacation. Despite the number of dinners and receptions she covered, the assignment was not her cup of tea. "If this is journalism, it's an awfully silly way to waste your life," she thought at the time. She may have planned to use her writing talent to further her studies and possibly forge a career in political science or government. After all, when she graduated from high school in 1926, few women had entered journalism full-time. Furthermore, journalism at the time consisted primarily of newspapers and magazines, although radio was poised to mature and challenge the dominance of the print media. With a few exceptions news reporting simply was not considered women's work. Broadcasting, in particular, relied on the deep, authoritative voices of men. It was assumed women had no business reporting on the air.

Still, the world of journalism attracted Frederick even when she was a girl—the addictive quality of a byline drew her in. She once described how she felt as an Edison Junior High student, when her teacher told her she was submitting a short story Frederick had written to the school newspaper. "I thought I would faint with excitement when my English teacher suggested that it should be sent to the *Edison Record*," she said. When she saw it in print, she said, "I had my second weak spell." This first taste of the exhilaration that came with seeing her byline was unmatched: "When interviews I was writing appeared with my name in the *New York Times*, I couldn't have been more excited that when I first saw my name in the *Edison Record*."

Frederick's outstanding high school record and her drive provided great insurance for someone who wanted a college degree and ultimately a professional career. After a months-long stint working at a department store while continuing her freelance writing work, she turned down a full-time job as a society editor at the *Telegraph* in Harrisburg to accept a small scholarship to American University, a college she selected because of its Methodist affiliation and because of the scholarship. She moved into a woman's dormitory and entered the College of Political Science in the fall of 1926 because the school offered no journalism classes. But Frederick's dedication to the Methodist religion began to wane in college. She had always been religious in a "sectarian sense," she said, and attended Foundry Methodist Church in Washington when she was a student at American University; as she grew older, however, she "put away those ways."

Frederick excelled as a college student, earning high grades and many accolades: "Frederick wins highest honors," read the page 1 banner headline of the *American* (University) *Eagle* on June 2, 1930. She received the highest prize given by the faculty, a fifty-dollar stipend awarded to the student who made the "largest contribution" to the university. As she had in high school, she served as the yearbook editor and was a key member of the debating club. She was also active in the campus International Relations Club. Frederick also wrote lyrics for one of the first versions of the university's alma mater. It begins:

> Firm on a sweep of campus
> Stands American U.,
> Built with vision and labor,
> Pioneer dreams come true;
> Namesake of our great nation,
> Nurturer in ideals high
> American—alma mater
> Behold—thy banners fly!

Frederick's undergraduate and later graduate years at American University were crucial for other reasons. While there, she further refined the art of networking, a talent she had cultivated while in junior and senior high school as an officer in several student groups. Even more important, the university's location just outside of the District of Columbia allowed her to spend most of her time out of class attending legislative meetings, speeches, and other political gatherings. Washington DC was an exciting and stimulating place for someone whose knowledge of its workings had come from books, classrooms, and discussions. And it was a great place for someone who understood the value of knowing the right people.

Still, nothing proved as educational for Frederick as her jobs following college—especially two that sent her to Europe shortly after V-E Day, May 8, 1945. Well educated and accomplished as she was as a student, trips overseas in 1945 and 1946 became the most eye-opening events of her young life, shaping her future and her world outlook. The two trips introduced her firsthand to the horrors of war. Later she became a vocal advocate of nuclear disarmament, and it was probably the time she spent in postwar Europe that led her to believe that a war could cause near-total annihilation.

During college Frederick cultivated contacts that would lead one by one to her career as a journalist. The first was an association with a favorite professor, Arthur Sherwood Flemming, a professor of government and coach of the university debating club, of which Frederick was a member. Flemming, who was only four years older than Frederick, was a lifelong Republican and civil rights activist. He was appointed by President Franklin Delano Roosevelt in 1939 to the Civil Service Commission and would hold policy positions in every administration through that of President Bill Clinton, where he was Clinton's advisor on the elderly. He also served as president of Ohio Wesleyan University, University of Oregon, and Macalaster College from the late 1940s until the early 1970s. He left government service during the administration of President Ronald Reagan, who fired him for his civil rights advocacy, replacing him with a conservative Republican.

Through Flemming's contacts Frederick got a job editing and writing for *Uncle Sam's Diary*, a weekly student-oriented publication that focused on news of interest to a college audience. She received thirty dollars a story for her work, which helped pay the bills, but her work for *Uncle Sam's Diary* was important in other ways. First, because its audience consisted primarily of college students, she was forced to distill complicated concepts and events into direct, understandable prose. Second, it was through *Uncle Sam's Diary* that she met one of its investors, Washington journalist David Lawrence, an insider who knew many important and influential people. Lawrence would serve as a valuable professional contact for her.

As she neared graduation in 1930, however, Frederick's future did not look so rosy. The stock market crash of October 29, 1929, triggered a collapse that ultimately paralyzed world economies. Unemployment soared to unprecedented levels in the United States, and prospects seemed particularly bleak for those about to enter the job market. Frederick was not sure what she would do with her degree in political science, despite her high grades and participation in extracurricular activities. Clearly, many young people felt that a college degree would shelter them from hard times. Although most of the college graduates of the era were men—only about 49,000 of the nation's 122,484 college graduates in 1930 were women—women and men had begun flocking to college in unprecedented numbers. The number of college graduates overall nearly tripled from 1920, when it was 48,000, to 1930; it doubled from 1940 to 1950. Although Frederick's college degree would no doubt help her find a job, she faced plenty of competition from other new graduates, and she began to rethink her career goals. Flemming, who at the time was studying in the evening for a law degree at George Washington University, suggested that she pursue a master's degree in international law. Flemming's interest in international law was contagious for Frederick. She applied for and received a fellowship for a master's degree in the field and stayed on at American University, earning nine hundred dollars in 1930–31 as a research assistant.

During that year as a graduate student, Frederick took more advice that would ultimately shape her life. Another of her favorite teachers, Charles Callan Tansill, a professor of early U.S. history who would publish more than twenty books on that subject, suggested to Frederick that she use her skills as a journalist—and, indirectly, her gender—to report on a topic that he believed would be of interest to many people in Washington: what life was like in the United States for the wives of foreign diplomats. Tansill noted that diplomats in Washington naturally wanted to cultivate positive images and would be eager to demonstrate that they had stable family lives.

Frederick had always disdained the conventional wisdom that men and women defined news differently, and she always gravitated toward hard news and political commentary rather than soft society or "women's page" fare. But she agreed that Tansill had a point, and she decided to give his idea a try. She lifted the telephone and called the Czech embassy and made her request. The voice on the other end, a secretary, seemed receptive but asked her in what media outlet the interview would be published. "That depends how good it is," Frederick replied. The interview was granted.

Frederick said later that she may have drawn the attention of the embassy secretary, because she mistook her for another Pauline Frederick, a silent screen actress popular during the early 1920s. During much of her early career people asked Frederick if she was the same Pauline Frederick who had acted in silent movies, and she sometimes received mail meant for the actress, even though the actress's career had waned considerably by the late 1920s. The actress died in 1938—but that did not stop people in the 1940s from continuing to mistake Pauline Frederick the journalist for Pauline Frederick the actress. Frederick had become accustomed to this confusion and accepted it with equal parts amusement and annoyance. But it appeared she was always gracious when correcting people who mistook her for the actress. Frederick often related how she had once visited Cuba for a hotel opening. As she stepped off the plane, a gaggle of photographers called her name and asked her to pose, and the next day a newspaper article, with the photo, announced that the star of a film called *Perils of Pauline* was in the country. Fortunately, a correction appeared the next day, but it was not the one Frederick expected. "They admitted it was not [actress] Pauline Frederick who was in *Perils*. It was Pearl White," she recalled. In 1940 the author of a biography of the actress wrote Frederick an odd letter asking her if the identical names were more than sheer coincidence. "Were you by chance named after our [actress] Pauline Frederick? If you were named after her—several people were at different times—you will perhaps be interested in the book on her life," wrote Muriel Elwood. There was no record in Frederick's archives of a response, although she usually sent a standard reply when she received fan mail that was apparently meant for the actress: "I am sorry to have to tell you that Pauline Frederick the actress died in 1938. I was not named for her nor am I any relation."

When Frederick became a well-known voice on NBC Radio in the mid-1950s, the network wrote a news release to its affiliates stating that the very-much-alive news correspondent Pauline Frederick was not the late actress by the same name: "Hear one, hear all, NBC's lady United Nations reporter—Pauline Frederick—is not the late stage and silent screen star of the same name."

If Frederick benefited from that early case of mistaken identity, she did not mind. It helped her get her foot in the door, as it were, as a reporter. She conducted the interview through the Czech embassy and two more with diplomats' wives, hoping that a news outlet would be more likely to publish her work if she gave editors several writing examples. When contemplating a venue for the stories, she decided to think big: she briefly had met Frederic William Wile, a newspaperman and radio reporter who knew people at the *Washington Star*, and sent him the article. He sent a letter of recommendation to the paper's managing editor.

More than fifty years after the event, Frederick could still recall in detail the moment she received the news that her interview would appear in the *Star*. She, her roommate Bernice Moeller, who was a bursar at American University and Flemming's fiancée, and Flemming were preparing dinner when a messenger knocked on the door with a package from the paper. Frederick was crestfallen, assuming that the editor had rejected her query and was returning her writing samples. Instead, she had hit the jackpot. A letter from the editor stated that not only would he publish the stories she sent—but he wanted more. He would publish one a week every Sunday if she could provide them. "I nearly collapsed," she recalled.

Frederick was thrilled to see her story in print in the largest paper in Washington. But even better, *Star* editors were so happy with the story that they wanted more just like it. Frederick continued to interview the wives of diplomats, cabinet heads, and other influential men, and the *Star* continued to publish them in a weekly column, "Women and Diplomacy," for which she earned ten dollars a column. Ultimately, the columns were syndicated through the North American News Alliance to member news outlets, so they appeared in newspapers around the country. The payment, while helpful to Frederick, was relatively unimportant to her. The initial excitement of seeing the *Star* newsroom and later having her story published was priceless to her. Her ambivalence about her career was over. She was determined to become a journalist.

The thrill Frederick felt trumped her awareness that she had few female role models in journalism in the early 1930s. Only a handful of women reported on the news then, particularly at the national level. Most women in the field were society or fashion writers, or they reported on issues considered to be of interest to women such as marriage, family, and home. In fact, one of the few well-known women who dared venture outside of "women's" news may indirectly have hurt Frederick's chances of entering the field. One of the leading national female journalists of the era was Dorothy Thompson. Thompson had traveled to Europe in the early 1920s, eventually serving as Paris bureau chief for the *Philadelphia Daily Ledger*. In 1924 she became Berlin bureau chief for the *Daily Ledger* and the *New York Evening Post*. Thompson was one of the few women foreign correspondents of the era—others were Anne O'Hare McCormick of the *New York Times*, Martha Gellhorn of *Collier's*, and Sigrid Schultz of the *Chicago Tribune*—and one of the most colorful. After a divorce, Thompson married author Sinclair Lewis, who reportedly had followed her around Europe in the 1920s until she agreed to marry him. But some thought Thompson a questionable role model. Her drive, talent, and courage were admirable, especially for a young journalist such as Frederick, but she was considered by some of her peers to be aggressive and shrill—qualities that were not always admired by the men in the media in the 1920s and 1930s.

By the early 1930s Thompson had returned to the United States and was writing a syndicated column through the *New York Herald Tribune* that reached eight million readers. But later her somewhat controversial opinions about people and topics in the news alienated her from some readers. Late in her career she changed from being a supporter of Zionism to becoming a critic of the creation of an Israeli state. Ultimately, her strong—and sometimes radical—positions led her syndicate to drop her column. Thompson also became the first woman to transfer her talents from print to broadcasting. NBC hired her in 1936 as a radio commentator, and as a result of that two-year stint, she became one of the most popular radio voices in the country. Frederick said that Thompson served as a negative role model in some ways for women, explaining in an interview that during a meeting of members of the Association of Radio and Television News Analysts in the 1940s, Thompson "spent the time telling [President] Roosevelt . . . what was wrong with his administration and how he should fix it up, and shaking her fingers at him." After the meeting, Frederick said, men in the association "decided never, never again would there be a woman in that organization, so for years and years [after becoming a radio reporter], I was banned."

Thompson's attitude might have served as an early warning for the young Frederick. She always treaded lightly when talking about her role as a female journalist, and she did not want to be known as aggressive or overbearing. She preferred to be thought of as an individual rather than a "woman" journalist. In an interview in 1975, when she was in her late sixties, she noted: "I dreaded the idea of being known as a suffragette— abrasive and militant. I wanted a chance to be a professional and I felt if I emphasized the sex angle I wouldn't be able to." Her reluctance to be known as strictly a woman journalist became an oft-repeated theme. A *New York Times* reporter once noted in a interview with her, "Miss Frederick does not wish to be considered as a 'woman reporter,' judged not just according to the feminine lights of her personality, but on her merit in her job."

After she graduated in 1931 with a master's degree in international law, Frederick continued to write profiles of diplomatic and cabinet wives for the *Star* as well as articles for *Uncle Sam's Diary*. But that work did not pay the costs of living in Washington DC, where she wanted to stay. Stubborn and determined, Frederick did not let poor economic times and limited job opportunities for journalists deter her. She subsidized her journalistic stints with a "real" full-time job—clerical work as an associate editor with the *Federal Register*. For a year, from 1933 to 1934, she also taught a journalism class at Fairmont Junior College in Washington DC. This cobbling together of paychecks to support a job she loved would become a way of life for her over the next decade.

Every time Frederick considered abandoning a career in journalism, fate always seemed to intervene. The decade of the 1930s brought major societal and cultural changes, many spearheaded by President Roosevelt's sweeping reform initiatives. They included major labor and minimum wage legislation and the enactment of Social Security. These were heady times for anyone interested in reporting on public affairs, government, or politics, and Frederick was not about to miss covering them. The contacts she established during her five years at American University would pay dividends by the mid-1930s. She would meet two people active in the newly emerging field of radio, and they would change her life.

Through her association with David Lawrence from *Uncle Sam's Diary*, Frederick began writing in 1934 for another of his publications: the *United States News*, a predecessor to *U.S. News and World Report* (where she used the gender-neutral byline "P. A. Frederick" because, as she would say decades later, she did not want readers to know she was female). She covered federal agencies for the *News*, including the Departments of State, War, and Navy, for thirty dollars a week and eventually covered White House press events. The stories Frederick wrote for *United States News* demonstrated her ability to write serious and multifaceted stories about world affairs at a time when the world was on the threshold of a major war. In a column titled "Tide of World Affairs" she offered a combination of facts and interpretation. One day, for instance, she wrote an extensive piece about the abdication of King Edward VIII—which had become one of the biggest stories of the decade. Frederick focused on the ramifications of the abdication on the British government and the world. Another column examined the Soviet Union's apparent breaking of a pledge of neutrality with the United States in 1935.

Through her freelance work, the *United States News* job, and her teaching, Frederick's income for 1934 was about twenty-four hundred dollars, about half the average of five thousand dollars annually that most full-time reporters earned. Frederick was a dedicated worker who let nothing stop her, according to Helen Brabrook, one of her roommates at the time. Brabrook noted that Frederick sometimes had debilitating headaches that caused nausea and vomiting, but they did not stop her from showing up to work every day. The many receptions, inaugurations, and other events Frederick attended opened doors for her and introduced her to many influential people. One person, a man named Hilmar Robert (H. R.) Baukhage, would have a major impact on her life and career.

The changing media landscape of the 1930s and 1940s, when radio news was coming of age, made it particularly difficult for women to succeed in the media. The prevailing wisdom among Frederick's professors and coworkers at the time was that women would never report news on the radio because their voices were not sufficiently authoritative, so they would not be taken seriously if they reported on anything but cooking, children, hosiery, or other issues of supposed importance to women. This situation frustrated Frederick, who once noted, perhaps jokingly, that even the microphones "are built to pick up men's voices more eloquently than women's." Decades later, after becoming a successful journalist, Frederick remarked that she wished she had had the nerve as a young woman to correct one high-ranking network executive in the 1930s when he told her a female voice did not carry authority. "I am terribly sorry I didn't have the courage to tell him . . . that I knew his wife's voice carried plenty of authority in his house," she said.

Radio had grown tremendously as a source of news by the early and mid-1930s, the era known as the golden age of radio. Radio advertising increased during this time, as did the number of radios in homes. In 1929 radio received only 4 percent of the national advertising dollars compared to 54 percent for newspapers and 42 percent for magazines. Ten years later radio received 27 percent of the national advertising dollars. In 1930 about fourteen million households had radios; that number more than doubled, to nearly thirty million, in 1940.

Because of radio's rapid growth and its relative newness as a delivery system for news, few reporters or editors were trained as broadcasters, so radio executives relied heavily on newspaper reporters as broadcasters. H. R. Baukhage, a former foreign correspondent, wire service reporter, and magazine writer, was certainly qualified to collect the news, but like most other radio reporters at the time, he was a novice at actually delivering it to the public over the air. He began work for NBC Blue Radio (which later became the American Broadcasting Company [ABC]) in 1932, when he gave five-minute news broadcasts Monday through Friday at 12:30 p.m. Eventually, he became the first radio broadcaster to host a live news show from the Capitol. The rangy Baukhage had cultivated a distinctive style and tone, opening every broadcast with the to-the-point greeting "Baukhage here." Hilmar Robert 'H. R.' Baukhage was known only as "Baukhage" to listeners, and his quick staccato verbal style and raspy baritone became his trademark: "Washington . . . August 4 . . . and in just a moment I'll tell you what we're thinking about here."

In 1938 David Lawrence introduced Baukhage to an enthusiastic young woman with knowledge of Washington politics, experience covering government, and the ability to write quickly and well. Baukhage hired Pauline Frederick as an editorial assistant, and the gruff reporter became a mentor to the young woman. But he parroted the prevailing wisdom of the era that radio was not the medium for a woman who wanted to report the news. Women's voices just did not carry authority, he told her, so they would never be on the air. "Stay away from radio. It doesn't like women," he told her repeatedly. It was a view that Frederick had heard before and had accepted. After all, she was a print reporter at heart. But as radio began to emerge in the 1930s as serious competition for newspapers and magazines, Frederick began to read the writing on the wall. If she wanted to succeed as a journalist, she would need skills in radio broadcasting.

Thus, Frederick became a "legman" for Baukhage, running to meetings and getting interviews, giving Baukhage written reports for broadcast, and writing scripts. It was tough and demanding work, but it helped her learn firsthand about the emerging medium of radio. She learned from Baukhage how to transfer her print skills to broadcasting, but their relationship was mutually beneficial: Frederick became a recognized presence in Washington journalism, and Baukhage was able to expand his journalistic activities because he had help from a quick and reliable assistant. Through the job with Baukhage, Frederick was becoming a Washington fixture. In fact, she spent so much time there that she moved from the outskirts of the District to an apartment in Foggy Bottom in the center of town. Baukhage, meanwhile, was also thriving. In addition to his radio report, he began writing a daily column for the North American News Alliance, which Frederick edited and for which she earned an additional forty dollars a week, a welcome added stipend she later missed when Baukhage discontinued the column. Ultimately, Frederick expanded her skills from print into radio, much as her male role model Baukhage had done. She had similar drive, skills, and now experience as the men in print who had transferred to radio. What she lacked was their advantage as men.

Nevertheless, most of the major strides Frederick made in her early career probably occurred because she was a woman. Philosophically, she believed that women's "news" should not be ghettoized or separated from men's news. But she also knew that her first major national stories—the interviews with diplomats' wives—developed because of her feminine touch. And that pattern repeated itself in 1939.

In New York City, Martha Cuthbert, who was in charge of "women's programming" at the NBC Red radio network (later NBC Radio) read Frederick's stories about the diplomats' wives and had an idea. She thought that similar topics could lend themselves well to radio, and she immediately contacted Baukhage to get in touch with Frederick. Cuthbert soon learned that Frederick had never performed in a broadcast studio, but that did not discourage her from asking Frederick if she could send her a 78 rpm celluloid audition platter. Cuthbert had come up with an idea for a fifteen-minute radio show tentatively titled "Women in the News," which she believed could have Frederick as its host. Many, but not necessarily all, of the subjects could be wives of influential men. But first she needed to know if Frederick had any talent as a broadcaster. A startled Frederick felt she had one option: she asked Baukhage, a sympathetic "subject," if she could interview him for the audition platter. Baukhage complied, and the interview was placed on a platter and sent to NBC in New York.

Cuthbert was impressed enough to ask Frederick to develop several ideas for subjects of this prospective show. A surprised Frederick was happy to comply, but she was a realist and knew that writing for radio and conducting an interview while broadcasting on radio were two different skills. The year was 1939, and Frederick's first idea was to interview the wife of Czech foreign minister Vladimir Hurban, who had refused to give up his legation as Germany was preparing to invade Czechoslovakia. Frederick persuaded the couple that such an interview would improve the morale of the Czech people and Americans of Czech background, so they reluctantly complied. But Frederick, the seasoned reporter who had interviewed top federal officials and shrewd politicians, was nervous. During a trial run interview with Olga Hurban, Frederick developed a fever of 104 degrees. "I had butterflies and the woman [Mrs. Hurban] was as frightened as I was," she remembered. The next day the interview was conducted from the legation itself. Frederick later recalled the interview: "'I haven't slept a wink,' [Hurban said,] and I said, 'I'm sorry,

I haven't either.'" The two women—interviewer and interviewee—had a glass of wine and then did the interview, which aired on NBC radio.

Frederick was a novice broadcaster, but it apparently did not show. Cuthbert saw her potential and eventually launched the fifteen-minute interview show called *Let's Talk It Over*, with plans for Frederick to be its regular host and to focus on women in the news. Although the two women only met a few times, Cuthbert and Frederick maintained a friendly relationship, and correspondence between them indicates that the NBC executive was nurturing and encouraging to Frederick during their two-year relationship. Frederick was happy to offer ideas for subjects for the show, and Cuthbert frequently praised her ideas and her performance. "It was nice meeting you the other day," Cuthbert wrote to her after their first meeting. "You more than filled our expectations." Cuthbert's assistant, June Hynd, was also encouraging: "It's a pleasure to deal with a person as intelligent as you who takes things in just the right way."

Frederick learned firsthand through her diplomatic connections in Washington government, and now in Washington media, how to do what today would be called "multitasking" when it came to stories and media outlets. She conducted the interview with Mrs. Hurban for NBC radio, for example, but also wrote it as an article for the *Washington Evening Star*. Similarly, Frederick used her connection to her former American University professor Charles Tansill—who by 1938 was an author and had served as an aide to the Senate Foreign Relations Committee—to write a story for the *Star* about his predictions concerning Germany and the possibility of another world war. As it turned out, the former professor and foreign affairs advisor was not the best prognosticator, indicating that he thought the United States could avoid another war. While Frederick's diplomatic wife profiles were popular on radio and with *Washington Star* readers, she was clearly happiest when she was writing longer and more comprehensive stories that employed several sources and oftentimes numbers to give them more credence and depth. She wrote an extensive story, for instance, for North American News Alliance about women in top professional jobs in Washington DC, a story that was picked up by the *New York Times*. In it Frederick noted that women by 1938 were making strides in Washington as "cabinet officer, diplomat, director, bureau head"—jobs that carried "financial reward for heavier responsibility." In the story—which focused on Frances Perkins, Roosevelt's secretary of labor and the first female cabinet chief—Frederick detailed the salaries of these top women, their specific job duties, and their personal backgrounds.

While few women were on the air nationally in the late 1930s, women held a variety of jobs on radio networks during that time—primarily programming, research, advertising, and clerical jobs. One of the few women who made the switch from print news to radio was Mary Margaret McBride, a pioneering woman in radio news. McBride had written for several newspapers and in 1934 was one of more than fifty women to audition to become "Martha Deane" on WOR Radio in New York. As Martha Deane, she was given a forty-five-minute interview show, in which she talked to local and national figures in the news. McBride began hosting a network radio show for the Columbia Broadcasting System (CBS) in 1940 and continued in radio until 1960.

Frederick's interview show, *Let's Talk It Over*, had as a recurring theme women's role in society and politics and the role of women in shaping culture and world events. By 1939 women had had the right to vote for fewer than twenty years. And the interviews, for the most part, portrayed them as an emerging but new voice in shaping government—a voice distinguishable from that of their husbands. In an interview with Martha Bowers Taft, wife of then-senator Robert Taft of Ohio, for instance, the topic of the fifteen-minute show was "How to make a woman's vote count." With the exception of small talk at the beginning of the interview, Frederick pressed Mrs. Taft, an important figure in the League of Women Voters at the time, on her answers and often asked her to elaborate on vague or general comments.

FREDERICK: How do you get a woman who's pretty much tied to the home to vote?

TAFT: She'll vote right away when you make her see that political questions have a personal application to her household—you dramatize for her.

FREDERICK: How could you dramatize a thing like taxes, for instance?

TAFT: All you need to do is to point out to a woman that her husband works four days a week for his family and one for the government—that his one-day wage which goes to the government is often being spent for certain services and functions which she may or may not approve [of]. Arouse her shopper's instinct—is she getting her money's worth in police and fire protection, in good schools, in federal relief for her community, or is the money . . . being wasted or trickling away in graft?

FREDERICK: But how do you get a woman to vote right?

[At this point Mrs. Taft, a Republican, acts annoyed.]

TAFT: Be careful, Miss Frederick, don't give me the wrong cue or I'll start off into a good rousing speech for the GOP. And I know perfectly well that this is supposed to be a non-partisan interview.

FREDERICK: I hope it is. What I meant was . . . how can the women who are especially tied down to their homes get their information . . . Do they have to get it from their husbands?

Frederick also interviewed Lucretia Grady, the wife of Assistant Secretary of State Henry Francis Grady. When she asked Mrs. Grady about women's biggest concerns, she may have been surprised at a portion of the answer she received. After mentioning that she believed that the country should stay away from the "isms" of the day—fascism, Nazism, communism—Mrs. Grady added that women are getting increasingly educated, thanks in part to radio as an emerging news source. "Radio should have more women commentators," she said. "After all, we have representation and a very large interest in the news." "Far be it from me to say we shouldn't," Frederick replied. Interestingly, Grady's comment about the lack of women in radio apparently caught Cuthbert's ear. "I particularly liked her comment on there not being enough women commentators on the air and sent it around to our program directors for their information!" she wrote Frederick.

One of the more informational interviews Frederick conducted for the show was with Dorothy McAllister, director of Women's Activities for the Democratic National Committee, and Marion E. Martin, assistant chairman of the Republican National Committee. Their comments about the philosophy of their respective political parties sound remarkably similar to those voiced today. Frederick asked each why they belonged to the political party they represented, noting that some people found little difference between the two parties. Her guests disagreed with her contention. "Democrats believe in a paternalistic type of government with a superstructure in Washington," Martin, the Republican, said. "The GOP believes in states' rights. Democrats believe in lavish spending, the GOP in prudent use of other people's money."

McAllister was equally concise in stating her party's philosophy. "The Republican party is based on the philosophy that if a few people at the top prosper, the benefits will trickle down through to the rest," she said. "The Democratic party says that if there is to be a permanent prosperity in the country, there must be a wider distribution of purchasing power so the people at the bottom will have a decent chance at a livelihood."

Over the course of twenty-one months Frederick wrote and hosted nine episodes of *Let's Talk It Over*. The show was canceled in 1941, when the network decided to concentrate on coverage of World War II. But the short stint on radio was addictive to Frederick. "It tasted very good to me," she said decades later. "I from that time on decided that I would like most of all to broadcast rather than write my stories."

Frederick did not give up, however, on print journalism. By 1939 her years in Washington had reinforced the idea that cultivating sources and contacts was the key to success in journalism. Through her contacts the publishers of a book about the future of America asked her to write five chapters. The book, *America Prepares for Tomorrow*, published by Harper & Brothers in 1941, was marketed as a complete overview of America's defense efforts as seen by six "experts," of whom Frederick was one. The book allowed Frederick to use the knowledge she had gained in college and on the job, and it further cemented her reputation as someone in the know. By 1940 war news had hit the airwaves, and even print reporters knew that the immediacy of radio was crucial because radio broadcasts could convey war news within seconds after events happened. Frederick, like many other Washington reporters and commentators, was itching to cover the war overseas. By 1941, the year of the Pearl Harbor bombing and of U.S. entry into the war, she had had about a decade of experience in both the print and broadcast media, but she was still not aligned with a media outlet that could send her overseas.

Frederick's association with Baukhage opened many doors for her and helped establish her name and reputation in the world of Washington journalism. He was well-known among Washington journalists and at any given time was working for a variety of news outlets, from NBC Blue radio (later ABC) to *United States News* to the Western News Union syndicate, which distributed stories to weekly newspapers across the country. In the early 1940s Frederick was working for Baukhage, covering politics and government in Washington, but she was still stitching together part-time jobs in journalism and had a full-time job at the *Federal Register*. In the summer of 1944, using Baukhage as a reference, she traveled to Chicago to persuade editors at the Western News Union to credential her to cover the war in Europe. Sorry, she was told, the organization already had enough war correspondents.

Her attempts to become a foreign correspondent were thwarted, but Pauline Frederick found no shortage of news to cover in the mid-1940s. Although her desire to cover World War II overseas had not been realized, the postwar period brought with it world-changing events, including a meeting of fifty-one delegates in San Francisco in April 1945 to form the charter for a new worldwide peacekeeping organization to be called the United Nations. The meeting was a major event designed to formulate the structure of the new body as well as define how it would operate. It was part of a continuing story for Frederick, who had covered a historic meeting in Quebec of British prime minister Winston Churchill and President Roosevelt in 1944, when they conceived of the idea to establish an international institution that many believed could ultimately prevent another major war. "To see them in the flesh was quite an experience, "she recalled many years later. "Roosevelt with his cape and cigarette at an angle at which he always carried it, and pudgy Churchill with his cigar." What Frederick remembered most vividly, however, was not the actions or sight of these two men but the activities of someone else: "As they sat there . . . the famous dog [Fala] of President Roosevelt wandered out, sniffed at the feet of the great men and then lay down in front of

Churchill with its legs extended and stayed there throughout the conference." Roosevelt's famous Scottish terrier drew everyone's attention, Frederick noted. "While everyone tried to be serious and listen to what was being said, I'm afraid there was more attention being paid to Fala than there was to the great man."

The development of the charter for this new peacekeeping organization was considered a major story. Baukhage decided to leave his perch in Washington briefly to cover parts of it, but he believed that his young assistant was the perfect person to chronicle such an event. So, he dispatched Frederick to San Francisco in April 1945 to cover the formation of a charter for the United Nations.

As she prepared to leave for the trip, Frederick received word from the Western Newspaper Union that editors there wanted to hire someone to fly on an Air Transport Command (ATC) airplane over the Himalayas from India to China. The journalist credentialed by the WNU would be one of thirteen who would observe the activities of ATC pilots, who flew over the mountains to supply Allied military bases in China. Traveling to Asia had never been part of Frederick's plans, although when the WNU made her the offer, she quickly contacted the North American News Agency (NANA) to see if it, too, would accept freelance articles from Asia if she decided to take the job.

Frederick was ambivalent about the WNU offer. After all, she was about to travel to San Francisco to cover what could be one of the biggest stories of the decade. Also, she did not want to let down Baukhage, who was depending on her for reports about the formation of the charter for NBC Blue. And it would be impossible for her to do both jobs because there was no telling how long the charter meeting would go on—possibly for weeks or longer. (In fact, it lasted about two months.) Frederick turned down the WNU offer before she left for California and before she had received a response from NANA.

Throughout her career Frederick observed that her success in journalism resulted from three factors: hard work and determination; good fortune; and happenstance. Indeed, fate intervened that spring of 1945 shortly after she arrived in San Francisco. Waiting for her at the hotel was a letter from the editor at NANA telling her that the news agency might be interested in her stories in Asia if she uncovered something interesting. He also said he would help open doors for her with Chinese government officials. Frederick was torn. She knew what Baukhage would say if she asked for his advice—he would advise against the overseas trip and tell her that even if she did go, she would never succeed as an on-air radio news correspondent because no man would hire a woman in that capacity. It is evident that Baukhage cared about Frederick and looked out for her welfare, but he also maintained the same paternal—some would say patronizing—attitude of some men that women were much more fragile than men and that they were not meant to do jobs that could put them in danger. (For a year after the invasion of Pearl Harbor, in fact, the U.S. War Department prohibited women from working as credentialed war correspondents overseas because of the possible danger of the assignment.) Baukhage had been one of the most important influences of Frederick's early career as well as a mentor and friend. But she could not get the WNU offer out of her mind, even though she had already turned it down. As she recalled six years later, the decision to go came suddenly—when she was getting a manicure: "Then I jumped up and from the beauty parlor called Washington to see if the place was still open." The reason? "I realized that the charge of the United Nations was not going to be ratified or approved in a few days, especially with 51 nations having their own points of view," she said forty years later.

In fact, the opportunity was not still open, but fate intervened again. The editor who had arranged the trip, Henry Snevily, assigned someone else to the job but agreed to consider Frederick's stories and credential her for the trip spanning nineteen countries. Although Baukhage could not have been pleased by Frederick's decision to leave the charter meeting in San Francisco and serve as the only woman on an all-male delegation around the world, the two remained friends. While she did not always take Baukhage's advice, letters and telegrams between the two during her trip indicate she considered him a trusted colleague and sounding board; his correspondence to her shows that he respected her as a colleague and reporter and also cared about her well-being.

Frederick spent the next nine months or so traveling, literally, around the world. She missed the signing of the UN charter as well as the first meetings of the newly formed United Nations, which were held in London.

But the overseas experience was alternately exhilarating, frustrating, eye-opening, physically demanding, and, most of all, educational. The thirty-seven-year-old Frederick was a relatively young woman when she left Washington DC on June 2, 1945, to begin her thirty-five thousand-mile Air Transport Command tour with the other reporters, but she, like them, found the trip across North Africa, Iran, India, and parts of Europe tremendously taxing mentally and physically.

Before they left, the War Department sent the correspondents a two-page, single-spaced directive outlining what they should take with them during their upcoming trip. They would all wear the official uniform of the war correspondent, but the government made many other "suggestions" beyond that. The directives themselves indicated that living conditions during the trip might be rough: "Make sure you have all your shots . . . Wear the war correspondent uniform . . . High or GI shoes are recommended and a raincoat is must . . . Bring your own portable typewriter and a supply of copy paper, a notebook, and pencils . . . A flashlight is essential . . . Take a jar of sunburn lotion and two pairs of sunglasses . . . Pack a large box of Lux or some soap."

At each stop the reporters were given story ideas from military officials, but most were expected to file stories continuously. Some, like Frederick, were freelance writers who were paid only for stories that were published. Others were expected to file background information for stories being written at home by their news organizations. The reporters had very little free time when they were not seeking stories, gathering information, interviewing, and writing. And the physical demands placed on them were tremendous. As Frederick said in letters to her sister, to her father, and to Baukhage (whom she addressed as "Buck"), they sweltered in India, where the temperatures reached as high as 118 degrees, and they turned yellow from antimalarial medication. As pilots prepared to fly the C-54 at fifteen thousand feet across what was called the "hump" of the Himalayas, they warned their passengers of the hazards of the trip and said they could forgo that portion of it if they desired. None did, Frederick wrote her sister, noting that the oxygen mask she wore felt surprisingly comfortable. She wrote to Baukhage about the thrilling trip: "How you would revel in a trip like this. It's the experience of a lifetime."

As a freelance writer, Frederick received about twenty-five dollars per story. As a uniformed and credentialed overseas correspondent, her accommodations and food were provided. But she and the other reporters had not anticipated the challenges of trying to operate in crashed world economies. Very early in the trip Frederick indicated in letters to her family and to Baukhage that little had prepared her for what she saw and experienced, some of which had not been reported in the United States. In addition to bombed-out streets and homes and other widespread physical damage, for instance, the economic problems in China were phenomenal, with inflation and theft out of control. When she arrived there, one American dollar equaled eighteen hundred Chinese dollars; that exchange rate rose to three thousand to one when she left two weeks later. When Frederick's typewriter was stolen, she learned it could sell for up to three hundred American dollars on China's black market. "Have just had my typewriter stolen out from under my nose," she wrote Henry Snevily, her NANA editor in the states. "I can get one over here on the black market for $150.00 and up, but I've decided to borrow typewriters as I go along."

Still, she said, the Chinese held their heads high, repeating the cry *ding-hao*, which means "everything's fine." The stop in China was particularly eventful for Frederick as well as the other reporters because they could talk to high-ranking Chinese officials and American and Chinese military leaders, including Gen. Chiang Kai-shek. That access, along with visits to hospitals and prison camps, gave them a realistic idea of the toll war had on citizens—so much so that Frederick thought ABC Radio might be interested in a broadcast from China.

As Frederick prospered throughout her career, she was to achieve many "firsts." She was, for instance, the first female network news reporter, the first female to head the UN Correspondents Association, the first newswoman to win the national duPont reporting award, the first woman to moderate a presidential debate, among others. In China she achieved her initial first: first woman to broadcast news from China to the United States. The broadcast was far from clear, but that did not bother a delighted Kitty, Pauline's sister. "We were so thrilled to hear your voice," Kitty wrote to her. "The reception was bad but we could hear you say some things and heard you give your name and place. B. [H. R. Baukhage] sent us the record and we played it over and over again and I think your voice sounds wonderful and only once did I detect your Pennsylvania Dutch inflection when you sang one of the 'afternoons.'" Baukhage apparently told her that as a newly minted broadcast journalist, she should adapt an on-the-air speech pattern that carried no regional affiliation.

Frederick's broadcast for ABC radio from Chungking was exciting, but in some ways it was a comedy of errors. It was broadcast through shortwave and picked up by a dentist in Ventura, California, who relayed it to NBC. A combination of the primitive equipment and the time change meant that neither Frederick nor anyone else could be sure if the broadcast even went through. And at least one aspect of her reporting provided unintentional humor, thanks to some confusion when it came to translation. Frederick herself was the subject of news coverage in China because she was a woman who traveled long distances to cover a story. A female war correspondent was very much a novelty to two part-time women Chinese reporters, who were intrigued by Frederick's dedication to her job rather than to a husband and family, but miscommunication and language problems caused them to misinterpret a facetious comment she made. When they asked Frederick if she was married, she responded, jokingly, "I'm an old maid and spinster by preference." Their story focused on that sentence, with the translation misinterpreting its meaning. "She's an old maid and a spinster and isn't married because she hasn't felt the need of it," one of the women wrote in her story.

The interaction with the Chinese reporters provided Frederick a rare moment of levity on the trip. The destruction the reporters saw in Europe was far worse than what they saw even in Asia. Much of the infrastructure—bridges, roads, and railroads—was destroyed, and thousands of European citizens were starving and homeless or living in the rubble of their homes. The devastation Frederick witnessed appalled her. Most Americans, unaware of some of the most horrifying aspects of World War II, did not know of the war's effects on thousands of children. In Italy, for instance, Frederick met a dozen children who were taken in by Italian royalty after they had been maimed and blinded by air force bombings. Several of them had lost limbs, and one child she met had lost both his arms and legs.

When Frederick returned to Washington at the end of the ten-week tour, she was in many ways a changed person. She gave a series of speeches in and around Washington and in her home region of central Pennsylvania, and she tried to convey the horror of what she had seen. Mostly, however, she emphasized that the end of the war did not mean the end of suffering, as many Americans thought, nor did the surrender of the Germans bring peace for Europeans. American citizens were obligated to help their neighbors overseas, she believed. "People in this country will have to learn that the people in other countries who are suffering most for food and fuel must be fed, not only as a humanitarian service, but as a matter of preserving that for which we already have sacrificed and fought," she said in a speech to the American Newspaper Women's Club in Washington. "Democracy means nothing to the man or woman who is hungry." In January 1946 she wrote to Farnham Dudgeon, her editor at the WNU, "If the people back home could look once in a while beyond their own strike-torn shores, they'd know that the war is far from won . . . We haven't succeeded in bringing democracy, or much of anything else to our poor benighted neighbors on this side of the water."

Most of all, she said, Americans must be willing to make sacrifices to avoid another world war, which she considered very possible. A reporter covering her speech wrote: "Miss Frederick observed during her trip . . . that the war is far from over and the hardest is yet to come—if the world is to be spared another and far worse war in the future. This will greatly depend on the willingness of the people of the United States, she thinks, to do without butter, steaks and other good and nurturing foods so that the starving peoples in the other countries may be sufficiently nourished to enable them to resume a normal view of life."

Despite the hardships she suffered during the tour—including a negative reaction to the antimalarial medication that delayed her trip back to the states—the comforts of home were not much of a draw for Frederick. Her limited time in postwar Europe only whetted her appetite to return there. When she and the others were in Germany, they learned that thousands of Nazis were incarcerated in camps throughout Europe, awaiting criminal trials. With the help of her sister, Frederick sublet her Washington apartment and set out as a freelance writer to cover postwar France, Poland, Denmark, and the Nuremburg trials in the Bavarian region of southern Germany.

Before she left for Western Europe, Frederick hired a New York–based literary agent named Faustina Orner to help place the stories she would write from overseas. In addition, editors at the Toronto-based newspaper the *Star Weekly* had also indicated they might be interested in some of her stories from Nuremburg and other parts of Germany. Still, despite this expansion of possible markets for her work, Frederick found herself in a difficult and sometimes no-win situation. Her constant traveling caused her to miss connections with some of her editors and with Orner, even though her sister and Baukhage tried to help from afar. And she found that editors were not interested in breaking news stories because most had their own correspondents covering them. More frustrating, editors simply rejected some story ideas—for instance, what Frederick saw as an increasingly close and dangerous relationship between American servicemen and German women, as well as the suffering of German citizens. Editors felt their readers were not interested in stories that could be construed as being sympathetic to the Germans, nor did they want stories that might be seen as placing Allied soldiers overseas in a negative light. In fact, Orner in particular was sensitive about trying to sell stories that she felt caused readers to relive the ordeal of the war. "This Week [Sunday newspaper supplement] has now established a policy of no controversial articles," she wrote in one letter to Frederick. "In general, the attitude of the American public and the editors is that the war is over, let's forget it."

Letters to her sister, her family, Baukhage, and some editors indicate that Frederick was deeply ambivalent about many aspects of her trip to Germany in the latter part of 1945 and 1946. She knew reporting from Europe was a once-in-a-lifetime experience, but she was often overwhelmed by what she saw and heard. On the other hand, her nomadic existence sometimes triggered deep feelings of loneliness. During the dozen or so months of her life spent covering postwar Western Europe, her devotion to her work and a peripatetic existence left her little opportunity for romance. Although she fell in love on her second trip overseas, it was not destined to last.

As a credentialed correspondent, Frederick traveled with military forces, so her expenses overseas were small because the government covered her food, housing, and transportation. But her lifestyle, like that of the troops, was at best primitive and uncomfortable and at worst potentially dangerous. Letters to Baukhage often described the numerous hardships she endured while traveling long distances by plane and train. The Nuremberg press camp, for instance, which housed reporters covering the trials, was an old hotel, and in February "it was bitterly cold," she wrote, "and no heat in my room." She returned to Hereford, England, just in time for floods: "[Floodwaters] came so high around the hotel that for two days we had no heat, light or water, and life was a little grim, except that there was no let-up at the hotel bar." Other letters to her family noted that regular bathing and a daily change of clothes were often luxuries.

She told WNU editor Farnham Dudgeon in January that all traveling was risky in Western Europe—even by jeep: "Jeep riding in this weather is anything but pleasant, as you can imagine. There are some trains, but usually they don't go all the way to the place you are heading, so you fill in the gaps by other means of transportation. Of course, flying over here now is risking your life . . . so all advise [sic] is for you to stay on the ground." But the experience overseas was well worth the hardships, as she wrote to Tom Velotta, director of news for ABC radio, after she had been overseas for nearly six months: "I get homesick as the dickens to drop in on New York or Washington for a spell, but then I would want to come back over here for a while longer. It's a priceless experience."

The sheer inconvenience of being out of the United States combined with missing regular paychecks and the comforts of home took a toll on Frederick and those close to her. Her correspondence shows that her checks were sent to her sister Kitty in Pennsylvania, so she was sometimes kept in the dark about which of her stories had been published and who was paying her. And when Kitty did not hear from Pauline for an extended period, she grew worried and contacted Baukhage by letter to locate her. Baukhage was usually quick to reassure her and gave her Pauline's latest location if he knew it. But sometimes Kitty's notes to Pauline had a desperate and worried tone: "This is the fifth letter I have written you and from the letter we received yesterday written while you were flying the 'hump,' you have not yet received any of them."

As Frederick's trip overseas progressed, however, Kitty apparently grew accustomed to periods of silence from her sister, and she filled the letters with news from home. In addition to reviewing typical family gatherings, Kitty also wrote frequently about the health of their father, Matthew, who had been ill on and off since the death of Mrs. Frederick in 1940 at age sixty-eight. (Susan Catharine Frederick had for many years been ill with what then was diagnosed as "hardening of the arteries" and had long been frail, according to her granddaughter Catharine Cole.) Kitty also provided her sister with some of the comforts of home—she indicated in one letter that she had shipped off some jam and clothes that Frederick had requested.

Seeing war-torn Western Europe probably first triggered in Frederick her lifelong disgust for the senselessness of war—and it led her to believe few heroes emerge during wartime. When she first arrived in Nuremberg in December 1945, she was stunned by what she saw, writing to Kitty's husband, Lynn Crowding: "It's 80 percent destroyed . . . The thing that breaks your heart is the utter, senseless destruction of the old inner city—the city behind the walls and the towers and the moat which was old before America was ever born. It is the city whose towers and quaint Bavarian houses were seen on Christmas decorations. It was the place where Christmas toys were made . . . And there is unanimous agreement that it was smashed for spite and nothing else—the RAF [Royal Air Force] hit it on January 2 and then we completed what they didn't do . . . It seems to me that the premeditated vengeance is almost worse than the . . . Germans . . . doing what they did."

And she could or would not sugarcoat what she saw, even to her young niece Virginia, her brother Stanley's daughter: "Can you find Berlin on your map of Germany? That is where I am now . . . Yesterday as I was driving along I saw a beautiful yard with boxwood and evergreen all draped in snow and the pillars and steps of a mansion were all white. But I looked and I saw there was no door, and I looked through and there was nothing behind it-all bombed out. There wasn't even a second story, it had just been cut off as though by a big knife. I saw some boys and girls sledding in the park just like you and [Virginia's brothers] Fred and Harry, and they all had warm leggings and hoods. But it was very strange to see the benches without any seats on them—the wood had been chopped up for firewood." She added one final somber note: For the first time she saw a

German woman put out crumbs for the birds. "People usually don't have enough food to do that," she said.

The most frustrating part of Frederick's trip, however, seems to have been her inability to gauge what interested editors at home—editors who themselves were walking a fine line in providing their readers and listeners with the news while not making the German people appear too sympathetic. She wrote Baukhage, for example, that she got an exclusive interview with the British food director, who predicted food riots in the British zone of Germany if that region did not get wheat within a few weeks. "NANA unwanted German food stories in response to my query," she wrote.

Because of her remote location, she could not talk to editors or her agent, so she received contradictory and confusing messages about what kind of stories they sought. She told Baukhage that she had an idea for a long explanatory piece about the reasons for Hitler's rise, but her agent rejected it. "Well, I'm afraid I'm not very hot on this writing business," she wrote. "I just had a letter from [her agent] Miss Orner . . . labeling the Hitler thing a 'think' piece in which editors are not interested . . . Up to that point she said I was writing news stuff and not mag[azine] pieces and there were thousands over there if I would only find them." She later explained the problem in a letter to Orner. "As I told Mr. Baukhage it is a little difficult working in the dark and not knowing wherein I am failing, or not, to meet market requirements. I'm therefore eagerly anticipating your evaluation of the material I have sent you from time to time."

She indicated to her family and friends that the continual rejections were puzzling and humbling. But Baukhage did try to encourage her, and he inquired on her behalf what types of stories editors wanted. He urged her, in particular, to focus on stories about the psychology of the German people and their tendency toward "militarism" because that was what editors wanted. In March 1946 he wrote a telegram and letter asking her to send collaborative material and interviews for a story he was working on about "the problem of demilitarizing Germany . . . with emphasis on the youth . . . from the teenage up to thirty year-olders, I suppose." In the telegram he referred to that age as "the Hitlerized age bracket." Within days of receiving that correspondence, Frederick conducted interviews with psychologists and educators, including the head of a German psychiatric hospital. She reported his comments to Baukhage in a letter. "Reeducation has to come very slowly," she wrote. "If we should start telling the students how bad the Nazis were and how bad they were to join them, there would be resistance . . . The mis-education of the Germans had been so great that young people cannot be sure what is German and what is Nazi."

Along with tips on what kinds of stories editors would accept, Baukhage's letters also included some pep talks. His correspondence indicates that he understood well Frederick's determination and dedication. "You have had a remarkable lot of experiences and have encountered what was to be expected and what you ought to arm yourself for—continued disappointment," he wrote in one. "You still have a splendid chance to get yourself started on something creative without which you'll never be happy, I'll bet a nickel." In the same letter he wrote, "You HAVE to take chances. You can work like a stier [sic] when you have to and I know what it is not to have a deadline, but good Lord, instead of lamenting all this remember you have a chance that a lot of people would give their eye teeth for."

Despite the hardships and frustrations, or perhaps because of them, Frederick did find some happiness during her second trip to Europe in the form of a romance. Based on letters she wrote to her family and friends, she began a serious relationship with an attorney in army intelligence, Maj. David Howard Sokolow, whom she met in Heidelberg, and the two contemplated marriage after a two-month courtship. "He said he . . . wanted to marry me because he had fallen in love with me," she wrote her father in January. "It came so suddenly, and marriage was so far from my thoughts as I was just getting adjusted to being a war correspondent that I said I thought we really ought to get acquainted." The letter to her father sounded downright giddy as she described Sokolow: "We would like to be married in Switzerland, but nothing can be settled yet. David wants me to go to Copenhagen sometime soon and pick out a fur coat which he says will be my belated Christmas gift. He has given me his onyx ring and he is wearing the one I got in Chengtu. It's all very wonderful—I feel like I'm in a daze, so much has happened." Frederick went on to give a detailed biographical and physical description of him, noting he was born on January 1, "11 months and 12 days" after her birth.

"We are the same height, he has very black hair and a lot of sparkle. He calls me Butch."

The relationship seemed to end as quickly as it had begun, but letters indicate that this whirlwind romance, uncharacteristic for the thirty-eight-year-old Frederick, made her happy, at least temporarily. In the letter to her father she referred to him as "your son-in-law to be" and glowingly described in detail Sokolow's background and upbringing. A University of Illinois law graduate, he had been in the army for five years and was raised in Chicago in a devout Russian Orthodox home. "I'm afraid his biggest fault will be that he will be too good to me—but I have buffaloed him into thinking I'm wonderful," she said. She indicated she greatly admired him. "He is one of the most intelligent men to talk to I have ever met. He is deeply sensitive to fine things—consideration of other people—graciousness. Absolutely refuses to discuss another person unless he can find something good to say about them . . . He longs for a home where there will be gracious living—where people know how to live—where there is culture, good talk, music, art, furnishings in excellent taste."

About three weeks later, however, she wrote her sister that she was about to call off the engagement. She gave no concrete reasons but hinted at one. "You were a little bit doubtful about the suddenness of it, and since I have had some time to think, I'm not sure about things," she wrote. She pointed to one aspect of her fiancé's background that bothered her: "David made most of his money defending the gangs in Chicago on the theory that a man who is accused has the right to an attorney whether he is guilty or not . . . I suppose that's true, but if he goes back to his practise [sic], I'm not sure that I could take it . . . I hate to get people's hopes so high and then let them down!!!" It is unclear whether Sokolow's background bothered her enough to break off the engagement or whether Frederick's desire for independence ultimately forced the separation. Much later in her life, when she was a well-known and respected NBC correspondent, Frederick made reference in a *Saturday Evening Post* profile to a man who broke off an engagement when he learned she could not have children. It is unknown if that man was Sokolow. Frederick's niece Catharine Cole remembered her mother telling her and her sister that "Aunt Polly" was getting married and that the little girls would get dresses for the wedding.

But the girls' glee was short-lived. "We were so excited—it was like the queen was going to get married," Cole recalled. Literally a few days or a week later, their mother informed them that the wedding was off. "I'm sorry. It's not going to happen," was all she said.

Frederick apparently cut all ties with Sokolow. But in letters to her sister and to her childhood friend Ann Cordell, she exhibited an uncharacteristic emotional display of homesickness and regret. "After I had been traveling around in the British Zone for three weeks an American AP man came into the Press Camp at Herford [*sic*] and said 'Hello, Yank,' and I could have wept," she wrote to her sister. "In Copenhagen, my escort at dinner twice told the orchestra there was an American in the audience, and he struck up *Over There* and *My Old Kentucky Home* and I just started to cry."

And she found it depressing to celebrate a birthday overseas. "I was awfully blue at being on the eve of another birthday—when I would be 38—much too old for not yet really having found myself," she wrote Cordell. Her sadness was relieved, however, when she struck up a conversation with a British military government official in the hotel lobby in Brussels. When she mentioned it was her birthday, "we had a very pleasant time—philosophical discussion—integrity, emotion and subjects like that. Then I dashed off to get my train." Some of Frederick's letters during the spring of 1946 were unusually wistful and even flighty. "I think I'll find me a sugar daddy and take a nice long stretch at the Riviera or in Switzerland," she wrote friends "George" and "Freda" in April. "I get a little wary of this rugged existence."

Frederick was not about to miss the trials at Nuremberg, however, which had begun in November 1945 and continued through much of the next year. Key parts of the proceedings were scheduled for the spring of 1946. Frederick and some other reporters discussed the possible long-term effects of the trials in Nuremberg on the German people. They feared that the almost-certain guilty verdicts for the twenty-four former Nazis on trial could instill sympathy for them on the part of Germans. A story in the trade publication *Publisher's Auxiliary* quotes Frederick, whom they identified as a correspondent for the Western Newspaper Union, as saying that most Germans simply did not believe the stories of atrocities outlined by the prosecution and that they considered such tales propaganda.

Frederick was lucky at least once during the trials when the regular ABC correspondent was not available to cover the testimony of Hermann Goering, the highest-ranking survivor of the Third Reich. Later in her career Frederick would find again that serving as an understudy and taking on assignments that others were forced to miss could be a key to success. As she recalled much later, she would never have been assigned the Goering broadcast if not for a combination of "work and luck." "I must have unconsciously been preparing for it my whole life, for everything I have done has led to it," she said. But that didn't break down the prejudice against a woman discussing world events. "They simply stood adamant that a woman's voice didn't carry authority in a man's field. And that was that. But then I filled in in an emergency and that's all." Frederick's ability to fill in during an emergency should not be taken lightly. At pivotal times in her career her willingness to uncomplainingly fill in for someone is what led to bigger and better things for her.

Goering's testimony generated particular interest because he was seen as a crafty and clever defendant who many thought outfoxed prosecutors. Frederick's ABC broadcast of the testimony, her first international broadcast since the one from China, was a major story for her and one of the great successes of her trip. It received mixed reviews, however, from Baukhage, who wrote her with a critique: "You sounded a little tense and nervous at first; later you relaxed . . . You are as good as any of the other ABC'ers, far better than some of the terribly naïve, sing-songer's [sic] ABC has to offer . . . I trust you have your foot in the door and that you will not expect many assignments and will get a lot." Frederick's written coverage of Goering's testimony was picked up by NANA, and that coverage, combined with the radio broadcast, made it her biggest story from postwar Europe.

Frederick's relatives back home were treated to some inside stories and descriptions about the Nuremberg trials that never made it into print. "I have been fascinated and impressed by some of the proceedings. It is almost unreal to sit there and listen to the unbelievable facts—stranger than fiction being unfolded," Frederick wrote her brother-in-law Lynn Crowding. "I hope the trial is getting the play it deserves back home . . . And the men who carried out these acts have to sit there in the prisoner's dock and listen to their own words that are going to convict them being entered into the record. Of course, I can't help but feel that the ghost of Hitler hangs heavily over the place." Frederick clearly had her own views of some of Hitler's leading lieutenants. "[Goering] said he was so devoted to Hitler he would do it all again and that seems to be the general attitude," she wrote Crowding. "Goering has an ugly licentious face although the guards testify that he is the kindest of them all in his conduct."

Frederick sent short dispatches from the trial to news outlets at home, but she remained determined that editors accept some of her more in-depth story ideas. One series of stories in particular focused on how five families in Belgium, Denmark, France, Germany, and Holland were rebuilding their lives after everything they owned had been destroyed in the war. WNU heavily promoted the series, branding it a syndicate "exclusive" and calling it "Europe's Little People—1946." This human interest series was not the type of hard news or interpretive story that Frederick preferred, but through it she managed to convey the scope of the devastation in Europe and explain how innocent citizens were affected by war. Another of her stories, published on the front page of the *New York Times*, revealed the shocking conditions in postwar Poland, where, she wrote, the Polish people seemed to have exchanged one form of subjugation for another. Frederick was so shocked that she wrote the story in first person, giving it a true sense of urgency. "I have just returned from an eight-day stay in Poland and I could scarcely believe . . . what I saw and heard," she wrote in the second paragraph. The country was on the brink of civil war, she said, after one hundred thousand demonstrators jammed the streets of Cracow protesting terrible living conditions, censorship of the news, and the Communist Party's military government. She quoted a Polish college professor: "The people of Poland have had subjugation, we have had occupation and now we want liberation. Poland . . . looks to the United States for salvation."

She was not so fortunate, however, when it came to another of her story ideas—a long piece about the relationship between young German women and American GIs stationed in Germany. Frederick witnessed the complicated sexual and psychological relationship between German women and American soldiers. Included among her personal papers is a typewritten copy of a very long story about the "fraternization" of American soldiers and German women, who were willing to provide sexual favors in exchange for such basic needs as food and clothing. American news managers did not seem interested in this story, which did not put American soldiers in a positive light and would no doubt cause pain for their families at home.

But Frederick had significant evidence of extensive fraternization, or "fratting," as it was called. In addition to bringing it up as a story idea, she alluded to it in letters to friends and family. In a letter to Baukhage, for instance, she raised the issue of German women "not wanting their babies any more."

Frederick tried to frame the story in practical terms, quoting a colonel as saying that chaos would result when the wives of soldiers visited them in Germany and could not avoid meeting their German "girlfriends." She wrote: "Thousands of American women . . . will join their occupation force husbands in Germany by the end of summer. The frauleins are German women who have been scrounging chocolate, cigarettes, army rations, warm places to sleep and affection from American men since V-E day." She noted that American wives would be "coming to communities in which war has let down the standards of behavior to the point where promiscuity is openly accepted, especially between the frauleins and American men. Normal jealousy is compounded by the fact that American women look down on the fraulein and the fraulein knows it. And the fraulein resents her social and economic security."

The fraternization story was accepted by the WNU syndicate but rejected by most editors. Mention of the series appeared in a brief story in the trade publication *Publishers' Auxiliary*, which discussed the plight of American news correspondents covering postwar Europe. Although the headline reads, "Hair-Pulling When GI's American Wives Meet Nazi Frauleins, WNU Writer Predicts," the story mentions Frederick's predictions of trouble between the German women and wives only in its last three paragraphs. "With keen feminine insight, Miss Frederick writes feelingly about the 'psychological war' which she claims German women are trying to win against American soldiers," the story says. Yet few newspapers published the story, despite the syndicate's attempts to couch it as a women's story. Some press reports at the time focused on the reputation of American soldiers overseas as "women-chasers" who, while on "R and R trips," drank and patronized prostitutes. The issue of fraternization between Americans and Germans overseas was mentioned less frequently, but it was considered a greater threat because wives and girlfriends back home feared this behavior could lead to lasting relationships. Wartime censors, of course, tried to keep reports of fraternization and philandering by GIs from the press.

The failure of the fraulein series to get traction in the American media exemplified Frederick's frustrations at being a freelance writer who had no full-time association with a specific news outlet. But her time in postwar Europe did further open her eyes to the ways of the world and to the horrors of war. And although she may not have known it at the time, the experience was indispensible for her in getting her foot in the door in radio. When she returned to the United States in the fall of 1946, she began work—without a full-time contract—for ABC Radio in New York. As soon as she became accustomed to reporting exclusively for radio, another job opportunity came along, this one with the emerging new medium of television.

3 *Talking about Serious Things*

We have a long list of women applicants and, as you know, little opportunity to use them. I am afraid that Miss Frederick's name cannot be put very near the top of the list.

EDWARD R. MURROW, August 29, 1946

Pauline Frederick returned to the United States from Europe in the late summer of 1946 exhausted and ill—she went directly to the home of her sister, Kitty, in Sunbury, Pennsylvania, where she spent the next few weeks recovering. Her niece Catharine, a teenager at the time, remembers her aunt's return and recalls how she spent the first few days of it on the family's living room couch, with Kitty caring for her. A few months before she returned home, Frederick had written to a friend that she had been hospitalized briefly for what she called "atabrine poisoning" (atabrine, or quinacrine, was a chemical used in antimalarial medications). The nature of her illness upon her return is unknown, but it required that she receive constant care.

Frederick's initial plans were to return to Washington to the apartment she had sublet for the last year or so, but she was clearly exhausted mentally. In speeches and interviews for the rest of her life, she would refer to the atrocities she had viewed in Europe as haunting experiences that reinforced her opinion that war was horrific and should be avoided at all costs. "I saw such terrible devastation . . . in so many countries that I couldn't believe it," she once said. "I couldn't believe that human beings could act this way, and as a consequence if I was ever sold on an effort to preventing war, I was sold then." The idea that war could be avoided at all was perhaps an idealistic philosophy but one she would maintain most of her life. While she always believed that war benefits no one, her idealism had been shattered by the time she retired. Decades after she returned from Western Europe, after she had become a respected and well-known NBC correspondent, transcripts of speeches she gave indicate that her memories from that era were still raw and vivid. In one typical speech in 1955 she said: "In Italy I looked on the jagged ruins of villages and . . . the human splinters of little children—children without arms and legs and eyes. In Britain and France and Germany and Poland I saw desolation and destruction. In the freight yards at Cracow I watched human beings crawl out of the straw of cattle cars to try to warm themselves besides the tracks . . . I saw in Germany the concentration camps, the ovens that bore mute testimony to the horror that had been perpetrated there."

It is difficult to gauge if, as a woman, Frederick's reporting differed in tone or subject from that of her almost exclusively male colleagues who also covered the aftermath of the war. But some studies have indicated that women reporters and editors do by nature have a different take on war than males and may be less content to rely on "official" government sources for information. As Steve Hallock notes in his study of government influence on the press in covering the buildup to wars after World War II, normally skeptical news managers may abandon their traditional watchdog functions in times of war (hence, the rejections Frederick received from many editors). He speculates on the reasons: "I understand . . . the weight and credibility that official sources lend to news reports . . . I understand how public officials try to use newspapers and their perceived influence to shape public opinion. I understand how and why newspapers buy into these officials' positions and arguments—because these same officials lay claim to the facts and often exclusive information behind their policies and thus assert the mantle of authority and credibility."

Frederick's home was Washington DC, an exciting and promising city for reporters looking for work. But many of the journalists who had covered the war returned to media jobs in New York City, home to many of the nation's largest media outlets. New York City was the epicenter of the storm that was overtaking journalism in the late 1940s—the rise of broadcast news. Frederick knew that if she wanted a job, she had to go where the jobs were, even though most of those jobs went to men. But she was optimistic. She had become accustomed to dealing with male news managers, and with few exceptions her bosses and coworkers were male. Baukhage, gruff and direct as he was, served as an important role model and sounding board for her, especially when she was in Europe. And the two professors who urged her to continue her education and pursue a career in journalism, Charles Callan Tansill and Arthur Flemming, were men. Also, Frederick was closer to her father than her mother. Matthew Frederick passed on his passion for world events to his daughter, who never cared much about mastering the domestic arts.

When Pauline Frederick returned to the United States, she was ready to continue what was an active and thriving, if not lucrative, career. She had become a reliable and steady source of stories for the North American News Agency, and she continued to write for the news service after she returned. Although she worked on a freelance basis for NANA, she obtained many exclusives for the news service and sometimes landed hard-to-get interviews. She obtained an interview, for instance, with author Elliott Roosevelt, son of the late president, who had stirred controversy when in his latest book manuscript he indicated that British prime minister Winston Churchill was a heavy drinker who had been imbibing during key meetings with President Roosevelt. A magazine had published excerpts from the yet-unpublished book, and many readers complained that the stories placed Churchill in an unflattering light. "I don't consider that I have made any derogatory statements about Mr. Churchill in my book," the author said in the first sentence of Frederick's story. Although Elliott Roosevelt denied to Frederick that he painted an unflattering picture of Churchill, she noted that the publisher of the book, to be called *As He Saw It*, had plans to delete many of the passages.

The interview with Elliott Roosevelt did not signal the end of the Roosevelt-Churchill controversy. When the prime minister's son, Randolph, visited Washington in 1946, Frederick interviewed him for ABC's radio show *Inside Edition*. Frederick—never one to shy away from controversy—asked him his opinion of the Roosevelt biography of his father. Randolph Churchill's reply was curt and somewhat snide. "My father is still alive. He can look after himself. The tragedy is that the

President is dead," he replied. Churchill implied that Eleanor Roosevelt might set the record straight about Winston Churchill: "Perhaps Mrs. Roosevelt will do something to look after his [Roosevelt's] memory." Frederick reminded him that Mrs. Roosevelt had written the foreword to her son's book. "Oh, dear, I didn't know that," Churchill responded. Frederick also asked him if he thought another war was possible. "Not imminent, but unavoidable," he replied, adding, "It seems as though war in 1946 is as inevitable as it was in 1936. But it could be as easily stopped now as it was then." When Frederick asked him to elaborate, he told her listeners to attend his U.S. lectures.

In another story for NANA Frederick linked the ramifications of World War II and the resulting fear and uncertainty to trends in women's hairstyles. Written with a wink, Frederick wrote that fear of another war, shortages of some grocery products, and uncertainty about who will be elected president "are starting to wind themselves into the American woman's hair!" As a result, she said, the glamorous and complicated hairstyles women wore to please their husbands when they returned from overseas were being replaced by simpler and shorter styles. Frederick was not above using a pun in the lead of her story: "There is being born a new style in coiffures in which milady takes down her hair—so to speak—to put it up simply, if at all."

One of Frederick's biggest scoops during her first year at home was an interview with first daughter Margaret Truman, who was notoriously shy with the press. Miss Truman, then twenty-three, was training to become an opera singer. Frederick quoted her as saying that she "never wanted any special consideration because I happen to be the daughter of the President. I want to stand on my own two feet." Frederick described Truman's "typical" day, down to what she had for breakfast (usually grapefruit, bacon and eggs, and coffee, prepared by her live-in companion, Mrs. T. J. Stricker, who held the vague title of "coach and lifelong friend"). That story earned her a congratulatory memo from the editor at NANA and fifteen extra dollars in her paycheck. An assistant to John Wheeler sent a message enclosed with a forty-dollar check for payment for the story: "Mr. Wheeler asked me to point out that this is a bonus for getting a good story to show our appreciation."

Despite her recent experience in broadcasting, Frederick was still more comfortable writing for print outlets. She had more space to tell the story, and she was more confident in her abilities as a writer for that medium. But as the end of World War II brought changes in many aspects of life, it also created explosive opportunities for news broadcasters. Radio during wartime had provided listeners an opportunity to get breaking news immediately, something newspapers could not do. Also, some of the manufacturing that had slowed or been stopped during the war picked up again—and this growth brought with it technological advances that would have far-reaching implications for radio and television.

As Edward Bliss Jr. wrote in his comprehensive history of broadcasting, *And Now the News*, radio had served the nation well during the war. The Federal Communications Commission (FCC) was flooded with AM and FM applications, and radio was becoming such a fixture for Americans that they were beginning to get radios installed in their cars. About thirty-four million Americans had radios in their homes in 1945, up by about four million from 1940. By 1952 forty-six million households, or about 96 percent of all homes, had radios. In what he labeled the "vintage" years of radio news, Bliss notes that some radio reporters, too, had high-profile and prestigious jobs. Some traveled around the world getting stories, and a job covering a foreign capital could mean lavish living with a large expense account. Radio allowed Americans to get news virtually around the clock, a phenomenon that was a boost to television. While the war postponed the development of television temporarily, that technology and the kind of programming it could provide grew tremendously after the war ended. As early as 1941, CBS had provided limited television news coverage, and Bliss writes that RCA introduced an improved television camera soon after the war.

Whether they understood it at the time, young journalists such as Frederick faced a brave new world in 1946—they could thrive if they fully appreciated the changes that were coming and if they were willing to take chances and learn new skills. The FCC had ruled in 1945 that NBC's operation of two networks, the Red and the Blue, was monopolistic, forcing the sale of the NBC Blue network and its ultimate renaming to the American Broadcasting Company. The new network needed top news managers who were hardworking, enthusiastic, and courageous. Frederick's work overseas had introduced her to two men who would ultimately be instrumental in shaping the arc of her career: Robert Kintner and Tom Velotta, men who would become news executives at ABC and later NBC.

Kintner, like Frederick and many other radio broadcasters, had a print background. He was a financial writer and Washington correspondent for the much-respected *New York Herald Tribune*, and he had served in U.S. Army Intelligence during the war. After his discharge from the army, he rose quickly in the ranks of ABC, becoming executive vice president in 1946 and president in 1950. Kintner was an innovative and bold executive, and he admired Frederick's work with ABC. In one of Kintner's experiments with news programming for the network, he developed an hour-long news show in 1952, created in part to compete with popular shows such as *I Love Lucy*. The show, called *All-Star News*, aired on four weekday evenings and featured four reporters: Gordon Fraser, Leo Cherne, Bryson Rash, and Pauline Frederick. It was canceled after a year because it failed to make money but is now considered a forerunner to the successful newsmagazine shows that came much later. Kintner was hardworking and creative, and he valued those qualities in others. And Kintner was known as someone who could spot talent: when he worked at NBC, it was he who first saw potential in the anchor team of Chet Huntley and David Brinkley, and it was he, with his attention to detail, who made sure that NBC News had a camera at the transfer of Lee Harvey Oswald from a Dallas jail, so that network alone was able to air the shooting in 1963 of Oswald by Jack Ruby. Tom Velotta, whom Frederick also knew from her reporting overseas after the war, was named special events chief for ABC. The three of them—Kintner, Velotta, and Frederick—would work together for many years after the war ended, both at ABC and NBC.

Most published photos of Frederick on the job in the late 1940s depict her surrounded by men—they are either her colleagues at ABC or the subjects of her stories. While the photos may imply that Frederick was one of the guys figuratively but not literally, this was not the case. Several years after the end of World War II, the networks still seemed ambivalent about women. While executives knew that women listened to broadcasts, they did not quite know what women wanted to hear, and they were unsure what to do with the women they employed. Frederick had certainly paid her dues in Washington before the war, covering federal agencies and legislative bodies, and she had traveled all over the world in the immediate aftermath of the war. Perhaps most important, she had made many contacts in the world of journalism. So, by August 1946, when she returned to the United States, all indications were that her gender would not hold her back. But a letter she received that month quashed any hope that her gender would not be an obstacle in her job search. It was a letter about her from CBS correspondent Edward R. Murrow, who had made a name for himself during the war and whom many still regard as one of the most influential figures in American broadcasting. Murrow, who in 1946 was thirty-eight, the same age as Frederick, had been sent by CBS to assemble a group of correspondents to report from the front lines of the war. That group, which came to be known as "Murrow's Boys," provided some of the most courageous and compelling accounts of the war, and most of Murrow's "boys" would become household names in broadcasting over the next four decades. When Murrow returned home, he was a star.

Frederick apparently sent audition plates to Murrow in mid-1946 seeking a job. She received a copy of the reply, sent from Murrow to Robert Kennett, who was in CBS's program relations department: "I have listened to the records submitted by Pauline Frederick. She reads well and her voice is pleasing but I would not call her material or manner particularly distinguished . . . We have a long list of women applicants and, as you know, little opportunity to use them. I am afraid that Miss Frederick's name cannot be put very near the top of the list. E.R.M." Kennett mailed a copy of the memo to Frederick in Pennsylvania, along with an apologetic note: "I am enclosing [Murrow's] brief and rather frank comment on your work. As you know, CBS has never gone in too heavily on the women's slant in the News Department. We did experiment with a Women's Club feature during the summer months, but it has gone off the air now. Don't let this discourage you in the least because I think eventually you will find a spot in the type of work you desire . . . I have shipped your Audition Records back."

For decades Frederick and a few other pioneering female broadcasters debated whether it was midlevel news managers or top network executives who determined that women would not make suitable network correspondents. Marlene Sanders, another broadcast pioneer who was one of a handful of female network television correspondents to come along in the mid-1960s, believes it was probably a decision made by top network executives. In her memoir and history of women in broadcasting, she speculates that based on his behavior, Murrow, specifically, did not seem to oppose hiring women. In the 1940s he hired Mary Marvin Breckinridge for CBS radio, and he tried to hire Helen Kirkpatrick before his efforts were vetoed by top CBS executives. Breckinridge had been a friend of Murrow's from college and was a top-notch radio correspondent; Kirkpatrick was a London correspondent for the *Chicago Daily News*.

If Frederick was "discouraged," as Kennett termed it, she did not show it—she applied for work at ABC in New York City and was given a job of sorts as a part-time correspondent with no contract and no promise of full-time work. But the note from Murrow must have had a dramatic effect on her—she kept it for the rest of her life and, decades later, made reference to it in interviews, mostly to illustrate how reluctant the networks were to acknowledge that men and women could be equals professionally. After she worked at ABC for three years and had become a well-known name there, she told an interviewer that the road was not easy. "When ABC hired her, they defied a prejudice against female news announcers as old as radio itself," the reporter wrote. "For Pauline it was a well-earned victory after many heartaches." He then quotes Frederick. "Sometimes I almost gave up and would go off for a good long cry," she told him. "But it was the anger more than anything else that made me stick it out."

While network officials were certainly willing to take advantage of women's talents and dedication to the job, they were unwilling to give them the same job duties and pay as men. Many women held important jobs, often in public affairs programming, but they were behind-the-scenes positions that did not carry the prestige of being on the air. Martha Cuthbert, who had given Frederick her first break in broadcasting on NBC Red radio, was one example. NBC was ahead of its time in establishing a department of "women's programming," and as head of that department, Cuthbert made sure the network treated both its male and female listeners as intelligent people who were interested in world affairs. As Bliss noted in his history of broadcasting, Cuthbert devoted her nearly thirty-year career to NBC, beginning as a receptionist and jack-of-all-trades at an NBC affiliate and working her way up to director of children's programming for the network and, eventually, head of public affairs programming. She retired in 1952.

Frederick clearly benefited from Cuthbert's pioneering work and her willingness to help other women at NBC. She often acknowledged Cuthbert's professional generosity, calling her "marvelous" and someone who had continually encouraged her. Still, when Frederick was hired by ABC in 1946 (without a contract), she stood out in the world of radio. "I was such an object of curiosity as to be completely rebuffed by NBC and CBS. Only ABC was willing to risk a female voice on the [radio] airwaves," she said.

In the fall of 1946 Frederick moved into a tiny apartment at 802 Ninth Avenue in Manhattan, to work for ABC. The network imposed two restrictions on her hiring. First, she would be hired as a freelance reporter only, and second, she would work on stories for women. "My occasional assignment was to cover so-called women's news; that is, fashion shows and the like," she said later, even though she made it known that she would rather report on news. One of her editors, John Dunn Jr., told her that his bosses had quietly given him orders not to use Frederick on the air in news stories. "I'll have to slit your throat if you ever tell anyone I told you this," he said. "When people turn on the radio and hear a woman talking about serious things, it just doesn't have the same authority." But Dunn also revealed to Frederick a trade secret: if she got an exclusive story, she could go on the air with it. It was valuable information.

When she started at ABC Radio in New York, one of her first assignments was to cover a forum about "How to Get a Husband." For decades Frederick would use this assignment as a source of humor. Because she remained single for most of her life, lessons of the forum apparently did not take, she would joke. And much later, after she married, she amended that quip to note that she was a slow learner.

Still, as Frederick struggled to broadcast hard news at ABC, network executives were not the only ones to build barriers; sometimes news sources resented her very existence. She was once assigned to cover the presidential inauguration of Tomás Berreta in Montevideo, Uruguay, and the assignment required that she fly with the army air force on a B-29 to that country. Because she would be the only woman among 130 officers and correspondents, air force officials at first refused to let her go, stating that policy prohibited women on board. Frederick appealed the decision in a self-described "stinging" letter in which she promised not to "corrupt the men," and air force officials relented. But her ordeal was not over— the general in charge became furious as soon as he saw her. But there was little he could do. Frederick's coup, however, was not making the trip but, instead, being congratulated after it ended. The same general who had opposed her participation praised her lavishly after it was over. She was a "good sport," according to a story about Frederick in the trade publication *Editor & Publisher*. "[The general] proposed a toast to her, and kissed her while the officer and male correspondents applauded," the story said. Frederick told that light anecdote many times in her life, but it had a serious point: the reason the general came to respect her, she explained, was that she had made sure to defy stereotypes. She was always punctual, she did not complain, and, above all, she did not make waves. "As a woman, I was very conscious of my responsibility to be self-reliant," she said. "And especially not to keep anyone waiting." And she was also proud of her self-sufficiency. "I've covered crime, fire and flood; war, Washington and Wall Street," she once told a reporter. "No editor has ever had to fish me out of trouble."

Frederick often said that luck played a major role in her success, but like many accomplished people, she did not acknowledge overtly that one must sometimes make one's own luck—or know when to take advantage of opportunities. This is what happened when ABC assigned her to what some news reporters labeled a junket: the last voyage of the *Queen Mary* as a troop ship before it was converted to a luxury liner and renamed the *Queen Elizabeth*. "Somebody had to go to England to cover the final voyage of the Queen Mary. ABC wouldn't spare a man, so I went," she said—but Frederick saw it as an opportunity to get exposure and to meet newsmakers, even though ABC had made it clear she would be paid only for copy it used. Unused stories would mean a waste of time and money for her. In September 1946 she and sixty-nine other American and British reporters—again, all of them male except for Frederick—boarded the *Queen Mary* to England and returned the following month on the *Queen Elizabeth*. As she had planned, Frederick did meet many current and future newsmakers on board, and she earned valuable experience by providing continual broadcasts from the *Queen Mary*. Dwight D. Eisenhower, then chief of staff of the army, was one passenger she met and one who would of course become an important newsmaker in the future. More important, however, was the fact that key diplomats who were instrumental in the activities of the newly formed United Nations were passengers on the *Queen Elizabeth*, including Russian diplomat Vyacheslav Molotov, who notoriously shunned the press and who, with the others, was on his way to the last meeting of the Big Four foreign ministers at the Waldorf Astoria hotel in New York. Members of the American delegation were returning from the Paris Peace Conference and headed to Lake Success, New York, for the first meeting of the United Nations General Assembly. Although Frederick had not yet begun covering the new United Nations on a regular basis, the contacts she made on the ships would prove to be of great value to her.

The broadcasts she made to ABC affiliate stations from the *Queen Elizabeth* demonstrated to network officials that Frederick was capable of working on her own and covering a continuing story in an innovative and concise way. But if she thought this success would earn her a regular beat on ABC or allow her to cover hard news, she was wrong.

On the evening of November 4, 1946, a combination of fate and opportunity converged, and as Frederick told it for years, her life and career would forever change as a result. By that time Pauline Frederick had covered numerous national and international stories, the aftermath of a war, and, of course, many forums and conferences about fashion and society. But she had never covered a trucking strike, and when truckers walked off the job one evening in late 1946, she was not assigned to cover it. Still, the decision by those truckers would indirectly change her life.

Two reporters were working for ABC local news manager Paul Scheffel that evening, but he knew which one he had to send to cover the strike. Violence could break out, and he could not send Pauline Frederick, a woman—it would be too dangerous. Instead, Scheffel sent the lady reporter on another major but more sedate story: coverage of the Big Four foreign ministers conference at the Waldorf Astoria in Manhattan. The group was composed of U.S. secretary of state James Byrnes, Vyacheslav Molotov of the Soviet Union, Ernest Bevin of Great Britain, and Georges Bidault of France.

Frederick was thrilled. Her studies in school, her experience covering the development of the United Nations charter meeting in San Francisco, and her chats with diplomats aboard the *Queen Elizabeth* had prepared her well for this assignment. That evening she went on the air with an account of the meeting. ABC news executives were so pleased with her lucid and comprehensive account that they continued to send her to these meetings on the thirty-seventh floor of the hotel.

Security was heavy for the first key gatherings of the newly formed United Nations, and it was hardly an action-packed event: Frederick and other reporters spent most of their time waiting for meetings to end. But Frederick had a clear advantage over many of the other reporters when it came to identifying sources, and her knowledge of and experience in international politics also gave her an edge. In addition to covering the breaking news at the gatherings, she broadcast many scoops and established valuable news sources during the weeks of the meetings. Afterward she was assigned by ABC to provide regular coverage of the United Nations, which then had its headquarters in Lake Success, New York, in Nassau County. (After the London conference UN sessions were held temporarily at Hunter College; then they were held in more permanent venues in Lake Success and, to a limited extent, Flushing Meadows.) The commute from midtown Manhattan to Lake Success may have been inconvenient for Frederick, but she did not mind. She quickly carved out a niche as the only female radio reporter to cover the meetings regularly.

By this time Frederick had been spending most of her time covering feature stories for ABC and writing on a freelance basis for NANA. Her income for 1946 was $1,456, with $769 of it from NANA. She hoped to earn more than that as a journalist and soon began to suspect that, with her experience overseas and a seemingly glamorous job, there were more ways for her to make additional money. She had always been adept at networking, and she had many friends in journalism in Washington DC.

Now, as a fixture in the New York journalistic scene, she mingled with other reporters and in the course of conversation got tips about how to thrive in the relatively new world of radio broadcasting. One piece of advice she received was to give speeches and lectures to earn extra money and to establish a high public profile. In late 1946, at the suggestion of Baukhage, she hired a law firm—Hall, Dickler, Kent, Friedman and Wood—to represent her in salary negotiations and a speakers' bureau to obtain lecture engagements for her. Both would pay off. She retained Hall, Dickler throughout her career, and the firm helped her greatly in salary negotiations as she became a well-known and sought-after network correspondent. And indeed, speaking engagements throughout her career provided her with extra income and helped build her reputation. Newspaper articles found among her papers show that even before she signed on with the speakers' bureau, Frederick had given numerous talks about her time overseas, mostly to groups in Pennsylvania, in the region where she was raised. In late 1949 she gave the keynote speech for the Conference on American Foreign Policy at Colgate University, a forum that also included John Foster Dulles, future U.S. secretary of state, who at the time was a U.S. delegate to the UN. Over the decades she would become an extremely popular speaker who gave literally hundreds of speeches in her life—about topics as diverse as international events, the United Nations, and the role of women in journalism.

Within eighteen months of her arrival in New York in 1946, at least two major media outlets wrote stories about Frederick's role as the sole female network news correspondent, and several other smaller publications published profiles of her. In October 1947 a *Newsweek* story headlined "Spinster at the Mike" recounted how, as the only woman network correspondent on radio, she had traveled extensively around the world. It described Frederick's interview with the two Chinese reporters in Chungking who had not realized she was joking when she called herself a "spinster." A little more than a year later *New York Times* reporter Nancy H. MacLennan wrote a story about Frederick, focusing on her status as the only female UN reporter: "Miss Frederick herself does not wish to be considered as a 'woman reporter' but rather as a 'regular reporter' judged not just according to the feminine lights of her personality but on her merit in her job."

Published interviews with Frederick raised her profile throughout her career and were important during this relatively early stage of it. As a reporter herself, Frederick knew how to charm interviewers and tell compelling anecdotes. Nearly all the stories written about her commented on her graciousness and warmth, her low-key personality and attractive appearance. MacLennan called her "a tall, lissome brunette of mellifluous voice and photogenic figure." *Newsweek* described her as "dark-haired, handsomely dressed." Most interviewers described her as "handsome," especially later in her career, and all indicated that her manner of dress, while stylish, was hardly flamboyant or attention seeking. Several describe her as supplementing simple A-line dresses with a few necklaces and bracelets. As one reporter noted in 1960, when Frederick was fifty-two, "Pauline is no modern counterpart to the suffragette who chained herself to lampposts. Her manners are as quiet as her voice. She has expressive gray eyes, a flawless delicate skin, a trim figure and a nice taste in clothes, utterly feminine." In a profile of her for the *Washington Post Magazine*, the *Post*'s well-known television critic Lawrence Laurent seemed to think Frederick was nervous giving a speech. And he may be the only reporter who ever described her as "intense." "An intense woman who has little patience with over-simplifications, Miss Frederick is much more at ease before the audience of millions on radio or TV than before a small public gathering," he wrote. "For public speeches, she is likely to fidget and to betray nervousness with hesitant jerky gestures." (Laurent also noted parenthetically that Frederick "is much lovelier in person than on camera.")

In a widely read interview with her in the *Saturday Evening Post*, popular writer Gay Talese wrote in 1963: "Miss Frederick's obvious reserve on camera, a holdover from her girlhood shyness, and her resistance to the employment of female charm while commenting on world events, are what distinguishes her from other lady reporters . . . She could pass as the headmistress of a school for girls." Marlene Sanders believes Frederick would not have been hired at ABC if she had been glamorous or beautiful in the conventional sense: "She wasn't masculine, but if she had been a glamour girl or overtly female, they wouldn't have put her in the job. They would have thought she wasn't qualified."

Frederick's voice may have also played a role in her being hired by ABC.

It was naturally low and well modulated (enough so that some early network executives may have thought it carried some "authority"). Whether Frederick learned to modulate her voice as a debater in high school or whether she began lowering it during her early days interviewing diplomats' wives for NBC is unknown, but the quality of her voice was one of her assets and served her well over the years. Frederick would say in speeches that the trick to getting listeners to pay attention to her was for her to pretend she was talking to them one on one. "I try to speak as though I were talking to a friend," she said. "Broadcasting is an intimate medium and a reporter should make his audience feel that he is talking directly to them."

Nonetheless, Frederick, the only female network news reporter in the United States was starting to get national publicity by 1947—not as an oddity but as a unique personality and voice. But she was nearly forty and still had no network contract to ensure job security.

4 *Television's Merciless Eye*

I have to condense a story when I tell it. Did you know that it only takes one minute, twenty-two seconds to deliver the Gettysburg Address? I timed it.

PAULINE FREDERICK, May 18, 1950

Frederick's decision to obtain the services of a speakers' bureau paid dividends. As she began covering the activities of the United Nations on a regular basis, she was able to use her extensive knowledge and background of international events on the lecture circuit. The topics of her talks varied widely and allowed her to address current and timely issues—including, ironically, the topic of why the broadcast industry employed so few women news broadcasters. As she would do throughout her life, Frederick armed herself with facts and figures to make a point, a habit she probably cultivated as a high school and college debater.

During a 1947 speech in New York she addressed head-on the reasons behind the mostly male world of radio broadcasting. "The other day I had the tables turned on me, or to be more exact, the microphone," she told a group at the Waldorf Astoria. "I was interviewed on the air. One question my male colleague put to me was: 'Since broadcasting about international affairs is usually a man's job, how come you're doing it?'" The question itself was off-putting, she implied: "Try as I can I have not been able to break down international problems—or domestic ones either—into classifications, saying 'these are men's problems,' or 'these are women's problems.'"

Frederick acknowledged that while "statistics show it's a man's world, the door is opening a little into this male inner sanctum." She outlined specific steps women must take to begin to achieve parity with their male colleagues in broadcasting. First, she said, women must want to be hired in radio based not on their gender alone but because they want to offer information and encourage understanding. Second, women who want to enter the business must have a qualified background that leads to gaining that information and understanding. And women must be prepared to put forth "twice as much effort and hard work as our male colleagues to win and hold a place in radio," she said. Finally, Frederick repeated her view that luck and fate will always play a role in one's life. Women will succeed in radio, she said, "if we have some luck—by that I mean if we happen to be at the right place at the right time."

Frederick was frustrated that broadcast news executives were reluctant to hire more women even though they were fully aware of the fact that many women listened to the radio. She once compared the plight of women broadcasters to that of Jane Austen heroines. "Broadcast programmers know women buy products offered by sponsors, and it would be natural that programmers pay special attention to them, but that may not be the case," she said. "As in Jane Austen's time, [they think] women are a species possessing limited abilities, and have brains altogether too fragile to be burdened with the problems of the day."

By late 1947 Frederick had been working at ABC regularly, but she still had not been offered a full-time contract. She had little job security, but she was taking full advantage of several opportunities the job presented: first, she was building up her public image—and getting extra paychecks—by becoming a regular on the lecture circuit; second, she was establishing contacts with sources and other reporters; and third, she was regularly covering international affairs, her dream beat.

The lectures she gave did indeed help supplement her income. A publicity flier from the Charles Pearson Lecture Management Agency touted her as a speaker "with so many experiences that it is difficult to enumerate them," although the brochure attempts to do so by listing a number of them, including covering the Nuremberg trials; traveling to Paris, Brussels, Copenhagen, Berlin, and Munich during the war; and traveling on the last voyage of the *Queen Mary* as a troop ship and subsequent maiden voyage of the *Queen Elizabeth*. Suggested topics were "A Woman in a Man's

World," "Can the United Nations Survive?" "Behind-the-Scenes of How Radio Gets Its Eyewitness, First-Hand Accounts of News," and others.

Contracts from the agency found among her personal papers show that she generally was paid $100 or $125 per speech, plus expenses, although the speakers' bureau received 30 percent of that fee. (By the early 1960s she was paid $1,000 or more per speech.) Frederick was apparently a natural and poised speaker. Correspondence found among her papers indicates that her audiences were pleased with what they heard and charmed by the speaker. The local coordinator of one of her speeches wrote to the speakers' bureau to note that she had received many positive comments about Frederick's talk from members of the audience. Frederick is "a most attractive and engaging personality. She speaks beautifully—with ease, humor and a bit of well-chosen seriousness." Several other letters noted Frederick's humor, grace, and professionalism. "We couldn't have been prouder of any speaker," one event organizer wrote. "She is a very charming person; she has a gracious ease of manner that wins an audience at once. The audience of 850 women was with her every minute." Throughout her life Frederick was not content to give the same canned speech to different groups. When she lectured, she usually tailored her comments to the group to whom she was speaking. While she did convey many of the same anecdotes, stories, and thoughts to multiple audiences if they were appropriate, she did not simply file one or two standard speeches that she rotated to different groups.

She was able to supplement her income not just through her speeches but also by continuing to write news stories for the North American News Alliance wire service, which by the late 1940s considered her a steady and reliable correspondent. Instead of getting paid a fee for each story that the news service used, she was now getting a flat fee of fifty dollars per week if she turned in a minimum of two stories, according to a memo from NANA news executive Joseph Agnelli. He also said that the news agency would provide payment "for time spent on stories that did not pan out." This arrangement was unusual, given that freelance correspondents are usually paid only for stories that are published or aired. More important, however, was the fact that Frederick was again demonstrating that she was a reliable, diligent, and productive correspondent. She had by this time become a fixture at meetings of the UN General Assembly and Security Council. She took a train nearly every day to Lake Success or Flushing Meadows and dutifully reported back to the news editor about what was going on. To Frederick the United Nations was more than just a beat or a way to get exclusive stories. She truly believed that nations around the world could work together in peace if they had some coordination and common ground, and she felt strongly that the new UN could arrange for that. The seeds of this idealism had been planted when Frederick was growing up and later when she attended college, and her hope for permanent peace intensified after she covered postwar Europe and viewed the everyday atrocities there that would haunt her for the rest of her life. Anyone who viewed what she had overseas would naturally be shocked and sickened, she thought.

Within a few years of the formation of the UN in 1945, Frederick and others began to detect cracks in its foundation. But one dedicated and charismatic leader, Dag Hammarskjöld, revived the idealism of many people shortly after he became secretary-general in 1953. In 1956, one year after the UN's tenth anniversary, Frederick summarized her concerns about the agency and indicated that the United States was not blameless for some of its problems: "There were high hopes; the charter was based on the assumption that the big five powers (Britain, France, China, Russia, the United States) would work together in peace as they had in war . . . Then the Cold War began to divide the world. The UN became for us an extension of the State Department dedicated to repelling Communist diplomacy." She added that the UN had, sadly, become one more instrument for carrying on the tradition of killing. "Those who remembered that the UN's purpose was to end this kind of thing, not participate in it, are heartsick," she said. If she was heartsick in 1956, her hope that international peace could be achieved on a permanent basis had been permanently destroyed by 1984. Nearly a decade after she retired, she reflected about what had gone wrong: "I don't think the UN was meant to be a place where you were supposed to outvote your opponent. The idea was to try to use it as a conference table, where you tried to achieve some sort of understanding with your opponent," she said, adding, "It's the one conference table in the world that's always available, if representatives of nations would only use it, but if they decide that if they can't get their own way, they're going to put guns on the table and maybe use them."

In interviews throughout her career Frederick indicated that the United Nations represented more than just a beat to her. She loved covering it and made many personal friends there, both reporters and UN diplomats and employees. As the Cold War intensified in the 1960s, making the relationship between the Communist and non-Communist worlds more complex, she gradually began to realize that perhaps the goal of all world leaders was not necessarily peace. Perhaps their goal was victory or dominance over other countries, a politicized goal that was anathema to Frederick. A journalist who interviewed her in 1949 quoted some of Frederick's friends as having said she was easily disillusioned by unsuccessful attempts at compromise in the world. "Pauline's friends speak of her seriousness and sincerity that sometimes get her terribly depressed," the reporter wrote. "When she sees hypocrisy and politics interfering with the supreme goal of a happy, peaceful world she feels as ill as if she herself had been suddenly struck by disease." As she became older and retired, Frederick indicated she was saddened by the UN's inability to do what it had initially intended: "I suppose in retrospect you can say it [the original goal of the UN] was unrealistic . . . But then the first hopes were unrealistic. There were people who believed that if you pressed a certain button you'd have peace and if you pressed another button you'd have war . . . To solve international problems and reduce the chances of conflict you had to work out some . . . differences. And that meant compromise and attempt to search out the views of the opposing parties, not just try to get our own position established."

Her emotional investment in the United Nations cut two ways: because of it, she found her job fascinating and felt that by interpreting the activities of the assembly for millions of viewers and listeners, she was contributing to society; but as she saw the agency's initial purpose and stature gradually diminish, she became disillusioned personally. This disillusionment was not evident in her news reporting, but she did ultimately express it in speeches she gave about the Vietnam War, which she viewed as a futile endeavor. Eventually, she became devastated that the UN was not living up to its initial expectations and, indeed, was toothless when it came to avoiding or ending the Vietnam War.

By 1947, however, Frederick's career and personal life were flourishing, and she was able to meld them seamlessly as she became a fixture in the Manhattan media world and in diplomatic circles. (The current UN complex in Manhattan on the East River was not completed until 1952.) She told interviewers at the time that she rose at four thirty each morning with the help of two alarm clocks, quickly dressed, usually in dark jacket and white blouse, caught a taxi, and was at her desk in the RCA Building by six o'clock, munching on a breakfast of toast and coffee and reading stories from the teletype machines. She then wrote and edited scripts for her morning news update, which she delivered live at eight fifty, and was then usually off to gather news. She rarely returned before nine at night to her small apartment in Manhattan's East Eighties—an apartment decorated with souvenirs from her world travels and which included a fireplace, two rooms, a kitchenette, and a small balcony. With her long hours and frequent travel, Frederick never became adept at the domestic arts of cooking, sewing, or decorating—she usually ate ham and eggs when she was at home by herself—but she did periodically entertain her friends at her home with a special recipe. "Tops on my list is French broiled chicken and it's very simple to make," she told a reporter. "You rub a cleaned chicken with garlic then take a pastry brush and coat it with olive oil. While it's broiling turn it often and keep brushing on olive oil."

Throughout her life Frederick kept in close contact with her sister and her sister's family in Pennsylvania as well as a handful of childhood friends who lived outside of New York. Although she was not close to her brother, Stanley, who also lived with his family in Pennsylvania, Frederick did occasionally visit his family and see them at family outings. Frederick's relationship with her father, Matthew, had always been close, and she said in interviews throughout her life that she felt that she had more in common with him than she did with her mother. It was Matthew to whom she could as a young woman talk about politics, international events, and social issues, while her mother, she said, was more focused on domestic issues and tending to her home and family. But their relationship was also problematic—when she was young, Matthew wanted her to marry and live what he considered a more conventional life than the one she was pursuing. But as she grew older and became successful, he grew to accept her lifestyle and was proud of her.

After Pauline became a reporter, she was in a position to help her father. As a state worker and a lifelong Republican, Matthew's livelihood was frequently based on which political party was in office in Pennsylvania, and in the late 1930s he lost his job after the Democrats took office in the state. In 1939, when Frederick was based in Washington, she wrote an impassioned letter to a "Dr. Dudley," who apparently was in a position of providing valuable recommendations for Matthew. "I'm . . . taking advantage of your repeated suggestion that I come to your office if there is anything one Pennsylvanian can do for another," she wrote. "This is about the swellest dad in the world." The long letter details her father's employment history, noting that as head of the state's Division of Bedding and Upholstery, "dad built the division from nothing to a live-wire bureau with more than a dozen inspectors and its own chemical laboratory for protecting consumers against unsanitary bedding and upholstery." The lengthy letter was polite but firm, and she noted at the end that she would follow up with a telephone call. It is unknown if the letter got results, but Matthew Frederick did ultimately get another job with the state. He died in 1946, shortly after Pauline returned from Europe, outliving his wife by six years.

During her first few years at ABC Frederick became particularly close to her sister Kitty's daughter, Catharine, who was then a philosophy major at Barnard College in New York. Catharine remembers many visits by subway to visit her aunt during that time and many shopping trips on which Pauline wanted the young Catharine's opinions about choosing outfits. She also remembers that her Aunt Pauline sometimes asked her to mend her clothes.

Although she did some freelance reporting for the North American News Alliance in 1946 and 1947, Frederick by 1948 was primarily a radio reporter. Times were changing, and journalism jobs in radio were expanding as the technology and popularity of radio grew. But it would take years before Frederick would label herself a "broadcaster." By 1947 she still considered herself a print reporter and was still unaccustomed to the brevity required in news broadcasting. She felt it was difficult, if not impossible, to tell an entire story in what would now be called a few "sound bites." She often said in lectures that Abraham Lincoln was her role model when it came to distilling complicated concepts to a few sentences: it would take most people one minute and twenty-two seconds to recite the Gettysburg Address, she said, and if Lincoln could be that concise, she could too.

By 1948 the continual exclusives she got from the United Nations beat meant she had permanently broken the barrier that kept her from reading news on the air. Not only did she broadcast live from the United Nations on many weekday afternoons; she was also given her own fifteen-minute radio broadcast, which aired on ABC's affiliate stations. It took her about two years to prove to ABC that she was worthy of a full-time employment contract. On May 30, 1949—less than three years after she returned from postwar Europe—ABC launched her ten-minute radio show, *Pauline Frederick Reports*, from 8:50 to 9 a.m. eastern time. She was also heard regularly on two of ABC's other radio shows, *Headline Edition* and *News of Tomorrow*. ABC's public relations unit, meanwhile, had begun touting its only female news broadcaster—and the only woman network news reporter in the United States—in press releases to affiliate stations.

Also by this time, the low-key Frederick apparently learned one lesson that many women in the workplace continue to find difficult: she needed to promote herself and call attention to her accomplishments. In one interoffice memo to her superiors, for instance, she highlighted several recent achievements: "I thought you might like a re-cap of the 'exclusives' on the United Nations that I have dug up for ABC in the last *two weeks*." She gave the date, the abbreviated name of the show on which it aired, and a two- or three-sentence summary of six stories.

Just as she was gaining fame as one of America's few female radio broadcasters, at a time when she was considering permanently abandoning print journalism for radio, fate intervened. And as she had done at other times in her life, Frederick met a new challenge and eventually embraced it, although in this case not necessarily willingly.

In his memoir about life in television news, legendary NBC News president Reuven Frank sounds hyperbolic at first when he talks about television news and the 1948 political conventions. "Television news began with the

1948 political conventions," he wrote in the first sentence of *Out of Thin Air*. But Frank meant it: known as a brilliant and innovative news executive, he served two separate stints as NBC News president and has been labeled a mentor to many of NBC's most high-profile journalists, including Tom Brokaw, Andrea Mitchell, and John Chancellor. Frank began his book by describing the chaotic, turbulent, crazy—and stiflingly hot—summer of 1948, when the four newborn television networks beamed their first major continuing news events into the homes of millions of Americans to cover the Democratic and Republican presidential conventions in Philadelphia. (The DuMont Television Network, owned by a TV manufacturer, joined the established networks of ABC, CBS, and NBC.)

Ever the newsman, Frank pinpointed exactly when the television networks were "born." It happened, he said, on May 1 of that year, when AT&T began regular commercial intercity transmission of pictures on television. Frank goes on to explain that it was on that day when the company's coaxial cable reached nine cities in the United States. In those cities eighteen stations carried live convention coverage, pioneering what is today known as gavel-to-gavel television coverage. Never mind, of course, that few people on camera or behind it knew what they were doing and were for the most part tightrope walking without a net. Experiments with new and rarely used equipment were being conducted under the watchful eye of millions of viewers, and all activities were taking place under bright floodlights in rooms that were not air-conditioned—this during a record heat wave the likes of which Philadelphia residents had not seen since 1787. It was a learning experience—and a profitable one—for nearly everyone involved. But the profits came first and the learning second.

Frank noted that radio news had been so profitable until 1948 that it did not need to offer continuing coverage of events such as the conventions. Television was so new and untested, however, that news executives were still unclear about its costs and how much revenue it would generate. In short, the novelty of television offered many exciting new ways to make money, and live coverage was one of them. By television standards continual coverage of the Republican convention, which began on June 25, and the Democratic convention, which followed on July 12, was an accountant's dream: actors need not be paid, elaborate sets were not needed, and hours of broadcast time could be filled easily and inexpensively. Each network had a broadcasting room inside the convention hotel, the Bellevue-Stratford, as well as studios in the adjoining convention hall building. (It should be noted that television was introduced on a very small scale during the 1940 Republican convention, but its introduction went all but unnoticed.)

Of course, the excitement of the 1948 political conventions—with their uncertainty, conflicts, and dramatic role call votes—made for great television. In previous years no one other than the participants had been privy to the nomination of presidential candidates. And although an incumbent was seeking reelection to the presidency, the campaign had the potential to become a real horse race. The Republicans nominated what many believed was the "dream" ticket of Thomas E. Dewey of New York and Earl Warren of California. Energized and optimistic, Republicans felt that they had a good chance of defeating the beleaguered Democratic incumbent, President Harry Truman. In the end, however, some viewers apparently thought the camera made the proceedings all too real—reading about political maneuvering was one thing, but seeing it in action was another. A story in *Broadcasting* magazine reported that radio stations received many letters from viewers who indicated they were shocked at the convention "shenanigans" that were beamed into their homes via television. "Writers [of the letters] were upset because choosing a presidential nominee is serious business," the story said.

Despite the sound and fury that accompanied the first live ongoing televised event in U.S. history, the event was not broadcast throughout the nation. Eighteen cities in fourteen states and Washington DC had television stations, but only nine of them were located along the coaxial cable line and could broadcast the events live. The other cities received their coverage in a more delayed and primitive way. A day or two later the U.S. Postal Service delivered to television stations an edited film version of a television picture called a kinescope.

To radio journalists of the era, the first televised convention offered opportunities and created trauma. Most of the seasoned and well-known radio reporters had already made the switch from print to broadcasting, and they were not anxious to make yet another transformation to television. They resisted assignments to the convention, although a few did participate. Even prominent radio broadcasters such as Edward R. Murrow, Charles Collingwood, and Howard K. Smith would occasionally appear on television, but they made it clear that radio was their medium of choice. Managers at each of the networks knew they had to send many people to cover the convention—a daunting task because no one had extensive experience reporting in front of a camera. Each network dispatched to Philadelphia large teams of producers, writers, reporters, and anchors (although the term *anchor* as it applied to journalism would not be used commonly until the 1952 political conventions, when it was coined by Don Hewitt of CBS to describe the arrangement of a relay team, in which the strongest runner is used in the final leg of the race as the "anchorman").

Serving as anchors for the conventions were Douglas Edwards for CBS and John Cameron Swayze for NBC. Many of the journalists who covered the political conventions were relatively new to broadcasting in 1948, but the roster included names that would become well-known in broadcasting for decades to come, including David Brinkley, Charles Collingwood, Richard C. Hottelet, Howard K. Smith, and Don Hewitt (who was then a director and would become executive producer of the enduring CBS newsmagazine *Sixty Minutes*).

The televising of the 1948 political conventions was a major story in the media world, and the performance of the networks would ultimately indicate whether television could seriously rival radio when it came to broadcasting the news. *Broadcasting* magazine published stories about preparations for the event weeks before the Republican convention began in late June, and the magazine critiqued the coverage of it and the Democratic convention in July after both had ended. The magazine also offered postmortem reviews of the coverage after both conventions, data about viewership, number of news professionals participating, and the faux pas involving equipment that took place before live audiences at home.

Pauline Frederick, one of the print journalists who had recently made the switch to radio, remembered decades later the day she saw a posting on the ABC bulletin board that sought personnel to participate in the televised convention. She also recalled being happy to read about it— not because she wanted to take part but because she would have more opportunities in radio if some of her colleagues moved to television. She said years later: "I was the only person who didn't sign up. I was the only woman of course. And when the men asked me why I didn't, I said, 'Well, if you guys would just get over into television, maybe there'd be more room for me in radio.'"

Frederick may not have wanted television, but it apparently wanted her. Convention coverage was coordinated by her friend and now boss, Robert Kintner, whom she had known from her time in Europe in 1946 and who was now an executive vice president at ABC; and Tom Velotta, another friend from her time in Europe, who was now vice president of news and special events at ABC. Velotta asked why she had not signed up to cover the televised convention. When she told him she had no interest or background in television, he asked her to join the ABC convention team. Her reaction to the request was one of great surprise. "I was horrified!" she said and confessed that she knew nothing about television. "That's perfectly all right," he responded. "Neither do we." "Research" into television broadcasting, she said, consisted of the convention reporters borrowing books from the library about the new media and attempting to read and understand them. But Velotta also wanted Frederick to put aside her broad knowledge of government and politics and focus what he called the "woman's angle."

For Frederick the experience must have been one of déjà vu. There she was, in a nearly all-male environment, being asked to focus her coverage on stories about the activities of the wives and families of the candidates and the fashions. Frederick was not the only woman journalist working at the convention, but most of the others served in behind-the-scenes capacities as writers and producers. In a story about the 1948 convention in *Broadcasting*, a photo of the ABC convention team tells the story: it depicts Velotta sitting behind a desk, surrounded by the ABC team. A lone woman, Frederick, stands slightly behind Velotta, surrounded by national news director John Madigan and nine male correspondents.

As broadcast historian Mike Conway noted, the introduction of television to the 1948 political conventions can be compared to another media event more than fifty years later: the use of blogging to deliver news and commentary during the 2004 presidential campaign. During both years the public began receiving news in a novel fashion, and longtime journalists used to doing things a certain way were discovering that the rules of the game might be changing. As was the case in 2004, when a number of print and broadcast media joined forces to provide political polling, some competing media organizations in 1948 found it might be to their advantage to pool their resources. The DuMont network, for instance, joined forces with *Newsweek* for coverage; *Life* magazine partnered with NBC.

All those who covered the 1948 political conventions had the task of converting their talents in radio onto the television screen. If that seemed daunting to the male correspondents, it must have seemed nearly impossible for a woman. Viewers would naturally pay more attention to the way a woman looked on the small screen—her hairstyle, her clothes, her makeup, and many other details that might go unobserved in a man. Men could certainly "get by" on camera if they were clean-shaven, conservatively dressed, and neatly groomed. Frederick learned a lesson during those early days in 1948 that she would be forced to remember for the rest of her career: her appearance was key to her survival and success in broadcast journalism—in simpler terms, looks would always be an issue. She had warned other women much earlier in her career that women had to put forth twice as much as men if they wanted to succeed in radio. She would learn that with the advent of television, they also had to work much harder than men to maintain a pleasing appearance.

One of the first things she did to prepare for the conventions was seek advice about clothes and makeup. A dutiful reporter, Frederick tried to collect a list of "dos" and "don'ts," but it was futile. "I began asking people what kind of makeup I should wear," she recalled. "Some said heavy pancake with very dark lipstick. Some said light pancake with medium shade lipstick. Some said rouge, others no rouge ... Some said no black-and-white [clothing], others said black was all right." She remembered years later that one "don't" involved the color red. "I knew there had to be some kind of special makeup and clothes and so on for television, or least so I had heard," she said. "One of the things that they were always snickering about in the office was that a woman shouldn't wear red on television because the light would go right through her and she'd be seen in all her native glory." Frederick thought it was best she seek professional advice, only to find that none was available. She went to the Elizabeth Arden makeup salon but was told that the makeup artists there could give her advice on makeup for the movies but did not know anything about television. The makeup artist there did, however, give her small packets of makeup with which she could experiment. Frederick also sought the counsel of fashion experts at the department store Bonwit Teller to try to determine what colors would look best on camera. Again, she had no luck—no one had experience in how to dress for the television camera.

So, Frederick became the resident makeup artist for herself as well as for the women she interviewed: before she talked to them, Frederick used the tiny Elizabeth Arden makeup packets she obtained on interview subjects such as Esther Stassen (wife of former Minnesota governor Harold Stassen), Frances Dewey (wife of GOP nominee Thomas Dewey), Congresswoman Helen Gahagan Douglas, and first daughter Margaret Truman. The high temperatures in the convention hall, combined with the heat generated by the camera lights, made the job of makeup artist even more difficult, as the heat could melt the makeup soon after it had been applied.

The fashion magazine *Vogue* weighed in about the convention in its August 1 issue, focusing on the appearance of those involved and the role of cosmetics—and its assessment was not positive: "Making up for television, speakers often looked unfinished, haggard, too blanched, too bearded," the story said. "The wiser ones . . . used a dark bronze foundation, a heavy pancake makeup, with the women using moist reddish-brown lipstick, no rouge, no eye-shadow, but heavy mascara."

Frederick also sought to learn what clothing would please the camera—and this time she received plenty of advice. Always conservatively attired while on camera, Frederick's wardrobe had never been designed to attract attention. Because she was tall, she frequently wore neutral colors such as taupe, but she accented her wardrobe with heavy rings and bracelets. Now, on television, she would have to walk the line between pleasing her audience and ensuring that her appearance did not distract from her words. "I was told I should wear navy with austere necklines," she recalled, noting that as she became a more permanent fixture on television over the years, she grew tired of navy. One day she appeared on camera wearing something "a little more jazzy"—only to receive a memo from the management the next day telling her to please return to navy.

Frederick made it through the makeup and wardrobe dilemmas of the 1948 conventions, but television's emphasis on appearance would bedevil and annoy her for the rest of her career. The conflicts she had with hair and makeup over the years ranged from battles she fought with contact lenses to hair color to hairstyle. Frederick needed eyeglasses to see, but as contact lenses were developed, she was told to wear them, even though she found them uncomfortable, because television executives feared viewers would disdain eyeglasses. At one point in her career, when she worked at NBC, *Today* show officials favored eyeglasses because they "made [her] look more like a newsperson," she recalled. Frederick's natural hair color was dark brown, but news managers thought light brown or blonde would work better on camera. (In fact, Frederick's hair grew progressively lighter as she grew older, apparently to cover the gradually encroaching gray.) And Frederick's self-described "flat-headed" hairstyle did not please all of her bosses. One of her first television producers insisted she tease it to give her coiffure a more rounded look. And just as Frederick and others were growing accustomed to the best makeup for black-and-white television, color television entered the scene in the early 1960s. As she noted in a 1961 interview, when color television first caught on, one of her first stops each day at work was to the makeup department of the network. "She has learned to ask for color makeup, which is much lighter (and thus more natural) than the paints and colors used for conventional black-and-white television," one reporter wrote.

One mysterious quirk of Frederick's on-camera appearance was the presence of a small diamond horseshoe pin she began to wear over her heart in 1956. When she was asked about its history or significance, she would say only that it was given to her by a good friend and that she wore it with its points up in a U-style "so the good luck won't spill out." She was uncharacteristically coy about its background, and often technicians in the studio covered it with dark dye to camouflage it to make sure it did not glisten on camera. She even once received an unintentionally humorous letter from a viewer who said she noticed the pin on Frederick and wondered if it was a pin that she, the viewer, had lost years before.

To Frederick, however, the stress on appearance was more than just literally cosmetic. She believed that television executives stressed form over style. As writer Gay Talese wrote in a 1963 profile of her, "[She is] both resentful of and rebellious against the glamour laws that must be obeyed by ladies on TV . . . She resents that she must sometimes rise at five a.m. for the *Today* show—an hour before her male colleagues—so that the makeup department will have the necessary time to darken her eyelashes, coat her skin with tawny coloring and fluff up her hair."

At the time of Talese's interview, Frederick was fifty-five and at the height of her career. It was also a time when women were beginning to make small inroads in broadcast journalism. Frederick made it clear that she still believed that men were listened to but women were watched. "She resents that it is not enough for a lady television commentator to be an astute reporter, or even a brilliant one," Talese wrote. "She must also seem wholesome to the home audience, should have sex appeal, and must never never seem the far side of forty." He quoted her as disdaining what she believed was a double standard in broadcasting. A male commentator can look like Bela Lugosi if he is talented, she said, but "when a man stands up to speak, people listen, then look. When a woman gets up, people look; then, if they like what they see, they listen." And indeed, Frederick received many letters from viewers during her career, and much of it was complimentary. But occasionally a viewer would comment about her appearance, and it was not always flattering. One viewer wrote: "I am your fan and you have done a wonderful job of reporting at the UN. But please go back to the beauty parlor. The new look doesn't do well in color." And Frederick responded, as she tried to for much of her mail: "I am sorry my appearance annoys you. The TV hairdresser and make-up artist do their best, but they cannot change the original."

Kintner, one of Frederick's biggest supporters, eventually became a legendary network executive who was known primarily for his hard-charging attitude about news and his desire for NBC to get the story first. But he apparently was also concerned with appearances. His obituary in *Broadcasting* magazine revealed an anecdote about Frederick, who, after attending a formal social gathering, appeared on camera with a large bow on her dress. Kintner saw it and grabbed the telephone, demanding that the producer in charge "get that bow off her dress."

When Frederick spoke about the 1948 conventions four years later, it was the intense heat combined with the exploratory nature of the reporting that stood out in her mind. She recalled giving her first broadcast at the convention hotel on the Saturday before the Republican event convened. It was a three-minute broadcast "in a steaming room . . . in the presence of a baby elephant." On her second night there she and fellow ABC correspondent Elmer Davis did a thirty-minute broadcast that consisted, she later recalled, of interviews with convention guests "in the public steam bath that was the studio." Davis, however, had an easier time than she did of coping with the heat: "When the cameras were off Elmer, the prop men mopped his face with a Turkish towel. They couldn't do the same for me because of my makeup. A veritable river was pouring down the back of my dinner gown." The heat was clearly a major player in the proceedings. As the *New York Times* noted in a headline above a story about the Democratic convention, "Convention Hall Is Rechristened as 'the Steamheated Iron Lung.'" The subhead read, "Perspiring Delegates Look like Sheiks in Handkerchiefs Head Gear—The Cold Drinks, Even, Warm Up."

If the 1948 conventions offered Frederick a crash course in how to look on camera, she was a seasoned veteran when it came to hustling to get stories. She did indeed interview politicians' wives, as she was assigned to do, but she also went beyond that, talking to delegates for background information that allowed her to interpret events more fully. And because broadcast technology was still relatively primitive, correspondents could not interview their subjects live in hallways or on the convention floor but, instead, had to herd their subjects to one of several makeshift broadcast studios set up at the convention center and at the hotel. The television correspondents walked around carrying large walkie-talkies so they could be in constant contact with control rooms.

Frederick worked so hard that she apparently became ill in the middle of the Democratic convention, according to a memo sent to her by Velotta, who wrote that he "was sorry that you were actually overworked." But, characteristically, the illness did not deter her. She saw a doctor, took medication, and returned to work. In the same memo Velotta congratulated her on a job well done. "This is to express our appreciation for the excellent job you did both in radio and television at the two conventions in Philadelphia," he wrote. "I am joining you in the hope that all the effort will pay off in the near future." And her hard work did pay off. In addition to receiving a grateful memo from Kintner thanking her for the "splendid job" she had done, four months after the convention she got what she was waiting for: a contract with ABC News. Frederick was now a full-time employee with the network, earning $158 a week, a 41 percent increase over her average weekly salary in 1947. (In 2013 dollars that would be worth about $1,600 a week.) She was forty years old.

It is difficult to pinpoint the number of people who watched the conventions on television or the number of television sets that broadcast the proceedings. *Broadcasting* magazine estimated that ten million people watched at least some of the convention coverage; Conway wrote that the events were aired on 350,000 television sets. Nevertheless, the number of television viewers paled in comparison to the number of radio listeners. The radio audience for the conventions was estimated to be about sixty million. But the numbers may not be as important as they seem. More telling was the fact that television forced news managers and correspondents to focus on pictures as well as words, an activity that was new to them. As the *Broadcasting* story noted: "Broadcasters swung away from the spot news approach to look for feature material. Interviewers ran the gamut from live donkey brays to busy bellhops, with the usual string of busy politicos in between."

The conventions were educational for nearly everyone involved—for those behind the camera as well as those in front of it. The novelty of the situation, combined with the stifling heat, forced technicians to improvise. The high temperatures in the convention hall caused largely untested videotape machines to overheat, forcing resourceful technicians to pack bags of ice around them. *Broadcasting* reported on several problems with giant floodlights that were used for the first time. On the opening day of the Republican convention, an ABC floodlight was so bright as it honed in on a broadcast booth that all images were killed; later a monitor blew out with a sharp bang.

In the bigger picture the networks succeeded at what they had set out to do, according to Reuven Frank: "It was by the convention coverage that network television . . . had proved it could record and report serious news." And participants learned lessons that would carry them through decades of television broadcasting. As ABC executive producer Burke Crotty noted, the correspondents involved could benefit from further training in televised events. "This is a delicate problem for men who are essentially news experts and not showmen," he said. But it was Democratic radio and television director Kenneth Fry who may have had the most accurate description of the new medium of television. Fry warned that candidates would be wise to be aware of the ubiquitous nature of television and its "merciless and complete eye." He quoted a story in *Time* magazine that noted that during the convention the television camera "peered and pried everywhere and its somewhat watery gaze was often unflattering. Good-looking women turned into witches and dapper men became unshaven bums . . . The camera caught occasional telltale traces of boredom, insincerity and petulance." He warned politicians to look alert and engaged at all times, in case the camera caught them at an unguarded moment.

After the pioneering coverage of the 1948 political conventions, it did not take a soothsayer to predict that television would forever change news, politics, and many other aspects of American culture—for better and for worse. It may have been a bit more difficult, however, to guess in 1948 that newscasters might someday be more newsworthy than newsmakers, but that is what *Broadcasting* magazine predicted. The magazine's staff sounded giddy in a post-convention editorial that described the profound effect the "miracle of video" would have on society and the media landscape: "To talk about television in other than superlatives is futile. The delegates who attended the convention, the newsmen who saw the miracle of video for the first time, returned home as TV zealots . . . In fact more words were written in newspapers and magazines (and on the editorial pages) about the political revolution wrought by television than about many of the candidates themselves. TV was newsworthy."

By 1952 the networks were more organized in their coverage of the political conventions in Chicago. Those conventions featured some high-profile and seasoned broadcasters, including Frederick, Elmer Davis, commentator Paul Harvey, and columnist Drew Pearson. For a change, however, Frederick was not the only woman on the list—pioneering radio broadcaster Mary Margaret McBride, who was then near retirement, also covered the event.

As a full-time ABC employee under contract, Frederick worked for both the network's radio and television stations. Within a month of the Democratic convention, ABC Radio launched *Pauline Frederick's Guest Book*, which aired from seven to seven fifteen on Sunday evenings. In publicity information ABC New York affiliate WJZ-TV publicity called the show "a witty and informative quarter hour." While the show did not focus on Frederick's forte, international news, she was able to conduct interviews in connection with news stories from the previous week and offer depth and interpretation to news that she and others had already reported.

Within a year of launching *Guest Book*, Frederick became the host of two more shows—one on radio and one on television. *Pauline Frederick Reports*, a weekday ten-minute radio show, debuted on May 30, 1949, at 8:50 p.m., and *Pauline Frederick's Feature Story*, a fifteen-minute weekly television show, began in January 1949 and aired on Wednesday evenings. Apparently, publicists at the network thought it appropriate to promote the fact that ABC employed the only female network correspondent. In *Feature Story* an announcer opened the show with a listing of her credentials: "The American Broadcasting Company presents 'Pauline Frederick's Feature Story.' Each Wednesday evening at this time, the American Broadcasting Company brings you Pauline Frederick, commentator, lecturer, and reporter, with a feature story she has covered in carrying out her assignments as the only woman network news broadcaster." And if viewers did not believe the announcer's words, Frederick is shown on the screen busily typing: "And here, still at her typewriter at this late hour, is Pauline Frederick!"

Frederick wrote a variety of feature stories for the show, including one in which she examined international visitors' impressions of Americans. As she typed, she looked at the camera and said: "You know, it's hard for us to believe that there are people in other countries who mistrust and fear us. We can't believe it because we think our motives are so right and our instincts so good. It's not that other people want to dislike us—but they frequently get such wrong ideas about us." She then noted that she had asked people from various nations to offer their opinions on the subject. "A woman from Poland told me, 'When I came to America, I expected to find gangsters everywhere'—Al Capones running wild so that it wouldn't be safe

5 *Crisis Pauline*

Television has introduced a new element into the diplomacy of the United Nations. The citizen in the television belt does not merely read or listen to the happenings at Lake Success: he participates in them.

New York Times columnist JAMES RESTON, August 13, 1950

By the time ABC gave Frederick a contract for full-time employment in October 1948, ABC's public relations department had intensified its efforts to announce to ABC affiliates and the public that the network was unique because it employed a woman as a full-time correspondent and host of her own radio shows. And why should ABC not take advantage of the possibility that Frederick, now a ubiquitous presence over the airwaves, would appeal to female viewers and listeners? One particularly compelling publicity photo depicts a glamorous Frederick in pearls, sitting behind a large ABC microphone with scripts in hand. When she traveled to give speeches, Frederick usually broadcast her daily shows from the studios of network affiliates in the cities she visited. In releases to those ABC affiliates, the network suggested ways to publicize Frederick's activities in local advertisements. By giving talks across the country and delivering news from affiliates, Frederick herself would be worthy of news stories, raising her professional profile. ABC executives were only too proud to announce to the world that they employed the only female network correspondent—but apparently not proud enough to hire more women.

The 1948 conventions showed that despite the newness of television, it was capable of effectively covering breaking news. Using numbers from the polling firm Audience Research Institute, which was owned by George

Gallup, *Broadcasting* magazine reported that as of mid-June, about 314,000 homes located in the eighteen cities with video programming capabilities had television sets, up a full 37 percent from the polling firm's May data. Between May 1 and June 15, 1.1 million people indicated that they had plans to purchase television sets within a year. The average cost of a television was high—about four hundred dollars, although that was expected to drop as more people purchased televisions. By 1955 nearly two-thirds of U.S. household had televisions.

While CBS and NBC had weekly televised news shows as early as 1946, the two networks began offering nightly newscasts in 1948. NBC, with host John Cameron Swayze, began airing a ten-minute nightly news roundup show at seven forty-five in February 1948, and that August CBS began offering a fifteen-minute nightly news roundup at seven thirty, hosted by Douglas Edwards. ABC, which had the fewest viewers of all the networks, was in some ways the most innovative. ABC did not come of age as a network until the 1970s. Until then it had fewer affiliates, a smaller news staff, and a much smaller budget than its rivals, CBS, NBC, and the DuMont network (which began to struggle in the late 1940s and was out of business by the mid-1950s). In his biography of newsman Harry Reasoner, Douglass K. Daniel quoted several former CBS newsmen as saying that ABC could not compete with the other networks in the 1940s and 1950s. "It was a laughing stock," one news veteran said. In his oral history of television broadcasting Jeff Kisseloff explained that ABC was chronically underfunded compared to its competition because of the frugality of its owner, Edward Noble, who had purchased the former NBC Blue network in 1943. Noble owned the Rexall Drug chain and became very wealthy with the development of Life Saver candies but apparently did not see fit to invest a great deal of his money in his new network. But he did put packets of Life Savers on the desks of his new employees soon after he bought the network.

Nevertheless, this laughingstock took chances that the other networks did not. ABC began its fifteen-minute nightly news show, *News and Views*, in 1948, featuring Jim Gibbons and Frederick's mentor H. R. Baukhage. (Frederick hosted a version of the show on Sundays.) *News and Views* went through several incarnations until 1951, when ABC, under another of Frederick's friends and mentors, Robert Kintner, took a chance and created the hour-long show he called *All-Star News*. The program featured, among others, Pauline Frederick, but it was doomed from the start for several reasons. It aired at eight o'clock one night and nine another night, confusing viewers, and it competed against some of the top television shows of the era: *I Love Lucy* and *Robert Montgomery Presents*. *All-Star News* lasted only a year, but it demonstrated the daring of the innovative Kintner and the network executives' willingness to do what he wanted. The show was ahead of its time—it took advantage of the longer time it had to offer a variety of news, commentary, feature stories, and even short documentary reports, making the program the "granddad," according to one historian, of Robert MacNeil and Jim Lehrer's *NewsHour* three decades later. And the short-lived *All-Star News* demonstrated something else too: ABC executives were more than willing to showcase the network's only female correspondent.

After the conventions, network executives may have been persuaded that a woman's voice could actually carry authority, thanks to Frederick. She also demonstrated that a woman could be cool under pressure. Frederick may have known she had made it when she became the subject of a short profile in the *New York Times* in late 1948. The reporter reviewed briefly her biggest story for ABC—coverage of the Big Four foreign ministers conference. The story also noted she defied the prevailing wisdom in radio that women's voices were not suitable for broadcasting. The story stressed Frederick's nonconfrontational nature: "She refrains from being temperamental even in the experimental world of television, and cultivates composure. Underneath her serenity, however, there is a fine percolating of ideas. She is not likely to brag about any of these ideas unless she should, perchance, come up with the answer to one of the biggest questions in television today: How can television best handle news?"

It should be noted that by the end of World War II, Frederick was not the only woman in broadcasting. According to U.S. Department of Labor figures, women made up 28 percent of the total employees in broadcasting. Local television and radio stations in some U.S. cities employed women, although few covered news or offered opinions about it. The most well-known local television news correspondents of the 1950s were Dorothy

Fuldheim in Cleveland, Ohio, and Zona B. Davis in Effingham, Illinois. Fuldheim, who worked for the Scripps-Howard station WEWS-TV, had been a household name in Cleveland for decades, known primarily for her commentary and insightful interviews. Davis, known for her broadcasts on WCRA Radio, was a well-known community leader and activist famous for her news broadcasts and her community service efforts.

Women in broadcasting were more likely to work in behind-the-scenes television jobs. Marian Glick, initially a writer for the United Press, eventually became the first woman news director, working for the short-lived DuMont network. She worked there for four years but left a year before the network went out of business in 1955. She eventually became a writer for CBS News. Lucy Jarvis of NBC was one of the first female news producers and later became executive producer of documentaries for NBC. Others who succeeded as writers after the war were Shirley Lubowitz, who wrote for CBS; Ruth Ashton, who began writing for CBS radio and later became a writer for CBS television; and Mary Laing, a writer and associate producer at ABC television.

In the coming years Frederick's theory that luck combined with opportunity can equal success proved to be true. It is unclear, however, whether she recognized that as the Cold War quickly intensified, so did her value as a reporter whose specialty was international events. But it was also the Cold War—the decades-long battle between the Communist and Western nations—that would ultimately water down the authority of the UN, leading to the ultimate decline in Frederick's prominence and authority as a newscaster.

In what many historians consider one of the first salvos in the Cold War, the Russians in June 1948 blocked the Western Allied nations' access to the city of Berlin with the intent of forcing their troops out of the city. Because access by road, railroad, and canal was not possible, British and American forces implemented what became known as the Berlin Airlift. Over a 324-day period the Allies delivered by air 2.3 million tons of food and supplies to the Germans. With the sudden removal of all barriers in the city's infrastructure on May 12, 1949, the lifting of the blockade was big news, and all the radio networks sent correspondents to Germany.

Frederick covered the story from its beginnings and was well qualified to do so. She had experience covering postwar Germany as well as a specialty in diplomatic reporting. Over a period of just three weeks, Frederick and ABC carried out a multipronged coverage of the event. Frederick started with stories about negotiations that led to the removal of the blockade, then flew with the airlift both ways and traveled on the first train into Berlin after the blockade was lifted. She ended her coverage of the event with a trip to Paris in May to cover meetings of the UN's top diplomats, the Council of Foreign Ministers.

To the network, publicizing the high-profile activities of its only female correspondent amounted to good publicity. To Frederick, however, those activities were more than just stunts. She was a firm believer that responsible reporters must travel to the source of news, if possible, in order to talk to people and absorb the environment. Her flights during the airlift drove home the enormity of the event, she said later. "I had read about the airlift, I had seen pictures of it, and talked with people who had flown it. But I never felt as though I could talk about the airlift the way I did after I had flown it." She said she considered the Berlin airlift one of the greatest humanitarian efforts in history, with "planes filled with food instead of bombs."

Adding to the drama of the blockade itself were the talks between representatives of the Soviets and the Allies, emphasizing the idea that with the existence of the UN, diplomacy and conflict could now go hand in hand. Philip Jessup, deputy chief of the U.S mission to the UN, and Jacob Malik, Russia's UN representative, attempted to reach a diplomatic solution, with the Soviets eventually agreeing to lift the blockade if the four major powers within the UN would set a meeting date to discuss Germany's future. When an agreement was reached and the Russians agreed to lift the blockade, a date was set for a meeting of the top foreign ministers. Frederick and reporters from around the world rushed to ride the first train into Berlin.

The lifting of the blockade became a major media event. A *New York Times* story about radio coverage of it noted that "on short notice, correspondents are being flown from New York to Germany to cover the event from both Berlin and Frankfurt, and special interviews are being set up with important personages involved in the operation." The networks differed on their decision about whom to send to cover this international event. CBS sent its White House correspondent, Charles Collingwood, to Germany, while NBC's London correspondent, Merrill Muller, was sent to Frankfurt, and its Berlin correspondent, Edwin Hasker, stayed in that city to report. Meanwhile, ABC's decision about whom to send may have spoken volumes about the network's attitude toward Frederick. As the *Times* story notes, correspondent Martin Agronsky "took off for Germany yesterday *to assist* the network's commentator, Pauline Frederick . . . and Lyford Moore, Berlin correspondent." The story implies that it was Frederick and Moore who led the coverage with Agronsky as an assistant. Within two weeks of her return to the states from the Paris talks, her news show, *Pauline Frederick Reports*, debuted, making Frederick the first woman to have her own daily news show on the radio airwaves.

With all her travels and long workweeks, Frederick still made sure that she sent about a half-dozen thank-you letters to those who had facilitated her coverage of the lifting of the blockade—Military Air Transport officials, foreign ambassadors, and others. In one case, when she later reported from a U.S. hospital ship in Pearl Harbor, she arranged for a Macy's department store in San Francisco to send a bottle of Haig & Haig Pinch scotch to a naval public information officer who had helped her. Based on the correspondence she left behind, it appears that part of her work philosophy was to be gracious at all times to those who gave her help—both fellow workers and news sources.

The lifting of the blockade and resulting division of Germany into two states—the German Democratic Republic, or East Germany, and the Federal Republic of Germany, or West Germany—was one of the first major battles in the Cold War. The Berlin Blockade demonstrated the need for experienced and qualified reporters who could cover and interpret complex international events. The advent of the Korean War a little later would further drive home the need for that kind of reporter.

Based on histories of American broadcasting and interviews with those who participated in the early years of television news, the major networks were ambivalent at first when it came to the newly formed United Nations.

On one hand, ABC, the weakest yet perhaps most daring network during the 1940s and early 1950s, thought the new peacekeeping agency was so important that news managers there allowed Frederick to make the trek regularly from Manhattan to Lake Success to report on UN activities. And before Frederick began working at ABC, correspondent Gordon Fraser covered diplomatic activities for the network. Fraser, who began in radio in New York, worked for NBC Blue, the network that eventually became ABC. He covered World War II for ABC Radio, and returned to New York after the war and continued to work for the network. John MacVane covered the UN beat for NBC from that agency's inception until 1953, the year he began covering it for ABC. The apparent reason he switched networks? It was that year that NBC hired a new NBC diplomatic correspondent named Pauline Frederick.

Still, as television news first came of age, it became increasingly evident that diplomats sitting at tables and giving speeches in large rooms made for less-than-compelling video. CBS correspondent Richard Hottelet, a World War II correspondent and one of the fabled Murrow's Boys who was assigned the United Nations in the early 1960s, noted in an interview decades later that the big stories coming out of the United Nations did not necessarily "come out" of the United Nations. That is, the action usually took place on the battlefield or in venues outside of the UN. Marlene Sanders, who followed Frederick in network news to ABC in the 1960s, felt most reporters shunned the UN beat. "Everyone considered it just a debating society," she said. It should be noted, however, that in the late 1940s and early 1950s, CBS correspondent Larry LeSueur, also one of Murrow's Boys, was a prominent UN reporter who won a prestigious Peabody Award as moderator of the television show *United Nations in Action*.

If network news managers were not sure how or when to cover the activities of the UN, they probably learned a lesson on June 25, 1950, when the communist armies of the Democratic People's Republic of Korea (North Korea) swarmed south of the 38th parallel, invading the Republic of Korea (South Korea) to launch the Korean War. The UN would play a key role in the conflict, and any news outlet that had correspondents who were familiar with the workings of the UN and its key players would no doubt have a leg up when breaking news happened. Immediately after the invasion, the UN Security Council went into emergency session and, despite a boycott of the meeting by Russian diplomat Jacob Malik, passed a resolution allowing military intervention in Korea after forces were not withdrawn. More than twenty countries represented by the UN sent soldiers to South Korea, with the United States providing the majority. In her broadcast on the day of the invasion, Frederick noted the speed with which the UN had gathered to condemn the invasion. "I've never seen the United Nations galvanized the way they were today," she reported from UN headquarters in Lake Success. Shortly after three in the morning the UN secretary-general, Trygve Lie, called a special Security Council meeting for two o'clock that afternoon, she reported, and all UN delegations were notified. In stifling heat—the air conditioners had been turned off over the weekend—the members met at two thirty, declared a "breach of peace and an act of aggression" on the part of North Korea, and called for withdrawal of the troops. All in all the meeting was short and to the point, she told listeners.

The invasion of South Korea was part of a larger political Cold War battle that Frederick and other diplomatic correspondents would cover for the next three decades. Russian diplomats had been boycotting UN Security Council meetings since January 1950, when they protested UN opposition to Security Council representation of the newly formed People's Republic of China (PRC), often known in the United States as "Red China," in favor of the National Republic of China (NRC). Ultimately, the PRC entered the war on behalf of North Korea, and while the Russians provided no forces, they did support the PRC intervention, and the Communist PRC was viewed in the United States as an arm of the Soviet Union. President Truman ordered troops to Korea under the command of Gen. Douglas MacArthur.

While Frederick was not sent to Korea to report on the war, she was responsible for "covering" the war from the UN—the diplomatic angle. The challenge for reporters covering the Korean War involved interpreting complex events and actions to an audience for whom the Cold War was new—as was the UN, the agency formed to prevent another world war. Viewers and listeners were frightened of the unknown and fearful of another world war, and they relied on Frederick and others to interpret for them resolutions, events, and comments by diplomats. And television added still more dimensions to the crisis—pictures and immediacy. Viewers trusted correspondents to act as gatekeepers who would tell them what was important and what was not.

Frederick and many of the other reporters covering the Korean War were accustomed to traveling overseas to unfamiliar environments and working hard; that was nothing new. The postwar reconfiguration of the world, however, *was* new, and no one could predict its ramifications. In fact, Frederick would say many times during her career that the most important part of her job was not simply to gather facts but to interpret them in an understandable way. "At the UN, it's not just a question of listening to speeches," she said in a 1958 interview. "The most important part of my job is getting the analysis, and to be able to interpret what happens through talks with the delegates behind the scenes." Another of her top priorities as a correspondent was to cultivate sources so she could gather information when news broke. "Getting the scoops isn't the important thing here [at the UN]," she said in one interview. "What is important is building up a relationship with these people so that when you do need information you can get it. Everyone here is cagey until they learn they can trust you."

Within the United States the Korean crisis also brought to light tension between Washington and the UN. The United States in some ways was hostile to diplomatic efforts by the UN in Korea because of a wish by Washington officials to punish China for its intervention in Korea. This conflict of interest on the part of the United States offered a glimpse into Cold War tactics and illustrated how the initial mission of the UN could be hampered by the influence and desires of the world's two superpowers and their allies.

Correspondents from around the world rushed to Asia to cover the war. ABC entrusted Frederick with a key role as "legman," stationed at the UN to provide instant coverage of events as they happened. For decades after the Korean War, Frederick would say in interviews that the immediate aftermath of the declaration of war was among the most grueling of her career because she worked almost around the clock for six weeks. After preparing for her morning radio show each day by reviewing the previous night's news and writing her script, she rushed to Lake Success to deliver and interpret news from the UN during the day. Then she would return to New York for a 7:00 p.m. news roundup on ABC's *Headline Edition* and then try to catch up on UN developments that evening. Years after she retired, Frederick spoke about her UN coverage in an oral history project, stressing her conviction that despite her travels around the globe, her perch at the UN offered her a unique perspective of the world. "You felt as though you were sitting there looking out on the world, and the world's problems were there right in front of you. You didn't have to travel to them," she said. "They were there, and representatives of the various nations were there exposing their views." She also believed that a grueling schedule was part of the job. "It's our job to bring you the news without your being aware of the trials and tribulations we've been through," she said.

More than thirty years later Frederick would say that covering the Korean crisis was one of the stories of which she was most proud. Because simultaneous translators did not exist then, she and other correspondents often had to fill airtime while translations became available. "We were called upon to fill in with analysis and description and history, anything we could think of," she said. "So, as a consequence, I did that for six weeks, and I thought that was quite a baptism by fire." That "baptism" also involved many hours of boning up on military history and strategy when she was off the air too, she recalled. "There was a real effort to try to keep a running story going without too much repetition, and sometimes it was quite difficult, but we did it."

At the time of the Korean conflict Frederick had become a familiar voice—and face—on ABC radio and television. She was host or contributor to six regular morning radio shows and three television broadcasts and "on call" for twenty-one, meaning she could be called on to contribute a story for any one of them. All were news shows except for *Pauline Frederick's Guest Book*, which aired on television on Sunday evenings. To the American public the Security Council discussions of the Korean crisis were riveting. After all, viewers had in the past read summaries of peace negotiations, but they had never actually seen them in progress. Further, the stakes were high—World War II had ended five years earlier, and citizens around the world were gun-shy, literally, about the possibility of another war. In fact, coverage of the crisis on television became a story itself. In his memoir,

Reuven Frank, head of NBC News from 1969 to 1974 and again in the early 1980s, wrote that three simultaneous events of the era would form a perfect confluence of fascinating events for Americans. "The Cold War in Europe, the hot war in Korea and infant television news were made for each other," he wrote.

It was clear that television itself was becoming a player in world events and one that was indirectly shaping public opinion. "Television has performed a great public service in bringing to a large number of people the debates of recent days within the Security Council of the United Nations," the *New York Times* wrote. "It carried into the living room and to many other vantage points a drama so absorbing, in spite of the long interruptions for consecutive translation, that other business or pleasure was forgotten." As with any conflict, heroes and villains quickly emerged. The villain to Americans was Malik, whom media critics quickly labeled the aggressor. As he addressed the Security Council, according to the *Times*, his lies were shocking. "Mr. Malik, under the camera, has given the complete answer . . . to those who used to argue that it was possible with good will and the open mind to 'get along' with Russia," the story said. "The result has been discouraging, disillusioning, terrifying in a way, as lie was piled on lie. This time we could see it happen before our own eyes. If there were doubters left, after all that had gone before in our relations with the Soviet Union, they must have been convinced at last of the perfidy that is Communist foreign policy."

The theatrics of the conflict combined with the identification of the Soviet Union as villain prompted the networks to interrupt television programming for special reports, an action so unusual that it caught the eye of newspaper commentators. James Reston, the well-respected and widely read *New York Times* columnist, called Malik "the most spectacular villain since Boris Karloff." While Reston's comments may have been made with tongue in cheek, he noted that the importance of the Korean negotiations could not be measured in dollars and cents—the networks felt viewers were so interested that they preempted some popular programming to air parts of them. Since Malik's testimony, "the radio and television chains have been tossing out well-paid commercial programs to make room for his tale of international crime and wickedness," wrote

Reston. "Social scientists may even wish to make note of the fact that in this week . . . Mr. Malik bumped *Howdy Doody* off the air for five or ten minutes. This is generally regarded as the greatest television triumph since Milton Berle." Reston went on to say that the international soap opera he described had captured the attention of U.S citizens. U.S ambassador Warren Austin normally received about thirty unsolicited telegrams a week on all subjects, he wrote, but since the Korean debate started at the UN, he had received nearly four hundred telegrams a week. And some were quite colorful. Reston quoted excerpts from several. "I urge you to cease temporizing with this unconscionable scoundrel [Malik] and restore American self-respect by denouncing him and his whole mob of murdering gangsters," wrote Robert Allerton of Lawrence, Massachusetts. From S. A. Pennock of Bloomfield, New Jersey: "Our tolerance has reached its limit. We want Malik and his kind removed, not in a month, but immediately." To Reston the televising of the UN proceedings gave the talks an added sense of urgency. "Television has introduced a new element into the diplomacy of the United Nations," he wrote. "The citizen in the television belt does not merely read or listen to the happenings at Lake Success: he participates in them."

As is the case with most major stories, winners and losers also emerged among those involved in the coverage. Jack Gould, a widely read and well-respected *New York Times* radio-television critic, wrote a column summarizing his views of the radio correspondents who covered the Korean crisis. It was headlined "Men of Opinion" because its subjects were almost all men—only one woman was mentioned. He noted that ratings for news broadcasts about the crisis were high. The coverage, he wrote, ranged from "first rate" to "miserable," and, unfortunately, those who excelled were "relatively few." "The intellectual rabble rousers and unabashed peddlers of sheer emotion are plentiful and, as is their wont, indulge in an orgy of superficiality," he wrote. "There are three gentlemen and one lady who are doing a preeminently sound job." The men were Edward R. Murrow and Eric Sevareid of CBS and Elmer Davis of ABC. Anyone familiar with the coverage could guess the identity of the woman because no other woman covered the crisis nationally. Gould praised Frederick's work. "Miss Frederick has been more the reporter than the analyst, but her background commentary on the United Nations proceedings has been sure and knowing," he wrote. "The ABC network, of course, has been the only radio chain to do a truly respectable job of covering the UN which admittedly has given Miss Frederick an edge."

Edge or not, that was high praise from one of the country's most respected media critics. In his critique Gould concentrated on news coverage as well as interpretation and commentary, noting that it was in the latter category that many broadcasters failed. Those who earned his praise "stick to the facts, carefully separate the straight news from their opinions and recognize that journalism should not be tainted by the soap opera approach." At least one participant in the events apparently agreed with Gould about ABC's coverage. In the fall of 1950 Frederick and her ABC colleague Gordon Fraser received kudos from an active player in the Korean negotiations—U.S. ambassador Austin. In a letter to Frederick he praised her and Fraser for "excellent radio coverage of the Security Council," writing, "I have followed your broadcasts with great interest and many of the letters that have come to me have praised you by name."

Frederick's reporting on the Korean conflict proved again that her diplomatic background and overseas experience, combined with her hard work and dogged determination, made her a genuine asset to ABC News in both radio and television. For Frederick several forces had conspired to provide her good luck: the Korean conflict was a diplomatic crisis and one for which she had prepared much of her life; ABC had begun to embrace her role as the only woman correspondent at a national network, and executives promoted her heavily to affiliates; and the new medium of television had allowed her to illustrate that she was versatile and could report under a variety of circumstances and in several media formats. By the time the Korean War ended in 1953, Frederick was a recognized name in broadcast journalism, and the beat she covered, the United Nations, would soon experience some of the most high profile and productive years of its history.

Television had not advanced enough technologically to allow live coverage on the battlefield in Korea, a phenomenon that most broadcast historians say originated with the war in Vietnam. But this new medium still brought war images into viewers' living rooms, according to Reuven Frank, who wrote in his memoir that film footage from the battlefield, although not live, was nevertheless riveting. Frank, a former radio correspondent who entered television news in the early 1950s, acknowledged that he and others were not sure initially how or if television could cover a war. But he became a convert during the Korean crisis, when he saw that visuals drove home the immediacy of the events. "They [viewers] liked the new experience of seeing things . . . That gives you a sense of participation that even the best-written and most carefully detailed written report does not give you," he said. "Until people were saturated [with television], they were fascinated."

With Frederick ABC news managers—particularly Kintner—knew they had someone who could report both soft and hard news from just about anywhere in the world. Near the end of the Korean War they sent her to Pearl Harbor for recorded broadcasts aboard the hospital ship the *USS Repose*, which was returning to the mainland with wounded veterans. In many of her assignments Frederick was indeed a multitasker who could get the most out of one event. As she told viewers on her morning radio show a few days before her trip, "Aboard the *Repose* I will learn firsthand not only the special medical techniques used for treating the wounded, but I expect to talk to many of those veterans about their views on the Korean War; and so, returning to New York, I hope to have a broader background and fresher point of view in discussing phases of this difficult problem facing us all." She planned to weave short segments about her *Repose* visit into a week or so of network news broadcasts, depending on the other news airing each day.

Frederick's trip began in San Francisco, a city that was dear to Frederick's heart—not because of the Golden Gate Bridge or the beautiful vistas but for the fact that it was the location of the signing of the UN charter. For the rest of her career, whenever she visited San Francisco on a story, Frederick would indicate that she had indeed left her heart there, when world leaders met there and pledged to do whatever was necessary to avoid war. Arriving in San Francisco early in the morning in February 1953, she eloquently recalled for listeners her own memories of that city in 1945: "Important visitors from all over the world were arriving. There was high purpose in the air. After two devastating wars that proved the futility of settling international differences by mass killing, revulsion against the war had created a dedication to the purpose of making peace possible. That day in 1945 seems so far away now as the same people who then were determined to destroy forever the belief that war is inevitable now question whether peace is possible."

Frederick made no secret of the fact that the stated mission of the United Nations had been a personal one for her—and the Korean crisis may have been the first concrete event that signaled that its goal of establishing peace worldwide might not be possible. As a reporter, she covered in detail nearly every anniversary of the signing of the UN charter, focusing naturally on the fifth, tenth, fifteenth, twentieth, and so on. With each succeeding commemoration, however, it became increasingly evident that the UN would never establish world peace.

But as she promised, Frederick taped segments from aboard the *Repose* for airing a week later, after she returned to New York. Frederick's broadcasts from the ship were very typical of her style of reporting on longer, more in-depth stories. She generally employed strong verbs and vivid adjectives and bolstered her general comments with facts, figures, and other data, and her reporting from the *Repose* was characteristically detailed. She noted, for instance, that while most of the injured men on the ship were returning home for further medical treatment, the facilities and personnel aboard the ship were top-notch: "With its gleaming white sides marked by huge red crosses, [the *Repose*] has come to be known as the Angel of the Orient—nearly 16,000 wounded veterans of the Korean War have gained health and comfort from her modern facilities."

Although ABC did not have the resources or the reputation of the other two major networks, the creativity, energy, and daring of Robert Kintner, head of its news division, ensured that it was a player in the competitive new world of broadcast journalism. Murrow by the early 1950s was vice president of news and public affairs for CBS and one of the most well-known broadcasters in the country. NBC's claim to fame, meanwhile, was a trio of early evening news programs heard over the network five times a week, hosted by Lowell Thomas, H .V. Kaltenborn, and the network's UN correspondent, John McVane, who hosted an 8:00 a.m. news roundup program. After the war the network hired a young news writer named Julian Goodman. Goodman, who was born and raised in Kentucky, would over the next three decades become a fixture and figurehead at NBC. A vocal and energetic First Amendment advocate, he ultimately became network president and chairman of the board.

While television at the time of the Korean conflict lacked the resources to report live from the battlefield, pioneers such as Murrow and his producer, Fred Friendly, nevertheless managed to portray graphic details of the war and its effects. Murrow's efforts later in taking on Senator Joseph McCarthy and exposing the lies and scaremongering of McCarthyism are well-known, thanks to many books and films on the subject, including the 2005 film *Good Night and Good Luck*. Murrow and Friendly's pioneering half-hour newsmagazine/documentary show *See It Now* was the first of its kind on television, with its mix of live studio interviews and commentary and reports and footage of events from around the world. The show, which was the television version of the CBS radio show *March of Time*, originally aired on Sunday afternoons but moved to prime time, first on Sunday evening and then on Tuesdays, as viewer response to it grew. Segments on the show drove home the humanity and horror of the Korean War through reports about the "average" people in the war. Reports included case histories of three wounded GIs, the view of war through the eyes of one marine division, and a detailed sequence about the trek of a pint of blood as it made its way from the United States to a military hospital in Korea. The show, which debuted on November 18, 1951, received numerous broadcasting awards.

As Jack Gould noted in his initial assessment of the coverage of the Korean crisis, Murrow's appeal lay in the fact that he was able to air compelling reports that were not mawkish or sensational. Frederick, too, viewed her job as interpreting and delivering the news in a straightforward manner that was designed to help her audiences make up their own minds about international events. In that way, she felt, she could help allay the fears viewers had about the war and other international crises. As she told an interviewer in her hometown of Harrisburg, Pennsylvania, in 1950, the advent of television contributed to transparency in government, allowing the public to get more than just "official" news of an event from news releases and communiqués. "[Viewers] are now getting a true picture of how the UN operates, and are learning the facts which before were kept behind the scenes," she said. That interview with Frederick referred to her idealism and her intense belief that permanent world peace was attainable with guidance from the UN. At the beginning of the story, the reporter noted, for instance, that one of the goals stated in the UN charter was to save succeeding generations from the scourge of war, saying it was a hope "dear to [Frederick] and *she'll talk for hours on the subject*." When the topic of negotiating with the Russians for peace in Korea came up in the interview, Frederick's "deep-set grey eyes [they were in fact brown] became more intense than usual as she warmed to her subject," according to the interviewer. "No matter how difficult it is," Frederick responded, "we should never be too tired to continue negotiating. The alternative is so horrible that we shouldn't even consider it." Frederick stressed that while the United States should not "appease" Russia, it should continue negotiations with that country. This story in particular illustrated her strong views that the formation of the UN could have been the first step in achieving world peace: "The ultimate ambition, Miss Frederick declared, must be a world government."

The perspective of time makes Frederick's ideas seem overly idealistic—especially her belief that countries represented in the UN would abandon politics to work for the greater good. But those were her hopes as the Cold War intensified in the late 1940s and early 1950s, and she took her role as a conduit for information very seriously. As she said in a 1953 speech, when a person steps in front of a microphone or camera, "what you do influences the thinking of others. You have the power to help stimulate hysteria with half-truths and distorted interpretations—which could yield a moment of popularity. You also have the power to foster a calm consideration of controversial issues by presenting the facts as you have been able to discover them, and a reasoned interpretation which contributes to calm judgment."

6 *Perils of Pauline*

It's one part protocol, one part alcohol, and one part Geritol.

ADLAI STEVENSON, about the role of a diplomat, April 4, 1984

The Korean War represented a major turning point for the media of the era. Although communication satellites were yet to be invented, technological advances had made it possible for broadcast outlets to bring the fighting into millions of living rooms. And as Pauline Frederick had learned during her travels to Germany in the aftermath of World War II, few major wars end when the fighting stops. This was the case in Korea when a cease-fire agreement was signed on July 27, 1953. That war may have been over, but the Cold War was raging, stoked by the conflict in Korea. As she noted in her first UN broadcast after the fighting ended, the real challenge was just beginning for the embattled nations: "The aggression has been halted," she told listeners. "Now comes the more complicated step of trying to restore peace and establish what has not been possible so far since the end of World War II—a united Korea."

As the Korean War wound down, Frederick had begun working at NBC. Her broadcasts were far from run-of-the-mill news bites. Using metaphors and colorful imagery, she often painted verbal pictures for her listeners. In June 1953, for instance, with the end of the war in sight, she described the paradox of what appeared to be the final month of fighting: "Deep night covers Korea again. Hopes for peace continue to grow, even as the battle mounted during the day. This may be the darkest hour of fighting before the dawn of the armistice."

Later in the broadcast, after a lead-in to a report from John Rich in Korea, Frederick continued: "Allied troops and supply trucks have been streaming into the base camp at Munsan to prepare for the exchange of prisoners. Gen. Maxwell Taylor is trying to prepare his Eighth Army troops for the cessation of hostilities by reminding them that an armistice would not necessarily mean the end of war. They must be reconciled to staying on, ready to fight again if necessary." Frederick tended to provide a distinct ending to her reports that linked the particular events to the listener, thus establishing a personal relationship with her audience. In this broadcast she ended with a directive by President Eisenhower: "The President has forth-rightly challenged Americans to stand forth with courage. And so, until this time tomorrow, when again I'll bring you the news, including direct and transcribed reports, this is Pauline Frederick, hoping your day is a courageous one." (Frederick occasionally closed with the wish that the audience's day be a "courageous one"; it is likely that she began doing that at NBC, although it is unknown how long or how frequently she ended her reports that way.) Transcripts of Frederick's typed, triple-spaced scripts indicate that she meticulously edited them. She often deleted entire sentences and paragraphs and crossed out adjectives and verbs and replaced them with stronger ones. In this way her background as a print journalist made her a better broadcaster.

Frederick's life was going well. She was being recognized for her work as a well-known ABC correspondent, and news managers at ABC could not afford to ignore or downplay her work simply because she was a woman. They knew they could depend on her to cover any story at any time. In 1950 Frederick received the first of what would be many national awards: the National Headliner Award for Outstanding Woman in Radio. The Headliner award, given by the women's honorary society Theta Sigma Phi (later to become Women in Communications, Inc., and then the Association for Women in Communications), honored outstanding women in the communications field. Frederick was given the award for coverage in 1950 of the Korean War and the United Nations.

According to a copy of her contract with ABC in 1952, she was earning $225 a week (an amount equal to about $1,800 a week in 2013), but as the contract spelled out, her duties were extensive: ABC expected her to provide five fifteen-minute radio broadcasts each week, with availability on her part for possibly two more each week. In addition, she was expected to air at least one five-minute television broadcast per week. Frederick did, however, have the opportunity to earn more than the $225. ABC Radio operated under what was called a "co-op" agreement with its affiliate stations, with individual stations selecting which shows they would buy and broadcast. (This is one reason why the network spent so much time and effort on public relations and marketing to sell programs to affiliates.) Frederick's ten-minute 8:45 a.m. radio program was sold on a co-op basis, and the network gave her 40 percent of all revenue it received from these broadcasts above $400 per week.

She was able to move in 1951 into a larger apartment at 77 Park Avenue, near the corner of East Eightieth Street, that had a view of the Hudson and East Rivers and a walled terrace in which she planted red geraniums. As one interviewer wrote, the apartment was homey yet sophisticated, decorated with modern art and furnished with a large deep sofa and over-stuffed chairs. "The apartment reflects the charm of a woman of culture," the reporter wrote. And there was a new addition to her life: a miniature poodle puppy named Patrick.

In the early 1950s Frederick decided to give up her longtime smoking habit. In letters to a childhood friend named Ann Cordell, who lived in Arkansas, she referred to a "bargain" the two women had made, evidently to give up cigarettes. "I've kept my cigarette bargain, starting with only one or two a day," she wrote, adding that she had not exceeded three cigarettes a day for three days. "However, the other night when I was nightclubbing, I indulged in Sunday's quota at 3 a.m." (Giving up smoking was apparently a lifelong struggle for Frederick, and she never fully succeeded.) Although they lived in different parts of the country, Cordell was a close friend and confidante to Frederick, and their frequent letters often discussed their political beliefs, their views on some of the stories Frederick covered, and even their health. Frederick clearly had to have been in good health to keep her hectic work and travel schedule, but letters to Cordell hint at some minor medical problems. In one 1954 letter she alluded to some numbness in parts of her body that required a doctor's care. "There is still some unpleasant grinding in the neck," she wrote. "And the index finger frequently goes cold from lack of circulation. All this is better when I don't pound a typewriter, but that is difficult to avoid." Letters between Cordell and Frederick show the affection that existed between the two: they often thanked each other for gifts and kept each other apprised of their daily activities. Frederick often wrote to Cordell about her social and personal life. In one letter, for instance, she noted that she had an "unusual number" of offers for evening social engagements that week—four—and had kept two. One that she turned down, she wrote, came from a "personable guy" she had met on an airplane as she flew from Atlanta to Philadelphia. "Very attractive native of Atlanta," she wrote to Cordell. "Yes, naturally—there's a wife—she's from Atlanta, too. So what's the use?"

Many of her letters to Cordell described just how busy Frederick's professional life had become in the early 1950s. In addition to the frequent travel for speaking engagements, her schedule with ABC kept expanding even though the network's staff did not. In one 1952 letter an exasperated Frederick described to Cordell how a new five-day-a-week ABC news show meant extra work for her. News managers wanted her to contribute UN and international news spots for the show, increasing her workload exponentially. Her comments also indicate how a seemingly short and effortless news broadcast could be the result of hours of work: "If you know anything about putting on a TV news show, you know the maddening details of viewing film and arranging for cuts—writing script to fit—and timing everything to the precise second so that when you are on camera you are saying what you're supposed to on camera, and when the switch is suddenly made to film, you are ready for that and talk behind the film." The problem was that the network was understaffed. "The film editing is all Greek to me, " she wrote. "And I shouldn't have to do that technical job, but as usual we are shorthanded." Frederick told Cordell that she started work early in the morning but was not finished until eight at night as she gathered news at the UN, dashed back to the studio, and did a run-through before her final news report in the evening. She added that a dinner date she had arranged one evening ended up taking place at 10:30 p.m. "I know this can't last—but I'll get it worked out someway [sic]. I cite all the sordid details to show you how I'm sort of mouse-trapped."

Frederick also believed she dare not slow down or refuse such a hectic schedule for fear of losing the assignment she was given. "As long as they give me the international slot on the TV show I feel that I can't turn them down—for females in the business usually get the cooking and sewing stint. But we shall see." Perhaps the letter to her friend presaged Frederick's feelings that she could not work forever for the cash-strapped and short-staffed ABC network. Indeed, within a year she would move on. By the fall of 1953 Frederick, a dog lover, wrote Cordell that she was forced to give away her beloved two-year-old poodle, Patrick. "I felt he would be happier with more and better attention," she wrote. "He's with friends in New Jersey, but I miss the little monkey." But Frederick would soon adopt another poodle, Sputnik, who would live a long life with her.

At this point in her life, however, she greatly benefited from the United Nations' move in 1952 from its temporary home in Lake Success to an eighteen-acre site overlooking the East River on Manhattan's East Side. The new complex, which would consist of four buildings, allowed Frederick easy access to the United Nations from her home. Frederick would have a permanent studio in the new United Nations complex, and she gradually began socializing with UN staff members and visitors. Her life as a UN correspondent became considerably easier and more productive after the move.

By the early 1950s the Cold War was taking a new and ugly turn. Americans were beginning to believe that a nuclear attack was a real possibility—an idea that was stoked by politicians and the media. The federal government outlined at length civil defense procedures, and the Russians were increasingly portrayed as enemies worthy of public hatred. Television took advantage of this fear in the form of special programming such as *Motorola Television Hour*'s "Atomic Attack," a fictionalized story of a New York–area family that flees their home after a nuclear attack. The episode, which stars a young Walter Matthau, seems cheesy and primitive when viewed today, but it played effectively into the fears of American viewers.

Frederick, meanwhile, thought it more important than ever to give listeners and viewers balanced and accurate reports of UN and world events. To her the nascent nuclear threat made it critical for the United States to act prudently when it came to atomic power. A letter she sent to a U.S.

senator and a segment of a radio broadcast she gave in early 1950 offered the first glimpse of what was to become a near-obsession with her: the arms race. At that time she sent a personal letter of support to U.S. senator Brien McMahon, a Democrat from Connecticut, who was chairman of the joint Committee on Atomic Energy. McMahon came out publicly with his belief that the country should question its use of hydrogen bombs under any circumstances and that it should seek safe uses only for nuclear power. It was a stand that was bound to cause controversy at a time when many government officials were trying to persuade Americans that the Soviet Union could very well develop a hydrogen bomb and use it against Americans. More telling of the intensity of Frederick's antinuclear stand, however, was the fact that the day after she wrote the letter she praised the senator in her radio broadcast: "Naturally, any stand as courageous as Senator McMahon's has shocked the Doubting Thomases—the old crystallized minds, that even before the 'hydrogen era' dawned, were closed to any new examination of the problems of the day." She urged listeners to write letters of support to McMahon and send copies to the White House and State Department. Frederick was equally as emphatic in her letter to the senator, writing, "I intend to keep on talking about your effort in the hope that every little bit of public opinion that can be stirred up will be of some help." McMahon responded to her in a letter, thanking her for the "encouragement" and the "nice words."

Frederick's efforts to publicize the dangers of nuclear power would intensify over the years as atomic technology improved, and she would gradually become more vocal in her opinions about that subject and others related to war. Her letter to McMahon and the related remarks she made on radio show that she was confident enough in her stature as a broadcaster to offer her opinion to viewers and that she believed that the arms competition between the United States and the Soviet Union was becoming dangerously volatile. But the 1950s would be one of the most active, productive, and happiest decades of her career and life. And once again, a pivotal figure and role model would enter her life.

To Pauline Frederick the United Nations held an almost religious sanctity. Because she covered the organization from its inception, she may have had protective feelings. Or perhaps she admired its relatively uncomplicated organizational structure and its inclusiveness. Or most likely, she hoped against hope that one entity could deter another catastrophic world war. But during these early years of the Cold War, even a true believer such as Frederick could probably see cracks in the foundation of the United Nations. At the very least she could see flaws in the makeup of the world's major powers that could render the UN nearly powerless to do its intended job.

The UN was a unique organization, but the idea for its existence was of course not unprecedented in U.S. history. After the end of World War I, President Woodrow Wilson had wished for the United States to join a similar peacekeeping world organization, the League of Nations, whose goal was to prevent another world war. Wilson's efforts for U.S participation in that organization ultimately failed, thwarted in large part by Republican senator Henry Cabot Lodge of Massachusetts. The two men had engaged in a long and bitter battle over the issue, with Wilson ultimately losing the fight.

By the early 1950s Frederick's most popular lecture topics dealt with women in the workplace and the role of the United Nations in the world. She never spoke completely off the cuff, despite her decades as a reporter and experienced lecturer, and she always came armed with facts and figures when she wanted to make a point. Frederick also frequently quoted philosophers, poets, and writers in her talks and relied heavily on notes and transcripts. In one 1959 speech she quoted Pulitzer Prize–winning poet (and fellow Pennsylvanian) Stephen Vincent Benét about war: "Our Earth is but a small star in a great universe. Yet of it we can make, if we choose, a planet unvexed by war, untroubled by hunger or fear, undivided by senseless distinctions of race, color, or theory." She explained why she had selected this passage: "You will note the emphasis on human choice [in Benét's words]." She also noted that at the start of World War II millions "who had lived in the valley of destruction" made a choice "that succeeding generations must be saved from the scourge of war. But important deeds are still needed to prove that a choice has been made between a world guided by the principles of human understanding and one influenced by nuclear threats." Frederick believed that most people around the world did not want to enter a large-scale war, so she found it frustrating that world leaders appeared willing to do so. When it came to disputes between the Soviet Union and the United States, she argued that irrational fear drove many decisions. "Fear begets fear," she said. "It shackles the fearful to a remembrance of hostilities and frustrations of the past."

By 1960 she expressed concern publicly that the Cold War was becoming an industry in the United States, so embedded in society and culture that the country was starting to depend on it economically. "To what extent have we made anti-Communism a vested interest" in the form of political careers and related jobs? she asked. "What would happen to our country if military contracts were curtailed or canceled? . . . To what extent is the Cold War a holding action because the cost of ending it is too high?" Frederick's comments in 1960 predated by a year President Dwight D. Eisenhower's 1961 often-quoted speech about the possibility that the nation could be reliant on what he labeled a "military-industrial complex" that depends on war to survive.

Each year for more than two decades Frederick broadcast a story commemorating the June 26, 1945, signing of the UN charter in San Francisco. Her idealism about the agency was evident in these broadcasts, most of which revisited the history of the signing. In her NBC broadcast marking the UN's fifteenth anniversary—aired in the middle of the Cold War—Frederick quoted President Truman from 1945 and his hope for the new international agency: "The charter is a declaration of the great faith by the nations of the earth—faith that war is not inevitable, faith that peace can be maintained. If we had the charter a few years ago—and above all the will to use it—millions now dead would be alive. If we should falter in the future in our will to use it, millions now living will surely die."

While Frederick believed the UN could do its job and promote peace if given the chance, her views that the United States was partially to blame for the world's problems remained as stringent as they had been when she covered post–World War II Germany. At that time she did not buy into the nationalistic view that the Allied forces could do no wrong during the Occupation and that once the war had ended, the suffering was over; as the Cold War intensified, she did not necessarily believe the Russians were always at fault—although she did say publicly on occasion that some Russian diplomats were stubborn or unyielding. She seemed to believe that to achieve world peace, all sides must compromise. "There will be no hope for the United Nations until the Soviet Union and the United States get together," she told an interviewer. "They are both equally at fault in not finding areas of agreement."

The fear generated by the Cold War began to trickle down to Frederick's home territory—the United Nations and her employer. In early 1953 President Eisenhower named Massachusetts senator Henry Cabot Lodge as U.S. ambassador to the UN, replacing Warren Austin, with whom Frederick had a friendly relationship. Frederick's earliest memory of Lodge, which she recalled more than three decades later in an interview, was one of near-disgust. He had ordered the fingerprinting of all American UN employees, apparently to make sure that none were Communists. Although the FBI had received permission from UN secretary-general Trygve Lie, it was, Frederick said later, an appalling action. "[The UN was] supposed to be a secure enclave, not to be violated by any of the nations," she said, and such an "intrusion" had not been conducted before or since. Frederick may have found it ironic that Lodge, the newly named U.S. ambassador to the UN, was the grandson of Henry Cabot Lodge, the ardent opponent of U.S. membership into the League of Nations.

Frederick also feared that the government would interject itself into network broadcasts. In a letter to her friend Ann Cordell, Frederick wrote in August 1954 that because one senator had announced he might soon "investigate" the networks, scripts written by correspondents were read by news managers at NBC to determine how correspondents portrayed the Bricker amendment." (Frederick was referring to a constitutional amendment proposed by Senator John W. Bricker of Ohio that would have limited the president's power to enter into treaties with other nations. The legislation was noninterventionist in nature and considered by many as a way to circumvent some activities of the United Nations. It did not pass the Senate.) Nothing more was mentioned about the news scripts. But Frederick's criticism of Lodge was unusual; over the years, as interviewers asked her opinion of former UN secretary-generals, she was generally complimentary, and rarely did she criticize anyone by name. In a 1985 interview with USA Today, conducted five years before her death, the reporter asked her opinion of a half-dozen UN diplomats. She tiptoed around criticism of Lodge in that interview: "Cabot Lodge was a very staunch supporter of the American policy in the United Nations."

Although Frederick reused parts of her lectures about the UN, transcripts of those speeches show that at least in part she tailored her talks to her specific audiences. At a luncheon of the American Public Relations Association in Philadelphia, for instance, she noted that the United Nations is a concept that cannot be "sold" to the public like a product. "Selling the United Nations is not like hawking a bar of soap that can be seen and used in our every-day life," she said. "Peace cannot be sold by the most efficient public relations firm in the world. It has to grow from the spirit of men and women everywhere, to the level where it becomes more desirable than anything that can be purchased."

But as Pauline Frederick and other Americans would soon learn, if anyone could "sell" the United Nations as a peacekeeping agency, it was Dag Hjalmar Agne Carl Hammarskjöld, the Swede who in April 1953 was named the UN's second secretary-general. As soon as Hammarskjöld took the reins at what he would refer to as "this house" on the East River, Frederick's increasing pessimism about the UN's role in world affairs eased. She knew almost immediately that Hammarskjöld was a born leader who could use his savvy negotiating skills, his intellect, and his energy to get member nations of the UN back on the right track. She was right in the short run, though sadly, fate would intervene.

Frederick worked hard, and she wore her dedication to her job as a badge of honor. But as she hinted in letters to Cordell, her job was exhausting, in part because ABC was short staffed, and network executives showed no sign of being willing to hire more employees. So, it may have surprised few at ABC when she announced in April 1953, at age forty-four, that she was taking a job as UN correspondent for NBC News. Frederick by this time had many contacts in broadcasting, and it was her acquaintance from her days in Washington covering government agencies, Bill McAndrew, who hired her. Frederick's hours would improve a bit—she would broadcast a daily fifteen-minute radio show at 1:30 p.m. as well as cover spot foreign news for NBC radio and television. ABC was gracious in letting her go—she was under contract with the network, and she could not have worked elsewhere unless ABC officials released her from that contract.

In a rough draft of a letter to ABC News president Robert Kintner found among Frederick's personal papers, she explained that the early morning hours of her job had become increasingly grueling: "The physical strain of getting up five mornings a week at 4:30 to prepare this broadcast has been serious—unless I sacrificed my social life. As a matter of fact, my doctor has been advising me increasingly of late that I cannot continue such a routine much longer . . . I now have an opportunity to undertake a news program at a later period in the day at NBC which would make it possible for me to live a more normal life. I don't regard lightly the fine consideration I have been given at ABC but I am sure you would be the first to recognize the importance of one's health and social existence in addition to professional responsibilities."

Kintner granted Frederick's request and released her from her ABC contract. Like Frederick's letter to him, his response was warm and appreciative. "We are of course terribly sorry to see you go because I think you are an able broadcaster in addition to being a nice person," he wrote. "I wish you lots of luck with NBC . . . I hope to see you in the course of months but in the meantime I wish you the best of everything." Kintner may not have seen Frederick over the next few months, but he would see her again within four years, when he, too, was hired by NBC and would eventually become network president. She noted to Cordell that she felt ABC officials were generous to release her from her contract and repeated her belief that her shorter, and later, hours might make her life easier. At NBC she would become host of a new show, *Pauline Frederick Reporting*, which was for the most part the same show as ABC's *Pauline Frederick Reports*.

Frederick joined NBC at the same time as Joseph Harsch, a former *Christian Science Monitor* Berlin bureau chief and a former BBC correspondent, according to a network news release. Interestingly, the same release announced the reassignment of NBC correspondent Clifton Utley, who reported from Chicago. Utley was the father of Garrick Utley, born in 1939, who would later join NBC and work there for nearly thirty years. Garrick Utley had met Frederick during his tenure at the network.

The news release quoted Frederick as saying that international relations are fundamentally human relations and that policies aimed at achieving world peace "must be faced with an appreciation of the backgrounds of people 'on the other side of the street.'" While the UN beat may have once been considered a staid or boring one by some correspondents and news executives, the increasing volatility of the world made it a much more interesting beat for reporters and the public. As Reuven Frank noted decades later, Americans by the mid-1950s were far more familiar with other parts of the world than they had ever been. During World War II millions of Americans in uniform had gone to what were once "strange places," he said. "Names [of countries] we had never heard before became reasonably familiar, not only to them but to their families back home. The war was fought around the globe."

The same month that Frederick gave her notice to ABC and a month before she joined NBC in June, the United Nations named Dag Hammarskjöld as secretary-general—and he immediately earned Frederick's respect; indeed, six decades after his appointment, he remains a legend at the United Nations. For the rest of her life Frederick would say that she admired Hammarskjöld more than any of the presidents, politicians, diplomats, or other government officials she had covered. And she was not alone. After his untimely death, the dynamic Hammarskjöld was given, posthumously, the Nobel Prize, and the UN library and a main UN plaza are named in his honor, as is a key UN scholarship. But Frederick and some people who worked at the UN did not quite know what to think of Hammarskjöld when he was named secretary-general in April 1953.

An economist and diplomat by training, he was seen by some as a classic bureaucrat who would be a placeholder at the UN. Brian Urquhart, a former UN staff member and former undersecretary-general who attended the 1945 signing of the UN charter, recalled nearly sixty years after Hammarskjöld's appointment that he had fooled many upon being named as secretary-general. He was relatively unknown at the time in the United States and Russia, was quiet, and looked much younger than forty-five, his age at the time. "He was extremely quiet, and in no sense a show-off," Urquhart said. "He started extremely quietly and people wondered how he would manage to deal with an organization that was split clean down the middle by the east-west political and ideological divide." Urquhart said that in the case of Hammarskjöld, first impressions by many at the UN were deceiving. "It was assumed that they'd elected a nice, competent

Swedish civil servant who wouldn't rock the boat and wouldn't be very independent and wouldn't create trouble," he said. "Well, I must say that was quite a surprise, the next eight years, because he actually turned out to be anything but that!"

Hammarskjöld's close assistants and his biographers have noted that he was at heart a spiritual man—but not in the conventional sense of the word. The product of a devout Lutheran family, he believed that human beings were capable of living together peacefully because that was their nature, and he believed that talking and negotiation were at the heart of conciliation. He also believed in the power of meditation. (When he died, his body was found with *The Life of Christ*, a book written in French, along with the oath he had taken when he assumed duties as UN secretary-general.) Frederick recalled decades later that she had learned early in his tenure as secretary-general that he was religious, and she was intrigued by this fact. As she was interviewing people for a magazine article about him, his assistant, Andrew Cordier, commented on Hammarskjöld's spirituality: "You know, Dag came in here the other day and he said, 'Of all the things that have been written about me, the most important has been missed. And that is that I have a very deep religious feeling.'" Frederick said that she then began to read some of his writings and to "listen to what he had to say to ferret out the religious aspects. And I found them."

Roger Lipsey, author of the biography *Hammarskjöld: A Life*, found that it was Hammarskjöld's spirituality that most defined him. And based on an extensive diary of personal thoughts that Hammarskjöld left behind, Lipsey claimed that Hammarskjöld felt a sense of fatalism, writing: "The evolving perspective of his journal recorded a struggle first to survive and then to be; to see without illusion both self and others; to know clearly, serve humbly, and lead firmly . . . And toward the end to accept the possibility of his own death in the line of duty."

One of her own favorite news broadcasts was one Frederick did about Hammarskjöld's development of the United Nations Meditation Room—a chapel for contemplation that was a favored project of Hammarskjöld, who believed it important that delegates have a quiet and calm place for contemplation and prayer. Frederick believed that the Meditation Room, as Hammarskjöld named it, was a symbol of his spirituality: "He said that 'this House'—which he referred to the UN frequently—must have one room dedicated to silence, in the outward sense, and stillness, in the inner sense." The room, on the west side of the visitor's lobby in the General Assembly building, down from the Assembly Hall, has at its focal point a simple block of iron ore; a single light from above shines on the structure. "He thought . . . that it was important to have a light shining on that altar," she remembered.

Hammarskjöld's personality, however, and to some degree his upbringing, bore striking parallels to Frederick's. Both became deeply interested in international law and politics at a relatively young age, earning advanced degrees in areas of international law; both shunned the spotlight even though they were very high achievers and excelled in anything that captured their interest; and most important, both were hardworking idealists who clung to their beliefs about the goodness of human beings.

Hammarskjöld was the youngest of four sons born into an aristocratic Swedish family. His father was a prime minister of Sweden and chairman of the board of the Nobel Foundation, and Dag often noted how his father's dedication to public service and his great accomplishments had influenced him, as did the family's devout Lutheranism. In college he studied humanities, with emphases on linguistics and languages, and obtained a law degree and later a doctorate in economics. Like Frederick, who briefly taught journalism after she graduated from college, he taught economics at the University of Stockholm for a year after graduation. Before being named UN secretary-general, he was secretary of a Swedish government commission on unemployment, secretary of the Bank of Sweden, and undersecretary of the Ministry of France. In 1949 he became the UN Swedish delegate.

Soon after being appointed, Hammarskjöld displayed his charisma, activism, and dedication to his position. Frederick and others knew that the tall, handsome Hammarskjöld—with his bow ties, ever-present cigarillo, and perennial tan—had his work cut out for him. The first UN secretary-general, Trygve Lie of Norway, had inadvertently been caught in the middle of two battling superpowers as a result of the Cold War. Soviet diplomats believed he favored the United States in the Korean War, and U.S officials did not trust him because he advocated a UN seat for the People's Republic of China. In 1951 the Soviets threatened to block his reappointment. Lie resigned in 1952.

Hammarskjöld hit the ground running. When he took office, it was near the end of the Korean War, timing that would be advantageous to any newly named secretary-general. One of his first actions, and one that earned him international attention, was negotiating for the release of fifteen American flyers who had been captured by the Chinese during the war. The situation was an awkward one for American political and diplomatic officials. Because the People's Republic of China was not a UN member, U.S. officials said they had no diplomatic links to the country so the United States could not negotiate for the release of the hostages. Ultimately, President Eisenhower suggested that the UN get involved. After meetings of UN officials and the Security Council, Hammarskjöld took matters into his own hands: he announced he would travel to China to talk to Foreign Minister Chou En-lai to gain release of the prisoners. As Frederick remembered decades later, the fact that the two men actually communicated by cable indicated a possible thawing of relations between the United Nations and China, and it spoke volumes in its symbolism. Hammarskjöld flew to China, met Chou En-lai, and persuaded him to allow the families of the flyers to visit them. But the State Department was not happy with this action—officials said they would not encourage Americans to travel to a country where their safety could not be guaranteed through a conventional diplomatic relationship. The flyers were released much later—and the willingness of Hammarskjöld to roll up his sleeves and dig in would become emblematic of his tenure as secretary-general. It also earned him the respect and admiration of many diplomats and government officials worldwide. But the incident demonstrated only too clearly the fine line any secretary-general had to walk. Despite Hammarskjöld's courage and his many successes at the UN, his violent death demonstrated how the Cold War and its ramifications placed any UN leader in a no-win situation.

Shortly after he took over as secretary-general, however, Hammarskjöld had become the closest thing to a rock star as any government official in the public eye, and he portrayed himself as a man of the people in ways big and small. First, he instituted an egalitarian leadership style that established him as just one of many UN employees. Unlike his predecessor, it was not his custom to ride the elevator solo to his thirty-eighth-floor office—he wanted the elevator operator to allow others waiting for an elevator to ride with him. An aficionado of modern art, he had the UN borrow great works of art from museums. He arranged for concerts on special occasions in the General Assembly Hall. Perhaps inadvertently, he cultivated an image as a Renaissance man—someone with a great knowledge of art, music, and literature—as well as an outdoorsman who enjoyed hiking, fishing, and other pursuits.

Frederick, like Hammarskjöld, was genteel and worldly, and she was immediately smitten with the aura of glamour and sophistication surrounding the new secretary-general. His strong belief that peace could be achieved not in the battlefield but in the conference room matched her own. And she, like him, had no use for meaningless political posturing, such as that done by the State Department during the attempted release of the flyers. Furthermore, Hammarskjöld, like Frederick, liked to quote from authors, philosophers, and statesmen to amplify his points. Sixteen months after his appointment, Frederick broadcast for NBC Radio a short but glowing profile of Hammarskjöld. She opened her report quoting Walt Whitman's "One Thought Ever at the Fore": "in the Divine Ship, the World . . . / All Peoples of the globe together sail, sail the same voyage, are bound to the same destination." Those words, she said, reflected Hammarskjöld's view of his job: "Stepping off the plane at Idlewilde [airport], Dag Hammarskjöld had become a representative of the peoples of the globe, sailing the same voyage to the same destination."

Hammarskjöld, she reported, was a private man with a very public job: his office in UN headquarters on the East River was glass "politically as well as architecturally." While the president of the United States was viewed by a mere 160 million people in one country, he, as secretary-general, was watched by a billion yet still had to conduct himself in a way that did not antagonize anyone: "He can't be called a communist or a capitalist," she said. In her nine years of reporting on Hammarskjöld's activities, Frederick frequently noted that the personality of the public secretary-general often clashed with the private nature of the man. "Now, after sixteen months on the job, he says today there is not much private life," she noted, commenting later that "he has resisted social exploitation . . . He has been known to return to his apartment on the Upper East Side after a party and settle down to reading UN documents." Frederick could not resist noting that over the last year and a half Hammarskjöld had caught the eye of many single women. "The tall handsome bachelor is regarded as a social prize. Blond, blue eyes enhanced by a face bronzed by sun and wind, a ready smile and easy conversationalist in several languages add to these attributes the dimension of secretary-general of the United Nations," she said. "Little wonder that socially conscious matrons have bid for his attention." Throughout her career—particularly in the immediate aftermath of Hammarskjöld's death—Frederick was asked by interviewers if her relationship with him was more than professional. Frederick always vehemently denied that the two had been involved romantically. In one 1969 interview, seven years after his death, she responded that the possibility that the two had had a personal relationship was "utterly ridiculous," adding that she did not think Hammarskjöld ever dated anyone. "I think I'd have known it if he did, for I followed him around so closely on my job."

In his biography of Hammarskjöld, Roger Lipsey addressed rumors that Hammarskjöld was gay—rumors that were at their height when he was named secretary-general. At Hammarskjöld's first news conference, according to Lipsey, after a UN official listed his accomplishments and was about to introduce him, a voice from the assembled crowd broke in, shouting: "And a fairy!" Lipsey quoted several sources, including the biographer of former secretary-general Lie, claiming that these rumors were spread or at least encouraged by Lie, who had secretly hoped that he could be reappointed secretary-general if Hammarskjöld's appointment were rescinded. In the 1950s knowledge or even rumors of a government official's homosexuality could open that person up to blackmail, Lipsey noted, although several of Hammarskjöld's close friends told Lipsey they never saw evidence that he was gay, and if the subject did come up, Hammarskjöld denied it and they believed him. In one telling anecdote Lipsey quoted a conversation the UN leader had had with a good friend of his in which Hammarskjöld said he could never fall in love or envision getting married after a woman with whom he was deeply in love had decided to marry someone else.

Frederick knew Hammarskjöld well enough to announce in her broadcast his daily routine: "The theater usually claims his interest, but when there are usually functions five days a week, leaving only Saturday, he frequently forgoes the theater for escape to the outdoors." Hammarskjöld could access a suite of rooms at the United Nations, but he was also given an apartment on East Sixty-Second Street near the United Nations complex as well as a weekend home in Brewster, New York. He went to that country home on weekends, Frederick reported, "leaving as much of the cares of the world behind him as possible, except for a bulging briefcase in which, as he quips, he carries his guilty conscience." There he would swim and bicycle and walk in the sun on the grass because he did not like walking on pavement: "He likes the good earth under his feet." Frederick went on to say that this man who came from a "distinguished line of Swedish diplomats" was trained to "emphasize the quiet intellectual approach to world problems rather than loud shouting . . . When passions are running high, it is not possible to intervene with hopes of success. The time to do it, Mr. Hammarskjöld believes, is during the valleys and not peaks of feeling."

Hammarskjöld could not have asked for better public relations than Frederick's report. At the end of the broadcast she noted that above the fireplace in his Manhattan apartment was the pick used by Tensing Norgay, sherpa to Edmund Hillary in his expedition up Mount Everest. Hammarskjöld, a climber himself, believed that mountain climbing and working for peace require similar personal qualities: perseverance, patience, a firm grip on reality, imaginative planning, clear awareness of dangers, and faith. "The safest climber is he who never questions his ability to overcome all difficulties," she reported.

If it was not already clear to Frederick's viewers and listeners that she admired Hammarskjöld, it would soon become obvious. Yet Frederick rarely let her personal views affect her reporting. During her first few years as a news correspondent, she kept her political opinions to herself, even when she was off the job. It was only after a nuclear war seemed a real possibility that she started criticizing in speeches the testing of bombs and warning of what she felt were the catastrophic consequences of a nuclear war. Frederick did, however, discuss politics with her friend Ann Cordell in letters. They reviewed the candidates and their parties in

1952, a presidential election year, after Cordell apparently sent Frederick a newspaper clipping quoting former first lady Eleanor Roosevelt as having said that she feared socialism as a political institution. "I do not share the blind fear and hatred of socialism which I feel is in the cards if we don't solve some of the inequities presented by capitalism—this is not treason, but an attempt to try to see where we are heading," Frederick wrote to Cordell. But she denied that she was a socialist. "But of one thing be assured—I am no more socialist than you are—or any other 'ist,'" she wrote. "I'm merely trying to keep down the barriers in my own thinking so as to try to be able to weigh issues on their own merits, and not on prejudices and preconceived notions which were readily available to me in my Orthodox Republican and Methodist youth."

During the 1952 presidential campaign Frederick took an instant liking to the Democratic candidate Adlai Stevenson, and he would become a favorite of hers when he was the U.S. ambassador to the UN in the early 1960s. "For the first time I have the urge to campaign for a man—Stevenson— but of course I can't do it in this business," she wrote Cordell, implying that as a journalist she could not publicly advocate or campaign for any candidate. "If the Republicans are going to persist in keeping their eyes glued to the past, I don't feel they deserve to win. Perhaps defeat this time will smash up the old guard and bring some new life into the party, although I'm beginning to fear that the old Republican stalwarts never even fade away, they just keep going on and on." A month later she wrote to Cordell that "the Republicans are still living in the bankrupt days of the thirties, with nothing new to offer in the way of a constructive program to meet the desperate needs of the times." She urged her friend to "read up on the Illinois governor [Stevenson] and see how he has tried to clean up the mess in Illinois and inaugurate constructive measures," adding, "I think you'll find him a man of real stature among the pigmies." Still, the daughter of a Republican indicated that it was not easy for her to vote Democratic: "I never believed I could look with favor on a Democratic candidate, especially at this time," she wrote Cordell. She indicated that she believed Eisenhower was being manipulated by what she called "the Three DS"—Republican senator from Illinois Everett Dirksen, New York governor Thomas Dewey, and former Republican senator John Foster

Dulles of New York. "I fear for the future if he [Eisenhower] gets into the White House," she said. "By contrast Stevenson has so many qualities of mind and heart that he is hard to resist. It is too bad he has to be a Democrat running at this time." (When Eisenhower was elected, he named Dulles as secretary of state.) Indeed, Frederick was no fan of Dwight D. Eisenhower. "I haven't changed my views on Ike . . . for it seems to me that he has been demonstrating how ignorant he is of issues and politics (necessary to our democratic procedures whether we like it or not)," she wrote Cordell.

Slightly more than six months after she wrote that letter, Frederick found herself covering newly elected President Eisenhower's first meeting with his cabinet and his vice president, Richard Nixon, at the Commodore Hotel in New York. If she was not a fan of Eisenhower, Eisenhower returned the sentiment—he apparently was not a big fan of the press, according to Frederick's ABC broadcast: "As has become his practice, the General [Eisenhower] has not chosen to take reporters into his confidence as to further details [of his cabinet], so as a consequence, it is not possible for the public to have a more complete picture of these important sessions. This brings up a matter that is disturbing the larger press and radio corps in Washington—namely the fear that General Eisenhower may choose to discontinue the Weekly White House News Conferences [held by the president] . . . General Eisenhower has never been known for his fondness for news conferences."

Frederick went on to say that reporters who had covered the new president before he was elected had indicated that he was not a fan of the media. As a reporter, Frederick was naturally concerned about government officials' willingness to be open with the press. When she became president of the United Nations Correspondents Association (UNCA) in 1959, one of her informal duties was to encourage UN officials and diplomats to be as transparent as possible with the press; her duties in this capacity included arranging news conferences and other public sessions for reporters.

Shortly after Eisenhower's first meeting with his cabinet, Frederick covered the first news conference of newly named secretary of state Dulles, who indicated that Frederick's comments to Cordell—that Republicans usually advocate the status quo—was prescient. Dulles announced that the country's Cold War policy, including its refusal to recognize the People's Republic of China, would remain unchanged. But Frederick was not necessarily prescient when it came to Eisenhower's coolness toward the press. It was he who in 1955 held the nation's first recorded presidential news conference. The news conference was not exactly televised—it was filmed, given to the White House to review and edit if it liked, and then returned to the networks to air. The thirty-one-minute event, which was newsworthy enough to merit a front-page *New York Times* story, was labeled an "experiment" by the Eisenhower administration, and the chief executive did indeed express reservations beforehand that he feared the existence of the cameras could be a "disturbing influence." But according to the *Times*'s account of the event, the news conference went smoothly: "Nothing was visible in the President's manner that is not customarily there on these occasions [press conferences]," the story said. It also noted that the White House did request, perhaps inexplicably, that broadcasters omit the airing of some parts of the news conference—most notably an exchange about the details of the nation's budget, references to a former Republican senator's criticism of the U.S. government's security measures, and a review of the Eisenhower administration's accomplishments in the two years it had been in office.

During Eisenhower's presidency an alliance of UN reporters began to come of age. The United Nations Correspondents Association was formed in 1947, two years after the UN charter was signed, but when the UN moved to its permanent complex on the East River, reporters had access to roomier and better accommodations and found it easier to form an alliance to improve coverage and accessibility of news sources. The UNCA became even better organized in the late 1950s—quite a feat considering that its members came from around the world and spoke many different languages. The maturation of the correspondents' association and Frederick's directing of it was one factor that contributed to her coming of age as a broadcaster. Hammarskjöld's appointment as secretary-general also helped, as the two formed a special professional bond and shared a common ideal. But some negative factors also contributed to Frederick's prominence and cachet as a network correspondent, including the intensifying of the Cold War and the accompanying threat of the spread of communism as well as advancing technology that could lead to the development of an atomic bomb. The fear generated by those phenomena fostered an interest by the public in international news and in finding a journalist whom they could trust.

The spacious and beautiful UN headquarters instilled in the United Nations a degree of sophistication and gravitas that it had previously lacked. The all-glass, thirty-nine-floor UN complex, on eighteen acres along First Avenue between Forty-Second and Forty-Eighth Streets in Manhattan, was designed by a group of architects from around the world, including the popular modern architect Le Corbusier. Frederick and other regular broadcasters had their own small studios in the complex (although Frederick did periodically report from NBC News offices at 30 Rockefeller Center in midtown Manhattan). But the new headquarters helped establish her as a respected authority on the UN and its actions—ultimately, she would become as much a fixture as the diplomats and bureaucrats who worked there.

Late in her life Frederick related in speeches what she called a "prized" cartoon that hung in her home library. She described it: "An agitated couple is shown watching television and the woman is crying out, 'Come quick, Ed. They're convening the Security Council and Pauline Frederick isn't even there yet.'" (Frederick referred to this cartoon as being from the *New Yorker*, but it was actually from Bil Keane's *Channel Chuckle*. Keane also referred to Frederick in another of his cartoons, *Family Circus*, depicting a man in front of a television as his wife peers from the kitchen: "I didn't say anything, dear. It's Pauline Frederick reporting from the United Nations." These cartoons, published in 1967 and 1965, respectively, speak to Frederick's fame as a UN correspondent and household name.) Frederick took pride that among other reporters she was known as "Crisis Pauline" as she careened from covering one crisis to the next. After Hammarskjöld took office at the United Nations in 1953, that appellation would become particularly apt.

Frederick worked for NBC for a little more than a year when she received the first of what would be a series of prestigious national awards and honors. In 1954 she was the first woman to receive the Alfred I. duPont Award for broadcast excellence; the following year she was the first woman to receive the Peabody Award, also for broadcasting.

The duPont Award, given by Washington and Lee University (later by Columbia University), came with a monetary award of one thousand dollars. The judges gave detailed reasons why they had selected Frederick, citing her for "exemplifying the best traditions of news commentary through thoughtful, original, objective and responsible reporting and interpretation of the news" and for "avoiding the slickness, automatic orthodoxy and superficial sensationalism characteristic of much news commentary today." Furthermore, the judges said, she "consistently succeeds in being interesting." She was in good company: past recipients included Edward R. Murrow, Lowell Thomas, H. V. Kaltenborn, and Frederick's colleague at ABC Elmer Davis; Howard K. Smith and Eric Sevareid were among the recipients after Frederick.

The duPont Award may have represented a turning point in Frederick's career—not necessarily because of the thousand-dollar prize money or the prestige of winning; instead, the award drew the attention and kudos of others in the business, including her bosses at NBC. She received letters of congratulations from current and former employers. Sylvester "Pat" Weaver, then president of NBC, seemed particularly happy: "I want you to know how proud and delighted we are [that you won] . . . and for being the first woman to do so," he wrote. Frederick's first employer and mentor in broadcasting, H. R. Baukhage, wrote to congratulate her; her response was heartfelt. "The most heartwarming praise comes from one's good friends. I can't tell you how much I appreciate your kind note. It was so unexpected that I still feel it was a wonderful dream," she wrote in a reply. (Baukhage at the time was working for the Mutual Broadcasting Company in Washington DC.)

At the duPont Awards dinner at the Mayflower Hotel in New York, Frederick's acceptance speech included a plea for "responsible" listening on the part of news consumers. In speeches Frederick had long encouraged viewers to contact the government with complaints or praise about the role of the United States in world events. "Networks and commentators may discharge their responsibilities, but unless listeners also assume the responsibility that goes with their citizenship, freedom of speech cannot be preserved in this country," she said.

If Frederick was surprised at receiving the duPont Award, she was perhaps more thrilled at winning what may have been an even more prestigious national award a year later, in 1955—the George Foster Peabody Award for broadcasting, which many considered the equivalent of the Pulitzer Prize, an award that was given only to print journalists. She was awarded the Peabody specifically for her "contribution to international understanding." The award was a feather in the cap of NBC—as *Broadcasting* magazine noted, an informal competition among networks took place to determine which won the most Peabody Awards each year. The magazine announced that CBS had received four Peabody Awards in 1955, while NBC and ABC had tied with three. Frederick received the award for her fifteen-minute Sunday morning radio show, *Pauline Frederick at the UN*. "Her independent mind and her consistently fair appraisal of the news. Her distinguished services in interpreting the United Nations and its agencies not only indicate her concern for world peace but reflect credit upon the NBC network for its recognition of Miss Frederick's integrity and skill," the judges said.

As was the case with the duPont Awards, Frederick received a flurry of congratulatory notes from friends and employers, past and present. Tom Velotta, her boss at ABC, wrote warmly: "It did [my] heart good to see you on the dais at the Peabody Awards yesterday. It isn't often that awards for radio and television go to well-deserving people. In this case, I am sure the proper person received it . . . P.S. You looked very pretty."

To Frederick, however, the most exciting aspect of being awarded the prestigious Peabody Award was receiving a congratulatory telegram from Dag Hammarskjöld. The one-sentence telegram—"Permit me to congratulate you upon receiving the distinguished Peabody Award for your coverage of the United Nations news"—was read aloud at the Peabody Awards dinner at the Roosevelt Hotel in New York City. Frederick wrote a short response to Hammarskjöld. "If anything added to the prestige of the Peabody Award . . . it was your telegram of congratulations." In her acceptance speech she subtly criticized Cold War maneuvering. "If there is ever to be peace in this world, all of us, all people, must learn a new language—and the key word in that language is understanding," she said. "Peace can never be had through the terms used in planning war, such as conflict and victory. Peace will come when our hearts and minds think and act in terms of cooperation and togetherness. The beginning is understanding. This is international wisdom."

Frederick's dedication to her job, combined with her true belief that another war could be catastrophic, came across when she was on camera. The tenor of the top awards she won in the 1950s indicated that she was successful in promoting understanding and helping listeners interpret and use facts they were given. Interestingly, she was not granted these awards for a specific story or for specific spot coverage of a pivotal event. In 1956 *McCall's* magazine awarded her with its "Golden Mike," given to the top female radio/television broadcaster—the one whom judges believed made top contributions to public service. To Frederick this third major award represented an embarrassment of riches. In a short congratulatory memo NBC president Pat Weaver wrote, "Congratulations on the McCall's Mike. Have you got them all yet?" At the awards dinner in Boston, judges said Frederick's show, *Pauline Frederick Reporting*, "has given her listeners some of the most competent and courageous news casting on the air. She has also scooped her male colleagues innumerable times."

In 1955 Frederick scooped many of her rivals in the broadcasting and print media. She got an "exclusive" in the true sense of the word—she nabbed a source that no one was able to get. During a commemoration of the UN's tenth anniversary in San Francisco, scores of reporters were hoping to talk to Vyacheslav M. Molotov, the Soviet foreign minister who was notoriously shy with the press—and who often stubbornly opposed UN initiatives. As he walked to his Cadillac, he allowed reporters to take his picture, but he said nothing. As his driver was departing, Frederick tapped on the window and presented her NBC microphone: "How does the United States look?" she asked. Molotov replied in Russian, and his interpreter translated in what would be his first U.S. broadcast. "Thank you for the welcome given by you [reporters] to all of the Soviet delegates on arrival here," he said. "Allow me to convey through you cordial greetings to the people of San Francisco, the city where the United Nations was born." It was hardly a major announcement, but it demonstrated the familiarity and trust that Frederick had established with foreign diplomats. And Frederick, who met many famous people while on the job, apparently treasured the encounter. She framed a photo of it and kept it separate from most of her papers and mementos. It was in her niece's home when she died, along with a handful of other special items.

Many of the awards Frederick received in her lifetime were given by her peers—people who saw her work and people who knew her well. In late 1955 she told Cordell in a letter that she was a finalist, along with reporters from both broadcast and print media, for recognition by the Overseas Press Club. She was to learn if she received the honor the next day at a dinner. (There is no evidence that she did receive it.) But as she indicated to Cordell, the dinner itself would be a festive occasion, and she planned to invite friends to her home afterward for drinks. "I've invited a gang from NBC from VP [vice president] down for night caps afterward—some thirty are coming." As an NBC correspondent, Frederick also had the honor of occasionally serving on the panel of *Meet the Press*, the respected Sunday news show. As she told Cordell, on one occasion she invited Lawrence Spivak, the program's moderator, and others to her home after the show. "The guest is [Indian diplomat] Krishna Menon," she told Cordell. "Afterward, he and the Spivaks and about fifteen others are coming back to my apartment for drinks and further discussion . . . So that should be fun."

During his tenure as secretary-general Hammarskjöld received extensive and, frankly, positive coverage from Frederick. But she was not alone in her tremendous affection and respect for him. Brian Urquhart, who worked in diplomatic positions at the UN for forty years and who wrote a biography of Hammarskjöld in 1972, believed no secretary-general before or since Hammarskjöld matched his brilliance and leadership abilities: "[Hammarskjöld] put the UN on the map as an organization that could actually take action in crises, one that didn't just pass resolutions, but actually got into the field and did things . . . [He was] the person who transformed the Secretary-General into a major player in international affairs on the political side and everything else." In his biography of Hammarskjöld,

Brian Lipsey referred to Frederick as "a journalist Hammarskjöld liked and trusted." Urquhart said Hammarskjöld enjoyed talking to Frederick because he viewed her as an outstanding correspondent and someone with a rare understanding of the UN. During the Suez crisis, when she was in Rome, Frederick wrote Hammarskjöld a note in longhand on Hotel Excelsior stationery, requesting a brief "chat" but not a formal interview. "It would serve to tie up some 'loose ends' in my mind and help me to adopt completely your 'don't worry' philosophy," she wrote. "I know your assignment is an exceedingly difficult one—and I continue to pledge my full cooperation. But in a much smaller way my job, too, has been one of the most difficult ones I have ever undertaken. With sincere appreciation, Pauline Frederick."

Hammarskjöld's response must have been important to her because it was one of the few pieces of professional correspondence that Frederick had framed. Hammarskjöld replied with a handwritten note on PanAm Airways stationery, apparently written when the two were passengers on a plane. The undated four-sentence note—some of which is nearly illegible—begins "Dear Miss Frederick" and is signed "Dag Hammar-skjöld." "I sincerely appreciate your message and I do appreciate your difficulties. Sorry that I may have added to them. Why not have a quick exchange of thoughts, sipping the brandy that PanAm is likely to pro-vide," he wrote. The remaining two sentences are difficult to decipher but appear to say, "Is it not true that there is a 'us worry' based on simple trust that somebody may use simple, honest service up to the limits of our capacity?" He signed it, "A biento" (translated roughly from the French as "see you soon").

The exact meaning and context of this note is unclear, but it is possible to decipher its probable meaning. As an admirer of Hammarskjöld, a journalist, and later head of the United Nations Correspondents Associa-tion, Frederick often played contradictory roles: she had to walk a fine line as a diplomat herself—someone who wanted to cultivate relation-ships within the UN yet whose job it was to report objectively on what she saw and what she was told. These jobs were in particular conflict when she covered Hammarskjöld's United Nations. Brian Urquhart said the secretary-general was adamant that no single member of the press receive preferential treatment. Although Hammarskjöld had invited Frederick to fly with him for an interview, much of what he told her was off the record, so she could not use it in stories That in itself might not have been the reason she kept and later framed that note, however. It is possible it had special significance for another reason.

7 *The Great Assembly Hall*

It is essential to visit the UN from time to time in order to reacquaint oneself with what is a separate world—and a world so vivid and hectic and compelling, so filled with excitement and crisis, that those who dwell in it all the time begin to believe that nothing else exists.

Historian and presidential advisor ARTHUR M. SCHLESINGER, 1977

Frederick loved the United Nations complex for its elegance and grandeur, which she believed conveyed its seriousness and sense of purpose—and never did the organization have as daunting a task as the one it faced with the intensifying of the Cold War. Often, when she broadcast from the UN, Frederick's script opened with more than just the news. "I'm reporting to you today from the NBC booth overlooking the great Assembly Hall here at United Nations headquarters in New York," she would say.

In 1955 Frederick took part in a great celebration at the UN—the tenth anniversary on June 26 of the signing of the charter. Throughout her career covering the UN, Frederick would periodically quote portions of the document—an idealist, she took its words seriously. One of the agency's reasons for being, according to the charter, was "to save succeeding generations from the scourge of war, which twice in our lifetime has brought untold sorrow to mankind." During the tenth anniversary of the signing, NBC and United Nations Radio, the in-house UN radio network, broadcast a thirty-minute program called "You and Article 71." With Frederick as the narrator and interviewer of several UN staff members, those who participated stressed two points: that the UN was an organization of people, not politicians or government leaders; and that part of its goal was to offer a voice to organizations around the world—religious groups, labor unions, educational alliances, and others. (Article 71 stresses that one of the purposes of the UN is to "make suitable arrangements for consultation with non-governmental organizations.") Frederick had always been adamant in her contention that activities of the UN affected tens of millions of people worldwide and that the ultimate objective of the complex organization was to serve people—and, more specifically, individuals. The fact that Frederick and NBC would participate so actively in that event, which was primarily a UN public relations activity, speaks to the UN's importance in the eyes of the network.

Despite her views of the crucial importance of the UN, there is no evidence that Frederick sensationalized activities or events at the agency. In fact, in interviews late in her career she would say that only a handful of events in UN history even merited worldwide interest or coverage— the advent of the Korean War and the resulting peace accord were two of them. And a third was the Suez crisis of 1956—a situation that allowed the body's novice secretary-general to show his mettle.

By 1956 Frederick was becoming a star at NBC, and her already busy lecture schedule was expanding. At least one new theme had emerged in some of her talks—the idea of a world paralyzed by fear of a hydrogen bomb. By 1953 both the United States and the Soviet Union had tested hydrogen bombs, and after the Soviets' launching of *Sputnik* four years later, many Americans came to the shocking realization that U.S. technology was falling behind Russia's when it came to nuclear weaponry. In speeches Frederick began to arm herself, as it were, with facts and figures about the bomb to describe the swath of utter devastation it could inflict worldwide. She spoke in vivid and stark terms. "If a bomb exploded near your house, there would be the burn and the blast, but also radioactive particles . . . would be carried downwind to fall onto the earth again . . . in a belt 20 miles wide, 140 miles long [and] all persons who had not taken protective measures would be destroyed," she said in 1955. "Half of those 160 miles away would probably die and 5 to 10 percent 190 miles away would perish." To graduates of Lynchburg College in Williamsport, Pennsylvania, she noted in 1956 that the United States had recently deployed a test bomb over the Pacific Ocean, and she quoted a *New York Times* story describing the sight of the bomb. First, she said, a giant fireball appeared, and then "the most startling and incredible phenomenon of all—a giant superearthly [*sic*] cloud that kept climbing and spreading outward and outward until it appeared as it would envelop the entire earth."

Throughout her career Frederick was quick to point out that she was a registered independent voter, and she obviously thought it important not to let her personal politics influence her reporting. As the Cold War heated up, however, so did her attitude against nuclear weapons—and as the conflict in Vietnam escalated in the mid-1960s, she became increasingly outspoken against that war in speeches and public appearances. In the early 1950s she, like other reporters, found it difficult to cover Senator Joseph McCarthy's claims of Soviet infiltration in U.S. government agencies "objectively." Although her beat was not Washington DC or Washington politics, the Wisconsin senator's activities did make their way into some of her broadcasts; during her early years at NBC she hosted a daily five-minute radio show at 11:25 a.m. featuring commentary, so she had some opportunity to inject opinion in her stories. In March 1953, a year before CBS aired Murrow's legendary *See It Now* episode on March 9, 1954, which exposed McCarthy, Frederick made her opinion of McCarthy clear to viewers when she reported on the senator's attempts to contact Greek ship owners to get them to stop delivering goods to the Communist People's Republic of China. She pointed out drily that his actions violated the Constitution. "Senator McCarthy says he is amazed if there is any misunderstanding over his activities in international affairs. The senator need not be amazed if he reads the Constitution of the United States which vets the conduct of international relations with the executive branch of the government with the advice and consent of all the Senate."

A year later Frederick became even more pointed in her criticism of McCarthy and top government officials, whom she felt had done little to stop him. "President Eisenhower has preferred to let his lieutenants deal with that controversy directly, while maintaining the moral position there must be fair play in congressional investigations," she said. Meanwhile,

Vice President Richard Nixon—who would become a frequent target of her criticism years later, when he became president—mimicked Eisenhower's "moral positions on behalf of fair play, following the President's practices of not mentioning the word 'McCarthy.'" In this broadcast, Frederick stressed that it was not communism dividing Americans, as the president and his men implied. "The overwhelming mass of Americans are united in opposition to Communism," she said. "Senator McCarthy exploited fear for purposes of achieving personal power . . . challenged the basic tenets of the Bill of Rights and outraged the feelings of decent people with his vicious attack." She went on to quote stories in the *New York Times* and the *New York Herald Tribune* asserting that the administration should not attempt to appease McCarthy.

In retrospect history has vilified McCarthy and his cohorts. But correspondence between Frederick and her friend Ann Cordell in 1954 indicate that the consensus among some apparently intelligent and informed people was that the senator's actions may have been merited, at least in part. After McCarthy and his chief counsel, Roy Cohn, began inquiries into possible Communist infiltration in the armed forces, army officials claimed that McCarthy and his staff had sought preferential treatment for Pvt. David Schine, a friend of Cohn. In the nation's first televised congressional hearings, beginning April 22, 1954, the Senate investigated the charges. It was during these thirty-six-day hearings, which drew a television audience of eighty million people, that public opinion against McCarthy began to turn. (In January 1954, before the army hearings, a Gallup Poll showed that 50 percent of those polled had a positive opinion of McCarthy and 29 percent had a negative opinion. Those numbers fell to 34 percent and 45 percent, respectively, after the army hearings ended.) Letters Frederick wrote to Cordell early that year indicate that Cordell may have had sympathy for McCarthy because she felt he was being treated unfairly by the media. In March, shortly before the hearings began, Frederick wrote to Cordell, "After the Army reported the McCarthy-Cohn efforts to blackmail it, if you still feel the whole thing has been stirred up by the press and radio I can add nothing that will change your mind." Later in the letter she said: "Forgive me if I sound a bit crisp. But I am so indignant over the persecution and ill-will engendered by our budding totalitarians that I can scarcely contain myself." In a P.S. she added sarcastically, "Do you think Edward R. Murrow is a Communist?"

The encouraging news worldwide, however, was that Dag Hammarskjöld was living up to the high expectations he had established when he first came to office as secretary-general. In April 1956 he turned his attention to the long-standing conflicts in the Mideast—particularly the conflicts between Israel and the Arab nations.

Frederick recalled years later that because Hammarskjöld sensed the volatility in the Mideast could escalate further, he began traveling early in 1956 to the nations involved to talk to leaders there about the importance of the UN-negotiated armistice agreements between Israel and the Arab nations. As Frederick recalled, he had some limited success in helping to establish a cease-fire between Israel and the Arab countries at borders and in allowing UN observers to have freer access to the region. But she also remembered that Hammarskjöld himself was not persuaded that hostilities would end solely through outside diplomacy—he believed the countries themselves needed to have a will to pursue peace.

And Hammarskjöld was proved correct. By the fall of 1956 the Suez Canal, strategically important for trade because it allowed the only direct means of travel from the Mediterranean to Indian oceans, became the focus of a major military confrontation. Gamal Abdel Nasser, who had recently become Egypt's president, decided to nationalize the Suez, which had previously allowed free passage, and charge a fee for its use. Nasser's action came after the United States and Great Britain had retracted aid they had pledged to Egypt for the building of the Aswan High Dam in the Nile. (The withdrawal of funds was announced after Egypt established ties with the People's Republic of China.) The move provoked an angry backlash by three nations—Israel, which immediately marched toward the Suez, and Great Britain and France, which gave reinforcements to Israel. British and French forces soon occupied the region, and Egypt sank forty ships in the canal, blocking all passage.

In an attempt to quell the conflict Hammarskjöld and UN Canadian delegate Lester Pearson established the first United Nations Emergency Force (UNEF), which was composed of military representatives of nations outside of the world's two major powers. Its purpose was to help restore peace in the region. Ultimately, control of the canal was returned to Egypt, which promised to restore free passage. But the Suez conflict was seen as a political victory for Egypt and is believed to have triggered the demise of the colonial tradition of Great Britain and France, a phenomenon that would ultimately exacerbate the Cold War and have long-lasting global ramifications. Many people were glued to their televisions and radios during the Suez conflict. Frederick worked around the clock getting updated information and trying to interpret it for listeners and viewers. "I never covered anything that changed so frequently," she said later. "I was chained to a microphone for six weeks—practically killed myself."

It was during the Suez crisis that Frederick would better get to know Hammarskjöld, and one incident presented her with her own conflict as a journalist. During the Suez crisis and after the formation of the UN Emergency Force, Hammarskjöld decided to travel with one of the UNEF contingents to the Suez region from a staging area near Naples, Italy. Frederick, who also made the trip, had a discussion with Hammarskjöld on one leg of the flight, from New York to Rome, when he acknowledged to Frederick his regret that he could not be more open to her about UN activities and noted that formation of the UNEF was an unusual step. And it is on this trip that he probably wrote Frederick the warm note on PanAm stationery inviting her for a drink on the plane. When the secretary-general and the contingent switched planes in Rome to an Italian Air Force plane headed for Naples, Frederick was able to arrange for a seat next to Hammarskjöld through an unnamed "friend" at the UN; NBC executives, of course, were thrilled and, she suggested later, expected it would generate a big story or two during the trip. Instead, Hammarskjöld gave her information off the record that she could not report. She never revealed what it was, even decades later. Frederick did say in a UN Oral History interview that Hammarskjöld had confided in her that he knew his job was a dangerous one and, in words that would prove sadly prescient, that he knew he could be a "target" for those who resented his activism.

Frederick told Gay Talese in a 1963 *Saturday Evening Post* profile of her that her bosses at NBC were not pleased that the discussion did not lead to an exclusive story. "I don't think some of them have ever forgiven me for not getting that scoop," she said. But Frederick made no secret of the fact that she would not report on something that might threaten the security of the public or of peace negotiations. As a *Newsweek* reporter wrote of her, "Miss Frederick has . . . built a reputation for keeping her lip buttoned when necessary."

Although there were always rumors, it is almost certain that Frederick and Hammarskjöld never had a relationship that went beyond friendly and professional. Frederick was always circumspect about her romantic relationships, other than stating that her job left her little time for personal relationships. In a few interviews she did comment that she had had a very close relationship with a man who had died in an airplane crash, although she never revealed his identity or anything else about him, other than to say it was not Hammarskjöld. Her niece Catharine Cole said she had a vague memory of her aunt talking about someone she had lost in a plane crash, but Frederick said little about it, possibly because he was married, Cole said, although that is speculation.

In his profile of her, Talese mentioned three men who were romantically involved with Frederick, including the mystery man who died in a plane crash and one who had died more recently of a heart attack. He also wrote about an unnamed man from Frederick's distant past who broke up with her when he learned she could not have children. (That man may have been David Sokolow, to whom Frederick had been briefly engaged when she was in Germany in 1946.) Talese related an anecdote about this unidentified former fiancé of Frederick who apparently visited her at the UN many years later. He called her from the lobby, asking her if she would like to go to lunch with him and meet his wife. "Miss Frederick coldly clicked down the receiver," Talese wrote.

In her many broadcasts about Hammarskjöld, Frederick stressed that despite the many social activities that were a part of his job—and despite his genial nature and charisma—the secretary-general was a loner at heart and greatly valued the rare hours of solitude he spent reading and writing. As she said in a 1959 broadcast, discovering the real man behind the secretary-general label "is not easy . . . because of his distaste for publicity and any inquiry into his life . . . Dag Hammarskjöld's name is now heard throughout the world and his picture is known to millions. Yet he remains a man few people know . . . And he stubbornly refuses all efforts to pull aside the cloak of privacy he insists on wrapping about himself." His "family," Frederick reported, was the UN family: "he has transferred family relationships to a larger context. To him, the United Nations headquarters is 'this House,' the Secretariat and delegates, the UN 'family.'"

By 1956 Frederick had been at NBC for three years, and her public profile as a correspondent continued to grow. Her status as the only woman network reporter, however, cut both ways for Frederick. The novelty of the situation made her a sought-after lecturer and probably a welcome anomaly for many viewers. But she was uneasy with the possibility that her status might reinforce the idea that women desired different types of news than their male counterparts and that news itself had to be targeted to either men or women. Early in her career she had stressed that news was gender neutral. Now more than ever, it seemed to her, the networks seemed to foster the view that news indeed had a gendered identity.

Nevertheless, in correspondence to her friends, she indicated that she was proud to be the first woman to be given many of the top awards she had received. By April 1956 she was to have another achievement bestowed upon her: she was named the first female "anchorman" at a political convention. NBC named her its radio anchor for the 1956 Democratic and Republican conventions. (In his short memorial tribute to her on the NBC *Nightly News* in 1990, Tom Brokaw noted that her title as anchor was one of her crowning achievements—as well as an achievement for NBC.) The Peabody Award–winning analyst Frederick was assigned the role of "coordinating all political developments for the radio network," according to an NBC news release, which announced this "first." (But Frederick would not be the only female network correspondent covering the convention; Ruth Geri Hagy, who moderated a local Philadelphia show called *College Press Conference*, was there for ABC as well as Shirley Lavine of CBS, who was an assistant to convention anchorman Walter Cronkite.) The network news release quoted Frederick about her view of the crucial role television and radio played in making government transparent. "The concept of the smoke-filled room has been outdated by radio and television," she said. "The public not only wants to see and hear what's happening, but also wants to understand." It is the duty of those covering the convention to interpret events for the public, she added. "There is an obligation imposed on broadcasters who are covering the conventions on a second-by-second basis to make the occurrences appear to follow a logical pattern of development . . . Radio and television have brought an end to the arbitrary control of old-time bosses."

The networks had come a long way in convention coverage by 1956; the mistakes they made during the 1948 and 1952 conventions proved to be learning experiences for them, and broadcast technology had grown tremendously since those earlier conventions. Television's power and its penetration into households during the era were measured by the number of miles of channels that were transmitted across the country. *Broadcasting* magazine reported that during the 1952 conventions, for instance, thirty thousand miles of channel carried television shows to 107 television stations in sixty-five cities, and more than 1,200 network radio stations could receive convention coverage. Four years later seventy-three thousand miles of channels transmitted telecasts to 400 television stations nationwide, and 1,500 radio stations were able to get convention coverage. The scope of the coverage was also increasing, according to *Broadcasting* magazine, which reported that radio and television networks would carry up to seventy hours of direct feeds from the two convention cities, as well as preconvention news and special features. (The hardware also improved over the years: "All networks will unveil for the first time midget tv cameras, some developed especially for these conventions," the magazine reported. "They range in weight from CBS's 1.5-pound flashlight size camera to ABC and NBC's 4 lb. hand viewers.") The combination of increased television penetration, more experienced and savvy correspondents, and rapidly improving technology naturally led to greater interest in corporate sponsorship for the event. Six national sponsors paid a total of $14.5 million for airtime during the conventions and on election night.

Despite all the preconvention publicity, the Democratic convention, held in Chicago, and the Republican convention, held in San Francisco, simply did not have the suspense of the previous two political conventions. Incumbent Republican president Dwight Eisenhower was expected to defeat Adlai Stevenson in the general election, forcing the scores of reporters covering the event to be particularly creative when coming up with stories that would build drama. From the opposite side of the camera, once-novice politicians and their advisors came into the conventions very aware of the camera's fickle eye and ubiquitous nature. "As was the case in Chicago, everything the Republicans did—and there wasn't much that was newsworthy—was geared for microphones and cameras," *Broadcasting* wrote after the Democratic convention. "It was a carefully calculated effort to reach maximum audiences in the populous East."

The growth of television audiences, combined with the fact that broadcasters were finally getting substantial experience in front of the camera, meant that network officials could turn their attention to practical matters such as beating their competition—they wanted their correspondents to get stories first, and they wanted them to establish themselves as familiar faces in the minds of audiences. NBC no doubt knew that it would get attention by naming Frederick as the first female anchor person at a convention, and it was right. A full six weeks before the election, well-known fashion editor Eugenia Sheppard of the *New York Herald Tribune* ran a story about her appointment, complete with three photos of Frederick in different designer convention wardrobes. "How to look smart, pretty, interesting and appropriate [at the conventions] is the next fashion problem to rear its head, " Sheppard wrote. For Frederick "the problem is double," she noted, because she had to travel to two different cities with two different climates. Frederick described her wardrobe style for the conventions as "smartly inconspicuous," with a focus on clothes that would remain flattering from early morning until late at night and would stay comfortable as she remained seated for hours at a time at the anchor desk. "Most of them are day-long costumes that will go anywhere if you add a hat or change an accessory," Sheppard wrote. A slim Frederick was depicted in a sheath dress, a sleek two-piece suit, and an evening gown complete with mink stole.

In a later column in the *Herald Tribune* Frederick spelled out to columnist Marie Torre her dilemma as the nation's first anchorwoman. Announcing Frederick's appointment, Torre opened her column with the "popular notion" among network executives that the way to draw female audiences to broadcast programs was to feature a female correspondent. To her that notion implied that "just as with clothes, colognes and what have you, there is 'news for men' and 'news for women.'" But Frederick, she wrote, was adamant in her style of "no frills" reporting. "News is news, and if it interests men, it's going to interest women, too," Frederick told Torre. "Why the dividing line? Female audiences too often are treated as secondary citizens, which is deplorable!" She continued: "I just can't fathom the theory that you have to sugar coat the news to appeal to women. It's nonsense. I'm covering the conventions not as a woman's reporter but as a reporter, period."

NBC's appointment of Frederick as anchorwoman was unquestionably a vote of confidence for her. She was one of several big guns covering the conventions. NBC sent Ned Brooks as an anchor and used popular broadcasters David Brinkley, Dave Garroway, Chet Huntley, and John Cameron Swayze; ABC sent John Daly and Quincy Howe; and Edward R. Murrow, Eric Sevareid, and Lowell Thomas provided coverage for CBS, along with anchorman Walter Cronkite. Despite the brief history of televised conventions—the 1948 and 1952 conventions were the only ones that had received extensive television network attention—by 1956 they were beginning to gain a reputation as the places where network news celebrities were born. Television critics commenting on coverage of the 1952 conventions gave uniformly high praise to the performance there of Cronkite, who, of course, would eventually become one of the most popular and high-profile network anchors in broadcasting history. Earning their stripes during the latest convention would be two relatively unknown NBC newsmen named Huntley and Brinkley.

The 1950s were a time of great change and upheaval for television networks. By the middle and end of the decade, broadcast technology had advanced to the point that network executives could finally focus on the "talent"—news personnel—and programming. CBS and NBC were serious competitors that battled each other for audience share and the kudos of critics. NBC news managers by the mid-1950s were beginning to tire of John Cameron Swayze, once the popular anchor of a nightly fifteen-minute evening news show called *News Caravan*. But network executives were fickle, and the fortunes of network anchors could change almost overnight. And so it was that Swayze's star began to plummet almost as soon as former advertising executive Sylvester "Pat" Weaver, who was hired at NBC in 1949, was named president of the network in 1953. Weaver, a dynamic and charismatic personality who was obsessed with good press as well as high ratings, saw Swayze as a competent but ho-hum journalist who had ceased getting favorable mentions in the press, and Bill McAndrew, head of news for the network, did not disagree. NBC could hold its own when it came to covering the news, but the fact was that the long shadow cast by Edward R. Murrow of CBS eclipsed everyone and everything at the other networks. Weaver tried luring Murrow away from CBS, but that did not work. So, he came to believe that NBC should find its own version of Murrow.

Weaver, meanwhile, already had success putting NBC on the map when it came to innovation. One of his legacies was his creation in 1952 of a morning news, feature, and entertainment program called *Today*. Weaver defied conventional wisdom when he came up with the idea for the hybrid show—it was widely believed that people did not watch television in the morning as they got ready for work or school. Although the show got off to a slow start (it was believed by some that ratings picked up when it started featuring a chimpanzee named J. Fred Muggs), the show eventually became habit forming to many Americans and remains, sixty years later, one of NBC's greatest success stories. Weaver lasted as president of NBC only until 1956, but he was a daring executive who is credited with endowing the network with a sophistication and worldliness it had lacked.

In 1955, as television viewership rose and radio audiences declined, Weaver developed the radio show *Monitor*, a block of news and entertainment shows on weekend radio that, against all odds, became popular among listeners. *Monitor*, which had a magazine format previously unheard of on radio, lasted until 1975. Weaver may have been prescient in his view that all communication forms would ultimately merge and become monolithic as well as in his belief in the tremendous influence television would have on all aspects of society. In 1954 the *New Yorker* published an exhaustive two-part profile of the outspoken and energetic Weaver, describing how his presence in some ways ran counter to the accepted ethos at NBC. A Phi Beta Kappa graduate of Dartmouth, he spouted philosophy and theology in his interoffice memos, which were rich in historical and literary allusions. A rare idealist in the world of television, Weaver once told a group of network employees that NBC "must do good . . . Television must be used to upgrade humanity across a broad base."

If *Today* boosted NBC's ratings, creation of what would be called the *Huntley-Brinkley Report* pushed it over the top to beat CBS, according to Reuven Frank, one of the news managers who initially had the idea to pair the two newsmen. As Frank tells it in his memoir, NBC's quest to replace Swayze and displace Murrow as top dog in the eyes of the public was born during the 1956 political conventions. NBC also wanted someone to compete with Cronkite, CBS television's convention anchor, who was a rising star. After some haggling among NBC news executives, they decided to pair Huntley and Brinkley—two personalities who, while not exactly opposites, did not appear to mesh at first. As broadcast historian Edward Bliss noted, Brinkley's wit and no-nonsense perceptions contrasted with Huntley's "solid, almost somber" manner. "It was sirloin and spice . . . so novel and refreshing, as well as informative, that critics gave NBC's coverage rave reviews." Two months after the conventions ended, the *Huntley-Brinkley Report* debuted in the evening, replacing Swayze's *News Caravan*. In his memoir Frank recalled that he had come up with the now legendary closing of the show after writers could not decide how to end it each night. "I wrote, [Huntley]: 'Good night, David.' [Brinkley]: 'Good night, Chet.' [Huntley]: 'And good night for NBC News.'" NBC executives were victorious in their quest to unseat Murrow as the voice of network news. In her history of network news Barbara Matusow named one chapter "Chet and David: The Superstars" and quoted a 1968 *New Yorker* story saying the news duo could take their place in American culture next to such immortal duos as Abbott and Costello, Roy Rogers and Trigger, and Fibber McGee and Molly.

These new and innovative NBC shows provided television venues for correspondents such as Frederick. She became a frequent correspondent for *Today*, particularly in the 1960s, and for the *Huntley-Brinkley Report*. Frederick was friends with Huntley, one of her contemporaries, who was three years younger than she and had joined NBC two years after she did. He once described her as "our dependable right arm in sorting out the legalities, the propaganda, the nationalistic sensitivities and the international nuances which frequent the UN." She did not know David Brinkley well; he was eleven years her junior, although she noted sardonically late in her life that he was one of the young male copy clerks who worked in the ABC radio newsroom in the early 1940s, when Frederick was advised that women would never be broadcasters and therefore had no place in the newsroom.

Frederick was not immune to the periodic shake-ups and personnel changes at NBC in the 1950s, even though she was well on her way to becoming a household name. The numerous awards she received and the many positive letters from viewers attest to the respect she earned from her colleagues and from viewers. In one profile of her, however, she indicated that the NBC power structure had not been happy with her performance at the 1956 political conventions. In his 1963 profile Gay Talese wrote that while some NBC officials applauded her convention performance, some criticized her inability to ad-lib well, so they did not assign her to cover the 1960 conventions. Although there is no evidence among her papers to corroborate this account, Frederick acknowledged to Talese that she had been blindsided and upset by the negative judgment. She told Talese that she was never told of the criticism and in fact had received a telegram of praise from NBC president Robert Sarnoff. She asked an NBC executive about these seemingly paradoxical messages. His response: "Everyone got a telegram like that!" Adding to her confusion must have been the fact that after the convention, she was asked to cover the general election, and her performance received high praise from *Washington Evening Star* columnist Bernie Harrison, who called her reports "concise, lucid and quietly delivered."

Navigating the corporate structure of NBC's news division and catering to the whims of vacillating news executives was not easy, and one of Frederick's talents was picking her battles carefully and handling unpleasantness politely and with a light touch. But she could not sidestep turf battles completely, and she was particularly territorial when it came to the United Nations in general and Dag Hammarskjöld in particular. One incident indicated that at NBC News, the right hand did not always know what the left hand was doing. In late 1956 NBC's publicity department sent out a news release publicizing a series of special shows on the radio series

Monitor devoted to Hammarskjöld. "His contribution to world peace will be outlined in a series of five feature stories" narrated by [*Today* host] Dave Garroway, the network announced. A news release explained that interviews would be done "with those who have worked with Hammarskjöld . . . [with] commentary by Leon Pearson and [Washington correspondent] Joseph C. Harsch." Pearson was, it explained, "the network's United Nations correspondent." Frederick, who had no role in this "tribute," as it was called, was surprised to read that it was Pearson and not she who was the network's United Nations correspondent. She fired off a memo to network news president Bill McAndrew, along with a copy of the news release. "I know the 'Monitor' goes its own merry way, but in view of the relationship I have with Mr. Hammarskjöld, the attached must be a little puzzling to the secretary-general and his associates on two counts: 1. Leon's designation, and 2. That I am not included." She noted that Pearson did occasionally report on the UN for NBC Radio and suggested "a little chat" about how to coordinate UN coverage in the future. (No response from McAndrew was found among her papers.) Frederick firmly believed in graciousness and tact at all times, but she evidently defended herself if she felt she had been wronged and promoted herself internally within the networks for which she worked. Robert Asman, who was a special events producer in Washington for NBC in the 1960s, occasionally worked with Frederick. "She was tough as a newswoman," he recalled. "In a huddle with competitors, she'd use her elbows. But she was also diplomatic, which is why she fit in at the UN."

There is little question that Frederick was adept at NBC interoffice politics. But as network television expanded its offerings and television itself matured and became part of the American culture, she began to spend more time at UN headquarters and less time in the NBC newsroom at 30 Rockefeller Center. Much of her work, of course, centered on activities inside the UN complex, so she naturally camped out there; beyond that, however, Frederick may have enjoyed the kinship and camaraderie she felt in the UN lounge and reporter's bullpen more than that of the mostly male NBC newsroom. Evidence among her papers indicates that she cultivated a friendly relationship with Gen. David Sarnoff, a legendary figure in American broadcasting history who was founder and chairman of NBC's parent company RCA and father of one-time NBC president Robert Sarnoff. She talked about him affectionately during a news broadcast shortly after she was hired at NBC, and photos found among her papers show them socializing at several formal occasions. In the first broadcast of her new NBC radio show *Pauline Frederick Reporting*, she spoke glowingly of David Sarnoff (who was known primarily as "General Sarnoff" because he had been named a brigadier general by Gen. Dwight D. Eisenhower), noting that several years earlier, while she was working without a full-time contract for ABC, she had met him and he had praised her work. Surprised, she assumed that he had mistaken her for the actress with the same name. When she started to explain to him that he probably had the "wrong" Pauline Frederick in mind, *he* corrected *her*: "But General Sarnoff interrupted me to explain he was talking about the broadcasts he had heard." His comments, she told listeners, boosted her confidence: "All the months of discouragement suddenly melted away. I took new hope in my efforts to try to prove that sex should not be a barrier to broadcasting." Their friendly relationship was somewhat unlikely considering that Frederick was an early and outspoken opponent of nuclear testing and, later, the war in Vietnam. RCA was a leading defense contractor.

Frederick apparently liked David Sarnoff—or at least respected him as a powerful figure at NBC—and she treaded lightly when dealing with him. In an interoffice memo she asked him to confirm statements about guided missiles that he had apparently made during a UN luncheon speech. She wrote the memo to confirm that the statements were on the record and therefore could be used in a story. One fact concerned the number of RCA engineers (two thousand) working on the guided missile, and one was a prediction by Sarnoff that within ten years both the United States and Russia would have missiles that could travel from five thousand to ten thousand miles. At that time the two nations would have reached "dreadful parity," he said. In handwritten notes to the original typewritten memo, Sarnoff asked Frederick not to use the statistic about the engineers. "This is correct but I do not wish it quoted as it may be objected to by the Defense Dept; so pls. forget it," he wrote. He confirmed and approved the other facts.

Even though she learned, belatedly, that network honchos may not have approved of her performance in the 1956 conventions, by the late 1950s and throughout most of the 1960s Frederick was one of the network's stars and nearly untouchable. NBC paid her $250 a week plus expenses in 1956 (a yearly salary of $13,000 in 1956 is equal to a yearly salary of about $111,250 in 2013, according to the Bureau of Labor Statistics. That agency also reported that the average income for men in 1956 was $3,600, and the average income for women was $1,100). NBC, which was hypervigilant about its reputation among viewers and critics, knew that she was a high-profile and popular newscaster. And the awards kept coming—in 1957 Frederick and popular entertainers Perry Como, Bob Hope, and Dinah Shore won top honors in a poll of the nation's radio and television editors. The group named Frederick "Woman of the Year" in radio, primarily for her role in NBC's coverage of the 1956 political conventions. She was given the same honor in 1959, 1960, 1961, and 1962. Also in 1957, Frederick was named *Ladies' Home Journal*'s "Woman of the Year," the first journalist to receive the honor.

Frederick's value as a broadcaster stemmed from the fact that she was talented and dedicated, but she was also a calming and rational presence to many viewers during a time of tremendous uncertainty. By 1956, its twelfth year of existence, many people still felt the United Nations could save the world from the catastrophe of war. To some critics, however, television coverage of the UN was schizophrenic at best and spotty at worst. Jack Gould, the respected *New York Times* critic, condemned the networks' coverage of the United Nations in general and, specifically, the 1956 Soviet attack on Hungary that quelled an uprising there. He called the coverage "dishearteningly erratic," even though it was clear that citizens craved coverage of UN activities in an increasingly volatile world. "Interest in the United Nations at what broadcasting's own commentators call history's crucial hour is intense," he wrote. Citizens should not dictate how news executives operate, he said, "but as thoughtful citizens neither can they quite understand why a medium that ordinarily and justifiably commands their loyalty should let them down when civilization's chips are down." Gould did not blame network news correspondents, however, and gave particular praise to Frederick, whom he called "the gifted United Nations observer" for NBC.

Judging by some of the mail she received from viewers, it seems clear that they also appreciated her. Some of the praise she received was probably unique to her as a network broadcaster—for instance, the gift and words of encouragement from R. E. Kell, president of Mary Grey Hosiery Mills in Bristol, Virginia. Kell was so impressed by her radio broadcast from Bristol and her luncheon speech at the Shelby Hotel there that he sent her a pair of panty hose. "I know you live a very busy life and I do not expect you to take the time to write a note of thanks for these hose," he wrote. "I am just assuming that every woman loves a wardrobe of beautiful stockings."

The day Kell wrote that note, Frederick was in Bristol, Tennessee, being presented with a scroll commemorating her honorary commission as a colonel in the Patton-Crosswhite Post of the Veterans of Foreign Wars. The NBC publicity department saw fit to write a news release about the honor, noting that "it's Colonel Pauline Frederick now." Frederick, the northerner from Pennsylvania, was given the honor after a lecture she gave in Bristol, the release noted. As an added bonus, she was given a deed to one tract of land located "in the center of the South Holston Lake" to ensure her return to the area.

Prominent in her fan mail were the themes of trust and calm she conveyed on the air. "Again this morning your broadcast encouraged us in our hope that a wise and just solution could be found for this terrific problem of world tension," wrote Alta M. and Charles Hancock. Or from Mrs. Robert Coody of Cincinnati: "What a pleasure to hear a voice of sanity pointing out that differences can be settled in the United Nations."

The fear and anxiety generated by the Cold War was obvious in the letters, as was the solace the writers apparently took from Frederick's reports. The height of the Cold War coincided with the tremendous growth spurt of television news—suggesting, perhaps, that viewers took comfort in hearing and seeing a trusted and ever-present "friend" offer explanations of events. "Just a note of thanks for your summations of the serious discussions at the United Nations," wrote Myrtle Henderson of Palmyra, New Jersey. "Sometimes I fail to understand the issues discussed at the meetings and you make everything so plain."

Many of the letters conveyed an intimate tone indicating that the writers felt they knew Frederick—for instance, the letter from the man who noted that she spoke "intelligently and beautifully. If a secretary is an

8 *If Not Miss Frederick, Who?*

[Frederick] was told that if we would stop bombing that they could sit down and talk.

PRESIDENT LYNDON JOHNSON to UN ambassador Arthur Goldberg, April 22, 1966

By the early 1960s Frederick had become a household name in television news and a well-respected correspondent who had been honored by her peers in the industry on several levels—in addition to numerous prestigious reporting awards, she was elected in 1959 as head of the United Nations Correspondents Association (UNCA), an international group composed of those who covered that agency. But if any one incident spoke to the power, authority, and respect Frederick had earned as a correspondent, it was a brouhaha she had with the UN's Soviet delegate Nikolai Fedorenko. What started as a possible misunderstanding between them grew into a media firestorm—a miniature international incident. Although its long-lasting ramifications are minor, it might have taught the Soviets a hard lesson in the way Western media worked.

The newly appointed Fedorenko, like other rookie delegates, was invited to appear as a guest at a luncheon held by UNCA. Traditionally, correspondents were asked to submit questions that the guest would answer at the lunch. Frederick, as the head of the group, submitted two questions and, by virtue of her role as head of the organization, was the first to ask a question: she asked, first, if the Soviets planned to ask the UN to play a role in intervening in Berlin (which was divided at the time); and second, she asked why the Soviet Union was behind on its dues payments to the UN. (In an attempt to protest UN action in the Congo, the Russians in the mid-1960s had refused to pay more than two million dollars in shared peacekeeping fees they owed.) Fedorenko apparently ignored the first question but called Frederick's second question "inaccurate," noting that she was obviously "not conversant with UN activities." He added that the Soviets had paid their assessed dues and that Frederick may have meant to ask about the Soviet Union's role in the UN Education Fund. "Even though we live in an age of electronics, it is difficult to penetrate your mind," he added, curiously. After the luncheon ended, Frederick walked up to Fedorenko, introduced herself, and told him that she did have her facts straight. "But your question was a bad one," he insisted, and then pointed out that "it was all a joke."

Stories in the national media followed their exchange, along with a critical news release from NBC and the gift to Frederick of a conciliatory bottle of vodka. (After the event Wieslaw Gornicki, a Polish news correspondent, came into her UN office, placed the bottle on her desk, and left without a word.) In a long memo to NBC vice president William McAndrew, Frederick wrote: "I thought it might amuse you to hear how [Fedorenko] apparently tried to insult me publicly today." Frederick noted in the memo that many of the correspondents present had laughed after the diplomat said she was "not conversant in UN activities" and that she initially thought he made his comments in jest. But "a *New York Times* correspondent who was sitting in front of him said it was an obvious attempt to insult me—that his face showed great anger when he talked," she told McAndrew. An irate McAndrew was quoted in an NBC news release as saying that NBC's correspondent was well-known for her competence and knowledge of that organization. "If Miss Frederick is not conversant in UN activities, I wonder who is," he said, in a comment that was picked up by several newspapers.

The incident sheds light on the awkward position of some UN reporters. By the late 1950s, with the expansion of the Cold War, Russia had intentionally become an international naysayer and obstructionist. The UN charter stated that if that agency were to use its power to keep peace through its informal police force, the Security Council, five major powers would become permanent members of that Security Council. In this capacity all five—Britain, China, France, Russia, and the United States—must agree on important UN actions. Russia consistently voted no on measures, so it exercised what amounted to a veto, resulting in gridlock and frustrating most UN diplomats.

Frederick had to be flattered that the extensive coverage of the incident painted her as the injured party—she was the seasoned and smart correspondent who had been insulted by a rookie, according to the reports. One television writer called Frederick "our favorite lady on TV." "Where were this diplomat's manners, especially when the question came from a lady?" he asked. A decade later, however, the icy relationship between NBC and Fedorenko apparently had thawed—or perhaps he learned how to work with the American media. As one reporter wrote in 1967, Frederick "has established a relationship with Soviet Ambassador Fedorenko; amazing since it's hard to be friends with the Soviets." Frederick was quoted as having said she was not his friend: "You don't get friendly with the Soviets."

The Cold War spawned a high-stakes tug of war between the world's two military superpowers, with the media sometimes playing the role of pawn. American and Soviet policy makers knew that the *Huntley-Brinkley Report*, as the highest-rated evening news show, had great influence on the thinking of the American public. The Soviets ordered NBC's Moscow bureau closed in 1963 after a run-in there between correspondents and Soviet officials. Russian officials seemed particularly sensitive to their portrayal in the American media and in popular culture—even light ribbing offended them. About a year after the bureau closed, Frederick asked Soviet ambassador Anatoly Dobrynin when it would reopen; Dobrynin replied that the bureau would not open in the near future because the Soviets had taken offense at a newspaper advertisement by WNBC, an NBC affiliate in New York City, for a program on the station. The ad, for a call-in radio program called the *Brad Crandall Show*, depicted a caricature of an angry Soviet premier Nikita Khrushchev shouting into the receiver of a telephone, with a vintage radio in the background: "Hotline, shmot-line," the caption reads. "Let me talk to Brad Crandall!" The Soviets were not amused. The bureau would reopen, Dobrynin said, "when you stop insulting our chief of state with those Brad Crandall ads." The exchange between Frederick and Dobrynin apparently amused NBC officials. Network president Robert Kintner sent out a staff-wide letter recounting the event, and it was retold in the trade publication *Editor & Publisher*.

As a United Nations correspondent during the Cold War, Frederick and others who covered wars and crises walked a fine line when it came to reporting the news and becoming part of it. They were very aware that they could be used by both sides to make a point or convey a message. Most veteran reporters knew that they sometimes played this role in high-stakes world events, and most believed it was part of the job.

When asked once if she thought she was "used" by sources, Frederick replied that she would always air a story that she thought would interest or affect her viewers, regardless of the motives of the sources who gave her the information. One very public example came in 1966 when Frederick got an exclusive story in the middle of a stalemate in the Vietnam War. She reported that an unnamed Soviet diplomat had told her that officials in Hanoi, in Communist North Vietnam, would negotiate with the United States if the United States stopped bombing in North Vietnam. The Soviets had no official comment for three days—an unusually long silence—and then issued a denial, declaring that Frederick's report was "complete fiction." The scoop was picked up by several news outlets, including the *New York Times*. Frederick was quoted as saying that Russians rarely gave reporters exclusive stories, so there must have been a reason behind this one: "Usually they won't even discuss the weather with you unless they've been directed to do so by the Kremlin." It was also unusual for them to wait such a long time before denying the story, she said. Frederick said in an interview that she believed the Soviet diplomat had given her the story because the Soviets did indeed want the Vietnam War to end.

President Lyndon Baines Johnson apparently thought Frederick *was* friendly with the Soviets. When he heard Frederick's report about the supposed willingness of the Soviets to negotiate in Vietnam, he was furious. David Brinkley apparently gave the White House press office a heads-up before the story was revealed in the April 22, 1966, *Huntley-Brinkley Report*. In a telephone recording from 6:45 p.m. that day, it is obvious Johnson was listening to *Huntley-Brinkley* when he asked his secretary to connect him immediately with U.S. ambassador to the UN Arthur

Goldberg. Goldberg answered the telephone. "You see this Fredericks [CQ] story on NBC?" an irate Johnson asked him. Goldberg appeared unaware of the report. "Pauline Fredericks, on *Brinkley*. *Huntley-Brinkley*. She says she was told by the Russian press attaché at the United Nations—all week he's been very friendly and suckin' up to her—and she was told that if we would stop bombing that they could sit down and talk," Johnson said. He told Goldberg that he did not tell NBC anything for the record but said that the news tip to Frederick was a ploy by the Russians: "They used NBC pretty well tonight; pretty effective propaganda and our state department had no comment." Goldberg said little but noted that the "little press attaché" from whom they believe Frederick got the information "doesn't talk with any authority." Johnson agreed but implied that it was irrelevant because "they [NBC News officials] cover 35 million people."

Goldberg reassured the president that he had told the American public repeatedly that the bombing of Hanoi was not an act of U.S. aggression but, instead, an act of retaliation for Soviet aggression. "You have made a statement that you are ready to stop everything if they are ready to negotiate a mutual cease fire," Goldberg said. Johnson asked Goldberg to examine Frederick's report and "get to her right quick and say now please point out that they have no proposal at all." "[That] it's propaganda," Goldberg said. Indeed, Goldberg did immediately call Frederick after his call from Johnson, as she noted years later. The ambassador was honest—he told Frederick that Johnson had just been listening to the NBC broadcast and had called him. "I had a call from Ambassador Goldberg chiding me for not telling him what I had," Frederick replied. "He said that if he had known what I was going to say on the air, he could have had a response from the United States which would have been, I suppose, the same kind of line they had followed for a long time." Frederick's report clearly irritated Johnson. About thirty minutes after he talked to Goldberg, he called Undersecretary of State George Ball and repeated much of what he had told Goldberg: "I'm calling about the Pauline Frederick propaganda story for Russia," he said. "Somebody [in the administration] said we have no comment; but NBC played it up that we have a new peace offer," he said, adding that "we ought to get it [the story] in the morning papers . . . They

[NBC] got it from a press attaché and that's not how you conduct serious diplomatic negotiations.'"

Through these phone calls Johnson gives the impression that he sat in the Oval Office, obsessed about what the media said about him—an accurate image, according to Chet Huntley. In an oral history interview in 1969, a year before Huntley retired from NBC, he talked at length about Johnson's relationship with the press and his obsession with trying to control what was said about him. "[Johnson] had three receivers [televisions] in [his] office and he watched all three networks, I think, virtually every night." Huntley added, however, that John F. Kennedy had done the same thing when he was president.

The Russian incident illustrates the degree to which the public and top policy makers viewed Frederick as one of the nation's main conduits to the American people. And, indeed, her role as a United Nations correspondent became embedded in popular culture. In addition to the Bil Keane cartoons, humorist Erma Bombeck mentioned her several times in her syndicated column "At Wit's End" as the punch line of a gentle joke. In one holiday column, for instance, Bombeck gives gift suggestions: "Thinking women on your list will appreciate the Pauline Frederick joke book with 1,000 funnies for all occasions including what Greece said to Turkey in the UN cafeteria."

Frederick's role as an intellectual and sophisticated broadcaster stemmed in part from her beat: the UN, with its international focus, had a tinge of glamour and Continental charm that other beats did not. And apparently it had a wide enough following that NBC Radio saw fit in 1957 to devote an entire weekly twenty-five-minute show to it, *Pauline Frederick at the UN*, which aired Wednesdays at 10:05 p.m. The show featured interviews with high-ranking UN officials and diplomats as well as recordings of portions of General Assembly meetings. When it debuted in 1957, at least one national outlet—the entertainment newspaper *Variety*—praised it and Frederick. "An informative, well-organized program on the activities of the world organization, helmed by vet woman commentator Pauline Frederick," the review began, noting, "Pauline Frederick as usual handled her running commentary and her interview . . . intelligently." By the time the show aired, Frederick was viewed as the ultimate expert on the UN—a role she maintained until her retirement from NBC in 1974. Periodic trips she and other NBC correspondents made to affiliate stations introduced them to local reporters across the country—and at least once one of those local reporters would rise to become a star at NBC. A young reporter who was beginning his career at KMTV in Omaha, Nebraska, sent a note of thanks to Frederick after she and several other NBC correspondents taped a special show about the United Nations from that city in 1964. "You all deserved combat pay for enduring the crush of cocktail parties and dinners that must have greeted you," wrote Tom Brokaw, who joined Frederick at NBC two years later. "Your charm, warmth and brilliance left a lasting impression on KMTV. For me, it was an inspiring experience."

News managers at NBC affiliate stations occasionally sent letters of praise directly to Frederick regarding her UN coverage, as did top brass at NBC News. A note such as the one from correspondent Ken Bernstein, who was passing on kudos to Frederick, was not uncommon in the late 1950s and 1960s: "Both Bill McAndrew and [NBC President] Julian Goodman called tonight to say that our endeavors at the United Nations have been excellent and they have been admiring them from afar."

Even some diplomats bowed to Frederick's expertise. Included among her personal papers is a photo of Frederick interviewing George H. W. Bush, who was the United States UN ambassador from 1971 to 1973. The autographed photo is inscribed, "Dear Pauline—Some day I'll know as much about the UN as you do! Would you believe almost as much? Best regards, George Bush." Throughout her career many congressmen, senators, and other political officials wrote her to compliment her coverage. Hubert Humphrey in 1962 requested a copy of a broadcast in which she discussed the job duties and dedication of UN employees. "I want to express my thanks and appreciation for the wonderful reporting that you do on the United Nations activities. Those of us who are concerned about the UN are indebted to you for your objective and responsible reports," he wrote.

Frederick also had some unlikely celebrity fans—she and poet Carl Sandburg were friends and occasionally wrote to each other, according to Catharine Cole. Included among Frederick's most treasured possessions is a framed series of photos of Frederick and Sandburg taken at his home in Flat Rock, North Carolina; in 1956 Sandburg wrote a short poem to her called "Isle of Patmos," and below the poem he inscribed, "A rare mind & spirit & I send this with love & blessings." A few brief letters from Sandburg are included among Frederick's personal papers, including a short note dated July 1960 sent from his home in North Carolina. "Dear Pauline: Several times we got your good full & rich voice again," he wrote. "You go on making your own archangels as you need 'em. Carl."

Frederick led a full and busy life during the late 1950s and 1960s, frequently socializing with top UN officials as well as some well-known broadcasters of the era, including Chet Huntley, Irving R. Levine, and Eric Sevareid , and she enjoyed hosting small gatherings at her home. By 1961, in addition to regular television appearances and reports on *Meet the Press* and *Today*, she broadcast a news report five times a week on radio as well as radio commentary three times a week, and she reported on the news on Saturdays for NBC's radio show *Monitor*.

To publicize the efforts of its foreign and international correspondents, NBC also sponsored a yearly tour in early January in which a panel of correspondents traveled to several cities to discuss a single topic in the news. The network billed this event as a meeting of its top correspondents, and the tours usually drew large audiences. Frederick was a member of this touring group for many years—and was always the only woman in a group of eight or nine correspondents. In 1967, for instance, the group included Frederick as well as London correspondent Elie Abel; Moscow correspondent Kenneth Bernstein; Rome correspondent Irving R. Levine; Jack Perkins, Southeast Asia correspondent; and Sander Vanocur, Washington correspondent. Based on memos in the Lyndon Johnson Presidential Library, the group also sought to speak with the president—either on or off the record—during their yearly visit to Washington DC.

When Frederick was asked in 1962 to donate a work of her art for a raffle to benefit the United Nations Children's Fund, she noted that she could barely draw a circle, but she did donate one of her radio scripts. More than three hundred listeners sent quarters and dollars to win the script, which drew more donations than any original work of art the group had sought from celebrities.

NBC would sometimes issue news releases to affiliates that came in the form of feature stories about Frederick's daily life. One noted that "she's in constant communication with NBC on weekends and does 'beeper' phone reports from her apartment at 77 Park Avenue for NBC Radio hourly news." Another described Frederick's role in providing a live broadcast each Saturday evening after the end of a televised basketball game. No one knew exactly what time the game would end, and that kept Frederick on her toes, the release noted. "Pretty soon NBC is going to think her Saturday TV stint ought to be called, 'Perils of Pauline,'" said it read. The news release described a scenario in which she "got caught in recent peril" as she sat calmly in the newsroom while the men watched the game on television. Suddenly, the producer ran out, shouting to an unsuspecting Frederick that she was to be on the air in five minutes. "It seems we had it [the television in the newsroom] turned to the wrong game," Pauline recalls shakily. (Frederick herself frequently told an anecdote about a time she was waiting to go on camera in her tiny NBC UN studio overlooking the General Assembly Hall, curlers in her hair, when an urgent press briefing was called. "I had no choice but to go as I was," she said.)

The networks were locked in a brutal competition for audience in the 1960s, and executives were sensitive about viewers' thoughts about their shows. The tremendous success of the *Huntley-Brinkley Report* was key in propelling NBC News to victory over its chief rival, CBS; after the *Huntley-Brinkley* report pulled ahead of the CBS evening news show anchored by Douglas Edwards in 1960, NBC immediately began airing a tagline to its show reminding viewers that it had more listeners than any broadcast in the world. But the fortunes of the networks would shift constantly over the next few decades. Murrow had quit CBS by 1962, as had Howard K. Smith. But Walter Cronkite was a rising star, even though CBS ratings fell immediately after he replaced Edwards as anchor in April 1962.

Each week NBC compiled a "Mail Report" summarizing viewer comments it had received about segments on the *Today* show. Each week's report listed the segments and show personalities that were the subjects of these comments and broke them down into "approval," "criticism," and "inquiry." For the week of February 6, 1967, for instance, the show received 795 comments by mail. Of the comments about the program in general, 727 were positive and none negative; of comments regarding the cast, 562 were positive and 55 negative. Each report specifically outlined the numbers for each cast member and segment. One week, for example, Floyd Kalber, a guest host, received sixty-five approving comments, three critical comments, and two inquiries; a segment with authors Will and Ariel Durant received eight positive comments, no negative comments, and three inquiries. During that week, Gen. Maxwell D. Taylor had appeared to discuss his book *Responsibility and Response* with Frederick. The week's report noted that "approvals reflect viewers' disagreement with Gen. Taylor's endorsement of U.S. Government policy in Vietnam and resounding accolades for Pauline Frederick."

Taylor's appearance was a controversial one. Appointed by President Kennedy as head of the Joint Chiefs of Staff, he played a key role in recommending that the United States send more troops to Vietnam as that war intensified. With such a controversial subject, it appeared that most viewers had trouble finding Frederick objective in her interview. "Bravo for standing toe to toe with General Taylor, throwing punch after punch, asking the questions we Americans would like to have answered by the administration," wrote one viewer from Moline, Kansas. A viewer from Johns Hopkins University wrote, "I want to thank you for expressing so eloquently and so firmly this morning on the *Today* program the serious misgivings and suspicions of many people I know and I'm sure of many serious-minded people throughout this country." Not everyone was so pleased, however. "I interpret your conversations with General Taylor on the *Today* program as meaning you are pro-Communist. Has Hanoi invited [UN secretary-general] U Thant and you to move to North Vietnam?" wrote an armed services veteran from Arkansas.

For more than a decade the war in Vietnam sparked debate among NBC viewers. In response to a *Today* show interview with U.S. ambassador George H. W. Bush in July 1972, Frederick herself received some letters from viewers who were less than pleased. "I am fully convinced that you are not working for the U.S. but are just as rotten as Jane Fonda and should travel all over the country with your venom against this country and then go to Hanoi and become one of their prize heroes," wrote an anonymous viewer calling himself "Just a Disgusted Listener" from Miami. "The war would have been over long ago but for the likes of you who are always against this country." From J. T. Johnston of San Antonio, "I am hoping that when the American people finally get wise to the purpose of the United Nations and throw that communistic outfit out of the country that they will take you along with them."

As the Vietnam War escalated in the early 1960s, Frederick was finding it increasingly difficult to keep her personal views out of her newscasts. In speeches she limited herself to describing in detail the horrors a nuclear war would bring, and she recounted how viewing the devastation in post-World War II Europe had changed her life and world outlook. More blatant criticism of the war would come later. Meanwhile, a reporter writing a profile of her asked her in 1963 "if it was hard to fight down the tendency to editorialize the womanly emotions." Apparently, it was. "Yes," she replied. "Occasionally I find myself stopping just short of giving my own views on a subject because I am so close to it."

In 1961 a publication called *National Business Woman* published a profile of her that focused on her personal feelings about the Cold War and the possibility that the world could enter another world war. Unlike others who wrote profiles of her and emphasized her accomplishments, her daily routine, and her background, the reporter this time focused on the emotional aspect of her job and noted that it was impossible for Frederick to remain "objective" about the world-changing issues she covered. "Miss Frederick is not just a reporter reading the happenings of the day to the listening audience, but a woman with deep feelings and convictions about people and their homelands, their hopes and hopelessness, their struggles for self-determination, and with a great yearning hope of her own for a lasting peace. This is a student of the world, working in her chosen field because her interest and firsthand knowledge tell her these happenings upon which she reports are vital to all life and the future world. Asked for a description of her, a friend said, 'she's literate—not just in words but in ideas—literate and high-minded. She has strong convictions and high ideals. This is not just a job.'"

Frederick was elected president of the United Nations Correspondents Association in March 1959, an organization of more than two hundred reporters worldwide who covered the UN. (It should be noted that when Frederick headed the UNCA, only about 50 of the 206 men and 24 women who covered the agency were there full-time; some covered breaking news at the UN, and others were stationed there in the fall when the General Assembly convened.) A story about Frederick in the *Connecticut Sunday Herald* reported that during her inauguration as UNCA president "some 200 press representatives . . . lined up to buss her on cheek and hand for an hour." The reporter called it the "kissingest scene witnessed in the glass house."

A story about the UN beat reporters in the *Overseas Press Bulletin*, the newsletter of the Overseas Press Association, echoed what Frederick had said for years: that it was the cultivation of sources and the knowledge of the inner workings of the UN—and not necessarily a consistent presence— that led to exclusive stories on the UN beat. As the story said, successful reporters "know the idiosyncrasies of the UN and . . . are on most intimate terms with the permanent representatives." The story, written in 1960, said that most of the men and women who covered the UN full-time then were former foreign correspondents who had extensive experience living and reporting overseas. They included Max Harrelson of the Associated Press, who had covered the UN since its inception in 1945; Bruce Munn of United Press International, who had covered the beat since 1949; and Tom Hamilton and Kathleen McLaughlin of the *New York Times*. Network correspondents, along with Frederick, included Larry LeSueur of CBS, Gordon Fraser of ABC, and Leon Pearson, who covered the beat for NBC along with Frederick, mostly for radio.

The reporters who regularly covered the United Nations were a self-contained and tightly knit group, even though they competed with each other. They had their own Press Club within the UN headquarters, complete with cafeteria and snacks. They also had access to the delegates' dining room and had their own press room—called the "bull-pen"—to get UN press releases, agendas, and running accounts of UN sessions compiled by the press office. Each correspondent had a small office on either the third or fourth floor of the Secretariat Building, with proceedings of meetings piped in as they happened. What truly bound the reporters together, however, was the schizophrenic nature of the work. On a normal day little happened before 10:30 a.m., but most correspondents stayed at least until seven o'clock in the evening. During crises they were on-call nearly twenty-four hours at a time—the Security Council could meet until four in the morning, with more activities scheduled for the same day. If breaking news occurred overnight, a press officer might call a news conference for 5:00 a.m., so UN correspondents might get a wake-up call in the middle of the night at their homes. Decades after he worked as Frederick's producer at NBC when she covered the UN, Jim Holton said she had an unmatched knowledge of the UN and near-exclusive access to UN officials. "Within a few years [of covering the UN], she was as much a part of the UN apparatus as was the secretary general," he said. "In fact, she had as much entrée to his office as most ambassadors."

Frederick often said she considered her term as UNCA president one of her highest honors because she had been elected to the position by her peers. Her election as head of the correspondents' association triggered a flurry of stories about her, many in national publications such as the *Washington Post* and the *Christian Science Monitor*. She became the first woman to hold that position, which was far from simply ceremonial. The president of the correspondents' group had distinct duties that included representing all reporters at formal dinners held by the UN for visiting dignitaries; asking the first and usually last question at news conferences; serving as the UN pool reporter at formal UN dinners and other occasions when only one reporter was permitted entry; arranging luncheons for visiting diplomats and reporters; and attempting to resolve any disputes that arose between reporters and UN officials. In fact, Frederick's appointment itself brought to light an issue of protocol that few had paid much attention to in the past. The formal dinners for visiting dignitaries were officially hosted by the UN secretary-general and were "stag" affairs—only men could attend. Frederick single-handedly violated that protocol when she began attending the dinners as UNCA president, an action she found amusing. She showed an interviewer her first invitation, a formal one from Hammarskjöld inviting her to a state dinner for King Hussein of Jordan: "[It says] white tie, tails, with decorations," she said. "What do they do with me?" Frederick attended the dinner as the men did—in "formal" black and white. She bought a black chiffon evening gown and wore white gloves and pearls. She was the only woman among "73 handsome, perfectly attired diplomats," she recalled. Numerous photos among her personal papers show Frederick in evening gown and gloves sitting at the dais of these formal UN dinners, surrounded by male diplomats, guests, and UN officials.

She no doubt took pleasure in inviting Hammarskjöld to speak at one of the correspondents' luncheons in September 1959, shortly before the UN General Assembly had convened for the fall. At the luncheon she introduced Hammarskjöld with a verbal wink and some ribbing. "Although we appreciate very much his news conferences when the General Assembly is not in session, we always hope that—in a slightly more intimate atmosphere, shall we say?—Mr. Hammarskjöld will be inclined to share even more of his substantive thoughts than usual," Frederick said, adding, "At this time of year, just before he takes his annual vow of silence . . . for the duration of the Assembly, we always like to give him one final opportunity to unburden himself of some of the thoughts which he has in mind." Hammarskjöld, a natural diplomat, focused his talk on the value of the UN correspondents: "The United Nations press corps is an absolutely essential part of the operations in this house. You are a service to the United Nations just as much as any member of the Secretariat or any member of the delegations, although in a different sense because just as we are servants of the organization and the legations are servants of their government, you are servants of the wide public and of your organization." The long-term common goal of all the parties, Hammarskjöld said, is to help "set this poor world of ours on the road which may finally lead to peace [and] to greater sanity in world affairs."

When it came to assessing personalities and character, Frederick's radar was usually right on target; thanks in part to a natural intelligence and years of experience covering people and their motivations, she was able to detect hypocrisy and phoniness. But apparently this innate talent abandoned her when it came to at least one man: Fidel Castro. In April 1959, as head of the UNCA, she invited Castro, then a handsome and lean revolutionary, to speak at a luncheon of UN correspondents while he was on a visit to the United States. Castro, who was then thirty-one, had been premier of Cuba for two months and was known around the world as the young freedom fighter who, against all odds, had organized the overthrow of the dictator Gen. Fulgencio Batista. The people of Cuba—and the free world—had high hopes for this attorney and newly named Cuban leader when he visited the United States in the spring of 1959. Many believed he would restore Cuba's constitution and civil liberties.

As Frederick introduced him on April 22, she noted the day was "Cuba Day" and that several Cuban officials, including the Cuban ambassador to the UN, the minister of the Treasury, the president of the National Bank of Cuba, and the commanders of the Cuban navy and air force, were visiting UN headquarters. Then she began speaking in superlatives: "This man has rekindled belief in some of the qualities that were admired before there were machines. Regardless of political beliefs, the world is stirred by personal bravery, by individual sacrifice, by dedication to ideals, by faith that pushed back the horizon of the hills." When "Dr. Castro," as she called him, was taking a tour of the UN's second floor, a group of workers saw him and spontaneously cheered, she said. "There was great cheering and affection . . . Tourists also cheered him in Security Council chambers." But she gave him the greatest compliment she could when she described his gait: "I remarked that he had a stride like Dr. Hammarskjöld's."

Photos of the luncheon show Castro and Frederick standing next to each other at the podium and smiling. The self-deprecating Castro apparently wowed the crowd as he spoke slowly in broken English, saying he wanted only to take questions. "It is important for me to speak clear to you [but] English is not my language," he said. "I don't presume to speak English. It is better to [take] questions. A prime minster is supposed to be wise, an encyclopedia, and know about all matters. [To speak] only the truth. Possibly in my own language I would speak better, but I hope I can answer clear." Frederick asked the first two questions, and despite her obvious admiration for Castro, they were not easy ones. Why, she asked, were reforms scheduled to take place in Cuba before elections rather than after, and why had Castro said in a television interview that the people of Cuba did not want elections? Castro replied that the new regime has the support of "more than 94 percent of the people" and that the country needed time before an election was held. "The people agree with one thing," he said. "With the revolution, with the finishing of tyranny, people in Cuba are living in happiness . . . At this minute, they're not interested in an election. People are afraid not of no election, but of the old vices of Cuba. They're afraid the vices could grow again."

Frederick said that after the ouster of Juan Perón in Argentina in 1955, the military men who overthrew the government said they would not seek public office because they did not want to create an appearance of having profited from the overthrow. "Are you prepared to do the same?" she asked. The slippery Castro turned on the charm. "That is a mistake, dear friend," he said. "Perón was overthrown by a military coup. In Cuba, the government was overthrown by the people fighting against the military . . . I am a civilian and a lawyer. The Cuban army does not have a general and colonels, but a lawyer leading the people. My profession is not military. It is the law."

Frederick may have been impressed by Castro's performance at the UN, but as history has shown, her probing questions were prescient. Within a year of Castro's celebratory visit to the United States, the clever self-described "lawyer" would show he was no friend of the United States. Two crises in the next two years involving Cuba—the Bay of Pigs and the Cuban Missile Crisis—marked that country's entry into the Cold War. Americans witnessed the self-deprecating "civilian" Castro become a wily and active player in world events, a role he would play for the next half-century.

The Bay of Pigs, as it became known, involved a program initiated by President Eisenhower in 1960 to overthrow Castro's newly formed and pro-Communist government. The plan, later approved in 1961 by newly elected President John F. Kennedy, involved training and using anti-Castro exiles in the United States to invade Cuba in April 1961 to overthrow the government and install a non-Communist government friendly to the United States. All of this would be done while hiding U.S. involvement. When the secret plan became known to Castro, the invasion forces came under heavy fire as they landed at beaches along Cuba's Bay of Pigs. Some escaped, some were captured and imprisoned by the Cubans, and others were killed. While it was not a worldwide crisis, the Bay of Pigs disaster had long-term ramifications: it was another salvo in the Cold War and one not soon forgotten by the Kennedy administration. And the distrust it generated on the part of the Soviets paved the way for the Cuban Missile Crisis a year later.

To Frederick the event diminished the reputation of someone for whom she had great respect: Adlai Stevenson. Shortly after the attack, U.S. government officials, in an attempt to camouflage their country's role in it, insisted that it was the Cuban Air Force that was the aggressor. Stevenson, who had just been named U.S. ambassador to the UN, believed his country's explanation and repeated it during a speech to the UN Security Council. Within a few hours the truth came out, and a shocked Stevenson was humiliated that he had unknowingly lied to the General Assembly. He also learned that President Kennedy had referred to him as "my official liar."

Frederick had long admired Stevenson, dating back to his days as a presidential hopeful in 1952 and 1956; eight weeks before his ill-fated UN speech, she had apparently sent him a birthday present. A thank-you note from him is included among her personal papers: "Dear Miss Frederick: You are too kind to have sent me such a magnificent birthday present! Your silver tray is certainly a most elegant addition to my new surroundings [at the UN] and I hope I'll have the pleasure of using it soon—to serve you! With many, many thanks."

Decades after Stevenson's Bay of Pigs speech, Frederick recalled in detail the respect UN officials had shown for Stevenson when he was named U.S. ambassador, noting that each member of the Security Council had stood up and applauded him when he first walked into that body's chamber—a demonstration of respect she had never witnessed before. "Adlai Stevenson came there as a man of the highest regard," she said. "He was an international citizen and it was looked upon as great evidence of the United States' belief in the United Nations that a man of this stature should be appointed to this particular post." His Bay of Pigs speech had diminished him, she noted, but did not ruin his reputation. "His own government kept him in ignorance about the facts of the Bay of Pigs invasion and he was allowed to testify falsely . . . about the invasion," she said. "As one sorrowful observer remarked to me, 'He came here as a superman and now he's been reduced to a man.' Well, Stevenson once said in my hearing 'I never thought they'd do this to me.'" Late in her life, when recalling the incident, Frederick revealed several times that she thought Stevenson should have offered his resignation after the Bay of Pigs incident. "I felt Adlai should have resigned," she said years later. "It would have given me a great lift if he brushed the dust of the connivers off of his feet, because he was so far above them."

The incident challenged the nationalistic view of some citizens that the

United States could do no wrong, and the country's failure in the execution of the Bay of Pigs was duly noted by Frederick and Walter Cronkite of CBS. Columnist Harriet Van Horn praised their coverage. "What impresses me the most is the blunt, no-nonsense reports of such commentators as Walter Cronkite and Pauline Frederick. Both are plain-dealing, downright types, a species television has not developed in legion," she wrote. "They minced no words in announcing that our Central Intelligence Agency had abetted the Cuban invasion and that it had gone awry because of CIA miscalculation. Worse, they reminded viewers the full truth had not been spoken in the United Nations. In consequence, they noted, our government had lost face around the world."

If the Bay of Pigs incident did not drive home the gravity of the Cold War to American citizens, an event eighteen months later, also involving Cuba, certainly did. The Cuban Missile Crisis of October 1962 was the closest the world had come to nuclear war. The crisis began on October 15, 1962, when reconnaissance photos revealed Soviet missiles under construction in Cuba, apparently as a result of a plan by Khrushchev to protect the Soviets from a U.S. attack. After the Bay of Pigs such an attack was inevitable, Khrushchev believed. President Kennedy immediately ordered a naval blockade around Cuba to prevent the Soviets from bringing in more supplies and demanded that they remove their missiles. The results of these actions by both nations were unknown; neither knew how the other would react, and after a tense thirteen days of high-level meetings in the United States, both sides backed down, apparently realizing the dire consequences of nuclear war.

While she was never a mindless cheerleader for her country, Frederick seemed to struggle at times to hide her patriotic feelings during her newscasts. On October 13, 1960, apparently in response to a speech by a Philippine delegate who had charged that the Soviets had "swallowed up" Eastern Europe, Soviet premier Khrushchev pulled off his right shoe, waved it, and banged it on the table in front of him. (Over time the date of the shoe banging, the speech that prompted it, and the fact that it even happened have been debated. Frederick suggested in speeches that she had witnessed it.) Frederick addressed the incident in a December 1960 speech, noting that the incident and others by the Soviets were a sign that they disdained the UN and wanted to get rid of it. "Apparently Khrushchev arrived in New York to make the United Nations pay for what he considered years of humiliation and frustration for the Soviet Union," she said. "He decided that the independent office of the Secretary-General, which had become the symbol of the UN's power, must be destroyed." Frederick acknowledged that she had grown tired of the Soviets' antics. "Sitting in the NBC booth, listening to his assaults day after day trying to report objectively, nevertheless, I could feel my own reaction mounting," she said. "And yet, a mature person knows that it is not in the heat of controversy [when] the truth emerges. It comes in the quiet moments of contemplation, away from battle."

Frederick was frustrated by the fact that the Soviets attempted to circumvent the very structure and process of the UN. They had successfully lobbied for the ouster of the first secretary-general, Trygve Lie (and she came to believe that they would not approve the reappointment of Hammarskjöld). It was their blocking of UN procedure and policy—rather than their ideology—that bothered Frederick the most.

As a reporter, Frederick no doubt appreciated candor from her sources, and it appeared that she spoke frankly to the many journalists who interviewed her over the years. But that candor could go too far, she learned. If any one interview gave an indication of the scope of her fame and visibility as a journalist, it was the lengthy one by writer Gay Talese that appeared in the *Saturday Evening Post* in January 1963. Talese was writing for the *New York Times* when he interviewed Frederick, although he contributed to several national magazines on a freelance basis. Talese was a practitioner of what was called the "New Journalism"—a type of long-form reporting that emerged in the 1960s. The New Journalism was a form of literary journalism that consisted of vivid writing with a focus on details and surroundings, often but not always placing the writer at the center of the story. Talese's profile, headlined, "Perils of Pauline," carried the provocative subhead, "America's highest paid female TV commentator, Pauline Frederick, fights skeptical bosses, prettier rivals and video's glamour code."

Indeed, the facts in the subhead were borne out in the story, but they were not as titillating as they seemed: Frederick, who reportedly earned sixty thousand dollars a year in salary *and* lecture income, was in fact the highest-paid female television correspondent, although she was also one of the few, and close to a fourth of that income came from lectures; yes, she had fought skeptical bosses, according to the story, when in the mid-1940s she was consistently told that women journalists could not cover news. Regarding "prettier rivals," the story mentioned the recent entrance of Nancy Hanschman (later Dickerson) of CBS and Lisa Howard of ABC. But both were newcomers and much younger and more inexperienced than Frederick. The only part of the subhead that Frederick had discussed at length previously in her life was the fighting of television's "glamour code." Frederick had in many previous interviews talked about her disdain for the contact lenses, teased hair, and other trappings of glamour that news executives demanded of her, and she considered her half-hour in hair and makeup each day a waste of time. "Think of what that means if you are trying to follow a breaking story," she once said. But the Talese profile was somewhat sensationalized and indirectly focused more on Frederick's personal life than her career. It opened with a description of her elegant Sutton Place apartment and offered her first quote at the start of the third paragraph. "Oh, I would like to be married," it read. "I would love to be married."

The story recounted Frederick's background as a print reporter and reviewed how, as a relatively unknown journalist, she had covered some key stories of the late 1940s and early 1950s. But it emphasized what Talese termed personal struggles, including the loss of two men she had loved, one who had died in an airplane crash and one who had had a fatal heart attack. The profile implied that despite her many and varied accomplishments, Frederick greatly missed having a family of her own. Other profiles suggested that while she would have valued a more conventional family life, she was satisfied with her success and fame as a journalist. After she married in 1969, at age sixty-one, according to later interviews, Frederick felt she finally had it all: a husband and a career.

Talese's story was at its best when it described the environment in which Frederick worked: "On almost any afternoon she can be seen heel-clacking through the UN's corridors, notebook in hand, en route to interview a delegate or in the UN delegates' lounge, sipping Scotch, smoking a cigarette and casually chatting with a maharaja, a chieftain, a prince. Later ... she may be seen leaning out of her small NBC booth that overlooks the General Assembly, coolly listening while a delegate, arms flailing, blasts forth with a vitriolic speech. Seconds later, having jotted down the gist of the debate, Pauline swings around in her chair and faces a television camera."

The article ended on a schizophrenic note, painting a picture of Frederick alone in her third-floor UN office on a day when the General Assembly was not in session. "She sits quietly at her desk answering her mail, rearranging her papers, and planning the work schedule she will follow once the UN activity resumes," wrote Talese. "Some people might think this depressing, but Miss Frederick does not seem at all depressed. Perhaps the reason is obvious. The United Nations is her home."

According to a letter from Talese to Frederick before the story was published, he had interviewed her first and then sold the story to the *Saturday Evening Post*. Frederick had apparently asked to see the story before it was published. Talese told her that showing sources stories prior to publication was against *Post* policy but that he was allowed to read her back her own quotes. "I'm happy to say the *Post* bought the piece and liked it and they're planning to run it soon," Talese wrote in January 1962. (Actually, the piece ran the following January.) "The *Post* turned down my request to show the piece to you first ... They said they had complete faith in the accurate reporting of those they hire to do pieces ... I'm sure you have nothing to worry about."

Perhaps she did have something to worry about. The *Saturday Evening Post* profile of Frederick exemplified the ambivalence society had in the early 1960s about women achievers. Frederick ostensibly was "news" to the magazine because of her accomplishments and her role as one of the few women to achieve top status in broadcasting. Yet these accomplishments were portrayed as secondary to the one achievement she lacked: having a family. The article implied that her devotion to her career had come at the cost of a fulfilling private life. Frederick, of course, contributed to this portrayal by having noted that she would welcome a more traditional life, an attitude that could be perceived as regret about the life she was leading.

Frederick received much mail about the Talese story, most of which was positive. Some readers felt the story was critical of Frederick, whose appeal, they believed, was not based solely on her looks. "It takes more than glamour to make a good reporter and you certainly project those many fine qualities in your reporting," wrote Voula Demas of Sacramento, California. Another fan, from Florence, South Carolina, wrote: "I think the article was good but failed to give the verve and inspiration which your personality deserves. Anyway, it has been greatly publicized here." C. H. Fox of Berkeley, California, asked, "Whoever told you that you are not good to look at and that you are not a good commentator?" adding: "I want to assure you that you don't need to take a back seat to anybody . . . I have always enjoyed your broadcasts from the United Nations and will say that when you open your mouth, you say something." Another letter writer, Therese Howe of Chester, New Jersey, was more blunt, noting that she admired Frederick as a reporter, but "I do feel sorry for you . . . You must be very lonely. Of course you can entertain and go out and have what one calls fun, but to have nobody to come home to, no children to love and watch grow up, seems very useless. You will always be remembered as a great lady reporter but after you are gone who will remember you as a person, not a reporter?"

The article prompted an offer from a publisher for a memoir. "Did you enjoy the article by Gay Talese in the current issue of *Saturday Evening Post* as much as I did?" Morrie Helitzer, assistant to the president of McGraw-Hill, wrote to Frederick. "Upon finishing it, I immediately telephoned Ed Kuhn, the editor in chief of our trade book department to ask if McGraw-Hill ever discussed a book with you." Helitzer told Frederick that such a book "would give you the opportunity to say as much as you chose about your professional experiences, while leaving ample elbow room for personal observations, reflections, and recollections." In fact, Frederick had years earlier agreed to write a book about the United Nations but had canceled her contract because she found she did not have the time to do it. Frederick wrote back, declining Helitzer's offer: "I have turned down several other offers. I don't think I can write a book unless I take a year off from all the other things I'm doing."

Nothing in Frederick's papers indicates whether she was pleased or not with the Talese story. But it is likely that its theme—that of Frederick as an accomplished but lonely woman—was one that probably bothered her. Throughout her life she was candid in her comments that she would like to have a family, but her love and passion for her job and for the mission of the United Nations always came through clearly in interviews. The vital role of her job and her love of it were secondary in the Talese story.

In at least one case NBC executives may have taken advantage of Frederick's gender to draw audiences to a project that seemingly had little or nothing to do with her areas of expertise. In the fall of 1960 Frederick hosted and narrated a series of seven hour-long daytime programs the network called the *Purex Special for Women*. In publicity for the show NBC made it clear that it was targeting women viewers. The show, sponsored by the Purex Corporation, examined issues "affecting large groups of women," including divorce and child rearing, according to a news release. Frederick was the narrator, with professional actors participating in dramas illustrating that episode's topic. But NBC apparently wanted to air the most provocative topic first—the first *Purex Special* dealt with female "frigidity" in a show called "The Cold Woman." (Other episodes were called, dramatically, "The Captive Mother" and "Ordeal of the Single Woman.") The first show "candidly" addressed the issue of "sexual and emotional frigidity which has been described as the 'most epidemic sickness in our society,' a major source of blame for thousands of marital breakups," according to NBC publicity. Frederick told a reporter late that year that she was alarmed when NBC executives asked her to host the program and that she had taken ribbing from her colleagues about it. "I thought NBC was slipping back into the old sex segregation days," she said. "I'm afraid I didn't mask my concern too well. I carefully explained that I was a reporter—not a women's reporter." (Frederick joked that the "biggest problem facing the United Nations is frigidity—the Cold War.") Nevertheless, the show's producer, Irving Gitlin, persuaded her to participate. "My next concern was that the program would be slanted in such a way that I would pick up some kind of stigma anyway by my mere association with it," she said candidly. She said she soon learned that the so-called women's problems dealt with in the shows had to do with relationships between men and women: "As we discussed the subject, I realized I was wrong in my assumptions."

If NBC had "used" Frederick to draw viewers, the tactic apparently

9 *Death of the Peacock*

Pauline . . . got information that others couldn't get, primarily with her friendships.

ROBERT ASMAN, former NBC special events producer

On the evening of July 13, 1960, Democratic convention delegates in Los Angeles held a roll call vote to nominate John F. Kennedy as their candidate for president. At the same time, on the opposite side of the country, more news was breaking: the United Nations Security Council was meeting in a crisis session to decide a matter that the secretary-general determined could threaten world peace. The issue was of such vital importance that updates about its progress prompted periodic interruptions in the proceedings at the Los Angeles Memorial Coliseum. Ultimately, the nomination of the man who would win the 1960 general election was the bigger story. But the Security Council measures taken that warm July evening would have long-term and dramatic consequences that few could have predicted. A confluence of events in the early 1960s, spawned a decade earlier with the advent of McCarthyism, had led to a decline of public support for the United Nations that had never been restored. The ramifications of the Cold War would be numerous and subtle, compounded by the tragic deaths of two beloved world leaders and the expansion of the U.S. role in the Vietnam War. As the Cold War escalated, the reputation of the UN among American citizens would deteriorate, accompanied by a decline in the agency's influence worldwide.

UN secretary-general Dag Hammarskjöld, however, was at the peak of his power in 1959, six years after his initial appointment to that post and one year into his second five-year term. His appointment had, at least temporarily, boosted the public profile of the UN, which was declining with the Cold War. The respected Hammarskjöld was known as an activist secretary-general who through his extensive travels and his focus on "quiet diplomacy"—much of which took place in conversations with world leaders in his suite of offices on the thirty-eighth floor of the UN Secretariat Building—made him a high-profile and effective leader. Several burgeoning crises, however, forced him to accelerate his travel schedule in late 1959. In a two-month period beginning in December 1959, he visited twenty-one countries and territories in Africa. His travels to that continent highlighted the new tenor and tone of the United Nations as an agency whose main function of representing the world's most powerful nations had begun to shift to one that would eventually be composed primarily of the world's smaller, emerging nations. When the UN was formed in 1945, fifty-one nations were members; by 1955 that number had grown to seventy-six and by 1960 ninety-nine. The decolonization of countries worldwide was a phenomenon that would fuel the Cold War, deepen the wedge between the world's two military superpowers, and indirectly lead to Hammarskjöld's death.

In her recollections decades later of that interesting and fateful few years, Frederick noted that a jingoistic mind-set first established during the McCarthy era of the 1950s remained dormant among some Americans long after McCarthy had been discredited and had instilled an ongoing fear among them of "foreigners," including those from emerging nations: "Many people then began to fear that the so-called foreigners within our midst were all spies . . . because a spy story especially centering on the United Nations was always a headline story . . . even though they were never real, as far as I know." Furthermore, the reason these emerging nations were welcomed into the UN had been subverted, she said years later. "You have nations trying to impose their own foreign policies on other nations in the UN instead of trying to find out if there is some way of easing the differences that have brought the clashes that could lead to war." Also, she noted, the smaller, younger, and usually impoverished nations had far different problems and concerns than the larger countries: "They thought about economic and social problems . . . Our emphasis was on political problems and conflict between the big powers."

On that July night in 1960 Hammarskjöld had called an emergency session of the Security Council by invoking for the first time Article 99 of the UN charter, which authorized the secretary-general to inform the council of any matter that he believed threatened world peace. Hammarskjöld asked the Security Council for UN military assistance for the two-week-old Republic of the Congo, formerly the Belgian Congo. Belgium had sent troops back into its former colony, and officials of the newly independent nation sought UN intervention. Hammarskjöld feared that the nation could descend into chaos and that the conflict there could devolve into a battle between the world's two superpowers. He asked for Security Council approval for the UN's largest peacekeeping force to date, but gaining that approval was only the first step in a highly politicized process that required Hammarskjöld to tread lightly.

The peacekeepers could be recruited only from small countries outside of those actively fighting the Cold War—the nations that were not allies of the United States or the Soviet Union. The Congo, like other small, newly decolonized nations of the era, was a pawn in an escalating Cold War struggle between the world's two major military powers, and battles of that war were often played out in these nations. The Soviets wanted to abolish colonial governments and replace them with what they said would be "non-imperialistic" Communist rule. The United States and other free countries wanted independent rule for the newly decolonized nations.

As Frederick and others pointed out in their reports, the nuances of decolonization and the propaganda from both sides were many and complex. The Soviets stressed that the Western capitalistic way of government favored the rich and powerful and explained that only through communism would those nations be free of "imperialism." The crisis in the Congo showed how ferocious the battles could get and illustrated how the emerging nations had become political footballs in the larger game of world domination, with the UN in the middle. In an article she wrote in 1960 for YWCA Magazine, Frederick noted the double irony of this manipulation of the poorer nations: "Smaller nations . . . have to be more concerned with giving their people enough to eat and clothes to wear and shelter on this earth rather than trying to reach the moon and the sun and the stars. It must be disillusioning for half the people of this world who will go to bed hungry to watch the two most powerful nations pouring hundreds of billions of dollars into armament instead of at least part of it into bread." In the article she blamed both the United States and the Soviet Union for the escalating Cold War. "The tragic fact is that the USSR fears the USA and the USA fears the USSR, and each acts as though the most important thing in the world is to surpass each other, whether it be in corn, weapons or moon probes," she wrote. "Fear begets fear. It shackles the fearful to a remembrance of hostilities and frustrations of the past."

Richard Hottelet, who covered the UN and international affairs for CBS for four decades, until 1985, claimed that while the UN was ostensibly a neutral organization, it represented mostly U.S. interests during its first fifteen to twenty years of existence. During that time, he said, "the UN did nothing which was against what the United States thought was in its interests," adding, "The UN was . . . used by the United States as an element of the projection of American power which was open to any country to do." Similarly, according to Hottelet, the Soviet Union exploited the political naïveté of these emerging nations: "There [were] all these young countries totally inexperienced running into problems and the Russians very cleverly seduced them all into getting a feeling of Third Worldism, of anti-colonialism which was then projected against the so-called colonialist countries." An anecdote Frederick told late in her life exemplified the neglectful and patronizing attitude of the larger nations toward these newly decolonized countries. A diplomat from Africa, Alex Quaison Sackey from Ghana, once told her: "When two small nations have a problem, the problem disappears. When a small nation and a large nation have a problem, the small nation disappears. But when two large nations have a problem, the United Nations disappears."

The Russians became furious at Hammarskjöld, as they had become a decade earlier with his predecessor, Trygve Lie, for siding with the West. And just as they had worked successfully to oust Lie from his post, they said they would work to remove Hammarskjöld from office. Frederick noted years later that the contingent that went to the Congo to keep the peace numbered more than twenty-three thousand and cost 360 million dollars.

The Congo crisis illustrates how, before the advent of technologically advanced equipment and satellite feeds, these Cold War battles became

1. Frederick (*left*) with her mother, Susan Catharine, her
brother, Stanley, and her sister, Catharine. Photo courtesy of
Catharine Cole.

2. Matthew Frederick, Pauline's father. Photo courtesy of
Catharine Cole.

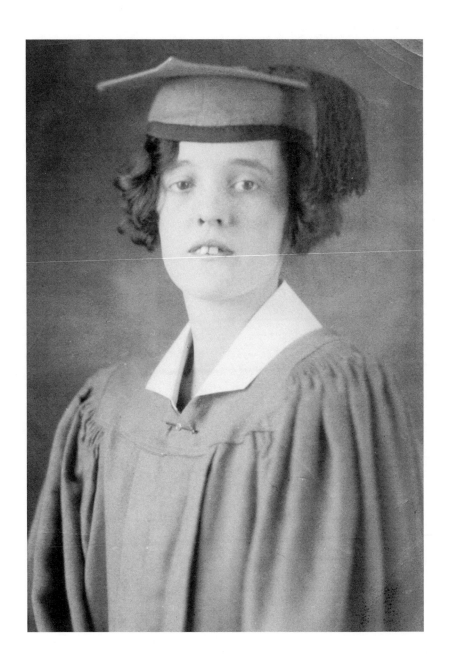

3. Pauline Frederick, high school graduation. Photo courtesy of Catharine Cole.

4. Frederick in high school. Photo courtesy of Catharine Cole.

5. Siblings Catharine (*left*), Stanley, and Pauline Frederick.
Photo courtesy of Catharine Cole.

6. Frederick in college. Photo courtesy of Catharine Cole.

7. Frederick with her mentor, radio broadcaster H. R.
Baukhage. Photo courtesy of Catharine Cole.

8. Frederick broadcasting for ABC Radio, late 1940s. Photo from the digital archives, Sophia Smith Collection, Smith College.

9. Frederick at the controls of a DC-9 over India, 1945. Photo from the digital archives, Sophia Smith Collection, Smith College.

10. Frederick (*right*) conducting her first radio interview (for NBC Radio) with Olga Hurban, wife of the Czech foreign minister. Photo from the Sophia Smith Collection, Smith College.

11. Frederick with Eleanor Roosevelt. Photo from the Sophia
Smith Collection, Smith College.

12. Frederick at a formal dinner as head of the United Nations
Correspondents Association, along with Dave Garroway of
NBC (*left*) and UN secretary-general Dag Hammarskjöld.
Photo from the Sophia Smith Collection, Smith College.

13. Frederick and Fidel Castro, who was a guest of the United
Nations Correspondents Association during his UN visit in
1959. Photo from the Sophia Smith Collection, Smith College.

14. Frederick (*right*) and her sister, Catharine "Kitty" Crowding. Photo from the Sophia Smith Collection, Smith College.

15. Frederick in NBC's United Nations studio, mid-1950s.
Photo from the Sophia Smith Collection, Smith College.

16. Frederick at home with her poodle, Sputnik. Photo from
the Sophia Smith Collection, Smith College.

17. Frederick with U.S. ambassador to the UN Adlai Stevenson.
Photo from the Sophia Smith Collection, Smith College.

18. Frederick outside of the UN complex in Manhattan. Photo
from the Sophia Smith Collection, Smith College.

19. Frederick at the 1969 YWCA Gold Medal Awards
ceremony in Philadelphia with Margaret Mead (*second from
left*), Coretta Scott King, and Grace Kelly. Photo from the
Sophia Smith Collection, Smith College.

20. Frederick in her UN office. Photo from the Sophia Smith
Collection, Smith College.

21. Frederick in the hall of the United Nations. Photo from the
Sophia Smith Collection, Smith College.

22. Frederick with UN secretary-general U Thant (*left*), 1962.
Photo courtesy of Catharine Cole.

23. Frederick with (*left to right*) Charles Robbins, broadcaster
Claude Mahoney, and David Brinkley, early 1960s. Photo
from the Sophia Smith Collection, Smith College.

24. Frederick with poet Carl Sandburg, at his home in South
Carolina, 1962. Photo courtesy of Catharine Cole.

25. Frederick and Charles Robbins at their wedding. Photo courtesy of Dick Robbins and Ann Forster Stevens.

26. Frederick with her step-grandchildren Bill (*left*) and John Robbins, 1972. Photo courtesy of Dick Robbins and Ann Forster Stevens.

27. Frederick on her wedding day. Photo courtesy of Catharine Cole.

28. Frederick and Charles Robbins with daughter-in-law, Ann, and their grandson John, 1973. Photo courtesy of Dick Robbins and Ann Forster Stevens.

29. Frederick during her days at National Public Radio. Photo from the Sophia Smith Collection, Smith College.

Dear Pauline – Some day I'll know as well about the UN as you do! Would you believe almost as much? Best regards. Geo Bush

30. Frederick with U.S. ambassador George H. W. Bush, 1971. Bush noted in this autographed photo that he hoped to one day be as knowledgeable about the UN as Frederick. Photo from the Sophia Smith Collection, Smith College.

31. Frederick after her retirement. Photo from the Sophia
Smith Collection, Smith College.

32. Frederick and UN secretary-general Dag Hammarskjöld
at a formal UN dinner, 1959 or 1960. Photo from the Sophia
Smith Collection, Smith College.

33. Frederick with future NBC news anchors Chet Huntley (*far left*) and David Brinkley (*second from right*) covering the 1956 Republican presidential convention. Photo from the Sophia Smith Collection, Smith College.

"Come quick, Ed! They're convening the Security Council and Pauline Frederick isn't even there yet."

34. *Channel Chuckles* cartoon about Frederick. Copyright 1967 by Bill Keane, Inc. King Features Syndicate, Inc. All rights reserved.

35. The Robbinses' home in Westport CT. Photo courtesy of
Dick Robbins and Ann Forster Stevens.

very public because they actually took place in the United Nations. News outlets could easily cover the progress and response to such international crises from UN headquarters in New York, and they could literally bring the crises into the living rooms of millions of viewers.

Fourteen months after that fateful day in July, the Congo remained on high alert, and it was taking up more and more of the secretary-general's time. In early September—four days before the General Assembly would convene—it appeared that Hammarskjöld could possibly broker a cease-fire there. He made plans with fifteen others to fly to Katanga on the evening of September 17. NBC News, apparently sensing the public's anxiety about world events and viewing the convening of the General Assembly as a news peg, aired a special prime-time program that night about the General Assembly and the uphill battle ahead. Frederick, who by this time had fifteen years' experience covering international events, appeared convinced that despite the outcome of the Congo crisis, Hammarskjöld would not be reappointed to a third term as secretary-general in 1963. Soviet officials had already called for his resignation, she and others had reported, and the Soviets were lobbying heavily for a change in the Secretariat, calling for the secretary-general's office to be composed of a "troika"—not one person but three people, who would represent what they considered the three major world forces: the East, the West, and the smaller emerging nations. On the NBC special the night of September 17, on what would be the eve of his death, Frederick predicted that Hammarskjöld would be ousted from his job, saying, metaphorically, that the "peacemaker," as she labeled him, would be "sacrificed." During that broadcast Frederick's thoughts about the dangers inherent in this new nuclear age came through, as did her talents as an eloquent and graceful writer: "Salvation in the nuclear age lies on the conference table, not on the battlefield; that this is the first resort of man of reason, not the last, as it is now; that in conciliation, mediation and arbitration there is common strength, not individual weakness."

Sadly, the literal interpretation of Frederick's prediction came true, although she explained countless times over the years that she meant it only to convey the idea that he would be "sacrificed" as the secretary-general because the Soviets would soon demand his ouster. Less than twenty-four hours after the first special program on September 17, NBC and the other networks would enter crisis mode, interrupting regular programming with news bulletins and ultimately airing a special program on the death of Hammarskjöld and the others who were on their way to that peacekeeping mission to the Congo. Their plane went down in Rhodesia (now Zambia).

In the half-century since that tragic crash, much has been written, discussed, and speculated about its cause and whether it was an accident or the result of sabotage. Investigations at the time—including one by a British commission and one by Rhodesia as well as several UN hearings— could not definitively determine the cause of the crash, or they concluded that it was either pilot error or a malfunction of the plane. An inquiry set up in 2012 to reexamine the incident based on new evidence indicated, however, that another plane piloted by mercenaries fighting for Katanga separatists who had revolted against the newly independent Congolese government may have opened fire on the plane.

Whenever Frederick discussed Hammarskjöld's life and career, she usually said little when asked if she believed his death was an accident, preferring to talk about the man himself. Yet during a speech six months after he died, she indicated that she did question whether the plane crash was an accident, pointing out that Katanga was rich in copper, further enhancing the desirability of the Congo to larger nations: "There are many unanswered questions as to what happened to this peacemaker, despite the Rhodesian investigation which assigned all blame to the pilot." Frederick, and others, noted at the time that the contingent had to fly at night in radio silence without an escort to avoid being seen "because of a marauding Katanga jet operated by French and Belgian mercenaries." Furthermore, authorities in the plane's destination of Ndola, Northern Rhodesia, had failed to report that the plane had still not arrived nine hours after it was expected to land. Frederick also said in the speech that various munitions and aviation experts reported that bullets were found in the bodies and holes in the plane.

Nearly twenty-five years later, when reminiscing about her own career, Frederick was reluctant to acknowledge the crash had been the result of sabotage, concluding only that "it's still a great mystery as to how his plane went down, and why—whether it was shot down or why . . . There were many . . . at the time who would have liked to have seen the secretary-general destroyed, but I just don't have enough information to go on [to judge the cause of the crash]." She added that despite many investigations, no one had come up with a conclusive reason for the crash.

Dag Hammarskjöld was buried on September 29, 1961, in his family's cemetery in Uppsala, Sweden. Nearly one hundred thousand people visited the grave that day, according to a wire service report, and two thousand mourners attended the service. "Weeping men and women lined the streets as Hammarskjöld's funeral procession moved to the churchyard cemetery from a solemn service in Uppsala's fourteenth-century cathedral," the wire report said. Vice President Lyndon B. Johnson, UN ambassador Adlai Stevenson, and Thomas Kuchel, U.S. senator from California, represented the United States.

Frederick and other newscasters said on that NBC thirty-minute special broadcast the evening after the crash that Hammarskjöld's death would have a great effect on the operations of the United Nations, even though most agreed that he would not have been reappointed to another term. In her eloquent tribute to him during that broadcast, Frederick said that it was also unlikely that the mission for which he had died would be resolved. "Unless by some miracle the Cold War suddenly ends, the possibility of this agreement [between Communist and non-Communist nations] is most forlorn, and the cause for which Dag Hammarskjöld gave his life becomes another threat to the existence of the United Nations." If one of Frederick's broadcasts could serve as an indicator of her skill as a writer and speaker, it was the one she gave that night. It was concise but graceful and thought provoking. The fact that it was heartfelt clearly came through to viewers, many of whom contacted her and the network to praise her and ask for a copy of her words. "I had any number of people tell me that I made them cry," she once said. For the rest of her life Frederick kept those letters from viewers; in one interview six years before her death, however, she modestly downplayed the response, attributing it to the fact that many people felt deeply about Hammarskjöld, so his death was naturally heartrending to them. But she did note once that she was particularly proud of one of the letters—a response from her boss, NBC

News president Bill McAndrew, who had been choked up by her words. "I felt as though I achieved something because he felt very strongly about it," she said. And it was natural that she wanted to please McAndrew; he, along with Robert Kintner, who then was president of the network, had been strong supporters of Frederick while the three worked at NBC.

While Frederick often denied that her comment about Hammarskjöld being sacrificed had predicted his demise, one other incident before his death was equally as eerie. In an undated typed report found among her personal papers, Frederick detailed the events of Hammarskjöld's last week alive. The notes outlined that on September 7, ten days before the plane crash, he had interrupted preparations to visit the Congo to host the author John Steinbeck for dinner at his New York apartment. The two were to discuss Steinbeck's latest—and what would be his last—novel, *The Winter of Our Discontent*. Five days later, on September 12, he had his last meal at the United Nations when he lunched with his trusted assistant, Andrew Cordier. Predictably, Hammarskjöld had suggested that the two take a walk after lunch in the UN gardens, one of his favorite locales. "His route invariably brought them to the fenced-in area near the children's playground where two proud peacocks strutted with their less glamorous hens," she wrote. (Hammarskjöld was particularly fond of the peacocks and had requested that they be moved from their original home at the UN's Palais de Nations in Geneva to New York, disregarding "lighthearted warnings from the superstitious" that peacocks were "birds of ill-omen," Frederick wrote.) During their walk Hammarskjöld "talked about the beauty of the landscape, as he frequently did—and the excitement of the wider view, with the river on the East and the towers of Manhattan on the West. The outlook from the United Nations always fascinated him." On September 17 Cordier reported that one of the peacocks had died. It is unknown if Frederick announced this news in one of her broadcasts, but it appears unlikely. Also, she did not attribute the information in those notes, but Cordier, with whom Frederick was friendly, was the likely source, as she had done an extensive interview with him not long after the plane crash.

Like many reporters, Pauline Frederick was accustomed to a "done-in-a-day" existence; that is, major stories that could take up entire days, weeks, or even months were gradually de-prioritized by reporters to make way for the next big crisis or event. Despite her interest in interpreting world events and capturing the subtlety of them if necessary, her hectic work schedule required that Frederick work that way. But the death of the man she so admired personally and professionally seemed to sadden Frederick for the rest of her life. It is unclear whether this was the case because a possible savior had died or because she realized that anyone who actively attempted to save the world would probably die trying.

About nine weeks after Hammarskjöld's death, the *Kansas City Star* quoted an uncharacteristically pessimistic and downbeat Frederick. "No longer can we be saved from the scourge of war by one man, no matter how great his skill," she said. "This responsibility belongs to all of us—and primarily to the big nations who boast of their power." She indicated that she hoped the newer emerging nations that had recently joined the UN might ultimately outnumber the major powers in votes: "Perhaps they can outvote the big powers." It was a hope that she had to realize was unrealistic based on the very structure of the UN; the Security Council, which had the power to send peacekeeping troops to war-torn areas, was by its nature the most powerful arm of the UN. Its voting members were only of China, France, Great Britain, the Soviet Union, and the United States. The story ended with harsh criticism from Frederick about the escalating arms race. She said the first reaction of the United States to any threat was to "add more billions to the defense budget" and that "we are prepared to kill millions and destroy half a world if need be."

Dag Hammarskjöld's death also changed the tenor of Frederick's many speeches. No longer did she tiptoe around what she felt was the growing threat of a catastrophic nuclear war, and no longer did she imply that both superpowers were to blame for the world's unrest. From then on the United States was possibly as big a villain as the Soviet Union, Frederick believed, and she was not afraid to say so in her many lectures and interviews, although not in her newscasts. One year after Hammarskjöld's death, she commemorated his passing by visiting his grave. Her broadcast over NBC Radio began as follows: "One year has passed. In a tree-shaded churchyard in the old university town of Uppsala, Sweden, a simple granite headstone marks the resting place of a favorite son between his parents, brooded over by a great slab, with one word, 'Hammarskjöld,' engraved on it. There are always flowers on the grave, frequently a single rose, sometimes a yellow rose, sometimes three yellow ones, tied together."

Immediately after the death of Hammarskjöld, the task at hand for the UN was to select his successor—or at least an acting secretary-general to serve in that capacity until April 10, 1963, when Hammarskjöld's term expired. And despite his death and the animosity the Soviets felt for him, the specter of the Russians' proposal to change the office of the secretary-general into a "troika" remained. But thanks to a bit of politicking on the part of the president of the General Assembly, Frederick Boland of Ireland, and U.S. ambassador Adlai Stevenson, the transition was relatively painless and received the approval of the Soviet representatives. Boland and Stevenson were friends with U Thant, the UN ambassador from Burma, a small neutral country in Asia. Boland and Stevenson believed that U Thant would be the politically prudent choice to get approval in the chaotic UN environment of the day—first, he represented a small country that had not drawn the ire of the Soviets, and second, he was head of an alliance of small UN nations called the "Afro-Asian Working Group," whose members had not yet held top posts in the UN hierarchy. The Security Council, which elects the UN secretary-general, unanimously approved his appointment as acting secretary-general, beginning November 3, 1961. U Thant was elected to a five-year term as secretary-general the following year and served in that position until 1971.

While he was low-key and different temperamentally from Hammarskjöld, U Thant was seen as a sincere and hardworking UN secretary-general and one who cultivated friendly relations with the media. But he came to that post during a turbulent era—in addition to the unrest in the Congo, the world had witnessed the Bay of Pigs incident earlier that spring, and U Thant would serve as informal negotiator in the Cuban Missile Crisis shortly after he took office. During the first few years of his tenure, however, the UN's influence and reputation began to wane again. The smaller Cold War "battles"—the chaos in the Congo, the Cuban Missile Crisis, and the Bay of Pigs, in which Stevenson's credibility was damaged—were taking their toll. Within the next few years the escalation of the Vietnam War and the UN's role, or lack thereof, in dealing with it would further erode its power. And as its influence became diminished, so did the role of many of the correspondents who covered it.

Until the latter part of the 1960s many major news stories traveled through the UN; most visiting dignitaries to the United States considered a visit to UN headquarters a must, and that agency had a voice in nearly all international events and crises. Also, in the middle part of the decade Frederick's friends and mentors—Robert Kintner, Bill McAndrew, and to a lesser degree Julian Goodman—still ran NBC News, so her role as a leading correspondent remained unchallenged. And another factor cemented her high-profile role as a network correspondent, at least for the time being: the expansion of the network evening news from fifteen to thirty minutes.

Frederick maintained her status as a dependable and knowledgeable correspondent in the early 1960s not only because the UN was the center of attention for much of the world. Her role was also a function of a changing environment in television news in 1963 and other related events that affected broadcasting. To some broadcast historians and former broadcasters the expansion of the fifteen-minute nightly newscast to thirty minutes was crucial for one reason: the longer format required more correspondents to provide more stories and more in-depth coverage, leading to a hiring boom and a change in focus to longer and more interpretive stories. Television had become a part of everyday life for most Americans by the early 1960s, and network executives were beginning to realize its tremendous cultural influence. (Also, the 114-day newspaper strike that idled nine New York–area newspapers in late 1962 and early 1963 indicated that many Americans could grow accustomed, indeed they had, to getting their news primarily from television rather than newspapers.) As Barbara Matusow noted in her history of news anchorpersons, 1963 marked the first year more people said they got their news from television than from newspapers.

In September 1963 CBS was the first network to announce plans to expand its evening news show to thirty minutes, and it was inevitable that NBC would follow quickly with its announcement. The networks, particularly NBC and CBS, were locked in head-to-head competition, for both viewers and prestige, and it is likely that CBS made the decision to expand the newscast because for the first time it had been upset in the ratings in 1960 by NBC. When it came to news, the "winner" was not simply the network that lured bigger audiences; it was also the one that received the most and biggest awards and best performed its public service duties. According to Matusow, the first few years of the 1960s, beginning roughly with the election of Kennedy, brought a certain glamour to network news, Kennedy being the first president who understood how to manipulate television to his advantage; as a consequence, he bestowed a certain sophistication on that medium. In addition, Kennedy's appointment of Newton Minow in 1961 as head of the Federal Communications Commission forced network officials to reassess their programming. His famous and often-quoted speech labeling television a "vast wasteland" was a call for increased public affairs programming, and one, some network officials feared, that was a veiled threat, warning broadcasters to clean up their act or else license renewal might no longer be a mere formality.

Many years after his retirement Reuven Frank said the golden years of network news came between the late 1950s and the early 1970s, "when the experimental times were over" and the "economic pressures had not closed in." He called the sharp competition among networks—especially the two leading networks—energizing: "It was a time of great esprit de corps and a time of great achievement."

In a lengthy memo to McAndrew in 1963, Frank, then executive producer of the *Huntley-Brinkley Report*, outlined his vision for a thirty-minute *Huntley-Brinkley Report*, stressing that NBC should not do it simply because CBS did and explaining that expanding the evening news would mean a complete revamping of it—not simply doubling the amount of time devoted to news. "Since June 1953 I have felt that the quarter hour dinner-time news program is irrelevant to television," he wrote. "It came to television because it was successful in radio." Frank called expansion of the evening news a major undertaking and one that "must proclaim and establish an individual identity ... It could let television journalism realize its potential." The expanded format "would build on the established authority of the regular television news report and exploit its unique capacity to transmit experience." Frank offered examples of how a longer broadcast could trump the staid and static qualities of newspapers. "The *Washington Post* can explain that the mainland Chinese are living on 1,200 calories a day. Television can show hunger," he wrote. "The *Kansas City Star* can feature a study of the trend toward larger farms in the Midwest. We can watch a farmer and his family while his farm is being auctioned."

Frank's memo is noteworthy because it outlined a sea change in the philosophy of NBC News. The conversion to a longer broadcast represented a change in direction of network news that would have long-term ramifications, according to one former NBC newsman of that era. Garrick Utley, who worked for NBC for three decades as a foreign correspondent and later *Meet the Press* moderator, called it a "generational shift" that led to the hiring of many people whose broadcast experience was exclusively on television rather than in radio. "The generational shift occurred because of the programming shift," Utley said. "It became a totally different industry when they went from fifteen to thirty minutes." He described himself as one of a new breed of reporters hired during that time who—unlike Frederick and many others—had cut their teeth in television broadcasting, so their outlook on the business was different than that of their predecessors.

That distinction and the change in news philosophy did not have an immediate effect on Frederick, but ultimately the changing environment of television broadcasting, combined with a shift in world events, would. At the beginning, however, the longer newscast was a boon to Frederick and others who had beats that required nuance and explanation. Charles Coates, an NBC writer and producer during much of Frederick's tenure there, worked with her occasionally on radio news reports. "She'd almost always run over [in length]," he said, and he would ask her to delete parts of her broadcasts. The switch to a half-hour evening report benefited her, he believed, because it gave her more time for explanation. "There's very little to actually show at the UN," he said. "When they [NBC officials] went to half an hour, it opened things up for coverage that might not have made it before."

In the fall of 1965 the visit of Pope Paul VI to the United States was one of the biggest stories of the year. During his one-day visit to the United States, the pope visited the UN, where he presented Secretary-General U Thant with a diamond cross and ring as gifts to that agency. He also addressed the UN Secretariat and urged the General Assembly to accept the Communist People's Republic of China (PRC) into the Security Council. The pope prayed with U Thant, who was a Buddhist, in the Meditation Room, which, Frederick reminded her viewers, had been developed and designed by Hammarskjöld and was one of his legacies. In her broadcast she noted that the room "is not a conventional chapel, but a sanctuary for prayer for all people of all faiths and lands—room of quiet where only thoughts are supposed to speak."

That simple broadcast, particularly its description of the two men praying together, drew many letters of praise from viewers. Mrs. Harvey K. Bleeker of Ossining, New York, asked for a transcript of the broadcast and praised Frederick in general. "I enjoyed every commentator, but would like to tell you how much pleasure you personally gave me," she wrote. "You have always been a favorite of mine. You are a knowledgeable reporter and your delivery most pleasant. It is time well spent to watch and listen to you." Francis Regis, a French teacher at Ursuline Academy in Springfield, Massachusetts, wrote to Frederick, informing her that her students watched the all-day coverage of the pope's visit. "When you described the Christian pope and the Buddhist secretary-general at prayer, together, the students cheered," she said. "When we all learn to pray to God in our own way, we shall have peace in our hearts. May God bless you in your great work for peace by our dissemination of truth."

Although Frederick routinely usually received kudos from media critics, at least one critic indicated that he thought she might have felt too much allegiance to the subculture she covered. Lawrence Laurent, a respected television critic for the *Washington Post*, criticized her broadcasts during the 1960 U-2 spy incident (although he had in the past praised her on several occasions.). The U-2 conflict, another by-product of the Cold War, was triggered when a U.S. U-2 spy plane was shot down over Soviet airspace. Although they denied the plane's purpose at first, Eisenhower administration officials eventually acknowledged its surveillance role, setting off a highly publicized dispute between the two nations. Interestingly, Laurent noted at the time that the incident "continues to be the best covered international story in television's brief history." He also commented on the crucial role of the UN in allowing viewers to see news as it happens: "There is no substitute for allowing the viewer to see and hear important speeches, simultaneously and with occurrence or utterance." But the subtle nature of the conflict, "with its complex imponderables," forced usually competent reporters to talk in empty generalities. Frederick, he said, "a deservedly praised reporter, is having the worst week of her career," remarking that "Pauline sounded like a press agent for the United Nations, harping gleefully on the failings of the summit meetings and the resulting new importance of the U.N." Laurent went on, explaining that while a UN reporter might be pleased by an increased role of the UN in the dispute, a halt in talks was frightening to the general public: "With a world threatening to burst into flames, the mere shift of scene is not likely to cause dancing in the streets."

Other television critics, however, praised NBC's coverage while noting the relatively newfound power of television to convey the gravity of the event vividly to viewers. Kay Gardella, in the *New York Daily News*, wrote that most local stations had rightfully preempted programming to bring viewers and radio listeners live coverage of comments by Soviet foreign minister Andrei Gromyko and U.S. ambassador Henry Cabot Lodge from the Security Council. "Kudos to the NBC-TV team of Pauline Frederick and Merrill Mueller," she wrote. Ben Gross, also of the *Daily News*, praised the three television networks for their public service in covering the U-2 incident and live coverage of UN activities related to it. He also singled out Frederick and NBC, noting that the network "gave us ... the lengthiest [and] also the most informative coverage. The chain's two aces, Pauline Frederick ... and [Washington correspondent] Frank Bourgholtzer stand out with their calm and incisive summaries of the situation." The familiarity Frederick had established with the UN and those who were a part of it apparently cut both ways: it made her an expert on the agency and gave her the ability to understand its nuances and subtleties; to some, however, this closeness hurt her objectivity.

The U-2 incident—and the resulting humiliation it caused the United States—seemed to accelerate Frederick's call in speeches for disarmament and her criticism of the Cold War. In a lengthy opinion piece she wrote for the *National Educational Association Journal*, she chastised both the Soviet Union and the United States for participating in what she believed was a childish and dangerous arms race. She noted that many people blamed the Communists for "all our trouble [in the world]." "Nevertheless, we must be neither afraid nor ashamed to take a look closer home for possible shortcomings." Frederick wrote that the U-2 incident was inevitable because of the arms race. "Any loss in prestige came not from an alleged missile gap but from frantic efforts to close one," she said, adding that an arms race would always lead to spying by both sides. "This time such risk resulted in an incident—the next time it could be an accident of cataclysmic proportions."

The volatility and emotionally charged atmosphere of the 1960s, with the escalating Cold War and deepening domestic instability, fueled public anxiety and naturally provided challenges for reporters covering national and international events. Most seasoned correspondents tried to provide complete and unbiased reports, but they were open to criticism from those who felt their reports were flawed or biased. Frederick said throughout her career that as a young reporter she had tried to remember the words of a seasoned veteran who had told her that when both sides of an issue complained about his coverage, he felt he was being fair. Frederick was not immune to these complaints, particularly when her reports aired on the popular *Today* show. In the fall of 1969, for instance, she conducted an interview with Israeli prime minister Golda Meir that sparked criticism from both pro-Israeli and pro-Arab viewers. The interview drew many comments from viewers, in part because she had asked Meir why she did not sign a nonnuclear treaty when she had said that she advocated peace in the Middle East. At least one viewer said the question was designed to put Meir "on the horns of a dilemma." The viewer, Edward Pearlstein of New York, said he had long admired Frederick, but now, he wrote, "your star has dropped so badly. I do hope you are not pro Arab." He asked Frederick to apologize to help improve her image. After Merton J. Segal of Southfield, Michigan, watched the interview, he wrote: "It is my opinion that [Frederick] is no longer capable of objective reporting. Miss Frederick's attempt to twist facts and put words in Mrs. Meir's mouth . . . were insulting. The fact that she threw the complete 'Arab line' at Mrs. Meir confirms my previous suspicions that she is no longer objective and unbiased. She needs a long vacation. How about Cairo?"

Other viewers praised her. "Bravo for you on the hard-line questioning [of Meir]," wrote Virginia Tanner of Baltimore. "I thought your questions were imminently [sic] fair, but closer to the truth than anything I have heard or read." The interview also drew a letter of thanks from the head of public information of the Israeli Embassy, who wrote to *Today* producer Stuart Schulberg to tell him that the interview had been one of the highlights of Meir's U.S. visit.

Covering the world's ongoing disputes among nations required a light touch; advocates on both sides measured in seconds the time given to each representative. Immediately after the Meir interview, one viewer, Margaret Mozzanini of Portland, Oregon, wrote that the *Today* show should have also included interviews from many other Mideast nations: "There are two sides to every story and the Arabian side gets short shrift in the U.S. press." Shortly after the Meir interview, Frederick did interview Egyptian foreign minister Mahmoud Riad on *Today*, drawing complaints from some viewers that the show had given more time to Meir. *Today* producer Schulberg, in response to the complaints, sent a wry note to Reuven Frank, then NBC News president, Frederick, and Don Meaney, executive vice president for special events, noting that the United Arab Republic mission in the United States had "held a stop watch to our . . . interviews and claimed foul because she [Meir] got 2½ more minutes than he [Riad]." He explained that its own investigation discovered that *Today* had devoted fifteen minutes, ten seconds to Meir—including a forty-five-second introduction—and fifteen minutes, nine seconds to Riad, including a forty-two-second introduction. "Nowhere is time more equal than on *Today*," he said in the memo.

Frederick's reports on *Today* seemed to draw more viewer reaction than her other broadcasts; it is unknown whether this was because of the large audience the show drew or because *Today* executives were particularly sensitive to what viewers thought of the show and actively tried to gauge audience reactions. After an interview dealing with another controversial world event—the U.S. invasion of Cambodia in April 1970—Frederick entered into a contentious exchange with show producer Schulberg. Memos between the two show that Frederick was able to stand her ground if she felt her professionalism was being questioned; they also illustrate the awkward and confusing role of the media in trying to cover a turbulent world of constantly shifting allegiances.

The subject of the dispute was an interview Frederick had done with two representatives of the Cambodian government. The United States had just begun bombing Cambodia, which was in the midst of a civil war, in an attempt to stop communism from encroaching in that country. (The unrest in Cambodia eventually led to the murderous Khmer Rouge regime, which had Communist Chinese and North Korean backing, although that guerrilla movement was small in 1970.) Two months after the U.S. invasion, Frederick conducted the interview, but apparently Schulberg felt that it shed little light on the conflict in Cambodia and that the men represented American interests in that country. He criticized the men's credentials and even their English. "I must confess that I was terribly distressed by the Cambodian 'intellectuals' who turned out to be second-rate hack mouthpieces for the current regime," he wrote. "Their interview— minus poor English (which didn't help either)—could have been scripted in [Nixon's director of communications Herb] Klein's office. I thought it was a disgraceful exhibition of thoughtless propaganda. NEVER AGAIN!"

The memo clearly unnerved—or perhaps enraged—Frederick, who responded, "I am shocked and hurt by the implication that I practiced journalistic dishonesty . . . in order to promote Administration propaganda. In the 17 years I have been with NBC my integrity as a correspondent has not been questioned as far as I know, and I am as jealous of that reputation as you are—and rightly so—of the integrity of the *Today* program." Frederick said she was not satisfied with the interview, adding, "I rarely am." She explained that she was trying to portray the idea that the Cambodians were seeking help from their past enemies, the South Vietnamese, in an attempt to ward off the Communists who were occupying more and more of Cambodia. "I could not be sorrier that you, *Today* and NBC were embarrassed by the interview."

Schulberg, upon receiving the memo, immediately backed down: "Good gracious, I must have escalated my language. I was only trying to express a sort of mutual disappointment, not a criticism of your judgment. I am surprised by your dismay at my note mainly because you have delivered so many good guests to *Today*, with such success and prestige, that I felt

I could register this one complaint without question as to your motives or professionalism. But in the meantime I do want you to know what respect and affection we have for you on *Today*, much too much to be tainted by a disappointing session with a few Cambodian hawks who obviously let you down as much as the rest of us."

Robert Asman, a special events producer for NBC in Washington DC who occasionally worked with Frederick, said she was capable of standing up for herself but that she was always professional. If Schulberg seemed cowed by Frederick's ire, it is an indication of how indispensible she was viewed by NBC. NBC marshaled the efforts of all its key correspondents, for instance, to cover the assassination of President Kennedy, and Frederick was one of a handful of correspondents who received a note of praise from Kintner, who was then NBC president. A generation of Americans may remember a tearful Walter Cronkite, on CBS, announcing that Kennedy had died. But NBC beat the other two networks in assassination coverage in other ways. As soon as he learned of the shooting, Kintner was the first network executive to take commercials off the air and to dictate twenty-four-hour programming, prompting the other networks to follow; and it was Kintner who ordered NBC to cover the transfer of Lee Harvey Oswald from police custody to the county jail, so that NBC was the only one to televise live his shooting by Jack Ruby. Of the three networks NBC devoted the most airtime to the assassination during the weekend of November 22, 1963. The assassination was also an important event in broadcast history: it marked the first time the world had viewed live images of a pivotal event as it happened. As Robert Caro wrote in his biography of Lyndon Johnson, the funeral and related events combined power and pageantry. Those images, Caro wrote, "were engraved, indelibly, on the consciousness of the nation, and . . . of the world, in a way that had never before happened with a major historical event, because the images were seen, seen live, as they were happening, which added to the drama, to the viewers' sense of involvement, and to the viewers' emotions."

NBC aired live reports from the UN, with U Thant expressing sorrow to the Kennedy family and U.S. citizens. Delegates from the 111 member nations observed a moment of silence. The coverage prompted Kintner to send appreciative memos to Frederick, and others, thanking them for their role in NBC's coverage of the assassination. When Robert Kennedy was shot five years later, NBC broadcast a statement by U Thant, who condemned the shooting as a function of violence in the world and of the controversial Vietnam War. "I regard the prevailing mood of violence in the United States and elsewhere as a consequence of the psychological climate created by the Vietnam war," he said. The Tet offensive of January 1968 spawned increasing pessimism that the war would not end soon and led to an intensified public outcry against the war.

But the escalating war was only one of several ongoing international stories of the times. The Paris peace talks between the United States and North Vietnam, launched in 1968 with the aim of ending the war, became a continuing story, as did debate over the admission into the UN of the Communist People's Republic of China. The Republic of China, whose government under Chiang Kai-shek had been forced to relocate to Taipei in 1949 after it lost the Chinese Civil War, had been one of the five members of the Security Council since the UN charter was formed in 1945.

Discussions were heating up in the late 1960s about whether the People's Republic of China, formed in 1949 and whose government was based in Peking, should replace the Republic of China, with Frederick and other foreign correspondents speculating by the late 1960s that public opinion would favor UN recognition of the PRC despite U.S. resistance to it. Frederick in 1970 predicted that it would be the last year the United States could block Communist China from being seated in the UN. She also said in interviews in the late 1960s that several Washington insiders had told her that the U.S. position on China would change. Since 1949 U.S. officials had been sharply critical of any suggestion that the PRC replace the Republic of China in the Security Council, even suggesting that admission be given to two Chinas, an idea that Frederick and others believed violated the UN charter. U.S. relations with the PRC had thawed considerably by 1971, the year Nixon's national security advisor, Henry Kissinger, visited Peking and U.S. ambassador George Bush publicly advocated the seating of the PRC on the Security Council (although he opposed expelling the Nationalist Chinese). On October 25, 1971, the People's Republic of China was seated on the National Security Council, replacing the Republic of China. Four months later, on February 22, 1972, President Nixon visited

Peking, becoming the first U.S. president to visit China. (Interestingly, in a May 1969 *Los Angeles Times* interview Frederick had kind words about Nixon after his first one hundred days in office. "He obviously is not trying to misuse the United Nations or use it for a propaganda platform," she said. Her only reservation about him was that he had said during his campaign that he supported the U.S. position opposed to giving the People's Republic of China a seat on the Security Council—a stand that he would reverse, she predicted.)

Meanwhile, the crisis in the Mideast had been ongoing and seemed continually on the verge of boiling over. Frederick had her hands full, as observed in a note to her by Julian Goodman, who by 1967 had replaced Kintner as NBC president: "I think you've been doing a splendid job covering the UN during the Middle East crisis," he wrote, praising her also for her coverage of Soviet premier Alexei Kosygin's visit to the UN. Goodman related in the memo that a friend of his had observed a tourist in UN headquarters pointing to Frederick and calling her "the head of the United Nations."

The de facto head of the United Nations was by the late 1960s becoming more public about her criticisms of the Vietnam War and the U.S. role in it. It is ironic that producer Schulman accused Frederick of mouthing the views of the Nixon administration in her broadcast with the Cambodian officials; she was no fan of Nixon when it came to his Vietnam policies, although she had already been critical in speeches of the United States's role in the war before Nixon came to office. But clearly NBC did not question her objectivity as a reporter. The network even issued a news release in 1969 reporting on Frederick's address to the World Affairs Council condemning the Nixon administration's development of antiballistic missiles, which she said deterred "meaningful negotiations on disarmament." The news release noted that in the speech she had called on the world's two superpowers to use the UN instead of the battlefield to settle their differences. The United States's new phase of rearmament, she pointed out, "comes at a time when [the two countries] have stockpiled nuclear power equivalent to fifteen tons of TNT explosives" for every person on the planet, and yet "security has continued to elude the Goliaths." By this time network executives and government

10 *Liberating the Airwaves*

> Put [women] in front of a microphone—and a camera as well—and
> something happens to them. They become affected, overdramatic,
> high-pitched. Some turn sexy and sultry. Others get patronizing
> and pseudo-charming.
>
> ROBERT WOGAN, NBC Radio Network, May 24, 1964

After the Tet offensive in January 1968 and the April 1970 invasion of
Cambodia (and the shooting deaths of student protesters a month later
at Kent State University), the Vietnam War was at its height. The influence of the United Nations worldwide had declined considerably, in part
because of its inability to help broker peace in Southeast Asia and in part
because of the attitudes of the administration of Richard Nixon, who was
elected president in 1968. His administration did not take the organization seriously as a player in world events. Frederick's high profile as a UN
correspondent began to fade as a result of these factors

But the Vietnam War and the resulting fall in prestige of the UN were
not the only reasons Frederick's influence at NBC was declining. It was not
until the early 1970s—a full two decades after she joined NBC and nearly
twenty-five years after she became a broadcaster—that women correspondents started becoming permanent fixtures on network television. The
television broadcasting environment was changing, and although Frederick
supported the entry of other women in the field, that phenomenon would
naturally change her position at NBC. But as one veteran broadcaster
noted, fashions change in news beats as they do in most other aspects of
society. Reporters on most beats face the reality that depending on societal and cultural events, once-valued areas of expertise can sometimes

195

be relegated to the background. "Her clout may have declined with [the intensifying of] Vietnam, but that's the nature of the job. Networks don't treat their correspondent with tender loving kindness," said Bob Zelnick, who was a correspondent for ABC for twenty years and who worked with Frederick at National Public Radio in the mid-1980s.

One incident that exemplifies her decline in stature was a decision by NBC about whom to send to cover Nixon's visit to China in 1972. This would be a historic event, and in his memoir, *Out of Thin Air*, Reuven Frank explained that NBC had wanted to send four high-profile correspondents, including one woman. Indeed, all three networks sent their heavyweight correspondents or anchors to China—Dan Rather, Eric Sevareid, and Walter Cronkite of CBS and Tom Jarriel, Ted Koppel, and Harry Reasoner for ABC. At the time the only newswomen at NBC other than Frederick were Nancy Dickerson, a Washington correspondent, and Aline Saarinen, a former art critic and NBC Paris correspondent. Barbara Walters, who joined the *Today* show in 1961 as a producer and writer, had become a regular on that show by 1972, and she was known as one of several "*Today* girls" whose job it was to do primarily feature stories. Walters's status as a journalist was debatable—*Today* was and is under the supervision of the NBC News division, but its primary role was to provide viewers soft news. Still, she had shown she was adept at covering hard news in the early 1960s, conducting an interview with Secretary of State Dean Rusk that so impressed the *Today* brass that they aired it over several days.

Frank selected Walters. Saarinen died later that year of a brain tumor, and apparently Dickerson had her hands full covering Washington. Frederick, Frank recalled in his memoir, "had never worked with film on a foreign assignment." His rationale is interesting: Frederick certainly had extensive journalistic experience overseas before she came to NBC, and occasionally she covered stories overseas for that network, although most of her duties were concentrated at the UN. And it is true that videotape and satellite feeds had not yet been developed before she came to NBC, and therefore her overseas experience with them was limited. (Walters and Saarinen—but not Frederick—had been a part of a *Today* team that participated in the first live broadcast via satellite from Europe. The historic broadcast marked the first time an event in Europe was seen live on television and remains one of the major breakthroughs in broadcast history.) But Frank could have made the case to send Frederick—for years she had covered the debate over whether the People's Republic of China should have a seat on the Security Council, so she was familiar with the politics and background of the U.S.-China relationship. And apparently NBC news managers thought she had done a good job. Julian Goodman, then vice president for news, sent her a handwritten note praising her for coverage of the UN vote in 1971 recognizing China, writing, "You were on top of the story all the time and put us well ahead."

Walters, however, was a known quantity whom NBC viewers saw five days a week. More important, however, was the fact that Walters was a "personality" and a celebrity of sorts; her style of reporting was as a participant, and she often became, indirectly, a part of the stories she covered, endearing her to viewers. In short she was a popular and ubiquitous on-air presence. Walters's trip represented a major turning point in her career, and in some ways it was a turning point for Frederick, too, or at least a symbol of what was to come.

Barbara Walters wrote at length in her own memoir about her trip to China, describing how apprehensive she was to be there in the company of some of the most powerful and respected newsmen in the world. During and after that historic China visit, she showed NBC officials and viewers why she would one day become one of the most high-profile journalists in the world; already she was energetic, innovative, and not afraid to cross boundaries. After the trip Frank described how CBS had sent Cronkite to talk to "high-powered" American businessmen about the untapped market of China—a brilliant move, Frank implied. No one at NBC had "had the wit to suggest something like that," he said—no one but Walters, who, on her own initiative, had persuaded network president Goodman to let her address NBC executives to test her "routine" and describe what she saw as an American woman in China, a routine she could display to businessmen. "China was Barbara's first big step out of the herd, and we in that room watched a television star on the verge of being born," Frank said. Another network executive, Lee Hanna, who was vice president for programming for NBC, recalled that when Walters was in China, she worked fifteen or sixteen hours a day and checked out every angle of every story.

If Barbara Walters emerged from the herd, Pauline Frederick was being forced back in. While network president Goodman had long admired and respected Frederick, continually sending her memos of praise and allowing her to cover the UN as she saw fit, her other main supporters were gone by 1972. Robert Kintner, whom she had known from their days at ABC in the 1940s, eventually left ABC to become NBC president in 1958, but he had been fired in 1966 and replaced by Goodman. (Kintner then served for about a year as a special assistant and cabinet secretary for President Johnson.) More important, and more detrimental to Frederick, NBC News vice president and later news president William McAndrew, whom Frederick had known since both covered Washington in the mid-1940s and who hired her at NBC, died tragically in 1968 of injuries he had sustained in a fall. He was fifty-three. McAndrew, who had served as a top NBC news executive for seventeen years, was replaced by Frank. So, Frederick's two biggest supporters were gone by mid-1968, and although Goodman remained and was later promoted to network president, it is likely he left the job of running the day-to-day activities of the news division to his lieutenants. But as Zelnick implied, news correspondents were not immune to the fickleness of time and chance. Frederick was not the first employee to become a casualty of changing times. Even Walters suffered a temporary career setback in 1971, before she was sent on that career-changing trip to China. She had been a popular *Today* girl, and she was a favorite of the show's host, Hugh Downs. When Downs left the show in 1971, he was replaced by newsman Frank McGee, who considered his transfer to the feature *Today* a demotion. McGee quickly elevated his own role on the show while downplaying Walters's. He selected his own interview subjects, leaving the "leftovers," as historian Barbara Matusow described them, to Walters. And he let Walters join in on interviews only if he granted permission, and even then, she was not allowed to ask the first question. Walters's star skyrocketed after the trip to China. She had always been smart, versatile, and hardworking, but after the China trip she proved she was also shrewd and aggressive. Frederick was hardly guileless, but she was not as cagey as Walters when it came to promoting herself. Walters may have had another advantage over Frederick when it came to being selected to cover Nixon's famous China visit. She was forty-two years old; Frederick was sixty-four.

By the time Nixon visited China, Frederick's role at NBC had been diminished. Her niece Catharine Cole said that her aunt had told her many times later in her life that she believed her age had been a hindrance during her last few years at NBC. When it came to employing women, she believed, television executives stressed youthful good looks over experience and wisdom (although as Frederick aged, she still dressed in a sophisticated manner and remained well groomed, slim, and attractive). The image and power of the United Nations had declined as well, and by that time it was no longer considered a key player on the world stage. Its failure to play a role in negotiating peace in Vietnam War was not the only reason the UN had lost its luster. By the late 1960s technological improvements had made the world smaller—live broadcasts, for instance, could originate from anywhere. As one magazine story said, because of improved technology, "the superpowers have elected to argue their problems in the UN, but settle them elsewhere." By that time correspondents could provide live coverage from "elsewhere."

If the UN had a chance to make a comeback on the world stage, it was on June 26, 1965, during a commemoration of the twentieth anniversary of the signing of its charter in San Francisco. In what Johnson administration officials billed as a major address, President Johnson spoke at opening ceremonies in the city's opera house. He asked the UN to bring North Vietnamese officials to the conference table to help broker a peace. Johnson said all attempts by the United States to negotiate had been rebuffed by North Vietnam and the People's Republic of China.

And indeed, his request was once again rebuffed. The Cuban delegation walked out during the speech, and delegates from several Eastern European nations labeled it a "Sunday school speech" filled with vague promises. More important, however, was the reaction the next day from the Soviet Union, whose representative, Nikolai Fedorenko, denounced it in his own address while decrying the United States's role in the "dirty aggressive war." Fedorenko's comments drew the thunderous applause of some delegates during the second day of the UN charter–signing commemoration. Fedorenko went on to say that bombing by the United States in Southeast Asia had led to the "barbarous annihilation" of "peace-loving hamlets." His speech came after Secretary-General U Thant, in a solemn address, had warned that the heightening of the Cold War could lead to a world crisis.

Richard Hottelet of CBS said the Soviets had gathered enough votes in the Security Council to keep the Vietnam War off its agenda. Frederick was a supporter of the United Nations throughout her career, and she continually justified its existence, even when the ranks of its defenders dwindled. The Sunday after Johnson's UN speech, Frederick, who had been a periodic panelist on the NBC Sunday show *Meet the Press*, appeared on the program with panelists William Frye of the *Washington Evening Star*, Peter Lisagor of the *Chicago Daily News*, *Meet the Press* host Lawrence Spivak, and guest Adlai Stevenson, the U.S. ambassador to the UN. The topic was the declining influence of the United Nations. Spivak opened the show stating the contention of many that the UN at the time was "in serious crisis and on the verge of collapse," an idea Stevenson vehemently denied, noting that the UN was a reflection of the world situation and that "if the world is tense, there will be tension in the United Nations." Frye asked Stevenson why, if President Johnson had asked the UN to intervene in Vietnam, the organization had not seriously discussed doing so. Stevenson replied that neither North Vietnam nor the People's Republic of China had entertained overtures by the UN the previous year to intervene in the war. "Indeed, they are doing their best to destroy the institution of the United Nations," he said.

Lisagor said that the UN had also been bypassed in dealing with world crises other than Vietnam and that the organization had "become so unwieldy and so preoccupied with the small powers" that it has "lost its peacekeeping capacity all together," another contention Stevenson denied. Frederick, who often asked difficult questions of *Meet the Press* guests, seemed oddly subdued. She asked Stevenson why the United States has not asked U Thant to issue a cease-fire appeal to all parties in Vietnam—an action that she probably realized would be futile. Stevenson replied that because the United States had already made negotiation offers to the North Vietnamese and the Chinese governments, he did not think such action by the UN would elicit a positive response.

If Frederick had a vested interest in the success of the United Nations, she was not alone. The reputations and dispensability of reporters are sometimes tied to the success or status of the areas they cover. And they often become personally tied to their beats. In a 1968 story about the United Nations press corps, *Newsweek* pointed out that the UN had lost its importance as a news beat for some major news outlets. The *Guardian* of London, for instance, had stopped covering it as a full-time beat. "The important things . . . just don't get considered seriously in the UN," its editor said. Still, the story noted, some major U.S. newspapers had increased coverage. Other editors said they believed UN coverage was still important but that its tone had changed since the mid-1950s. "The interest now is not in the decisions, but in watching how diplomats tip off the attitudes of their countries," said one correspondent who covered the beat for French and Israeli news outlets. Hottelet pointed to 1967 as the year many Americans had turned against the UN, as a result of the Arab-Israeli war. "It was quite a thing, the real hostility toward the UN in American public opinion," he said, noting that by the early 1970s some major news outlets—including ABC, the *Los Angeles Times*, the *Chicago Tribune*, and the *Chicago Daily News*—had removed their permanent correspondents from the UN and sent reporters there only when news broke.

The UN, of course, had played a major role in the Mideast throughout most of its existence; it had worked to guide the peace process there since the Palestine crisis in 1947. In the aftermath of the 1967 war, when the Israelis became focused on the Palestinians, the General Assembly had been seen as increasingly hostile toward Israel, passing the controversial 1975 resolution equating Zionism with racism. These actions, in turn, influenced public opinion of the organization in the United States.

In the *Newsweek* story Frederick was quoted as having said that the staid—some might say boring—atmosphere of the UN could make it a decidedly unsexy beat. Diplomats are by nature diplomatic, she explained, and they tended to shy away from controversy at all costs, making them undesirable news sources. "It's difficult to compete for air time with a story from somewhere else in which you can say either the house burned down or it didn't," she said in the story. As a matter of fact, this house-burning-down nature of television news was intensifying by the late 1960s; as broadcast technology improved, so did news executives' demands for exciting and provocative video to accompany stories.

In her memoir and history of women in broadcasting, *Waiting for Primetime*, Marlene Sanders wrote that she could literally count on one hand the number of female network correspondents in 1964, when she joined ABC after having worked in local television news. One of them, of course, was Frederick, who by 1964 had been in the business full-time for sixteen years. The others were Lisa Howard, who had worked at ABC when Sanders joined the network, and Aline Saarinen and Nancy Dickerson at NBC. (Dickerson became a CBS correspondent in 1960 and worked there until 1963.) Sanders did not include Barbara Walters in that count because in 1964 she worked at *Today*, and as such, her role was not strictly as a news reporter. But even if she had included Walters, Sanders's point was that the networks were surprisingly behind the times when it came to equal opportunity hiring. Two more women—Marya McLaughlin, a Washington correspondent, and Liz Trotta—had joined the ranks of female network reporters by 1965, at CBS and NBC, respectively, and many more were hired by the networks by the mid-1970s.

It should also be noted that NBC had employed at least one other woman full-time in the 1950s—Lee Hall, a foreign correspondent who worked for the network in the 1950s and early 1960s. Hall, who worked mostly overseas for NBC Radio, was part of the NBC team that covered the 1960 political conventions. Hall quit the network to join the Voice of America in 1962. Two of the early women network correspondents Sanders discussed in her book died young. Saarinen was an art and architecture critic for several news outlets, including the *New York Times*, who appeared on television in 1962 discussing art; her appearance was so popular among viewers that NBC hired her full-time in 1963 to cover news. Saarinen died in 1972 at age fifty-eight. Howard was a former stage and television actress who was fired from CBS in 1964 for partisan political activity that involved her campaigning for a political candidate; she committed suicide a year later, at the age of thirty-five.

As women started joining the network in greater numbers, they themselves became the subject of many news stories. And those stories were eye-opening, ironic, and sometimes downright odd. In one of the first national stories about female network correspondents—whose ranks consisted of

Dickerson, Frederick, and Howard—*TV Guide* described some of the women as indignant that they might be loved by television executives for their beauty rather than their brains. The same *TV Guide* reporter who decried the sexism of broadcast journalism called Howard the "prettiest" of the group profiled, although the writer noted that Dickerson was "equally as curvy" and "sleek." One of the points of the story was that many women broadcasters thought their male counterparts resented them because the men believed they used their femininity rather than their talent to get stories. Howard, for instance, who landed several exclusive interviews with world figures including Fidel Castro and Nikita Khrushchev, accused her male counterparts of thinking she had used her looks to get those interviews. The story quoted one unnamed Washington newspaperman as having said that Dickerson, too, used her "very feminine appeal" to get politicians to open up to her. The story labeled Frederick the "pleasant-looking but non-glamorous dean of female TV reporters." Frederick was fifty-three when the story was written; Dickerson and Howard were in their midthirties.

The story pointed out, somewhat insultingly, that no one had accused Frederick of using her good looks to get a scoop. "Frederick is spared the professional handshake of being a 'looker,'" the reporter says, noting that "the condescending 'word' in masculine circles is that 'Pauline covers the news like a man'—a highly dubious compliment." In this story Frederick repeated her contention that women in broadcasting were held to a higher standard than men when it came to appearance. "In the middle of a crisis, you have to stop working on your story and rush in and have your hair done," she said. "I don't want to be appreciated for my glamour. I want to be appreciated for my work." Sanders said decades later that she believed Frederick's appearance did in fact help her get hired at the networks—because she was not overtly sexual or threatening to the men with whom she worked. Male network executives apparently did not think brains and great beauty could go together.

As late as 1962, the myth endured that a woman's voice lacked authority. In a speech that year Frederick noted that through much of broadcast history executives thought women were supposed to "listen, not talk." And in a profile of Frederick written in 1960, an unnamed female journalist was quoted as having said that women had not been able to benefit fully from the civil rights and other movements that had begun to gain momentum in society. "The same editor who will campaign for civil rights claims a personal exemption from women's rights," she wrote. Indeed, in 1964, in a story about women and journalism, the reporter quoted Elmer Lower, then president of news, special events, and public affairs for ABC, as having said that while women may possess "knowledge and authority," they could rarely convey it through their voices. "Even the best-trained actress can't compare with men in this respect," he said. "Her voice is naturally thinner, with less timbre and range . . . for hard-core news, the depth and resonance of the male voice are indispensible." The apparent sexism in hiring in broadcast news indeed might have come from the top: throughout her career Frederick noted that the men she worked with in the newsroom had always been helpful to her and were for the most part "sweethearts," as she once called them. Network executives may have been a different story, she said.

Women broadcasters were in a no-win situation in the 1960s, when they first joined networks and local stations in large numbers. On one hand, it was crucial that they look attractive; on the other hand, great beauty was threatening—to network managers and possibly their female viewers. In a long story about women in broadcasting, *Ms.* magazine in 1974 pointed out that the new group of women in broadcasting walked a narrow line. The story quoted Sylvia Chase of CBS: "The fact that you're presentable works against you. You're a cute little girl. You don't sound believable. You sound young, naïve. Thank God I'm attractive . . . but it's a curse to my credibility." In a 1968 *TV Guide* story about women in broadcasting, author and critic Marya Mannes wrote that the few women in broadcasting at the time were in a no-win situation. "Put a woman behind one of those desks with buttons and monitors and let her rip?" Mannes wrote sarcastically. "For one thing, she should look young and smooth-faced, and who can be that after 20 or 30 years of training, involvement and experience."

By the time ABC hired Sanders, the network was only too happy to announce to its affiliates that they had another woman reporter. In a news release about her hiring, the network listed information about her that officials there apparently thought was vital: her experience in broadcasting, developed a distinct star quality. Dickerson, with her impressive personal contacts in Washington, did much the same thing. The two ushered in a new breed of female correspondent. Dickerson and Walters did not rely solely on their looks and personality—both were smart, hardworking, and aggressive—but they did not recede into the background as disinterested "objective" reporters. Throughout her career Frederick always returned to her roots as a print reporter: the story came first, and she, the reporter, remained almost invisible. As she matured into a widely recognized broadcaster, she became a familiar face to viewers, but the process was gradual.

In his candid and perceptive memoir about his mother, Dickerson's son John, also a journalist, talked about the requirement that high-profile female broadcasters be attractive. He noted that while his mother was the first woman news correspondent for CBS, Frederick was the first female network correspondent and that she "had suffered indignities." Perhaps more telling is his comment about Frederick's appearance. In most profiles of his mother her beauty was mentioned. Frederick, he wrote, was usually described as pleasant looking: "The faint praise says it all: Frederick was hired for her 'award-winning' talent, not her looks or glamour." The subtitle of John Dickerson's book, *On Her Trail*, is also revealing: *My Mother, Nancy Dickerson, TV News' First Woman Star*. Frederick was actually the first woman network correspondent, as he acknowledged, but Dickerson was, debatably, the first female broadcasting *star*. Indeed, a 1960 story in a Connecticut newspaper about the only two women network news reporters, Dickerson and Frederick, noted that Frederick was "distinguished"; Dickerson was described as "the capital's best looking correspondent."

The quality of being a "personality" did not always appeal to some people—or at least to some critics. In a 1961 column *New York Herald Tribune* television critic Marie Torre praised the two broadcasters, Frederick and Lee Hall, whom she felt delivered straight news stories without the frills. Torre criticized Lisa Howard's "beeline" toward Khrushchev in an attempt to interview him. "Viewers learned more about Miss Howard than about Khrushchev," Torre wrote. Happily, she acknowledged, not all female broadcasters were as "breathless" as some of the newcomers. Frederick "can always be relied on to do a man-like job," and Hall "also removes the frills from her reporting." Torre quoted an NBC representative as having said that the network is "not out for the flashy type in lady reporters."

Sanders remembered that the few female network correspondents employed in the 1960s and early 1970s focused on getting the job done and beating their competitors rather than being "flashy." "We were competitive," she said. "I was trying to get my story and they were trying to get theirs. We had practically no interaction." As more women joined the networks throughout the 1970s, they formed the American Women in Radio and Television, an organization designed to let them meet, host speakers, and help each other. Sanders was active in that organization, and Frederick addressed the group several times at Sanders's invitation.

Some of Frederick's correspondence indicates that the first few women broadcasters at NBC may have had cordial if not close relationships. In one undated note, for instance, Dickerson thanked Frederick for her thoughtfulness about some matter. "I appreciate it deeply and will phone you when next in NY. Please do the same when you come to Washington." And when Frederick broke her knee in 1971, among the many get-well cards was one, with a warm note, from Barbara Walters.

At least one of these pioneering women broadcasters, Liz Trotta, said that Frederick gave her some good advice when she was a fledgling network reporter. After she returned from one of her stints in Vietnam, Trotta was selected to participate in NBC's correspondents tours, in which a handful of the network's top international reporters traveled around the country to the network's affiliates, talking about current world events. Frederick had been a member of that mostly male panel many times. When Trotta was selected to participate in 1968, she was nervous about being in the company of such established correspondents. The men, Frederick advised, would be quick to namedrop and parrot the "official" word—but Trotta could tell audiences the *real* story: "[John] Chancellor and that crowd are going to talk about what the president said to them last week. What you should do is tell them what a GI in the Mekong Delta said to you last week."

But a few of the pioneering women broadcasters indicated that relations among them were not always nurturing. Sanders wrote that when she and Lisa Howard were the only two women correspondents for ABC, they rarely saw each other because Sanders was frequently out of the office.

The only contact the two women had was when Howard tried to persuade her to support the campaign of a political candidate—an obvious conflict of interest that later would lead to Howard's firing.

By the 1970s, as women began entering broadcasting in larger numbers, some of the stories about them questioned why the networks employed so few of them in an age of feminism. As Frederick read these stories, she may have experienced a sense of déjà vu. The good news was that more women were now employed by the network; the bad news was that as late as the early 1970s, some broadcasting executives still felt their voices lacked authority. And the issue of competition for jobs also emerged— among men and women.

In an often-quoted 1965 *New York Times* opinion piece called "Nylons in the Newsroom," Gloria Steinem addressed the relatively recent entrance of women into television news. The upbeat column noted that while the numbers of women in television news were low in 1965, women had finally begun to establish a foothold in the industry. (Steinem mentioned Frederick twice as a pioneer in the industry.) She specifically pointed out the ways women could enter the field: they could start at the bottom—"get a job [in television]—any job"—and work their way up; they could get a big scoop, thereby forcing television managers to use them to air their story; or if they had newspaper experience, as many female broadcasters did, they could use that to leverage a job in broadcasting.

Steinem was optimistic, quoting Barbara Walters as having said that "we're friendlier as a group than most men. I root for [her NBC colleague] Aline Saarinen and the others because I know every success of theirs will open more doors for me." In hindsight it appears that some of Steinem's optimism may have been misplaced. Five years after she wrote that article, more women were entering broadcasting, but the pace was still slow, and it did not accelerate until the FCC in 1971 said it would require applications for station renewal to include affirmative action plans for women. (It had already required such plans for ethnic and racial minorities.) Nevertheless, numbers did not tell the whole story. The first group of women did pave the way for the entrance of other women, but Walters and Steinem may have downplayed the problems women still faced even if they could get hired—problems that included the fear by some male broadcasters that women would steal their jobs and the age-old belief by some *female* viewers that women were not meant to cover news.

A year before Steinem's article was published, Lee Graham, a woman broadcaster who worked for WNYC in New York, wrote a story for the *Times* that was not as optimistic. Graham interviewed television executives, critics, psychologists, and others to shed light on the reasons more women were not seen on television even though more were entering the workplace and more were graduating from college. The title of the article, "Women Don't Like to Look at Women," describes why the news networks did not employ more women. "It's jealousy," according to *New York Herald Tribune* radio-television editor Richard K. Doan. He said most busy women resented seeing attractive, well-groomed women report the news on television while they were at home with their hands full, taking care of children and homes: "How do you think they like it when they turn on the TV set and there sits this goddess with the right hairdo, makeup and dress, plenty of poise—and a brain besides? Take it from me, they don't." Furthermore, Graham wrote, this attitude was pervasive: "Professors at one of the best schools of journalism advise their girl students to get jobs at newspapers and magazines when job-hunting instead of breaking their hearts over broadcasting."

At least one television critic said the insecurity of men kept more women from entering broadcast journalism. Women are qualified, *TV Guide* critic Cleveland Amory said, "but men keep the top jobs in a state of self-perpetuation," a contention backed by two psychologists. If men feared losing their jobs to women, it was the same fear women in the business might have, too, about other women, one of the psychologists said. Frederick, in a speech she gave to women journalists in 1983 after she retired, said she was pleased that more women than ever were entering broadcast journalism. But half-kiddingly, she added: "I was born too early to take advantage of the lowered barriers . . . But I did have one advantage. I had to compete only against the men. You have to compete against the women as well." But perhaps the most unfortunate reason women still lagged behind in broadcasting, the story noted, was one with which Frederick was too familiar: in her story Graham quoted several network executives that women's voices still lacked that elusive tone of "authority." "A woman's manner isn't suited to news and serious discussions," said Giraud Chester, formerly a vice president of television program administration for NBC. Chester claimed it was "all right" for a woman to serve as a panelist on a game show or even a public affairs show, but other women found it unfeminine for a woman to be forceful or to ask probing questions. "She'd rather have her hair in place than her brains," Chester said. Graham wrote that all but one of the four television executives she quoted in the story agreed with Chester. "Who likes an authoritative woman anyway?" asked Joseph Cook, program manager of WCBS radio. Another executive, Robert Wogan of the NBC Radio Network, apparently believed that women underwent a strange transformation when they were put on the air: "Put them in front of a microphone—and a camera as well—and something happens to them. They become affected overdramatic, high-pitched. Some turn sexy and sultry. Others get patronizing and pseudo-charming." Apparently, Frederick was none of these things, as she still did some reporting for NBC Radio in the mid-1960s. But her low-modulated voice may have also seemed somewhat androgynous and therefore "safe" to network officials.

Whether it was because of federal legislation, the success of these few pioneering women in television, or other factors, the trickle of women into broadcasting in the early 1970s accelerated into a flow by the middle of the decade. Joining the networks by then were Sylvia Chase, Connie Chung, Ann Compton, Cassie Mackin, Jessica Savitch, Lesley Stahl, Judy Woodruff, and others. Studies done in the early 1970s indicated that broadcast executives at local stations were beginning to hire more and more women by 1970, although newsrooms were still filled mostly with men. One study showed that in 1970 women covered news at 45 percent of the nation's newsrooms (although the study did not provide the actual number of women in each newsroom). Another study showed that in 1973, 23 percent of employees in the nation's 614 commercial television stations were women—but 69 percent of them were clerical or office workers.

Just because women were hired as news correspondents did not mean their assignments were equal to those of their male counterparts. Sanders said most network newswomen in the early years were assigned stories that were supposedly of interest to women viewers—subjects such as food, delivering the news did not matter. The authors of the study concluded that "it made no difference to [viewers] whether the newscaster was a man or a woman." In an often-quoted statement in the mid-1974, Reuven Frank claimed in *Newsweek* that audiences were less prepared to accept news from a woman's voice than a man's. A survey of viewers taken that year and cited by *Ms.* magazine negated that theory, showing that newswomen had more support from their viewers than from their employers.

Interestingly, most articles written in the early 1970s about these newly hired female network correspondents observed one new phenomenon—that it was the job of anchor that cultivated the most loyalty among viewers. Much has been written over the years about the competition at major networks for the position of anchor, and it had been a coveted position as early as the mid-1950s, when the popularity of the team of Chet Huntley and David Brinkley propelled NBC to the position of number one news outlet. So, it is no surprise that by the mid-1970s women began to seek that position, lured by the added prestige and the money. In interviews and speeches Frederick never mentioned seeking an anchor position.

In her memoir Jessica Savitch, who joined NBC in 1977 as a reporter and anchor of the Sunday evening news, observed that an anchor spot frequently engendered viewer loyalty for a reporter, thus ensuring professional longevity. Savitch wrote in 1982 that the previous crop of women correspondents, which included Frederick and Dickerson, had lost career momentum as they grew older because they did not anchor: "They were not seen with predictable frequency in key assignments. There was little chance for them to inspire and foster viewer allegiance." (Savitch became a controversial figure at NBC before she drowned during a car accident in 1983 at age thirty-six. Prior to being removed from the weekend anchor position in 1983, there had been rumors that she had a drug problem after she had appeared on the air slurring her words.) Even by the mid-1970s, however, the anchor jobs that went to women were in less-than-coveted time slots. As *Ms.* magazine wrote in a 1974 story about female broadcasters: "Women are anchoring early morning, midday, weekend, and wee-hour newscasts on local stations. All these shows have one thing in common—nobody watches them." Barbara Walters was the first female broadcaster to cash in on her celebrity-reporter status and turn it into a prime-time network anchor position. She left NBC in 1976 for a million-dollar contract to coanchor the evening news at ABC.

Yet the influx of women in broadcast journalism and other societal factors that helped to open doors for women professionally could not immediately erase the long-ingrained sexism in television news. Men still set the agenda when it came to hiring in broadcasting and many other fields. Still, some male executives may have been paying attention: in a speech in 1973 to the American Women in Radio and Television, NBC president Julian Goodman pledged to continue to hire and promote women, quoting a statistic that said 42 percent of the promotions at NBC the previous year had gone to women. "Too often your skills have been underutilized. There has been discrimination," he said. "But as society has changed, so have ... corporate attitudes." It is true that NBC was a pacesetter of sorts when it came to hiring women as on-air correspondents, although none of the three networks had a surplus of female correspondents, even by the early 1970s. In 1965 Goodman reminded a reporter for the *New York Herald Tribune* that NBC had the most women reporters of the three networks—four. (The network had recently hired Trotta, who joined Frederick, Dickerson, and Saarinen.) "Julian Goodman maintains that the recent increase in women in TV news is due largely to the Frederick-Dickerson-Saarinen success, not as cute number or weak sisters but as journalistic peers of men," the story said.

But not all attitudes had changed. One media historian reported that when Lesley Stahl of CBS sought out her desk for election night coverage in 1974, she found the anchor desks labeled "Cronkite, Rather, Wallace and Female." And on the back cover of Savitch's memoir is a quote from an unnamed station advisor at the Ithaca College radio station. "There's no place for broads in broadcasting," he said. By the late 1970s veteran broadcasters such as Frederick acknowledged that women had made great strides in journalism, but they believed the fight was far from over. "You've come a long way, baby, to paraphrase Mrs. Gerald Ford's recent comment," Frederick said in a 1976 lecture. "But I must add, you still have a long way to go, baby, to reach equality with your male colleagues in hiring, promotions and assignments in the broadcast media." And in her 2012 book, *Lots of Candles, Plenty of Cake*, Anna Quindlen, the first woman assistant metropolitan editor at the *New York Times*, recalled how excited, proud, and smug she had been decades earlier when she was named to that job—that is, until she had lunch with another pioneering woman at the *Times*, Charlotte Curtis. Curtis, the first woman to have her name on the *Times* masthead as associate editor, had served as a women's page editor, op-ed editor, and columnist, and she was accustomed to being the only woman in the room during meetings of top *Times* editors. But times had not changed so much, Curtis reminded Quindlen at that lunch. Curtis told her something she would always remember: "You should never forget that you will only have as much power as they are willing to give you."

Curtis's words may have proven prescient for Jill Abramson, who had been a longtime *New York Times* reporter and news manager when she was named that newspaper's first female executive editor in 2011. Less than three years later, however, she was abruptly dismissed amid speculation that top *Times* officials did not agree with her management style. The reason for her dismissal, and whether her gender played a role, remains unclear.

As a sought-after lecturer, Frederick frequently talked about the role of women in society and in journalism. She often said that she did not consider herself a pioneer or trailblazer; instead, she just worked hard at a job she loved. But as she grew older, she became more outspoken about her belief that she had faced discrimination in the newsroom and that it still existed after she retired. Although Frederick stated her opinion in her lectures—something she did not have the luxury to do in her news reports—she always came armed with facts and figures to support her points. She also used this tactic as she became increasingly outspoken in the late 1960s and early 1970s against the Vietnam War. In 1963 Frederick had been part of a panel, with feminist author Betty Friedan, on an NBC public affairs show called *The Open Mind*. Frederick said that part of her frustration stemmed from the fact that it was sometimes outside sources that kept women from achieving equality in the workplace and not women themselves. "I think the statistics are particularly telling," she said, quoting the fact that at the time 2 percent of the U.S. Senate was made up of women, 11 percent of the population of college and university presidents were women, 2.6 percent of lawyers were women, and 6 percent of doctors were women. "These figures are indicative of the fact that women are not making the breakthroughs in important positions," she explained. "No woman has a high policy-making position in the State Department." The last statistic was particularly discomfiting, she said, because "the question of war and peace is too important to be left just to men."

The role of women as activists and peacemakers was one that Frederick stressed throughout much of her career. To her the idea that women should hold top positions in public affairs and culture was not just one of simple fairness; she thought it was vital for world peace. At a YWCA awards dinner in 1969, for instance, she chided the audience about what she viewed as the dangerous complacence of some women: "I suppose there will always be women who argue that it is not possible to run a home and the world, too. This may be true for some women, but unless more women begin trying to run the world there may not be homes to run some day. Too many women . . . have been willing to abstain from involvement in the search for ways to ease human afflictions. Such women have been content to remain in a comfortable niche assigned to them by luck and tradition. They are satisfied with being admitted no-nothings and show little interest in breaking through the barriers of discrimination to help turn the world around."

The *Today* show held a special broadcast on August 26, 1970, to commemorate the fiftieth anniversary of the Nineteenth Amendment, which gave women the vote. The show was hosted only by women—correspondents Frederick, Aline Saarinen, and Barbara Walters. Hugh Downs, Frank Blair, and Joe Garagiola were given the day off. The show did not bang the drum for women and simply praise them for achievements but instead emphasized the slow pace of equality. Frederick interviewed National League of Women Voters president Lucy Wilson Benson, who noted that women are not as active politically as they should be. Dickerson, from Washington, provided two conflicting viewpoints. She talked to a male physician who said that policy decisions should not be left to women ("I'm not for the irrational libbers who want to lure the housewife away from the home," he said) and also to a female physician who disagreed with the contention that "women have a fatal flaw that assigns them to the home or nursery."

Frederick indicated on the show that while women had made strides in affecting world events, they had a long way to go. She repeated her oft-made claim that women, astonishingly, had had few roles in shaping the course of history. "After thousands of years, only three women today really rule—Prime Minister [Golda] Meir of Israel, Prime Minister [Indira] Gandhi of India and Prime Minister [Sirimavo] Bandaranaike of Ceylon," she said. "And who have been the so-called peacemakers of our time? No women participated in the negotiations following the two World Wars and the Korean conflict—and no woman has been designated to take part in the propaganda give-and-take that passes for peace talks over Vietnam . . . and the fluttering efforts to try to bring Israel and the Arab states to the conference table." No woman had ever been a secretary of state, she continued, and no woman had ever been named an undersecretary-general of the United Nations. Furthermore, she pointed out, only one woman— Agda Rossel of Sweden—had served as a permanent representative to the United Nations, and only two women had been elected president of the General Assembly, Madame Vijaya Lakshmi Pandit of India and Angie Brooks of Liberia. Frederick ended her report by asserting that "the world does not seem to be making much progress toward peace when it spends two hundred billion dollars ever year on arms to kill people . . . Qualified women should be admitted to the sanctum where the decisions are made about war and peace. Women are a necessary to the creation of life. They should have some say in the saving of it."

When Frederick first became interested in journalism in the 1940s, a series of profiles she wrote of the wives of diplomats jump-started her career. Interestingly, she did not often do "wife" stories as she became better known in broadcasting, although occasionally she interviewed the wives of top world figures. An interview with Khrushchev's wife, Nina, in 1963, which aired on an NBC radio show called *Emphasis*, indicated that she and Frederick may have been kindred souls when it came to the belief that women had superior negotiating skills. "Nina believes that 'war must be banned forever from the life of mankind' and we [women] are the ones to do this," Frederick said in the broadcast. Mrs. Khrushchev believed that meetings between "ordinary people"—such as mothers—could be the most efficient means of bringing countries closer and building trust,

Frederick explained. Such meetings could take place over a cup of tea or in a nursery. Frederick certainly humanized Mrs. Khrushchev in the report, noting that the Russian first lady had received many letters from American women who were frightened about the possibility of another major war. "'I can easily understand you,' Mrs. Khrushchev writes [to these women]. 'As a mother and grandmother, I value peace as much as you do . . . You American people must try to understand us. The Soviet people have no need of war. We do not threaten anyone and have no intention of doing so.'"

In the mid-1960s Frederick decided to compile a book of profiles of the wives of world leaders. *Ten First Ladies of the World*, published in 1967 by Meredith Press, focused on the wives of nine world leaders, including Yvonne de Gaulle, Lady Bird Johnson, Imelda Marcos, Tahia Nasser, and Mme Thant. Indian prime minister Indira Gandhi was also profiled. It is interesting and odd that Frederick decided to write this; over the years she had been asked periodically to write books, either about herself, about the United Nations, or about world events, but she always declined the offers, citing a hectic work schedule as the reason. She did, however, occasionally write essays or book reviews for general interest magazines. The contract she entered into with Meredith gave her about fourteen months to write the eighty-thousand–word book—it was due to the publisher by January 1, 1966, with the contract dated October 2, 1964. (The fact that the book was published in 1967 indicates that it might have come to the publisher after January 1966.)

Although there is no evidence that Frederick needed the money, she may have agreed to write the book in part for extra cash. She would receive 10 percent of the profits for all copies sold up to five thousand; 12.5 percent for all copies from five to ten thousand; and 15 percent for more than ten thousand copies sold. It is unknown how many were sold. In the introduction Frederick explained that she had decided to write the book in part to shed light on how these women had influenced their powerful husbands: "It is hoped to illuminate through their wives characteristics of influential leaders that have escaped notice in the usual biographies of these men," she wrote. The 134-page book is small, but it features interviews with each woman and background about her family and how she came to marry a powerful man. For the most part it was reviewed well, although a few reviews considered it bland; *Library Journal*, in one summary, called it "brief, up to date and readable" and in another summary characterized it as "readable and discerning" (this capsulized review suggested it as a possible Young Adult book). The *Los Angeles Examiner* called it "worth double the price." The *Raleigh News and Observer* said that Frederick had portrayed the women "with the terseness of the knowledgeable journalist."

But the *Providence Journal* reviewer wrote that while those who liked biography would find it "a well-prepared ten-course meal," others would find it "bland if not altogether indigestible." And the *Tampa Tribune* reviewer wrote that while Frederick had the proper background to write the book, she seemed to lack a warm personal interaction with many of her subjects and relied too much on research for combining collected material. "While she has done a commendable job, someone expects more," the review said.

In 1970 Frederick was asked by an interviewer from her alma mater, American University, if she felt she had helped pave the way for other women broadcasters and if she believed other female broadcasters had finally achieved equality with their male counterparts. "I do hope I cleared some way for them," she replied. "I do think they have somewhat of an easier time in that they're considered for . . . positions without the hurdle of being a woman. But I still feel women don't have full equality in this profession and that it's still more difficult for a woman to get a job and to advance than it is for men." It would be more than ten years after that interview that women in broadcasting would begin to achieve parity with men when it came to jobs and assignments. By that time Frederick would return to her roots in radio.

11 *Good News, Bad News, and Agnews*

> I never want to hear her again as I don't think she could be trusted
> to give the straight news or a balanced report.
>
> HOWARD MCCAULEY, in a letter complaining about Frederick's
> commencement speech at his daughter's graduation, June 9, 1972

The late 1960s were in some ways the best of times and the worst of times
for NBC's news division. Television had by this time become a permanent
part of the fabric of American society—more than six hundred commercial
stations served more than fifty-seven million homes, compared to a mere
ninety-two stations serving four million homes just twenty years earlier.
Color television was becoming the norm in many households, and studies showed Americans had their television sets turned on an average of
six hours a day. Television's coming of age of course benefited all three
networks. But several factors, including the retirement of one of its most
popular newscasters, led to a decline in NBC's ratings.

Frederick, meanwhile, watched in dismay as the power and prestige of
the United Nations continued to diminish in the eyes of the public and the
U.S. government. She held the Nixon administration partially responsible,
although she had witnessed the organization's steep decline earlier in the
decade. But Frederick would consider 1969 a banner year personally: on
March 31 she married Charles Robbins, a former newspaper editor and
founder and president of the Atomic Industrial Forum, a consortium that
promoted the peaceful use of nuclear power. Frederick was sixty-one on
her wedding day on the island of Granada, and she was surrounded by
her close friends and some family. As a journalist, Frederick had traveled
widely and had met many of the most powerful people in the world. But

her wedding was something she had waited for her entire life. She changed her name to Pauline Frederick Robbins on that day, although she remained Pauline Frederick on the air.

Things were not so rosy for her professionally, however. She was four years away from NBC's mandatory retirement age, and she had no desire to leave her job. And she knew that big changes at NBC could affect her. Chet Huntley—who of course was one half of the enormously successful team that anchored NBC's evening newscast—would retire from NBC in July 1970, and the network faced the task of naming a replacement for the popular anchorman and rebranding the immensely popular *Huntley-Brinkley Report*. The retirement of Huntley represented a turning point for NBC, and not simply because Huntley was a much-watched and popular anchorman. In her memoir NBC correspondent Liz Trotta noted that because of what she called his "easy and commanding" personality, Huntley was an informal leader at NBC News, and his departure triggered an intangible shift in the atmosphere there. Immediately after his retirement, NBC executives renamed the evening news broadcast the NBC *Nightly News* and initially selected a trio of broadcasters—David Brinkley, Frank McGee, and John Chancellor—to anchor it. But that tactic did not restore the program to its previous dominance.

More damaging to NBC's ratings, however, was the tremendous rise in popularity by the late 1960s of Walter Cronkite of CBS and a resulting emphasis by that network to invest more money into its news gathering operation; and the emergence of ABC, finally, as a true player in network news competition. Harry Reasoner, of CBS's popular *Sixty Minutes* program, who was once touted as Cronkite's possible replacement, left that network in 1970 to anchor ABC's evening news show. His arrival breathed new life into ABC's news-gathering operation, which since its inception had invested only a fraction of the money, time, and effort its two competitors had. While ABC News did not emerge immediately from its third-place slot in the ratings, its viewership rose dramatically shortly after Reasoner became anchor there. The networks were now in a three-horse race when it came to news ratings—and after Huntley left, CBS News outpaced NBC in that competition. Cronkite and folksy correspondent Charles Kuralt, with his *On the Road* show, helped propel that network to the number one spot.

But perhaps the biggest change for the networks in the early 1970s was one that was intangible: the relationship between these large news gathering organizations and the federal government, a changing relationship that was precipitated by the Vietnam War and, later, the Watergate scandal. From a practical point of view the war made it possible for the news divisions to get extra money from the networks for the manpower and technology required to cover the conflict, according to former NBC president Reuven Frank, who said years later that the Vietnam War "changed how we covered news." Newly designed satellite and recording technology existed before the war, he said, but it was not used successfully on a regular basis until Vietnam.

But the war forced news managers to rethink more than just how to use the new technology effectively. That conflict imposed a change on the relationship between news personnel and the government. According to journalist Barbara Matusow, until Vietnam the press had been a reliable cheerleader for the government, even on such presumably divisive issues as the Cuban Missile Crisis. "Reporters referred to 'the administration,' 'the government,' and 'we' (meaning 'our side') interchangeably," Matusow wrote. The combination of a lack of an endgame plan for Vietnam and the emergence of a new breed of young iconoclastic reporters led to a deep distrust between the media and the government during the Vietnam War. In addition, she noted, this group of young reporters refused to close their eyes to what they believed were lies by government officials about many aspects of the war, including the number of deaths resulting from it.

Cronkite, as anchorman, had an enormous impact on the public's view of the war. In a now-famous February 27, 1968, broadcast, he said that after returning from a recent trip to Vietnam, he was convinced that a U.S. victory there was impossible: "It seems now more certain than ever that the bloody experience of Vietnam is to end in a stalemate." As Cronkite biographer Douglas Brinkley noted, the public reaction to his comments were "seismic." Liz Trotta, the first woman to cover combat activities in Vietnam, acknowledged that Cronkite's comments that evening represented a turning point in American journalism because they "plant[ed] a seed" of partiality. "Cronkite, in those days in the middle of really the hottest story of our generation, did nudge that line of objectivity," she said.

"That was a real first, especially for a broadcaster." Cronkite's comments horrified and dismayed Johnson administration officials. Gen. William Westmoreland was "disgusted" with Cronkite and CBS, according to Brinkley, and soon after the broadcast, Johnson was overheard to have made the legendary comment, "If I've lost Cronkite, I've lost the country." Johnson realized that television did, indeed, bring the horrors of the war home to viewers in a way other media never had—it was, as *TV Guide* labeled it, "the living-room war."

Cronkite's comments and the resulting reaction by other U.S media outlets may have also contributed to the deepening of the divide between Americans who supported the war and those who opposed it. Cronkite's words came at a time of societal discontent, when government officials were keeping a particularly close eye on what journalists were writing and airing. An apparently beleaguered Julian Goodman, who had risen to NBC president by 1969, gave a best-of-times-worst-of-times speech to a group of television executives and broadcasters in Omaha in early 1969, pointing out that media messengers should not be blamed in times of social and political unrest. Goodman's viewership statistics indicated sharp growth, but he also indicated that he feared that a divided citizenry and social unrest could lead to increased regulation of the media. "Television has reported the national unrest because it is our function and our obligation to do so," he said. But because much of what Americans see on the news is disturbing and because television now brings viewers into close contact with those events, "the medium is too often associated with the disagreeable news it transmits, and too often held accountable, in some strange way, for the events it reports." He added, "It is dangerous for any of us to conclude that the serious problems our nation faces would recede if television stopped showing or talking about them."

Throughout his long journalistic career Goodman was a tireless proponent of First Amendment rights and the right of the press to do its job with as little government regulation as possible. Goodman and other top broadcasting executives had long been fighting a battle over their opposition to the Fairness Doctrine, a set of rules imposed by the Federal Communications Commission (FCC) that required broadcasters to air a minimum amount of public affairs television spots and offer contrasting viewpoints when controversial issues were discussed. Goodman, CBS president Richard Salant, and other top broadcasting executives were unified in their opposition to the Fairness Doctrine, which was eventually abolished in 1989, claiming that it introduced government into the process of journalism and pointing out that no similar guidelines had applied to the print media. But apparently Goodman and others saw that their coverage of an unpopular war, civil disobedience, and unrest in the streets might lead to some further retaliatory FCC "regulation."

Vice President Spiro T. Agnew's famous tirade against the press in the fall of 1970—in which he called its members "an effete corps of impudent snobs" who engaged in "nattering nabobs of negativism"—chilled further an already cold relationship between President Nixon and members of the media. During the Watergate scandal the relationship between Nixon and the press reached "radioactive levels," as Brinkley put it. Much of Nixon's ire was directed at the *Washington Post*, which broke the story, and CBS, which broadcast it extensively, thus legitimizing it. Johnson's relationship with the networks was more nuanced and in some ways more complex. According to Brinkley, Johnson rather liked Cronkite for the first few years of his presidency, until their relationship also soured. The relationship between Johnson and NBC appears to have been just as complicated. Shortly before Goodman's retirement in 1979, he was asked in an interview if Johnson had ever conducted any "arm-twisting" to manipulate coverage. He replied that Johnson had "a long arm around everyone's shoulder, and Lyndon was very tender and sensitive about what happened on the air," adding, "But he always stopped short of doing anything that . . . smacked of intimidation." Longtime NBC correspondent John Chancellor, who served as political reporter and anchorman, believed that it was Johnson's large and controlling personality that alienated reporters. "He overwhelmed the press. He was guilty of very serious overkill in his relation with reporters," Chancellor said.

When it came to influencing media coverage, Nixon may have been more subtle than his predecessor in the Oval Office. Johnson was more direct—he was not above spontaneously calling top news executives on the telephone to lodge complaints about coverage, which is what he did on the morning of June 21, 1967, after Frederick aired what Johnson labeled an erroneous report about a meeting in New York between Johnson and Alexei Kosygin, who was then Soviet chairman (along with Leonid Brezhnev). Such a meeting was never arranged, Johnson said. In a ten-minute call to Goodman, Johnson expressed outrage on two fronts: that Kosygin had apparently violated protocol by traveling to the United States without notifying the White House of the trip; and that Frederick would rely on an anonymous source to report erroneously that the Soviet official was meeting with Johnson in New York, rather than confirming the information with the White House press office. Johnson began the call by stating that he hoped Goodman would keep the call confidential, a pledge Goodman kept. "We're just getting all kinds of pressure on the morning shows with Pauline and Frank Blair stating emphatically that we are having a meeting with Mr. Kosygin," Johnson said. He then chastised NBC for relying on unnamed sources at the Carlisle Hotel: "Now there's no sense in quoting some drunk or some diplomat or somebody else, when you can get it direct from the horse's mouth, if you'll ask for it. And I'll guarantee not to mislead you. I'll guarantee to tell you the facts." Goodman said very little during the call, other than to agree that the exchange would be off the record and to offer that Frederick's sources were frequently "the Poles" (Polish diplomats at the UN), but he told the president that he did not know who the source was for this story. Johnson reminded Goodman that it was not protocol for the president to travel to New York to meet with a visiting world leader—that person would travel to Washington, he said, although he would have invited Kosygin to the White House if the Soviets had informed him of the visit.

Johnson was candid with Goodman about his fear that the report made him look bad in the eyes of the public. "And they'll say 'well, Johnson's petulant' or 'he's irritable' or 'he's moody' or something else. That's what happens, it's this damn press credibility. It's not our credibility." Although Goodman said that he wanted to make sure NBC reported the story accurately, he did assure Johnson that Frederick had "pretty good sources," adding, "She is not as you know irresponsible." Johnson agreed, saying, "All I want is a correction of the facts." Near the end of the conversation, however, Johnson became vaguely intimidating, referring to himself in the third person and telling Goodman: "I don't think you have a license to tell what the president's going to do when the president pays a man around the clock to answer you and they don't even ask him. And they quote some irresponsible diplomat or some hotel fella." He then told Goodman that he wanted a correction. "I want a denial that just says the chairman [Kosygin] has not been able to accept the invitation of the president to come to Washington, to Camp David, to Philadelphia or any other mutually agreeable place; it is likely Secretary [of State Dean] Rusk will see him at the United Nations. Period." Goodman said he understood his point and that the network would "straighten it out." (Johnson clearly had no knowledge of a complimentary memo Goodman had sent Frederick several days earlier, praising her for her coverage of the UN's role in the Mideast crisis and the Kosygin story.)

This incident—which revolved around the rulers of the world's two superpowers getting into an argument about who would visit whom—is emblematic of the type of Cold War skirmishes that Frederick and others covered. And it shows how reporters frequently were caught in the middle of the warring factions. Nobody in the United States seemed to know the reason Kosygin had flown to New York, but Johnson and others speculated that the reason was to inform the UN that the Soviets backed the Arabs in the ongoing Arab-Israeli war. In the end Johnson and Kosygin did arrange a meeting—in a venue that was supposedly halfway between New York and Washington: in Glassboro, New Jersey, at the home of the president of Glassboro State College. They had no fixed agenda but spoke for five hours about Vietnam, the Mideast war, and arms control, emerging arm in arm and smiling. The brouhaha—which made the front page of the *New York Times* and many other newspapers for nearly a week—generated a lot of sound and fury but signified very little actual progress.

The nature of Frederick's relationship with Johnson by the time he made that call to Goodman is unknown. But three years earlier he apparently had attempted to curry favor with her, just two months after he assumed office. In a long memo to her boss, William McAndrew, with a copy to Goodman, Frederick described how Johnson and the first lady had spent time with her after a White House luncheon held for Maryon Pearson, the wife of Canadian prime minister Lester Pearson. In addition to Frederick, thirty women attended the luncheon, including the wives of top administration officials such as Secretary of State Dean Rusk, Undersecretary of State George Ball, Senator Abe Ribicoff of Connecticut, and wives of other congressmen and State Department officials. Frederick had a brief and joking conversation with Johnson before the lunch, she told McAndrew. But as the gathering was breaking up, Liz Carpenter, the first lady's press secretary, suggested she stay to accompany Mrs. Johnson on a tour of the White House living quarters. Frederick and a Canadian Broadcast Corporation reporter were then given a private tour by Mrs. Johnson and had coffee with her. The president soon joined them—"by this time he was calling me Pauline," she said—and invited them to the White House Treaty Room for a formal signing of a treaty establishing a commission of the joint administration of Campobello Park in Canada. After the signing, he gave Frederick one of the pens. "When the ceremony was over, he warmly shook my hand and expressed pleasure over my coming to the White House," she told McAndrew.

As the Vietnam War escalated in the late 1960s, so did the resulting cold war between the press and the U.S. government. According to transcripts of speeches and NBC news releases summarizing them, Goodman's speeches warning of government interference in the media intensified. By the time President Johnson announced in 1968 that he would not seek reelection, paving the way for the election of Richard Nixon, the government and the press had developed a sharp and mutual distrust of each other, and Cronkite's legendary broadcast announcing his belief to Americans that the war was unwinnable opened up more floodgates. Now many journalists, including Frederick, pulled no punches when voicing their opinions about what they felt was the brutality and futility of the war, blurring the always vague line between subjective reporting and interpretation.

Frederick's comments about the war became increasingly harsh in the lectures she delivered across the country. By the 1970s her criticism of the war had seeped into all of her lectures, no matter the audience she addressed. She slammed the war to Rotarians, doctors, educators, and graduating college seniors, quoting specific figures about the damage bombing can do and had done to innocent citizens in Southeast Asia and the tremendous cost of the war in dollars for Americans. She relived for audiences her time in post–World War II Europe twenty-five years earlier, painting graphic verbal pictures of the death and devastation she had witnessed as a young reporter and predicting that the next global war would most certainly be the last one for civilization. Before 1967, when Frederick addressed the topic of war in her speeches, it was usually in the context of the role, or lack thereof, of the UN in preventing war. The UN was created "for mature nations presumably ready to leave behind a childhood of violence and unite their adult strength in saving the world from war," she said in July 1965 to an audience at Ohio University. "Instead, the UN is often a façade in which the old self-interest game goes on as usual." Six months later, at a town hall meeting in Fresno, California, titled "The United Nations in a World of Conflict," her rhetoric became bolder and more direct. "The most extensive and destructive power competition . . . emerged after World War II," she said. "When the guns of that holocaust were silenced, the allies that had crushed Nazism and Fascism split into two bitter camps. The proponents of communism and democracy squared off against one another. Allies became enemies and enemies, allies. [Now] a nuclear confrontation could leave 100 million Americans and 100 million Russians dead."

Fifteen months later Frederick's lectures contained unequivocal antiwar themes. In a speech in Houston in April 1967, for instance, she said the Vietnam War was distinctly different from other wars fought by Americans—in a terrible way: "The United States is bombing a country that never attacked the United States, that never declared war on the United States. Nor has the United States ever declared war against North Vietnam." Furthermore, "success" in Vietnam was being measured by deaths, rather than property claimed. "In more modern wars, progress was measured by land taken," she said, adding that the Vietcong still held more than half the territory of South Vietnam despite the continual bombing. What troubled Frederick the most was the number of civilian casualties in both North and South Vietnam and Americans' disinterest in the civilians injured or killed in North Vietnam: "The civilian casualties are regrettable, we hear, as we digest the body count of the Viet Cong with our martinis and cornflakes. The little innocent people just would not get out of the way of those 700-pound bombs dropped from thousands of feet above them . . . The question, for those of us who feel some responsibility to humanity, is how to spare people such hell . . . We must ask, why is there a war in Vietnam, 10,000 miles from the shores of the richest, most civilized, most powerful nation on the earth when the United States and the Soviet Union and China took a pledge twenty-two years ago to save the world from war?"

Using body counts as a measure of victory in war deeply troubled Frederick, and she spoke of it often. In a speech at the Westchester Country Club in New York, for instance, she related an anecdote about a lieutenant who was accused of killing a Vietnamese civilian. He said at his pretrial hearing that he kept a record on the wall of his room of the number of kills by his platoon, noting that he was proud that his platoon had more kills than any other. This numbness about, and even delight in, death and destruction had spread to Americans at home, Frederick said.

The violence and apparent senselessness of the war were not the only things that bothered Frederick—she also discussed the tremendous cost of the war in dollars. And she may have found a sympathetic audience at a Savings Bond Luncheon in New York in 1970, during which she offered a detailed account of the cost of war. The amount spent for defense and war around the world equaled fifty-six dollars for every person on the planet. The United States was spending three million dollars an hour to make war in Vietnam, Laos, and Cambodia in the costliest war in American history. One had to wonder if officials at RCA, then the parent company of NBC, found Frederick's comments about the cost of the war interesting. RCA at the time was one of the nation's biggest defense contractors. She apparently never mentioned her employer's indirect relationship to the war, although Frederick usually did take pains to adapt her speeches to her audiences. Sometimes that adaptation took an ironic twist. In 1978, for instance, addressing an audience of the Iowa Veterinary Medical Association, in Des Moines, she told an apocryphal anecdote about former Nixon advisor Henry Kissinger. He had been hired, so the joke went, to run the Tel Aviv Zoo and received national attention soon after he assumed that post. He had a lion and a lamb lying together in peace—for the first time in history. People had come from far and wide to witness this phenomenon, when a zoo aide finally made a confession. "It's the darndest thing," he said. "We have to put a new lamb in that cage every morning."

It took only a few years before Frederick got personal about the Nixon administration's role in the Vietnam War and its disdain of the UN. In one 1971 speech she related an anecdote she believed illustrated the president's disregard for the UN. When that organization held its gala twenty-fifth anniversary celebration in San Francisco in June 1970, Nixon, who was invited, was a no-show, even though he was on the West Coast in San Clemente at the time. Four months later, at festivities in New York, he made a short, last-minute trip to the United Nations to address the General Assembly, only to tell its members that competition between the United States and the Soviet Union could ultimately lead to peace in Vietnam—not any activity by the UN. Adding insult to injury, on the last day of the event chiefs of state from around the world were celebrating in New York, as they had traditionally done to commemorate the anniversary of the organization, when Nixon unexpectedly invited them to a special White House dinner the next evening. For political expediency most accepted the invitation, thus ruining what had been a decades-long celebratory custom.

Like other journalists, Frederick was appalled by the Nixon administration's charge that the news media was composed of the liberal elite. In 1971, a year after Spiro Agnew's famous "nattering nabobs of negativism" speech, Frederick was still talking about it. As she received the Carr Van Anda journalism award at Ohio University, she noted that "most of us broadcasters would like to report good news . . . There is no joy and little profit in being a permanent Cassandra; however, our job is not to make the news, despite freewheeling charges that that's become our profession when we do not report good news." Frederick said that she as a reporter was aware of the Orwellian rationale used to justify the Vietnam War. "A war is wound down by winding it up," she said. "The way to peace in one country is to invade two other countries." She added, jokingly, that a Soviet diplomat told her he believed there were three kinds of news in the United States: good news, bad news, and Agnews. She corrected him, pointing out that Nixon wanted only two kinds of news: good news and Agnews—the type that benefited the Nixon administration. By 1977—after Frederick had retired from NBC—she described Agnew in starker terms: "Big brother Spiro was looking over the shoulder of every journalist to make sure his reportage of this great American tragedy was the correct one—that is, correct according to the dogma of those paragons of official virtue, Nixon and Agnew."

Frederick was always a practical woman and as such would not indulge in fiery rhetoric about the war or the Nixon administration without a reason—especially to audiences of college students. As she told members of the American Association of Retired Persons (AARP) in 1973, she voiced her opinions to encourage members of the audience to ponder world events—and, she said, her audiences were frequently in the position to make a difference. The AARP members she addressed, for instance, had "attained the privileged position of being able to spend more time on reading and thinking about the issues that confront our nation and our world; it is my hope that you may be prepared to re-examine views that may have been too easily accepted when there was so little time to evaluate them in the rush of daily business or professional activities." She also told the group that a man who heard a recent speech she had given in Indiana told her after her talk that if Jane Fonda, then an antiwar activist, had given the speech he just heard, he would be angry. "But I'll take it from Pauline Frederick," he said. In other words, she felt she could make a difference in part because of her authority as a longtime newswoman.

The possibility of individuals making a difference and helping to change the world was one that Frederick stressed in the many graduation speeches she gave. She repeated her antiwar sentiments, usually to receptive audiences, some of whom spoke to her afterward to voice their agreement. But that was not always the case. A commencement speech she gave in 1972 drew the ire of many in the audience and caused a brouhaha that made its way into the news media. At San Diego State College, Frederick repeated her contention that the United States had no business being in Vietnam, and she quoted the toll of the war in lives and money. Some audience members booed her, and a few others walked out in the middle of the speech. Some wrote letters to university and network officials criticizing her speech. "Your Correspondent, Pauline Frederick, spoiled our daughters [sic] graduation for us and many others, evidenced by those who walked out or boo'd," Howard McCauley of Chula Vista, California, wrote to "the President" of NBC, in a page-long single-spaced letter, with copies to Governor Ronald Reagan, the chancellor of the university, the state superintendent of public instruction, and Frederick. The talk, he wrote, was biased and inappropriate, with its "one-sided discourse on the Vietnam War in which the U.S. was entirely in the wrong . . . She likened us to the Russians taking over the Baltic states . . . we were accused of un-believable destruction, cruelty and wanton killing; she recited the statistics of explosions." Further, he wrote, "I never want to hear her again as I don't think she could be trusted to give the straight news or a balanced report."

Someone else wrote a long letter to Frederick, commenting that on the day of graduation the weather was misty, "but it was nothing compared to the mist or cloud-effect you unleashed on a captive audience." This writer, Stanley Price, a teacher, said he wanted a copy of the speech so that he could use it in class "to illustrate what bias and out of context look like" and to have students challenge her statements. He would have left the talk, he said, if his daughter had not been graduating, and he accused Frederick of being "self-righteous" and partisan. In the two-page, single-spaced letter, Price spoke of World War II and other necessary wars "where people died for the betterment of society and to fight evil." About two dozen letters to the editor—most criticizing but some praising Frederick's speech—appeared in the *Copley Press* and other newspapers over the next few days. Several people wrote Frederick and university officials praising the speech. Mrs. Douglas Barker of La Mesa, the mother of a graduating senior, wrote to "express my deep admiration and respect for the moving message you imparted" to graduating seniors and their parents. "Your words carried a message of universal importance, one that each of us should listen to and digest. You zeroed in on the most distressing issue this country faces, the war."

A few short letters from Frederick found among her papers indicate that she did reply to some of those who criticized her, thanking them for their letters. University officials and the woman who served as Frederick's host also wrote her, thanking her for the talk. The acting president of the university sent her copies of the letters to the editor. "These [letters to the editor] seem to be all the negative fall-out that has appeared in the local press," he wrote in a note. "You can't win them all." Dr. Dorothy

Holman, a faculty member who was chairwoman of the commencement committee, wrote a long and somewhat apologetic letter to Frederick and sent her more press clippings. "Those of us who have lived here for several years are conditioned to the . . . 'right-wing extremists' who are so prevalent from here to L.A.," she said. She added that several people wrote to the university expressing their appreciation for her address and requesting transcripts of it.

It is not known if others who attended Frederick's speeches took offense to her remarks—if so, she did not get or did not retain written correspondence from them. Frederick's niece, Catharine Cole, and her husband, Dan, attended one of Frederick's speeches in 1971 at Barat College in Lake Forest, Illinois, and remember hearing some negative comments from faculty members in the audience, some of whom found her comments about the war "simplistic," Catharine recalled. Frederick lectured so frequently and reached so many audiences that it is unlikely that NBC officials were unaware of her comments about the war. Among Frederick's papers is a four-paragraph response from Harold Queen, NBC's director of corporate communications, to Howard McCauley, one of the parents who criticized her speech in San Diego. Queen said that while NBC can sympathize with the feelings of parents who felt the commencement ceremony was disappointing, "whether or not Pauline Frederick Robbins' speech was appropriate is not for us to comment on." He called her a "distinguished journalist" who had participated in the commencement as a private citizen. "[It] in no way reflected [opinions] of NBC . . . Of course she has views on the Vietnam War and any number of other issues. But as a professional journalist, we can assure you these views are not allowed to color her presentation of the facts." He concluded the letter by saying that "we trust you will appreciate the distinction between Miss Frederick, commencement speaker, and Miss Frederick, NBC correspondent." Queen sent copies of the letter to Goodman and Robert Kasmire, NBC vice president of corporate communications.

But what did NBC think about correspondents stating their opinions when they were not on the job? Nothing among Frederick's papers indicates that she was chastised by NBC management for her appraisal of the U.S. role in the war; perhaps the network felt the way Queen said it did—when correspondents were off the clock, the network had no interest or say in their comments. But Queen may have protested too much—he did repeat twice in a short letter that her comments would not influence her news reports.

Viewers who praised Frederick in letters often said that she explained and interpreted complicated events to them, thus illuminating the news. Her job as a correspondent meant she was more than a stenographer who simply mimicked what sources told her. But the line between personal interpretation and analysis can be vague. By the early 1970s Americans had grown accustomed to *seeing* their news messengers rather than just hearing them on the radio or reading their words in newspapers; this created an intimacy that led many viewers to establish what they considered personal relationships with the reporters. After all, television broadcasters appeared in their living rooms each day, endowing the broadcasters with a power and influence that their print and radio counterparts never had. As popular correspondent Frank McGee observed in 1966, television journalists were not just reporters but were instead stars to many viewers—a phenomenon that seemed to trouble him. Programs such as NBC's *Meet the Press* and others like it were developed to offer viewers analysis and interpretation.

Edward R. Murrow had earned a reputation as one of the most respected and credible journalists in the country when he offered opinionated commentary and went beyond mere recitation of facts. In fact, as television first came of age, some of its correspondents were criticized precisely because they focused too much on presenting "objective" facts with no interpretation. In a 1960 column about network correspondents, a *Dallas Morning News* writer bemoaned the fact that the era's most popular broadcasters lacked Murrow's habit of going beyond mere news reporting. (But the writer did say that Frederick, NBC's David Brinkley and Joseph Harsch, and Eric Sevareid and Howard K. Smith of CBS might effectively offer commentary if the networks gave them a venue to do so.) "An analyst is the rarest of the TV news birds, and some say—a fast dying breed," the writer said. "Certainly television does not provide a gamut of comment like in the good old days of radio when, with a flick of the dial, one could hear and mull over pundit after pundit." She also wrote that the public might not even want informed commentary because "it's a strain on the viewee and viewer to probe and place in perspective events of the day." In her memoir Marlene Sanders agreed that radio correspondents were more likely than their television counterparts to express their opinions about current events. Television news correspondents were prohibited from taking public positions on controversial issues, she said, to avoid the appearance of bias. "There is something about television that gives opinion more weight than a comparable statement on radio," she wrote. "Networks are skittish about antagonizing large segments of the population, and a strong opinion on almost everything is bound to have that effect."

NBC officials were clearly skittish about its correspondents venturing into the area of opinion during the volatile 1960s. In a speech to the Radio and Television News Directors Association at Columbia University in 1966, Goodman addressed the issue of objective reporting and interpretation, noting that NBC allowed and even encouraged its news correspondents, with their "experience and responsibility," to "go beyond the immediate news of the day to explain it, to put forth related information which could otherwise be ignored, to evaluate what is going on, not in the sense of exhortation or the pleading of personal opinion, but so that the audience can get something more than the uncritical regurgitation of the official handout."

As Frederick neared NBC's mandatory retirement age of sixty-five, the amount of time she was seen on the air had already begun to decline. In 1972, shortly before the war ended, she was sixty-four; whether her diminished stature at NBC was a function of her age, her comments about the war, the result of a changing landscaping overall in television news, or other factors is unknown. At least one veteran former newscaster who worked in network news in the 1970s believed it was unlikely that her anti-war comments would have alienated NBC officials, and another claimed that NBC correspondents were indeed encouraged to offer analysis of news events. "I can't conceive of [network executives] getting angry at her," said Richard Valeriani, a White House and diplomatic correspondent for NBC in the 1960s and 1970s. "Being a network correspondent in the 1960s was a big deal . . . She was unique. They were delighted to have her." Further, he said, the working atmosphere at NBC was more laid-back than the working environment at its chief competitor of that era, CBS: "It was much more competitive at CBS," he said. "I never got that sense of competition [among its own correspondents] at NBC." Valeriani said that top NBC officials, including Goodman, respected their correspondents and were "protective about them from outside sources." He also pointed out that others, including Cronkite, had also spoken against the war.

In her memoir Liz Trotta corroborated Valeriani's views, explaining that the news divisions of the two networks had specific reputations in the 1960s: CBS was the "producer's" network and NBC the "correspondent's network"; NBC, under the direction of Robert Kintner and Bill McAndrew, valued its correspondents. "Bill McAndrew is so proud of his correspondents you'd have to pee on his desk to get fired," she wrote. Trotta also noted that NBC in the 1960s was known as the "gentleman" of the three networks, "a place where people didn't throw tantrums, as did their unpolished brethren over at CBS or the funny folk with the almost-news department at ABC."

Garrick Utley, a former NBC correspondent, anchorman, and *Meet the Press* moderator who covered the Vietnam War, said that correspondents were not permitted to make what he called "moral values" about the war, but they could offer analysis. "We would get back from Vietnam and say things that were critical," he said. "We [the United States] had a right to be there, but I didn't think we were going to be successful. I had a right to say that. We trapped ourselves in Vietnam. So that was our analysis." Utley said a line existed between claiming the war was unjust or saying the United States had no right to be there—which were moral values—and saying the war probably would not be won.

During an interview in *TV Guide* in 1966, NBC correspondent Frank McGee made reference to that line between analysis and personal opinion. The *TV Guide* profile of McGee referred to comments he had made at the end of an NBC special about the war called "Vietnam: December, 1965." After an hour of impartiality, the story said, McGee summed up his feelings about the war. He said that the nation was mature enough to be spared "the doubtful arguments" and instead be told the truth about "why this sacrifice of life and treasure is vital to its survival." If the reasons for the sacrifice are not there, the United States should "retire with honor from untenable positions." Peter Benchley, who wrote the *TV Guide* story, said NBC tried to gloss over the fact that McGee had delivered an opinion, which is rare for a network correspondent. McGee said that his comments were responsible, explaining that "television must put things into their proper context and express a point of view . . . We have a voice, a responsibility."

Marriage apparently did not mellow Frederick. By 1969, the year of her wedding, her rhetoric had intensified considerably. In Robbins she found a kindred spirit: a former advertising executive and then a newsman, he had worked as an editor at the *Wall Street Journal* and was a World War II navy veteran. Frederick said in interviews that she had known him for years but that it had been only a year or so before their marriage that the two grew closer. And indeed, the tone of letters and notes between the two quickly changed from merely courteous to more intimate. A note she typed on NBC stationery in August 1968, for instance, thanked Robbins, apparently for a complimentary note he had written to her. "I do hope the sailing is especially good" and that "the Saratoga race was particularly pleasant." Less than a year later, in May of the next year, she handwrote a note to Charles—to whom she had been married for five weeks—on Highlands Inn stationery from Carmel, California, telling him she had a "good, but lonely" breakfast while she watched the waves "breaking in great white pikes of foam against cliffs and rocks." Before settling down to a typewriter, she wrote, "I just want to let you know how much I love and miss you!!" Two days later, while she was still away, she wrote: "Why do we have to be a continent apart—or even a room apart . . . I'm counting the days and hours until I see you—but they are all much too long. I love, love, love you."

Both Frederick and Robbins were accustomed to living alone. When they married, Robbins had been divorced for more than two decades and had one child, Charles "Dick" Robbins, who was married. (Robbins became a grandfather within a few months of the wedding). The tall, handsome Robbins, who was an avid sailor, had been living in New York City at the Phi Gam Club when he and Frederick married, and he was a much sought-after bachelor, according to his former daughter-in-law, Ann Stevens, who was Dick's wife at the time. While Frederick and her husband shared antiwar sentiments and were no fans of Richard Nixon,

Dick Robbins described his father as "middle-of-the-road-to-left" politically. At their home, when Nixon took office, the two posted a calendar marking off the days until the end of his term.

The wedding of Pauline Frederick and Charles Robbins took place on the secluded island of Granada. The venue was selected at the suggestion of a mutual friend of the couple, a former *London Times* journalist who had retired there. Frederick wanted to keep the wedding small and simple—and like many brides, she found that difficult. Guests included the couple's close friends and relatives, including Dick Robbins, who was best man, and his wife, Ann; Frederick's sister, Kitty Crowding, was the matron of honor. Catharine's husband, Lynn Crowding, who was a minister, officiated at the ceremony at St. George's Church, as did the pastor of St. George's. (The existence of not one but two ministers was ironic, said Cole, because Frederick had wanted a nonreligious wedding ceremony.) Frederick wore a lightly colored, summer-weight, knee-length dress with flowers around the neckline. An organ played a few bars of the traditional wedding march as a prelude to the ceremony, and afterward the pastor's wife sang a hymn—although Frederick had hoped there would be no music at the event. The tropical wedding may not have been as simple as the bride had hoped, but it was beautiful, according to the guests who attended. The couple received congratulatory telegrams and cards from friends and acquaintances around the world, including her NBC colleagues Floyd Kalber ("As long as it doesn't take you out of NBC and the news business, I will give it my sanction") and Barbara Walters ("I learned with such joy of your marriage. I congratulate the very lucky Mr. Robbins and hope that I have the chance very soon to see you and personally express my great happiness for you"), and from UN diplomats from Ethiopia, France, Greece, Iran, and Pakistan.

Within two years after their marriage, however, events worldwide exploded, and Frederick was as busy as she had ever been. The conflict in the Middle East hit a crisis stage, and a special UN envoy, Gunnar Jarring, Sweden's ambassador to the Soviet Union, was called in that summer to help arrange a temporary cease-fire, during which peace talks were held at the United Nations. Later that fall, on September 28, 1970, Frederick covered breaking news that made headlines around the world: Egyptian president Gamal Abdul Nasser had died after suffering a heart attack. Nasser, a popular and moderate leader, had helped modernize Egypt and ruled in an era of great economic growth. Frederick's reports over the days following his death stressed that his passing could threaten the ongoing Mideast peace talks and usher in uncertainty in Egypt. She said that his death "struck the United Nations with shock and uncertainty comparable with that of two similar occasions: the death of Dag Hammarskjöld and President John F. Kennedy." She added that Secretary-General U Thant had called Egypt's loss "incalculable because of the historic part Nasser played in events of the last two decades in the Middle East."

In 1971 U Thant retired, but because the power of the UN had diminished so radically by then, his retirement was not the major news story it might have been fifteen years earlier. Frederick, however, covered it extensively. Throughout his ten-year tenure as secretary-general, she had respected and admired the low-key U Thant, who did not have the charisma and influence of his predecessor, Hammarskjöld, but whom Frederick believed was a man of integrity. She noted that he had directed the UN in some of the most turbulent years of its history: "He has been confronted with some of the major trials of the world organization—the winding up of the UN peacekeeping operation in the Congo, the Cuban Missile Crisis, the 1967 War in the Mideast—and the tragedy that he could do nothing about and which probably came closest to him as an Asian—the Vietnam War." Frederick felt that U Thant understood the role of reporters—in 1970, at the request of UN correspondents, he had appealed for the safety of journalists who worked overseas in war zones after several had been captured, and he was accessible and helpful to reporters. Among Frederick's papers are several warm letters and cards between the two thanking each other for such things as get-well wishes, small gifts, and press receptions.

Robbins and Frederick bought a house overlooking the Saugatuck River in Westport, Connecticut. The house was big—it had five bedrooms and three bathrooms. In a letter to his family Robbins sounded happy to have found a nice home in an upscale and beautiful community. Westport's relatively close proximity to Manhattan—forty-seven miles from the city— was convenient for Frederick, and the home's location on a river pleased Robbins because he could keep a boat near his home. Summer was a slow time at the UN, he said, so the couple had made plans to travel in August to England, Geneva, and Ireland. They were happy for a while, according to a few of their relatives, but their differing hobbies and lifestyles, and later illnesses, would intervene. But as Frederick said in an interview in 1970, she was only too pleased to have the opportunity finally to combine marriage and career: "I think it's wonderful. If I had known I would have done it long, long ago." Marriage was so wonderful, in fact, that meeting her future husband made all the "heartbreak" of her very early days in journalism worth it. "That's the best reward," she said.

If corporate or news officials ever asked her to stop lecturing about Vietnam, Frederick never mentioned it to her niece Catharine. Her aunt had always been against war, Cole explained, but her resistance to U.S. involvement in Vietnam may have been about something other than that war—Vietnam represented Frederick's lost idealism and her lost faith in the UN. "There was a place where these things [conflicts between nations] were going to be worked out, it wasn't happening, and it made her angry," Cole said. Frederick also found her dwindling role at NBC increasingly frustrating. An index of news segments on the NBC *Nightly News* indicates that she had very few stories on that program by 1972. Still, in 1971, when she was sixty-three, she continued to work long days and energetically cover the UN—so energetically, in fact, that on December 4, when she was hurrying to NBC's broadcast booth in the UN, as she had done for twenty years, to report the latest developments on the India-Pakistani conflict, she tripped on a cane on the floor and fell. Frederick quickly gathered iced towels for her leg and was transported via wheelchair to deliver her newscast. Immediately after the broadcast—which she delivered "white as a sheet," one colleague said—she was transported to the Roosevelt Hospital emergency room, where she learned she had a broken kneecap. She had surgery immediately and was told she would remain in the hospital for two weeks and have her leg in a cast for four more. Correspondent Wilson Hall was sent in to cover the UN while she recuperated.

12 *Full Circle*

> It was a privilege to work with you at NBC—and is always a privilege
> to work with a true pro.
>
> NBC correspondent EDWIN NEWMAN to Pauline Frederick, May
> 25, 1977

Because of her fall, Frederick was out of commission for the latter part
of 1971 and the early portion of the next year. But she might have taken
some comfort in the number—and quality—of get-well wishes friends,
colleagues, and diplomats sent to her at Roosevelt Hospital. Some were
joking, but many noted they realized how difficult it would be for her to
sit out covering the UN. "Ouch—fractured knee. I was sorry to hear about
it. If this pace continues, I may fracture something and join you," wrote
George H. W. Bush, who was then the U.S. representative to the UN. "We
miss you and know that despite the change of pace I suspect you miss the
pace here. Holler if I can help you in any way." "What a lousy break, figuratively and literally," Barbara Walters said in a handwritten note. "I hope
your knee heals soon. You will be very much missed." And she received a
joking get-well message from Bruce Munn of United Press International
(UPI), who wrote on behalf of the UN Correspondents Association: "We
hope they have enough spit and chewing gum to put you together for a
well-earned Caribbean holiday from which we are sure you'll return hale
and hearty . . . It is different to hear of some UN personality suffering from
a game leg. There are so many lame brains—both within and without the
international civil service!" Get-well wishes from two top NBC executives
were both humorous and serious in their guess that Frederick would miss
her job: "Next time you are brought to your knees at the UN, you ought to

at least have whiskey on your breath," Richard Wald, NBC vice president, scribbled on network stationery. Network president Julian Goodman was more serious: "I know you miss being active during the current India-Pakistan development, but one thing we can be assured of is that there will be other crises at the UN and if you take good care of yourself, you'll be back quickly to cover them."

After a second knee operation, Frederick returned to the United Nations beat in 1972, but her role at NBC was diminished. (And she would later say that it took two full years for her leg to heal.) She did little if any reporting for the *Nightly News*, although her reports continued to air on *Today*, and she remained a periodic panelist on *Meet the Press*. Less time on the air, however, did not translate into fewer awards—Frederick kept receiving them, once again living up to her childhood nickname Polly the Prizewinner. In 1971 she was named by *Harper's Bazaar* magazine as one of the "100 Women in Touch with Our Times." And her home state honored her: she received a "Famous Sons and Daughters of Pennsylvania" award along with golfer Arnold Palmer; artist Andrew Wyeth; scientist Jonas Salk; opera singer Marian Anderson; labor leader George W. Taylor; Scott Paper Company chairman Thomas Macabe; and John C. Warner, president emeritus of the Carnegie Institute. She had been honored before in her home state, in 1966, with the Pennsylvania Award for Excellence in Journalism. Completing the list of other awards from the late 1960s and early 1970s were a national YWCA Centennial Medal; a Westchester County Women's Clubs award as Women of the Year in 1968; and awards from individual city organizations, including the Detroit Central Business District Association; the downtown St. Louis, Inc., Outstanding Working Woman Award; the American Association of University Women Woman of the Year Award; and a dozen or so journalism awards from colleges and universities. Notes among her papers indicate that Frederick always sent gracious and personal thank-you notes to her hosts when she traveled to receive these honors.

And she was still a popular lecturer. A 1972 White House memo from Nixon assistant David Gergen speaks to her stature as a respected female journalist. In a memo to Nixon aide Dave Parker, Gergen referred to White House plans for a special dinner President Nixon would host for some of the nation's most prominent women. Gergen noted that the idea for a dinner "never got off the ground," but "it occurs to me that there may still be a number of opportunities when you would want to have prominent women invited to state dinners on an individual basis." He enclosed a list of more than fifty names of women and corresponding categories. Frederick's name was mentioned in reference to her appearance a year earlier as part of a White House Conference on Youth held in Estes Park, Colorado, featuring more than one thousand delegates appointed by the president and nominated by governors. It is not known if Nixon hosted any such dinner or dinners for prominent women, and no evidence exists in Frederick's files to show that she attended one.

While her role at NBC had diminished by 1972, Frederick believed she finally knew what it was like to have it all: a meaningful job and a happy marriage. As she told an interviewer shortly after her marriage, "I always said I would be quite happy to give up my career for a good marriage," adding, "Well, I have the good marriage and the career, too."

The adjustment to marriage may not have been quite as easy as Frederick envisioned. Robbins was an accomplished cook—a talent Frederick never cultivated because she did not have time. At some early point in their marriage, however, the two decided that she should do the cooking, so she attempted to learn. They eventually hired a couple to live in their home and cook for them, according to Robbins's daughter-in-law Ann Stevens. (The couple owned a restaurant and worked there during the day.) One of the biggest wedges in their relationship, however, was one they may have predicted: Charles was an avid sailor and naturally owned a sailboat. ("We sailed in all kinds of weather," Ann Stevens remembered.) It was a hobby his new wife did not share, although she had pledged from the start of their marriage that she would take up sailing. (In the affectionate note she wrote Robbins from California shortly after their marriage, she included, parenthetically, that her NBC colleague Liz Trotta "feels about flying the way I feel about sailing—but she is trying, also.") Married life had to have been an adjustment for both of them. And the home in Westport may have been a blessing and curse. While it gave them a chance to live in a beautiful home in an upscale community, Frederick no longer had the easy access to the United Nations once they gave up her apartment on the East Side of Manhattan, and the house eventually became too difficult for them to maintain. But it did serve its purpose for several years; they entertained there, and Frederick, a dog lover, kept two beloved Yorkshire terriers as pets there after the death of her poodle Sputnik.

By the time she had fully recovered from the knee injury, most of Frederick's broadcasts were limited to the *Today* show. Jim Holton, an NBC producer who often worked with Frederick at the UN, recalled many years later that although she survived several "house cleanings" at NBC, network executives' growing obsession with ratings combined with a trend toward hiring young and very attractive correspondents led to Frederick's marginalization at the network. "She served out her NBC time virtually in exile in her office at the UN, which by then seldom warranted network pickups," he wrote.

Yet Frederick remained a sought-after lecturer, and she was an active member of the American University Alumni Board. In 1973 she agreed to serve as trustee at the university, with the chairman of the trustees assuring her there would be limited activity and only three meetings a year. By this point in her life Frederick had been awarded honorary degrees by twenty colleges and universities—the number would total twenty-three by the end of her life.

By 1973 Frederick could surely read the writing on the wall when it came to her job at NBC. A new breed of younger women—including Jane Pauley, Jessica Savitch, Lesley Stahl, and Barbara Walters—had joined the networks either as anchors or highly visible correspondents. And her age, sixty-five, was considered very old for a broadcast correspondent— especially for a woman. (Stahl, in her memoir, described how she felt old by network standards when she turned forty-two.) Anchor jobs were coveted by many correspondents, but Frederick often said that she never wanted to anchor the news—the job was too stationary and dull, she believed. "I'm a reporter. I've always been a reporter," she said in one interview.

On February 13, 1974, Frederick would turn sixty-six, one year older than the mandatory retirement age at NBC. She remained stately and handsome in appearance and demeanor, according to Holton, who described her as "refined and erudite," adding that even then, "there was no male in the UN press corps who was as good as she was." As the new year dawned, no one at NBC had said a word to her about retiring. Then, one January day, eighteen days before her birthday, she learned from the *New York Times* that she would be retiring from NBC. Frederick had differing versions of the way she learned of her retirement, but it is likely that a friend called her to ask if she had read the story in the paper (she had not). At least once, however, she said she learned about it when the *Times* reporter working on the story called her for confirmation. But one fact remains: the announcement was sudden, and she did not learn about it from NBC. The *Times* story, which was part of a longer story that contained media industry short items, carried the subhead "Pauline Frederick Retires at NBC." The three-paragraph story identified her as "one of the first news personalities in television" and said she had "announced" the retirement. It also noted that she would be replaced by Richard Hunt, who had covered the Mideast for NBC. Interestingly, it quoted an NBC representative as saying that she planned to lecture and write in her retirement. "Before joining NBC—long before the movement for equal opportunity for women—she had been a reporter with the North American Newspaper Alliance," read the last paragraph of the story. "She was also the first woman to be elected president of the United Nations Correspondents Association."

Naturally, Frederick received many congratulatory notes after that item appeared in the *Times*, although it was hardly cause for celebration. Included was a gracious one from President Nixon's press secretary, Ron Ziegler, who said the "whole journalistic community would miss your seasoned observations and articulate reporting." It is unlikely the warm note from Ziegler made its way into the group of Frederick's most cherished possessions. She said much later that the letter—sent unfolded so she could frame it—had a misspelled word: *irreplacable*.

But all the notes were probably cold comfort. For a decade Frederick expressed her hurt and anger about her retirement and the way it was handled. Five years after she retired, however, she did acknowledge that she took comfort in the fact that broadcasting pioneer and CBS executive Frank Stanton also took mandatory retirement at age sixty-five. She greatly admired Stanton, and "if it could happen to him, it could happen to me," she said.

In interviews late in her life Frederick labeled the circumstances of her retirement announcement a low point in her career. But it was probably inevitable. Frederick's role at the network had begun to decline in the late 1960s when her main supporters were gone—Robert Kintner had left the network to work for President Johnson, and William McAndrew had died suddenly. Also, longtime NBC executive Julian Goodman had retired as network president in 1974 to become chairman of the board of NBC. In his roles as news president and later network president, Goodman had established himself as a strong leader and one who respected and appreciated Frederick's talent and strong work ethic. And the environment at NBC was also changing. As Barbara Matusow wrote in her history of the networks, morale was already declining when Herb Schlosser took over as NBC president in 1974, and "indecision reached epic proportions." By the mid-1970s NBC News was second in the ratings, *Today* ratings were "sluggish," and NBC unsuccessfully sought a newsmagazine program to compete with the successful CBS show *Sixty Minutes*. Worse, Matusow wrote, "a lethargy had settled over the organization; the drive that had characterized it in the Kintner era seemed to have vanished. It was Kintner who ignited the fire under NBC News, but the effect of his departure in 1966 was not immediately noticed."

Considering Frederick's newly changed personal situation—her marriage and her new home—her unceremonious departure from NBC would not prove to be as unfortunate as it first appeared. She would soon be given an opportunity that she later referred to as one of the high points in her career.

Frederick continued lecturing during the year after her retirement, and she continued making antiwar comments in speeches and some newspaper interviews. Robbins, head of an organization that promoted the peaceful use of nuclear power, shared his wife's disdain for the war and her dismay at the decline in the clout of the United Nations. The two were particularly chagrined in late 1974 when the United States ambassador to the UN, Nixon appointee John Scali, warned in a speech that U.S. support for the UN would continue to decline if the dominance of the smaller developing nations in that organization continued. Shortly after Scali's address, Frederick and Robbins urged government officials to propose a "Declaration of Interdependence" and suggest Congress appoint a panel like the Continental Congress of 1776 to draft a new declaration. Their request came as the nation was approaching its bicentennial. What they proposed was not simply a call for the nations of the world to hold hands and come together—it was an attempt to change the voting procedures of the UN in a way that would protect the emerging nations yet still placate the superpowers. Earlier that year, in October, Robbins had written President Gerald Ford with the idea. The declaration, he said, could be drawn up by a "prestigious group of eminent citizens" and would "give new life and spirit to the world, and chart a course . . . inspired and unfettered by what had gone before." No response from Ford was found among Frederick's papers.

Frederick and Robbins began a letter writing campaign about the matter to senators later that year in which the two were a bit more specific about their suggestions and goals. In a letter to Stuart Symington of Missouri, for instance, Frederick pointed out that she had followed international events for more than thirty years and was "convinced that the world is at a crossroads insofar as the UN is concerned." The proposal was an attempt to revitalize the UN, make voting rights more equitable and, ultimately, "justify our country, and others of the industrialized nations, to depend more on the UN in international situations." A few of the senators responded, but none made any promises. "I share your concern for the future of the United Nations and I will discuss your suggestions with colleagues," wrote Senator Charles Percy of Illinois. Connecticut senator Lowell Weicker Jr. agreed with Frederick in a letter to her but made no commitment. "We are truly becoming, as Marshall McLuhan has said, 'a global village,'" he wrote. Ditto for Senator Abraham Ribicoff, also of Connecticut, who acknowledged in his response letter that "the oil crisis of last winter was a shock to most Americans, but it awakened in us the recognition that . . . we are dependent on many nations, large and small, across the globe." No evidence exists that the couple's proposals bore fruit. By 1975, however, Frederick would find another way to influence public opinion. She would do it the way she always had—by interpreting events, translating complex ideas, and reporting the news to the public.

Shortly after she started working at NBC in 1953, Frederick received a string of national awards—including the prestigious duPont and Peabody awards. Her boss at the time, NBC president Sylvester "Pat" Weaver, sent her a memo: "Congratulations . . . Have you got them all yet?" A year after she retired, Frederick was still getting awards and was on her way to getting them all. In 1975 she was selected for the Deadline Club's Hall of Fame, an honor given to journalists who had made a "unique and lasting contribution" to journalism. She was in good company; also selected that year were journalism heavyweights Walter Cronkite and Lowell Thomas, both of CBS; Homer Bigart and James Reston of the *New York Times*; Bob Considine of Hearst Headline Service; Wes Gallagher of the Associated Press; Roger Tatarian of United Press International; syndicated business writer Sylvia Porter; and Frederick's former boss Julian Goodman. Also that year, she received an award that must have been close to her heart: she was honored by the United Nations Association, a group of presidents of national organizations such as the League of Women Voters, the American Association of University Professors, and B'nai B'rith, who periodically met with UN representatives.

If Frederick felt she had been put out to pasture by NBC, apparently others did not feel that way. A year after her retirement, when she was lecturing and still visiting the UN to keep up to date on events there, she received a call from a producer at what the *Los Angeles Times* described as the "upstart" network National Public Radio (NPR), asking her if she would help cover a special session of the UN General Assembly. "Next thing I knew, I was part of the staff," she told an interviewer. Frederick, like many others, was not familiar with NPR in 1974; the network had been incorporated in February 1970 by 90 charter stations and set up as a private nonprofit corporation. A year later the popular show *All Things Considered* debuted, and by 1975 NPR had 179 member stations. When Frederick joined the radio network as its international affairs analyst, its audience was growing, and the network was becoming known for its in-depth and innovative broadcasts—particularly of live public affairs events. The year 1977 in particular was a banner year for NPR. Frank Mankiewicz, a former press secretary to Robert F. Kennedy, became its director, and he is credited with raising NPR's profile in Congress and dramatically boosting federal funding for the network—and also for helping to expand its audience from 3.1 million per week when he took over to five million within a few years.

As radio overall was coming of age when Frederick joined that medium in the late 1940s, NPR was beginning to mature when she joined its staff in 1975. And apparently it came in the nick of time, for both Frederick and the network. "I couldn't stand the thought of sitting around in retirement," she told an interviewer. NPR, meanwhile, was seeking someone who had experience and gravitas, according to Bob Zelnick, then manager of national news, who hired Frederick. According to the first contract she signed with NPR, she would serve as an independent contractor and earn a thousand dollars a month plus expenses and train fare for occasional trips from her home in Westport to NPR's Washington DC studios. Josh Darsa, who was head of live events coverage, wrote a long memo to Frederick outlining her duties and telling her that her job would entail contributing to three NPR offerings: the Mid-Day News module, a fifteen- to twenty-minute closed-circuit transmission to member stations, consisting of eight to twelve news spots or actualities (sound bites); *All Things Considered*, which Darsa explained was a "major" ninety-minute public affairs program (thirty minutes on weekends); and occasional special event and live broadcasts. Overall, *All Things Considered* "emphasizes substance in reportage rather than speed," Darsa wrote. Zelnick said he and Darsa assumed Frederick was a seasoned professional when they hired her, and indeed she lived up to that image. "When I think of Pauline Frederick the word pro comes to mind," he said nearly four decades later. But the idea of hiring such an old pro did not necessarily go over well at first with the young NPR staff, Zelnick recalled. "NPR was the epitome of the youthful generation taking over from an older attitude," he said. "To have a sixty-year-old barge in with the reputation of Pauline obviously caused trepidation among the regulars. It seemed to be counter to the direction we were going." Still, Zelnick was not the only news manager who advocated her hiring, he said. Darsa and Zelnick were among the few NPR news managers older than thirty (but not by much), and they thought of her as an institution. "This may be the greatest TV reporter of all time," Darsa told the NPR staff.

And NPR seemed eager to publicize its new correspondent shortly after Frederick started working there in the fall of 1975. "Beginning September 1, that familiar voice saying, 'This is Pauline Frederick at the United Nations' will be heard again," an NPR news release announced. And soon,

Zelnick recalled, Frederick had won everyone over with her professional attitude and her energy. In fact, it was her physical stamina as well as her mental toughness that impressed news managers throughout her career, according to James Holton. When he was her producer at the UN, he had been "unforgettably impressed with . . . her physical fortitude during those all-night Security Council sessions."

At NPR Frederick not only endured; she prevailed. Within a year she received a warm memo from producer Jim Russell telling her that he had been pleased by her "insightful analysis and interviews that have produced the kind of pieces which exemplify the kind of journalism for which *All Things Considered* strives." Throughout her high-profile television career she had intimated that she preferred radio to television because she could provide longer and more in-depth stories over radio. At NPR she had the luxury of time once again. And soon what had started as a part-time job had morphed into much more. The job did require physical stamina—Frederick traveled regularly to New York City from Westport, and at least once a week she took a train to Washington DC to the NPR studios. By May 1976, less than two years after she started working at NPR, she apparently felt her job was no longer a part-time one and appealed to Russell for a pay raise. (Interestingly, throughout much of her career Frederick had suggested that the size of her paycheck was not a major concern to her. While she never admitted that to network officials, she said after she retired that she realized she was probably underpaid. "I doubt my salary ever matched the male reporters, but the funny thing is, that never bothered me," she said in a 1979 interview. "I was always more interested in getting the story, in doing the job.") Frederick reminded Russell that her constant presence at the UN allowed her to talk to delegates and UN officials and, ultimately, get stories. That constant presence also led to in-depth analysis, she said, adding that she realized a pay raise may not come immediately but that "some adjustment would be appreciated and indicate a willingness to be fair . . . I enjoy working with NPR and its staff." Russell increased her monthly retainer from $1,200 to $1,250 and promised to look into further increases when a budget was passed later that year.

Her hiring and success at NPR clearly gave Frederick a boost in confidence—and persuaded her that she was not too old to do a job she had been doing for decades. A letter she wrote to an old friend, however, suggests that she still longed for the good old days. After she had worked for NPR a little less than a year, she wrote to a friend and former NBC colleague Lawrence Spivak, moderator of *Meet the Press*, asking if it was possible for her to once again make appearances on the panel of that show. The letter was newsy and friendly at the beginning, making reference to his wife, Charlotte, but she soon brought up NBC's mandatory retirement age. "I'm pleased . . . that there appears to be no retirement age for you with NBC as there was for me." (Spivak was three years younger than Frederick, so he would have been sixty-three when he received the letter in 1975—two years younger than the mandatory retirement age.) Frederick included a paragraph about her work for NPR and its 175 affiliates and noted that she had recently testified before the U.S. Senate Foreign Relations Committee about U.S policy in the UN. Spivak sent her a response within a week, but it was not promising. He said that he had plans to leave the show and NBC in two months and would serve as a consultant to the network and appear periodically on *Meet the Press*. Spivak's attitude toward his retirement was apparently less harsh than Frederick's about her own: "I will have been on television for 28 years by November and for almost 30 on radio—and frankly I think that that is more than enough . . . I am tired of listening to my own voice." Spivak said he would give her letter to the new producers of the show but doubted they would use a panel member who did not have an affiliation with a newspaper or with NBC.

Still, Frederick was thriving at NPR, and officials there clearly wanted her to stay. In January 1977 she became producer of the weekly *Pauline Frederick and Colleagues*, a half-hour public affairs show that focused on international issues. Her salary for the year became a flat $22,000, a dramatic increase from her previous pay of $1,250 a month—although she received no additional benefits. As part of her contract, she was given four weeks of vacation a year and during lectures would identify herself as an NPR correspondent. Her annual salary increased to $24,000 in 1978 and $26,400 in 1979. The relationship between Frederick and NPR was clearly a symbiotic one: it allowed Frederick to continue doing what she loved to do, and it gave NPR the opportunity to publicize a correspondent who upon her arrival at the network already had many followers. As she had done for decades at NBC, Frederick periodically hosted special events when she traveled for speaking engagements, including, for example, a panel discussion about President Jimmy Carter's role in foreign affairs and an appearance on a panel with Hubert Humphrey. She also participated in several NPR documentaries, including one about the career of Henry Kissinger.

NPR executives had to be pleased that Frederick got several national scoops as part of her reporting for the organization. Comments made to her and during her show were occasionally picked up by the wire services, with credit given to her and NPR. In 1978, for instance, an NPR news release announced that Chaim Herzog, the Israeli representative to the UN, had made news worldwide when he told Frederick and a few other reporters he disagreed with President Carter's recent statement that "peace seems far away." In another national story she generated, Donald B. Sole, South Africa's UN ambassador, announced that his nation would move quickly to improve race relations after elections were held that month and that the nation was "not going to preserve some kind of segregated way of life." But none of these scoops could match the event that put Frederick back on the map as a television broadcaster and beamed her once again into millions of living rooms: the 1976 presidential debate between incumbent president Gerald Ford and Georgia governor Jimmy Carter.

Frederick insisted that no one was more surprised than she when James Karayn, project director for the League of Women Voters–sponsored presidential debates, asked her to moderate the second presidential debate between Ford and Carter. The decision came somewhat late—Frederick had only a few weeks to prepare—but the announcement quickly made national news, in part because she was the first woman to moderate a presidential debate and in part because these three debates were the first to be held since John F. Kennedy and Richard Nixon had debated in 1960. Frederick said afterward that her first reaction upon being asked was that she was not sure she could do it. The announcement generated many congratulatory notes from friends and colleagues as well as telegrams from several special interest groups asking her to include particular questions—odd requests because as moderator she was not permitted to question the debaters. Although she was well prepared, the prospect of moderating a presidential debate was daunting even to the poised and experienced Frederick. She said the following year that she had enjoyed the experience—after it was over. Frederick saw her role primarily as "traffic cop"—"I was supposed to keep things moving and avoid tie-ups and smash-ups." To extend her metaphor, it was one of the debaters and not Frederick who had a smash-up of sorts. A comment made in the debate by President Ford has been discussed for decades since, and many think to this day that it led to his defeat in the election.

If Frederick was nervous on the evening of the debate, she did not show it. She wore a light-blue dress and a string of pearls, noting in an interview that she had selected the color because she felt it would go well with the beige background of the studio. The October 6 debate, held in the Palace of Fine Arts in San Francisco, took place at 9:30 p.m. local time and was to focus primarily on foreign and military issues. It would be televised live by CBS. The panelists were *New York Times* associate editor Max Frankel; Henry Trewhitt, diplomatic correspondent for the *Baltimore Sun*; and Frederick's former NBC colleague Richard Valeriani, that network's diplomatic correspondent. When she first took the microphone to make introductory remarks, Frederick made note of the beautiful setting, observing, as perhaps only Frederick would, that the city had been the venue thirty-one years earlier to the signing of the United Nations charter so the topic of international issues was particularly appropriate. Frederick's traffic cop duties meant that she was to enforce the debate ground rules stating that each candidate had three minutes to answer a panelist's question and his opponent has two minutes to respond if needed. The candidates were not permitted to consult notes, but they could take notes and refer to them.

The debate began innocently enough, with Carter—who called the President "Mr. Ford"—accusing Ford of allowing his advisor Henry Kissinger to conduct foreign policy in a way that "denies there's a Cold War." The first time Ford spoke, he went slightly over his time limit, putting traffic cop Frederick in a quandary. When a special stoplight indicated he had met his time limit, Frederick felt paralyzed. "President Ford was speaking and I was confronted with the awful prospect of having to tell the President of the United States to shut up from coast to coast," she recalled later. Fortunately, Ford finished his thought only a few seconds beyond his limit. But a now-historic gaffe by the president came about twenty-five minutes into the debate, when Ford was responding to a question from Frankel asking him to justify the signing of the Helsinki Accords with the Soviet Union. (The Helsinki Accords were a nonbinding declaration signed by thirty-five nations in an attempt to improve cooperation between the United States and the Soviet Union.) Ford declared that "there is no Soviet domination of Eastern Europe and never will be under a Ford administration." Ford continued talking after this error and eventually moved on to another topic.

Carter, in his rebuttal, did not immediately contradict the president. It was only after Carter's response that Frankel interjected, asking if he had misunderstood Ford's erroneous comment. "Excuse me—did I understand you to say, sir, that the Russians aren't using Eastern Europe for their own sphere of influence and occupying most of the countries there and making sure with their troops that it's a communist zone?" In his response Ford dug himself in deeper, elaborating that he did not think the Romanians or the Poles considered themselves dominated by the Soviets: "Each of those countries is independent, autonomous," he said, and each "has its own territorial integrity and the United States does not concede that those countries are under the domination of the Soviet Union." In his memoir Frankel wrote that he was surprised at Ford's response and deliberately asked him to clarify it in an attempt to get him to backtrack on it. Frankel assumed at first that Ford had unintentionally misspoken. In his rebuttal Carter criticized the Ford administration's overall foreign policy, adding, "I would like to see Mr. Ford convince the Polish-Americans and the Czechoslovakian-Americans and the Hungarian-Americans that those countries don't live under domination." Neither of the other panelists referred to his gaffe, nor did Walter Cronkite in a brief wrap-up of the debate. But the major newspapers exploded with it the next day, most leading their stories with Ford's mistake: "Debate Bolsters Carter as Ford Slips on Soviets," read the *Washington Star* headline of the Jack Germond story. The *New York Times* published two stories: one with an overall wrap-up of the debate and one sidebar about the gaffe: "Ford Denies Moscow

Dominates East Europe; Carter Rebuts Him," the headline read. Shortly after the debate, major polls suggested that the public may have been bothered by the mistake. Ford's poll numbers from the first debate to the second dropped dramatically, according to the *New York Post*.

Frederick, meanwhile, received numerous letters and telegrams of congratulations the next day for her performance, including notes from her NPR bosses Zelnick and Russell. Zelnick's was gently ironic: "Congratulations on a great job last night. You ought to consider a career in broadcast journalism. Love, Bob Zelnick." Russell said station officials "were thrilled . . . that you were selected; beyond that we all felt that your moderating of the debate was superb and a credit to the professional that you are. I look forward to a long and satisfying relationship between you and National Public Radio." She also received notes from several of her childhood friends, including Helen Cowles who lived in Lincoln, Nebraska. "I was so glad to see you, past the magic retirement age," she wrote. "It's terrific that your talent is still recognized." When the debate was finished, Frederick was not: the next day she moderated a panel of foreign policy and defense experts for a debate postmortem at the Washington studios of WETA-FM, a public radio station.

To the networks the three presidential debates were a success, even though the first had been marred by technical difficulties, including a twenty-six-minute audio gap. Although viewership declined slightly after each debate, millions of viewers still watched: the first drew an audience of ninety-four million viewers, the second seventy-four million, and the final fifty-five million. And the debates may have influenced voter behavior at the polls. A story in *Broadcasting* magazine after all three debates quoted officials from both political parties saying that they believed the candidates' debate performances had contributed to Carter's victory.

Frederick said many times that moderating the debate was one of the high points of her career—although she also maintained that the overall format of such debates was not practical. "It's as though we were trying to test [the candidates'] physical, intellectual, and emotional endurance by having them mauled in the public ring by every conceivable instrument of pressure from partisans, press and polls. Is this the way to find a leader in the United States?" she asked in speeches. These comments were emblematic of Frederick's sense of the direction the broadcast media were heading. She had long disdained the focus on superficial appearances that the television camera dictated. By the 1970s, however, she felt that the tail was wagging the dog when it came to television news content: high-profile correspondents and anchors often became the main story, she believed, with the actual story becoming secondary. It was what she referred to friends and relatives as the "Hollywoodization" of news. The phenomenon hindered the democratic process, she believed. After the election of Carter, Frederick said in lectures that she had seen little discussion of serious issues during the campaign: "There is little surprise that with the emphasis on style, form and trivia, issues were frequently overshadowed or ignored." She added that the "blame" is shared by candidates and the media. But NPR was a unique news organization that provided her one last opportunity to report on the news in a way with which she was comfortable.

Frederick and Robbins were firmly ensconced in life in Connecticut by the mid-1970s. The local newspaper periodically interviewed her, and she was a local hero at Connecticut Public Radio. In 1978 officials there wrote a long and laudatory news release about her that it apparently sent to its affiliates. After listing some of the details of her long career—at NBC, "for 21 years . . . her lucid understanding of world affairs caused her reputation to soar"—the press release pulled no punches when it described her unceremonious departure from NBC. "Four years ago, NBC decided to enforce a mandatory retirement rule," the release said. "The network didn't have the nerve to fire her; it announced her retirement in the *New York Times*, where she read about it." The release ended with her advice to women who wanted to enter journalism: focus on a liberal education, then try to get tools for the job by starting at a small station or newspaper. "When the opportunity comes, seize it," she said.

Despite a few setbacks, Frederick and Robbins's life together appeared to be happy for the first decade or so. Although Frederick never did come to enjoy sailing—or cooking for that matter—the two traveled extensively, and he often accompanied her to speaking engagements. Letters she kept also indicate that the couple had an active social life, often attending birthdays and anniversary events for friends and longtime acquaintances.

For her seventieth birthday, on February 13, 1978, Robbins held a surprise birthday brunch for his wife at their home. And it indeed was a surprise, as Robbins worked hard to arrange it without her knowledge. About thirty friends and relatives attended, many from out of state, including Frederick's sister, Kitty, and brother-in-law, Lynn, from Florida; her niece Catharine and her husband, Dan, from Illinois; her stepson, Dick, and his wife, Ann, from Texas. Her NPR colleague Josh Darsa attended, as did her former NBC colleague Edwin Newman. Perhaps taking into account Frederick's ancestral roots, Robbins read from Irish poet Robert Burns's "Saw Ye Bonie Lesley":

> To see her is to love her,
> And love but her for ever;
> For Nature made her what she is,
> And never made anither!

The group also wrote an original verse, taking license, they said, from the Spanish epigram writer Martial:

> Believing what you deserve to hear
> Your birthday as our own to us is dear . . .
> But yours gives most; for ours did only lend
> us to the world; yours gave us a friend.

Frederick received a warm note from Kurt Waldheim, then UN secretary-general, who sent best wishes and noted that "all of us at the United Nations appreciate your efforts for peace and justice by our calm and reasoned analyses which have been heard by so many millions of people over the years, indeed from the beginning of the United Nations . . . We are fortunate to have people of our high purpose and talents who are so dedicated to the cause of peace."

By the late 1970s Frederick's rhetoric in lectures was still as fiery as it had been during the height of the Vietnam War. By this time she focused on the declining status of the United Nations and the growth of the arms race: "The Arms Race or the Human Race?" was the topic of several of her talks. Carter was president at this time, and although he was hardly a hawk when it came to matters of war, Frederick told an audience at the

University of Alabama, for instance, that two men dominated the news at the time: Carter and Pope John Paul II. As Carter was announcing that he approved development of the biggest land-based missile in history, she said, the pope visited Auschwitz and "knelt in memory of the world's greatest obscenity while millions around him repeated 'Peace! Peace! Peace!'" A year earlier she noted in a graduation speech that Carter had just visited the UN for the first time, pledging to cooperate with other nations to curb the arms race and to contribute to an upcoming UN assembly on disarmament. But at the last minute, she said, Carter canceled his appearance there, probably because the United States had just pledged weapons to all sides if there was another Mideast war.

Frederick may have been hurt and angry about her retirement from NBC, but she never directed that anger toward the many women who had joined the network during her last years there or those who joined shortly thereafter. She was gracious in interviews when discussing these women, even though she was candid in her criticism of what she felt was the sensationalizing of broadcast news. Frederick had long been active in the American Women in Radio and Television (AWRT). The New York chapter of that organization named her its Woman of the Year in 1977, a high honor considering the increasing numbers of women who had entered the field by that time. The AWRT honored her as "an inspiration to the women who have followed her." In her acceptance speech Frederick reviewed her history as a correspondent in the 1940s who could get on the air only if she had an exclusive story—otherwise, it was only men who reported the news. And as she had often done in speeches, she reminded the audience that she had been rejected by Edward R. Murrow in her bid for employment at CBS. The AWRT recognition drew congratulatory correspondence from several of her former bosses at NBC. Whether these messages were heartfelt or an opportunity for NBC to salve its conscience will never be known. But the notes were gracious and warm, including two lengthy ones from Julian Goodman, then chairman of NBC, and David C. Adams, vice chairman. Goodman wrote: "In more than three decades of reporting you have helped give the American people a better understanding of international politics and the crucial issues of global peace and security. We are proud that two of those decades were spent with NBC and glad that the public continues to benefit from your insight and experience through your broadcasts on National Public Radio." Adams noted Frederick's role as a broadcast pioneer: "This must be especially gratifying for you, signifying not only your accomplishments as a journalist of the first mark but as a trailblazer for women's careers in broadcasting."

Richard Wald, then president of NBC News, wrote that the organization "could not have made a better choice . . . Your United Nations reporting will always be a shining chapter in NBC News history." Reuven Frank, her former boss at NBC, also wrote her: "There are, I am told, unnumbered thousands now working their way into the news craft who were inspired by you as their role model." She also received a telegram from Carter press secretary Jody Powell, who wrote to the AWRT on behalf of the president: "The President appreciates the remarkable talent, dedication and sensitivity that have made Pauline Frederick so admired by so many as the first lady of broadcasting in the country."

It is impossible to say how Frederick reacted to this congratulatory correspondence from high-ranking executives and the president of the United States. But it is likely she valued more the words of friends who knew her best. Her former NBC colleague Edwin Newman, who had been a close friend for many years and who was on hand for the ceremony, wrote her to tell her that AWRT came into existence because "there were walls to be breached, obstacles to be overcome. You were one of those who did the breaching and the overcoming and you did it with talent, persistence and devotion to journalism's highest standards . . . It was a privilege to work with you at NBC—and is always a privilege to work with a true pro." And Jane Barton, who was a program director who worked with Frederick at AWRT, recounted in detail the gestures large and small that Frederick had made because of their friendship and because of her devotion to the organization. In twenty-five years, Barton wrote, "you have never said no to a request that would benefit your colleagues [in AWRT]. With your quiet modesty, you would be the last to be aware of what is recognized by those who have benefitted from your knowledge, who have basked in the warmth of your friendship. You, Pauline Fredrick, are the epitome of greatness, the epitome of nobleness, the epitome of love. There are very few in this world today about whom that can be said."

At age sixty-nine Frederick was still doing what she had always done—reporting on foreign affairs, running back and forth from her home to the UN to broadcasting studios, and winning top national awards. But time was running out.

13 Out of the Box

She taught me how to . . . sniff news in the making, how to separate
the wheat of truth from the chaff of public relations.

JOSEPH DEMBO, on learning from Frederick, May 24, 1990

In her speeches and occasionally in her broadcasts Frederick often quoted
famous poets, writers, and philosophers. But one of her favorite quotes
came from a little boy who was the son of friends of hers. He had met
his parents' friend Pauline when she visited, but he was puzzled by her
appearance on television. "Why is Pauline in that black box and when is
she coming out?" he once asked his parents. Frederick was apparently
amused at the existential nature of the question. "There are strong implications to that question," she said. As the 1980s progressed, she emerged
from the "black boxes" of radio and television, although not necessarily
voluntarily. As she reached her early seventies, her health began to decline
to the point where she could not maintain the hectic schedule she had kept
for most of her life. By 1980, when she was seventy-two, she gave up her
regular stint on NPR to become a weekly contributor there, but her new
role meant she would offer only one three-minute commentary broadcast
per week, for which she would be paid one hundred dollars. In 1981 she
stepped down as a trustee of her beloved alma mater, an indication that
she was not well. "My health does not permit me to be as active as I once
was," she wrote American University president Richard Berendzen. "I feel
I should withdraw from the board of trustees to permit someone who can
be more useful to take my place." The board then bestowed upon her the
title of "trustee emerita," a designation that was a great comfort to her,
she told the board chairman.

The daily upkeep of the big house in Connecticut was increasingly becoming a problem for Frederick and Robbins, as was navigating the home's steep staircase. Still, while Frederick and Robbins were forced to slow down physically, that did not stop them from continuing as enthusiastic and spirited advocates of the UN and of the de-escalation of the arms race. Throughout the mid-1980s Frederick appeared occasionally as a guest on network morning news shows, and she wrote opinion columns for her hometown paper in Westport. Robbins, meanwhile, continued some of his work as a proponent for the peaceful use of nuclear power. He wrote a long op-ed piece for the *Christian Science Monitor* in 1984 about President Eisenhower's 1953 "Atoms for Peace" speech and its parallels to the current world environment. Eisenhower, fearing the massive devastation of a nuclear war, had proposed an initiative that would employ the peaceful use of nuclear power. Robbins wrote that after that speech to the UN General Assembly—which his wife had covered—hopes were high that humanity could actually benefit from nuclear power. He quoted Frederick as saying that many people at the time believed that Eisenhower's speech could trigger a new beginning for world peace. Alas, that new era of peace never materialized, Robbins wrote, just as he feared it would not materialize in 1984, despite some talk of a nuclear freeze.

Robbins and Frederick were true believers when it came to their faith in the United Nations and their fear that another world war must be stopped because it would be catastrophic. In September 1974, shortly after she retired from NBC, Frederick entered the lion's den to debate conservative icon William F. Buckley about the value of the UN. Buckley, seen as one of the nation's great intellectuals—and a champion debater—was host of the long-running public affairs television show *Firing Line*, which had moved to PBS in 1971. Appearing with Frederick on the show was John Scali, Nixon's appointee as U.S. ambassador to the United Nations and a man who had echoed Nixon's disdain for the UN. Although she had long declared herself a political independent, Frederick's politics and belief system were the opposite of those of the two men whom she debated that day. That she would agree to appear on the program speaks to her dedication to her beliefs and her confidence in her knowledge and ability to express herself. Frederick may have been outnumbered, but she performed with characteristic grace, humor, and dignity. After Buckley introduced his two guests, he selected Scali to speak first, but the former ambassador deferred to Frederick. "Pauline, I'll let you tee off," Scali said. "You mean there's sexism here today?" she asked, to laughter from the studio audience. "Thank you anyway." Frederick, predictably, came armed with facts and figures, including data from a Harris public opinion poll stating that 76 percent of the public thought the UN was worthwhile. Buckley countered with data stating that 47 percent thought it was doing a poor job. Despite their reliance on data, their geopolitical savvy, and their knowledge of history, the three participants did not change each other's minds as a result of the show. Frederick did not convince Buckley and Scali of the value of the UN, and the two men did not persuade her that it was a toothless organization that had lost the respect of the world. But the discussion remained civil and at times even humorous; it never turned bitter or condescending.

At this time in her life Frederick was growing increasingly impatient with the way the major media in the United States covered stories, although she was careful not to name specific names. In 1985 the professional journalism organization Society of Professional Journalists / Sigma Delta Chi was celebrating its seventy-fifth anniversary with a collection of essays about "What a Free Press Means to Society." (The New York chapter of the organization had already honored Frederick seven years earlier by inducting her into its Hall of Fame and praising her ability "to make complex and controversial issues understandable.") For its anniversary the organization asked a handful of seasoned media professionals to describe briefly what they felt a free press means to America. Most who answered—a list that included Daniel Schorr, then a CNN anchor; Mike Wallace of CBS; and former CBS commentator Eric Sevareid—focused on the civil liberties aspect of the question. Frederick, however, indirectly chastised her colleagues with her answer: like the others, she noted that a free press is the backbone of a democracy, but, she said, "it can be sustained best through restraint in competitive overkill, invasion of privacy, news embellishment and partisan image building."

Despite her criticism of the media and her view that it was abandoning traditional news values by becoming obsessed with competition, appearances, and personality, Frederick would always remain, first and foremost, a journalist and steadfast in her view that fair and objective reporting helped sustain a democracy. It must have been gratifying to her therefore that in 1980, after an up-and-down year with her health, she was honored by her peers and given one of the top journalism awards in the country for lifelong achievements in journalism: the Paul White Award, given by the Radio-Television News Directors Association (RTDNA). Because of the award's prestige, and the fact that she was the first woman to receive it, her selection made international news, and the NBC *Nightly News* spread word of it to millions of viewers—fittingly, considering Frederick used to be a regular contributor to that program. "The former NBC United Nations correspondent Pauline Frederick will be the first woman to receive the highest award given by the Radio and Television News Directors Association," said Jane Pauley, who anchored the news that night. "Ms. Frederick was an important broadcasting correspondent for 33 years. She retired last year from her assignment as an international affairs analyst for National Public Radio."

In a letter to longtime friends in Missouri, Robbins noted that Frederick was "overwhelmed" by congratulatory notes and messages, including some from friends overseas who read about her achievement in the *International Herald Tribune*. And the announcement came at a perfect time, Robbins implied to friends in a letter—when her health appeared to be improving. "The doctor has given Pauline a pretty good bill of health, which is not what her previous doctor had," he said, adding jokingly, "She reckons that was one reason to change doctors."

Unlike the two other national broadcasting awards she received in the 1950s—the Peabody and duPont Awards—the Paul White Award honored not one specific story or series of stories but a lifetime of contributions. It was given not only to journalists. Previous recipients included journalists Edward R. Murrow, Walter Cronkite, and Eric Sevareid but also John F. Kennedy and former senator Sam Ervin. Frederick was to accept the award at the annual RTNDA convention in Hollywood, Florida, a gala event that was the broadcasters' equivalent of the Academy Awards ceremony. Frederick was expected to give a speech—and she used the occasion to both praise and criticize the press. While she acknowledged that recent coverage of "moon landings, coronations and elections" has been "superb," she was not so complimentary when it came to what she felt was media hype that gave viewers a steady diet of "rape, pillage, destruction, drugs, incest, life beyond the pill, teenage suicide, child molesting, battered parents, the degradation of people and how to game the system for the sake of profit." Frederick was eerily prescient in that speech when she predicted that improved media technology would cut both ways for both news consumers and those reporting the news. Sophisticated equipment can take millions of viewers to the scene of historic events, she said, but "the question . . . is whether in our eagerness to use these instruments the importance of the message may become confused with the messenger, who could be perceived as trying to make and shape the news." Further, the ease in which reporters could travel to cover news allowed them to multiply exponentially; during the recent election, she said, the number of accredited correspondents was fifteen times greater than the number of delegates: "Little wonder that correspondents were reduced to interviewing each other." Finally, she decried what she called "what if" journalism based on speculation, fear, and baseless projection, predicting that it might one day overtake "what is" journalism.

In speeches and interviews late in her life Frederick often alluded to the respect she had for the women in journalism who had recently filed lawsuits against several news organizations in an attempt to get treatment equal to that of their male colleagues. But as the second wave of feminism heated up in the 1970s, she was also quick to point out—as she always had—that her aim was not to be a "leader of a movement."

And while she maintained that her marriage was one of the happiest and most fulfilling aspects of her life, she also acknowledged that she realized it would have never been possible for her to have it all—that is, it would have been difficult or impossible for her to have had a family and the career that she had: the math simply did not work out. If she had married younger, she said, "I don't think I could have done many of the things I did. The hours weren't so great, and it would have been impossible to take care of a family."

Frederick's low-key personality and laser-like focus on her job set her apart from many women who were joining the networks in the 1970s and

1980s—women who believed high-profile anchor jobs, a glamorous appearance, and heavy self-promotion were required for a successful career in broadcasting. The media environment of the 1980s was different from the era in which Frederick was at her peak professionally. In 1970, when she was still working full-time for NBC, Frederick said she hoped she helped other women at the network and implied that these women faced slightly different obstacles than she had. "I do hope I cleared some way [for other women]," she said. "I do think they have a somewhat easier time in that they're considered for positions without the hurdle of being a woman." But she believed women still faced subtle yet harsh discrimination when it came to age and appearance.

Many women of the era did recognize the pioneering contributions of Frederick and often mentioned them in speeches and interviews. The fact that she had succeeded in the business and had always maintained her professionalism indicated that other women could do the same, they said. In nearly all of their large gatherings, women speakers addressing the American Women in Radio and Television (AWRT) and the Radio-Television News Directors Association noted her contributions. Most acknowledged the contradictory nature of the progress made by women broadcasters over the years; for instance, Judy Woodruff, formerly a correspondent for the *MacNeil/Lehrer Report* on PBS, told an AWRT audience in 1984 that they had come a long way since the days of Frederick, who was consistently told by male news executives that her voice did not carry authority. Yet ageism still existed in the industry, Woodruff said. The litmus test for women in broadcasting by the 1980s was to "break the age barrier" and keep their jobs in their fifties and beyond. (Frederick held on to her job in her fifties and slightly beyond—but throughout her career she maintained that female broadcasters had a much shorter shelf life than their male counterparts.)

One television critic in the late 1990s had praise for then up-and-coming correspondent Christiane Amanpour of CNN because of her focus on reporting rather than on the glitz and glamour of the job. Amanpour reminded *Rocky Mountain News* writer Dusty Saunders of Frederick. The "low-key" Frederick, Saunders wrote in 1996, "was anything but a glamour girl . . . She was never involved in the big bucks of news broadcasting.

People Magazine would have ignored her." But she covered some of the biggest stories of her times with a hard-driving, no-nonsense style of reporting rare for many of the current network correspondents—with the exception of Amanpour, he said.

Shortly after her death, several men who worked with Frederick related how she had supported them early in their careers. Jim Holton, who had been one of Frederick's producers at NBC, wrote in a newspaper tribute to her that she probably would not have achieved great success in the turbulent media environment of the 1990s. "Frederick was a handsome woman but she had few of the cosmetic superficialities that are so important to the hucksters who run broadcast news today," he wrote. The rising network stars of the 1990s—Jane Pauley at NBC; Lesley Stahl at CBS; Connie Chung, then with CBS; and Diane Sawyer at ABC—"owe Pauline Frederick the acknowledgment that she paved the way for them in the once rarified precincts of broadcasting's big leagues."

Joseph Dembo, who eventually became vice president of CBS Radio, related how Frederick was one of the first people he met in the NBC newsroom, room 404 of 30 Rockefeller Center, when he joined NBC as a twenty-six-year-old rookie reporter in the early 1950s. And she was intimidating. "You could sense the 'no nonsense' in her walk, in her talk, in her eyes," he wrote after Frederick's death. Frederick soon became a trusted friend who consistently offered him support and nuggets of advice about reporting. "By the time I left room 404, she had become my mentor, my treasured colleague, my role model," he wrote. "She taught me how to write for broadcast, how to sniff news in the making, how to separate the wheat of truth from the chaff of public relations."

For nearly fifty years Frederick had, literally, a front seat to history. When she was off the clock, she usually kept quiet about her views of the famous people she covered. But after she retired, she was frequently asked about the people who shaped world events. She made it clear that her hero was Dag Hammarskjöld, with Adlai Stevenson a close second. Beyond that she played it close to the vest when it came to her personal opinions of those she had covered. Interestingly, she rarely discussed publicly her view of John F. Kennedy, a man whom American history has painted as a hero. But Frederick may not have been one of his fans, especially after his treatment of Stevenson, who unknowingly gave false information to the UN General Assembly after Kennedy had lied to him about details of the Bay of Pigs incident. Stevenson, she often said, was a principled and honest man whom Kennedy used and manipulated. In an interview late in her life Frederick asked, rhetorically: "Why would [Kennedy] have had the Bay of Pigs if he believed in the UN? He destroyed Adlai." Kennedy's predecessor, Dwight D. Eisenhower, "was a dear old grandfather who liked to play golf," she said, adding wryly that "he had done his job during World War II and it was really a shame to have had to interrupt his retirement for the Presidency." And Richard Nixon and some in his administration evoked in her mixed feelings. While she apparently kept a calendar marking off the days of his administration, according to her daughter-in-law, and she had been critical of his vice president, Spiro Agnew, Frederick commended Nixon and his aide Henry Kissinger for recognizing the People's Republic of China and backing its UN membership. Shortly after he took office, a newspaper reporter asked Frederick and her NBC colleague Liz Trotta what they thought of Nixon. Frederick was noncommittal. "On the balance . . . the administration has been correct in dealing with the United Nations," she said. Frederick and Lyndon Johnson had run-ins, although none were public. Frederick found Johnson "crude," according to her niece Catharine Cole. "My impression was that there was little love lost between them," Cole said, adding that Frederick occasionally told her stories about Johnson's personal rudeness when talking to reporters.

In some speeches in the late 1970s Frederick criticized President Jimmy Carter for paying only lip service to nuclear disarmament and defense cuts, but she gave him mixed reviews in one 1978 interview. Carter had a better understanding than his immediate predecessors of the role of the UN, she said. "Previous administrations regarded it as a sop to the conscience of mankind, when in fact it is an agency trying to work to avoid war."

When it came to U.S. ambassadors to the UN and U.S. secretaries of state, Frederick apparently favored those who worked hard, opposed U.S. military intervention, and displayed real diplomacy. Arthur Goldberg, who was appointed U.S. ambassador to the UN by Lyndon Johnson, gave up his seat on the U.S. Supreme Court after Johnson persuaded him to join his administration, apparently to help end the Vietnam War. Ultimately, Frederick said, "he didn't succeed and he left quite a disappointed man." And although George H. W. Bush knew little about the workings of the UN when he was first appointed ambassador, he worked hard to understand its mission and its subtleties, Frederick said. "He did his homework and made friends and, really, quite an impression on the United Nations . . . He was a good ambassador." Frederick's views about some ambassadors indicate that she respected those who acted diplomatically. She praised the "quiet diplomacy" of Cyrus Vance, secretary of state under Jimmy Carter, but she had few nice words to say about Daniel Patrick Moynihan, whom she described as overly confrontational. Paraphrasing Winston Churchill, she described him as "the only bull I knew who carried his china closet with him." Jeane Kirkpatrick, who was appointed U.S. ambassador to the UN by Ronald Reagan, was the first woman to hold that post. But she had the same problem as Moynihan, Frederick said. The UN was not meant to be a place of confrontation, she said. "It was meant to be a place for conciliation, and I don't think she worked very hard at that."

Frederick was a realist, but she apparently never recognized what one veteran reporter viewed as the simple reason the United Nations never lived up to its initial promise. Richard Hottelet, who worked with Edward R. Murrow during World War II, in the early days of radio, and who had a long career covering international affairs for CBS, reflected on the reason the UN had faltered: the organization was composed of human beings. "The United Nations is a human institution," he said on the occasion of his retirement from television in 1985. "If you don't expect it to solve all the problems of the world you're not going to slash your wrist when you realize that it's not."

Pauline Frederick's faith in the United Nations endured throughout her life, even when it became painfully obvious that the public viewed the UN not as an agency that would save the world from itself but, instead, as one devoted to furthering human rights. Late in her life, Frederick of course had the benefit of hindsight. In 1974, when she speaking in Chicago as part of the city's celebration of United Nations Day, she reflected on her more than thirty years of covering the UN. She told the group that she had last addressed a UN Day audience in Chicago in the fall of 1961, a month after Dag Hammarskjöld was killed in a plane crash over the Congo. She read an excerpt from her speech thirteen years earlier: "I cannot tell you whether the United Nations died in a flaming crash in Africa on the dark night of September 17, but I am afraid I must tell you that the United Nations we Americans have so comfortably accepted did die that night." Frederick's prediction that the UN would change dramatically almost overnight was realized. The UN did indeed change after Hammarskjöld's tragic death, as did public perception of it. But when she spoke in Chicago in 1974, she said the UN's goal was as it always had been—to save lives and improve the quality of life worldwide. Now, she implied, only its tactics had changed: it would achieve its goal by providing programs and resources for food, shelter, and education. As she had often done in speeches when pointing out irony, Frederick invoked George Orwell with her observation that as the world grew more technologically advanced, more people became homeless and hungry. Yet she was still optimistic that day, labeling the UN "the conscience of mankind and the instrument through which all people may find hope of a decent life."

Eventually, as their health declined, Robbins and Frederick found their house in Westport too difficult to maintain. Frederick had developed osteoporosis and occasionally wore a back brace, according to her daughter-in-law Ann Stevens, and Charles had developed prostate cancer, although it was not fatal. Keeping their home in Westport eventually became too much for them. And the house, while beautiful, had become a source of contention between Frederick and Robbins. Frederick missed the energy of Manhattan and the convenience of living there. Robbins, an outdoorsman, was happy to have a home away from the city and one that allowed him to keep his boat nearby. Frederick never did develop a love of sailing, and an outdoor pool that Robbins had built for her for exercise was unheated, so she eventually stopped using it. Despite their difficulties and deteriorating health, however, the Robbinses still entertained and met with friends for meals and drinks. Ann Stevens remembers that Frederick came to even casual outings impeccably dressed and well groomed. And on social occasions she never dominated the conversation or reminisced about what many would consider an impressive career. "She could compartmentalize," Dick Robbins recalled, although she would join conversations if they turned to current events. "She was very unassuming," he said. By the mid-1980s the couple sold the Westport home, auctioned its contents, and moved to Sarasota, Florida, to a condominium.

After the move to Florida, Frederick's health continued to deteriorate. Catharine Cole believes she probably had a series of small strokes; at one point Robbins had rented a villa in Hawaii, apparently against her wishes, and wanted her to travel there. Frederick resisted but eventually did fly to Hawaii, according to Cole, but she suffered what may have been a heart attack while she was there, so Cole traveled from her home in Lake Forest, Illinois, to pick up her aunt and help her move back to Sarasota. By that time, however, Frederick was quite ill, and Robbins had suffered a recurrence of cancer and had to have extensive surgery on his face and neck. When he returned home, both were too ill to live unassisted in the condominium, and they moved into a retirement facility. Robbins soon learned his illness was terminal, and he immediately began making financial and living arrangements for Frederick, fearing she would be alone after he died. He asked Cole if she would move Frederick to Lake Forest after his death, and she agreed. Charles Robbins died on August 9, 1989, at age eighty-three.

Frederick was very ill when Cole moved her to Lake Forest after Robbins's death, and she survived less than a year. Frederick's health deteriorated at the same time as that of her sister, Kitty, who was in a nursing home in Lake Forest when Frederick moved to Illinois. (Catharine "Kitty" Crowding was four years older than Frederick. She died two months before Frederick.) While Frederick was weak physically in the last year of her life, she, like Robbins, had been lucid and alert mentally through her illness. Cole and Frederick were close through much of their lives, and Frederick often confided in her niece. Cole said that the last few conversations the two had were downbeat, with Frederick denigrating her own accomplishments and regretting she had not done more in her life: "She said to me near the end, 'I don't feel like I have accomplished anything I started out to do.'" She believes the UN's inability to create a peaceful world ultimately crushed her aunt, who had always had high hopes for the organization, despite all of its setbacks. Cole reminded Frederick that she was considered a trailblazer by many people. "Yes, but it hasn't made any difference," Frederick said. Still, Cole thinks that Frederick did not believe what she said and that her illness and the resulting feelings of powerlessness contributed to this pessimism.

Indeed, Frederick maintained her optimism and idealism throughout her life, despite her comments at the very end. Frederick met and worked with some of the most powerful people in the world—many who had the same beliefs as she—and she covered some of the biggest news stories of the century. Although she continually said she would have liked to have had a conventional family, her job gave her tremendous satisfaction and fulfillment. Cole believes her aunt's happiest days were in the late 1950s and early 1960s, when the UN generated tremendous hope in the world and radiated glamour and genteel civility.

Frederick was able to converse with her close friends and relatives not long before she died. Ann Stevens remembers talking to a lucid Frederick several days before she passed away, and Cole said that Frederick remained an intrepid and objective reporter up until the end: several days before her death, she calmly told Cole that she had just talked to the doctor, who told her she had had another heart attack and had only a few days to live.

Pauline Frederick died on May 9, 1990, in Lake Forest, Illinois, at age eighty-two. She was buried in Grandview Cemetery in Tyrone, Pennsylvania, in a plot with her parents and grandfather. At a short graveside service her niece Catharine Cole read excerpts from the writings of Dag Hammarskjöld.

Notes and Sources

It is important for readers to identify the source from which information comes. The specific sources in these notes follow a short phrase describing material taken from each chapter.

Many of the sources cited here come from archives that house documents, recordings, and other information about Pauline Frederick and the history of American broadcasting. I also obtained valuable information related to the Cold War from three National Archives and Records Administration presidential libraries—the John F. Kennedy Library and Museum, the LBJ Presidential Library, and the Nixon Library and Museum. I obtained network information and debate recordings from the Paley Center for Media in New York City and the Vanderbilt University Television News Archive.

ABBREVIATIONS

CC: Catharine Cole
CFC: Catharine "Kitty" Frederick Crowding
CR: Charles Robbins
DH: Dag Hammarskjöld
HRB: H. R. Baukhage
JG: Julian Goodman
LAB: Library of American Broadcasting, University of Maryland
LBJ: Lyndon Baines Johnson
LOC: Library of Congress
NPR: National Public Radio
NYT: *New York Times*
OHist: Oral History
PF: Pauline Frederick
RK: Robert Kintner
SSC: Sophia Smith Collection, Smith College
UN: United Nations
WM: William McAndrew

1. A QUIRK OF FATE

Epigraph: Quoted in Hosley and Yamada, *Hard News*, 62.

PF's description of hearing the plane was missing: This was given in interviews done in three phases: in April–May 1986; on June 20, 1986; and on July 11, 1986. The interviewer for all phases was Norman Ho. During the interview on July 11, 1986, he was joined by Leonore Silvian. Transcript UN OHist. The transcripts of the interviews as well as the audio are at the UN website, www.un.org/depts/dhl/dag/docs/history /frederick1.pdf (accessed July 1, 2012).

PF's comments on the timing of DH's death: UN OHist, June 20, 1986.

Dan Cole's comments about PF and DH: Interview with the author in Evanston IL, April 6, 2013.

Time of the plane crash: See Thorpe, *Dag Hammarskjöld*, 42.

PF's broadcast the day before DH's death: UN OHist, June 20, 1986.

The background of DH's tenure as secretary-general: UN Department of Public Information news release, "Commemorating the Fiftieth Anniversary of Dag Hammarskjöld's Death," October 12, 2011, www.un.org (accessed July 1, 2012).

PF denying speculation that she and DH had had a personal relationship: PF was asked this occasionally throughout her later career. See, e.g., Jean Henniger's story in the *Oregonian*, May 10, 1969. Information about the congratulatory message from DH to PF came from Julie Ransom, "Pauline Frederick" *TV Star Parade* (September 1956): 12.

Brokaw's comments about PF: These remarks were broadcast on the NBC *Nightly News*, May 9, 1990, Vanderbilt University Television News Archive, http://tvnews .vanderbilt.edu/. Murrow's letter is dated August 29, 1946, and is in ssc, box 38, folder 7.

PF's comments on DH's low-key personality: UN OHist, June 20, 1986.

Marlene Sanders's comments about PF: These were made in an interview with the author on October 23, 2011, by telephone.

Critical acclaim for the NBC special broadcast: Many television critics of the era praised NBC's special report. See, e.g., Walter Hawver, "Aircasters Come through in Crisis," *Knickerbocker (NY) News*, September 19, 1961.

PF's comments about the death of DH: These are taken from a transcript of the special NBC News broadcast on September 18, 1961, SSC, box 11, folder 15. Kennedy's words were quoted in Martin, *Adlai Stevenson and the World*, 665.

Correspondence from viewers expressing sympathy about DH's death: All of these letters and cards are in SSC, box 11, folder 17.

Information about DH's life: This is taken from the Nobel Prize website, www.nobelprize.org/nobel_prizes/ (accessed July 9, 2012); and from Thorpe, *Dag Hammarskjöld*.

Matthew Frederick's background: Interview by the author with CC, December 9, 2012. See also Matthew Frederick's obituary in the *Waynesboro (PA)Record-Herald*, "Matthew Frederick Succumbs, Father of Mrs. Crowding," June 25, 1946.

Details about PF's view of herself growing up: Interview by the author with CC, December 9, 2012.

PF on her "churchy" upbringing: Broadcast Pioneers Library OHist, LAB. She also talked at length about her upbringing in the UN OHist, April 1984.

PF crying over Hindenburg: See Anthony Mancini, "Daily Closeup," *New York Post*, October 22, 1976.

PF's father as an avid reader and follower of politics: UN OHist, April 1984.

Inscription in her yearbook: PF's yearbook, the *Argus*, is in SSC, box 42, folder 5.

PF's physical ailments and her belief that her sister was prettier: Tozier, "Pauline Frederick and the Rise of Network Television News." CC also commented on this in the interview with the author, December 9, 2012.

PF's wariness about women broadcasters having to be attractive: See Gay Talese, "Perils of Pauline," *Saturday Evening Post*, September 26, 1963, 20–22.

Comments about the hysterectomy: Interview by the author with CC, December 9, 2012.

2. POLLY THE PRIZEWINNER

Epigraphs: Letter, Faustina Orner (PF's agent) to PF, January 4, 1946; and response from PF, letter, PF to Farnham Dudgeon, January 7, 1946, both in SSC, box 1, folder 13.

PF's writing activities in school: Copies of the yearbook, school newspapers, and other examples of her writing were found among her personal papers at Smith College, box 42.

"Polly the Prizewinner": PF talked about this in UN OHist, April–May 1984.

PF souring on journalism: She said this many times to interviewers. See, e.g., Martin Cohen, "In a Man's World," *Radio and Television Mirror*, December 1949, 6.

PF's exhilaration upon seeing her byline in the Edison school newspaper: She discussed this in a speech to Edison Junior High students on February 12, 1952, SSC, box 23, folder 3.

PF's recollections about the "pretentiousness" of journalism and why she attended American University: UN OHist, April–May 1984.

PF's religious activities in college: She discussed this in an interview with Carol Bennett, September 8, 1984, transcript in LAB, William S. Hedges Collection—No. 36.

Story about PF in the American University newspaper: This clipping was found among her personal papers, SSC, box 23, folder 3.

PF's authorship of American's alma mater: This version can be found in Abdul K. Bangura, *The American University Alma Mater and Fight Song* (Lincoln NE: iUniverse, 2002), 45.

Background of Flemming: See Flemming's obituary, Eric Pace, "Arthur S. Flemming," 91. "Served in Eisenhower's Cabinet," NYT, September 9, 1996.

Numbers of college graduates in the 1930s, '40s, and '50s: These are taken from U.S. Department of Education statistics.

PF's assistantship at American University: See the *Washington (PA) Evening News*, "College Honors Harrisburg Girl," June 3, 1930.

PF taking advice from history professor Tansill: She talked about this during interviews throughout her life. See, e.g., Doris Willens, "Pauline Frederick: Only Woman Who . . . ," *Editor & Publisher*, February 23, 1949, 42.

PF's link to actress Pauline Frederick: PF frequently mentioned in interviews early in her career that people asked her if she was the actress. The anecdote from Cuba is quoted in Don Vance, "Pauline Finds Horses, Men Equal to the UN," *Tucson Daily Citizen*, December 30, 1952. The letter from the author was found among PF's personal papers: Muriel Elwood to PF, January 11, 1940, SSC, box 1, folder 7.

NBC News release about the actress Pauline Frederick: This is dated January 20, 1955, SSC, box 14, folder 16.

Frederic William Wile's offer to PF: PF noted this in an interview with Carolyn Tozier, in "Pauline Frederick and the Rise of Network Television News."

PF's recollection of being told her interview series with diplomats' wives would be printed regularly by the *Star* and of her payment for the stories: UN OHist project interview by Norman Ho, April 1984.

Activities of Dorothy Thompson and review of women in journalism in the 1930s: Marzolf, *Up from the Footnote*, 52–55.

PF's comments about Thompson: These were made in a speech to the American Women in Radio and Television on September 20, 1983, in New York City. The transcript is available from LAB, Women in the History of Broadcasting project.

PF's comments about her reluctance to be abrasive: See Shirley-Anne Owden, "Pauline Frederick Recalls Life in a Man's Field," *Palo Alto Times*, January 12, 1975.

Times story about PF: Nancy H. MacLennan, "Only One of Her Kind," NYT, December 5, 1948.

PF as teacher at Fairmont Junior College: Copies of tests and lesson plans were found among her personal papers, SSC, box 1, folder 1.

PF's 1934 income and the average income of reporters of the era: Tozier reported on this, based on records on PF's pay in the National Archives, in "Pauline Frederick and the Rise of Network Television News."

PF's stories in *United States News*: "Tide of World Affairs: Problem of Communism," September 5, 1935; and "Tide of World Affairs: Another George Reigns in Britain," December 14, 1936. Her comments about wanting to use a first initial only in the byline were made during a talk, "The Influence of Women in Foreign Affairs," on January 24, 1945, at De Anza College in Cupertino CA. Transcript of this is in SSC, box 35, folder 3.

Brabrook's comments about PF: Taken from an interview with Brabrook by Tozier, in "Pauline Frederick and the Rise of Network Television News."

PF's comments about women's voices and microphones: MacLennan, "Only One of Her Kind."

PF's comments about the network executive's voice carrying authority at his home: See Marlane, *Women in Television News Revisited*, 17. PF also talked about this during an interview for the University of Maryland Broadcast Pioneers Library OHist Project conducted on September 8, 1984, by Carol Bennett. The transcript for this interview is available at LAB.

Growth in radio advertising and number of radios in homes: These figures were taken from Sloan, *Media in America*, 296–97, 350.

HRB's career: See Fang, *Those Radio Commentators*, 275–82.

PF's recollection of Baukhage's comments about women and radio: PF said this many times in interviews and speeches. See, e.g., her speech to the American Women in Radio and Television, September 20, 1983. HRB's comments to PF were also discussed in O'Dell, *Women Pioneers in Television*, 95.

PF's recollections about her radio interview with Mrs. Hurban: PF mentioned this frequently in interviews. She also discussed it at length in UN OHist, April–May 1984.

Cuthbert telling PF she enjoyed meeting her: Letter, Margaret Cuthbert to PF, October 3, 1939, SSC, box 1, folder 13.

Hynd praising PF: Letter, June Hynd to PF, August 7, 1939, SSC, box 1, folder 13.

PF's *Star* story about Mrs. Hurban: "New Czecho-Slovakia Visioned by Wife of Minister Hurban," April 1, 1938.

Predictions of Charles Tansill: "Dr. Tansill Sees No General War," *Washington Evening Star*, September 13, 1938.

PF's *Star* story about women in high-ranking Washington jobs: "Career Women in Washington Fill Men's Jobs, Get Men's Pay," appeared on December 18, 1938.

Summary of McBride's career: See Hosley and Yamada, *Hard News*, 3–4, 30.

Transcripts of "Let's Talk It Over": These are among PF's personal papers, SSC, box 1, folder 4. The interview with Mrs. Taft that aired is dated May 26, 1939; the interview with Mrs. Grady is dated August 25, 1939; the interview with McAllister and Martin is dated November 30, 1939.

Cuthbert telling PF that she distributed memo about lack of women in radio: Memo, Martha Cuthbert to PF, August 26, 1939, SSC, box 1, folder 13.

Radio "tasting good" to PF: University of Maryland Broadcast Pioneers OHist interview with PF.

Background of the UN charter meeting in San Francisco: O'Sullivan, *United Nations*, 7–20.

PF's recollections of Roosevelt, Churchill, and Fala: UN OHist interview. April–May, 1984.

PF's turning down of the wire service offer: She discussed this in her interview with Tozier, in "Pauline Frederick and the Rise of Network Television News." Tozier also noted there that an NANA editor offered indirectly to open doors for PF if she went to China.

War Department restrictions on women war correspondents: Edwards, *Women of the World*, 270.

PF's decision while sitting under a hair dryer: Latimer Watson, "Woman Finds Man's World of Radio a Challenging Field," *Columbus (GA) Ledger*, January 22, 1951.

PF's reason for leaving the UN charter meeting: UN OHist, April–May 1984.

Snevily's willingness to credential PF for China trip: PF related this to Tozier in "Pauline Frederick and the Rise of Network Television News."

Instruction to PF about what to take on ATC trip: Letter, U.S. Department of War, Bureau of Public Relations, to PF, May 25, 1945, SSC, box 1, folder 9.

PF's tales of uncomfortable conditions during her travels: See, e.g., letters from PF to her sister, CFC, June 25, 1945, and from PF to her family, June 10, 1945, SSC, box 1, folder 9. Letters to her family about similar topics are in box 39, folder 6.

PF's comments about the warnings from pilots: Letter, PF to CFC, June 25, 1945, SSC, box 1, folder 9.

PF telling HRB he would "revel" in the trip: PF to HRB, undated, but believed to be late June 1945, SSC, box 1, folder 9.

PF's stolen typewriter and economic inflation in China: This was discussed in the undated story in the *Sunbury (PA) Daily Item*, "Writer Here after 35,000-Mile Tour to 19 Countries," believed to be from August 1945, SSC, box 1, folder 9.

PF's letter home about the typewriter: Letter, PF to Henry Snevily, July 8, 1945, SSC, box 1, folder 9.

Kitty's letter to PF about her China broadcast: Letter, CFC to PF, March 24, 1946, SSC, box 39, folder 6.

PF reported as "spinster": This was reported in "Spinster at the News Mike," *Newsweek*, October 27, 1947, 66.

PF's speech to the American Newspaper Women's Club: This was covered in a story in the *Washington Evening Star*, "Miss Frederick Tells of Tour," August 28, 1945.

PF noting that the United States did not bring democracy to countries overseas: Letter, PF to Farnham Dudgeon, January 7, 1946, SSC, box 1, folder 13.

PF noting that the war "is far from over": This appeared in "Miss Frederick Tells of Tour," *Washington Evening Star*, August 28, 1945, SSC, box 1, folder 13.

PF's negative reaction to antimalarial medication: Tozier noted this in "Pauline Frederick and the Rise of Network Television News."

PF on almost "freezing to death" and noting floods: Letter, PF to HRB, February 21, 1946, SSC, box 1, folder 13.

PF's comments about jeep riding and other forms of transportation: Letter, PF to Farnham Dudgeon, January 7, 1946, SSC, box 1, folder 13.

PF getting "homesick as the dickens": Letter, PF to Tom Velotta, April 1, 1946, SSC, box 1, folder 13.

Kitty's worried letter to PF: Letter, CFC to PF, July 6, 1945, SSC, box 39, folder 6.

Kitty's letter about the fishing and their father's health: Letter, CFC to PF, July 15, 1945, SSC, box 39, folder 6.

Cause of Mrs. Frederick's death: Interview by the author with CC, April 6, 2013, Evanston IL. See also her obituary, "Mrs. M. P. Frederick," *Record Herald*, July 20, 1940.

PF's comments on the destruction of Nuremberg: Letter, PF to "Lynn" (no last name given but believed to be Lynn Crowding), December 9, 1945, SSC, box 39, folder 6.

PF's letter to her niece: Letter, PF to Virginia Frederick, February 22, 1946, SSC, box 39, folder 6.

NANA's disinterest in German food story: Letter, PF to HRB, February 21, 1946, SSC, box 1, folder 13.

PF relating rejection letter from Orner: Letter, PF to HRB: February 21, 1946, SSC, box 1, folder 13.

Comments about "working in the dark": Letter, PF to Faustina Orner, January 17, 1946, SSC, box 1, folder 13.

HRB's advice on what kind of stories to write: Letter, HRB to PF, March 4, 1946, SSC, box 1, folder 13. He also sent her a telegram on that date with similar content as the letter.

PF on "reeducation" of Germany: Letter, PF to HRB, March 24, 1946, SSC, box 1, folder 13.

HRB's advice to stop lamenting: Letter, HRB to PF, March 4, 1946, SSC, box 1, folder 13.

PF on her fiancé and wedding plans: Letter, PF to her father, Matthew Frederick, January 4, 1946, SSC, box 39, folder 6.

The Crowding girls preparing for a wedding: Interview by the author with CC, December 9, 2012.

PF's news of her broken engagement: Letter, PF to CFC, February 21, 1946, SSC, box 39, folder 6. She also mentioned her homesickness and her tears at hearing "Over There" in this letter.

Saturday Evening Post **story:** Talese, "Perils of Pauline," 21.

PF's comments about her birthday: Letter, PF to Ann Cordell, March 23, 1946, SSC, box 37, folder 11.

PF's wish to find a "sugar daddy": These comments were made in a letter to "George and Freda" (last name unknown), April 1, 1946, SSC, box 37, folder 11.

Journalists' concern for trials' effect on German citizens: See "Newsmen Worried over Nuernberg [sic] Trials' Effect on German People," *Publisher's Auxiliary*, April 13, 1946.

PF on "filling in" during emergencies: Watson, "Woman Finds Man's World of Radio a Challenging Field."

HRB's critique of PF's Nuremberg broadcast: Letter, HRB to PF, March 20, 1946, SSC, box 1, folder 13.

PF's commentary on the trial to her brother-in-law: Letter, PF to Lynn Crowding, December 9, 1945, SSC, box 39, folder 6.

PF's coverage of Goering's testimony: In addition to the ABC radio broadcast, clippings among PF's personal papers indicate that many newspapers also picked up her coverage of the testimony through NANA. See, e.g., the *Louisville Times* magazine, January 2, 1946; the *Ottawa (Canada) Daily Citizen*, January 2, 1946; and the *Canton Repository*, January 2, 1946.

PF's story about Poland: This appeared in the NYT with PF's byline on May 22, 1946, with the headline "Visitor in Poland Reports Coercion." PF also described the trials in a story in one of her hometown papers, the *Sunbury Daily Item*, "Woman Newspaper Writer Tells of Nurenberg [sic] Trials," undated but believed to be from May 1946.

German women not wanting their babies: Letter, PF to HRB, February 21, 1946, SSC, box 1, folder 13.

PF's fraternization story: The draft of a long and detailed story written by PF about the topic was found among her personal papers (SSC, box 1, folder 17), but it apparently was never published. The *Publisher's Auxiliary* story, "Hair-Pulling When GIs American Wives Meet Nazi Frauleins, WNU Writer Predicts," which briefly discusses the issue of fraternization, is dated March 23, 1946. For more information about sociologists' comments about the relationship between American GIs and European women in the mid-1940s and press coverage of it, see Richard K. Popp, "Domesticating Vacations: Gender, Travel, and Consumption in Post-War Magazines," *Journalism History* 36 (Fall 2010): 128–29.

3. TALKING ABOUT SERIOUS THINGS

Epigraph: Memo, Edward R. to Robert Kennett, August 29, 1946, SSC, box 38, folder 7.

CC's recollection of PF's illness: Interview by the author with CC, December 9, 2012.

Description of PF's drug poisoning: This is discussed in a letter from PF to "Pat" (no last name given) on April 23, 1946, SSC, box 1, folder 13.

PF's view of war devastation "selling" her on peace: UN OHist, April–May 1984.

PF's speech about war atrocities: She gave this talk on May 1, 1955, in Chicago to the Katherine Legge Memorial Association, SSC, box 23, folder 6.

Hallock's view on the role of publicity in wartime: See Hallock, *Press March to War*, xvi.

Men returning to their journalism jobs after the war: See, e.g., Maurine Beasley, "Women and Journalism in World War II: Discrimination and Progress," *American Journalism* (Summer 1995): 321–33; and Hosley and Yamada, *Hard News*, 5.

PF's story about Elliott Roosevelt: North American News Alliance hard copy dated September 13, 1946, SSC, box 35, folder 5.

Interview with Randolph Churchill: A video of this September 30, 1946, interview is in SSC, box 52.

Coiffure story: Hard copy, North American News Alliance, October 31, 1946, SSC, box 35, folder 5.

Margaret Truman interview: This interview was distributed by the North American News Alliance and appeared in many newspapers. See, e.g., the *Louisville Times*, "Margaret Stands on Her Own in Bid for Fame," May 20, 1947.

Congratulatory memo: Memo, T. Rahl to PF, May 21, 1947, SSC, box 35, folder 5.

The effect of the aftermath of the war on broadcasting: See Bliss, *Now the News*, 179.

Numbers of radios in the United States: See figures from the University of Memphis, https://umdrive.memphis.edu/mbensman/public/homes40.html (accessed January 28, 2012).

Development of ABC: Bliss, *Now the News*, 149.

Kintner's background: Bliss, *Now the News*, 307–8.

Letter from Murrow: Letter, Edward R. Murrow to Robert Kennett, August 27, 1946, SSC, box 38, folder 7.

Kennett's note: Robert Kennett to PF, August 29, 1946, SSC, box 38, folder 7.

Sanders's thoughts about hiring of women: Sanders and Rock, *Waiting for Prime Time*, 9.

Story about PF in tears: Cohen, "In a Man's World," 6, 74, 76.

Martha Cuthbert's career: Bliss, *Now the News*, 103. See also her obituary, "Martha Cuthbert, 81, Is Dead; Ex-Executive of NBC Radio," *NYT*, April 26, 1968.

PF's recollections of Cuthbert: See, e.g., the Broadcast Pioneers OHist interview with PF by Carol Bennett, LAB.

PF as a "curiosity" in the radio world: She described herself this way in a speech to De Anza College in California in 1976, SSC, box 23, folder 1 (specific date unknown).

PF's comment that a network executive would quit his job before hiring a woman: She said this in her interview with Cohen, in "In a Man's World."

PF's editor telling her that he had instructions not to use her on the air: PF related this anecdote many times in her life. See, e.g., Gloria Cole, "Pauline Frederick: A View from the Sidelines," *Free Press* (CT), March 27, 1974. But PF also indicated that she had affection for John Dunn, the editor who told her this.

Description of the general in the trip to Uruguay: See "Pauline Frederick: The Only Woman Who . . . ," *Editor & Publisher*, July 23, 1949, 42.

PF quotation about being self-reliant: Cohen, "In a Man's World."

PF being "fished" out of trouble: She was quoted as having said this in Lilla Anderson's story, "Pauline Frederick: Reporter," in *TV Radio Mirror*, January 1960, 62–64.

ABC not "sparing a man" to go on the *Queen Elizabeth*: PF made that comment during an interview with Latimer Watson in the *Columbus (GA) Ledger*, "There's Something in a Name, Says ABC's Pauline Frederick," November 11, 1950.

Details about the *Queen Mary* press junket: Many stories were written about this. See, e.g., "*Queen Elizabeth* Voyage No Joyride for Newsmen," *World's Press News*, November 17, 1946, written by "a special correspondent."

PF's earnings in 1947: This was taken from Tozier, "Pauline Frederick and the Rise of Network Television News." Tozier got the information from the files of the law firm of Hall, Dickler, Kent, Friedman and Wood, a firm that represented PF and that has since dissolved. Its name changed several times over the years.

"Spinster at the Mike": This was published in *Newsweek* on October 27, 1947, 66.

PF as "no modern counterpart to the suffragette": Anderson, "Pauline Frederick, Reporter," *TV Radio Mirror*.

Laurent's profile of her: "UN Is Pauline's Beat," *Washington Post Magazine*, March 12–18, 1961, H-3.

Talese's profile: This appeared in the *Saturday Evening Post* on January 26, 1963.

Marlene Sanders's view of PF's appearance: Telephone interview by the author with Marlene Sanders, October 23, 2011.

Broadcasting as an "intimate" medium: Jerry Stein, *Cincinnati Post and Times-Star*, September 22, 1967, headline unknown. This clipping is in SSC, box 39, folder 12.

4. TELEVISION'S MERCILESS EYE

Epigraph: PF made this comment frequently in speeches and interviews. See, e.g., Margaret Paschke, "Hear NBC's Gal at the UN," *Kentucky Post*, January 12, 1974. PF frequently noted in speeches that Lincoln had given the Gettysburg Address in one minute and twenty-five seconds. See, e.g., the speech she gave at the Miami Heart Dinner cardiologist seminar, May 18, 1950, SSC, box 23, folder 1.

Ways women can succeed in radio: PF gave this speech at the twenty-first annual Friendship Dinner on November 9, 1947, in New York City, SSC, box 23, folder 1.

PF's comments about modern women broadcasters and Jane Austen: She said this in a speech to the Institute for Education by Radio and Television in Columbus OH, April 9, 1954, SSC, box 23, folder 5.

Contract and fliers from the lecture agency: These were found among PF's personal papers, SSC, box 27, folder 5.

Letters from audience members complimenting PF on her lectures: These came from Gertrude Strandberg of the Munsey Park Women's Club in Manhasset, Long Island, 1948 (exact date unknown); and Margretta S. Claflin of Columbus OH, March 3, 1949. Both are in SSC, box 27, folder 5.

Memo outlining NANA payments: Memo, Joseph Agnelli to PF, November 18, 1946, LAB, box 1, folder 13.

Trips to Lake Success: PF described these in the Broadcast Pioneers OHist Project, LAB, September 8, 1984.

PF "heartsick" at the idea of the UN as an instrument of war: She said this in a speech to the twenty-seventh annual convention of the Southern Interscholastic Press Association, Washington and Lee University, Lexington VA, May 4, 1956, SSC, box 23, folder 7.

The UN as a "conference table": PF said this during the Broadcast Pioneers OHist, LAB.

Article that described PF's reaction to "hypocrisy" at the UN: See Cohen, "In a Man's World," 6, 74, 76.

PF's views of the initial goals of the UN: Broadcast Pioneers OHist, LAB.

PF's daily routine and the description of her apartment: Cohen, "In a Man's World."

PF's self-promoting memo: Memo, PF to John T. Madigan, February 19, 1948, SSC, box 3, folder 21.

Reuven Frank's recollections of the 1948 political conventions: These are discussed in detail in his memoir, *Out of Thin Air*, 1–27.

Cole's recollections of visits with her aunt when she attended Barnard: Telephone interview by the author with CC, December 9, 2012.

PF's relationship with her father: Interview by the author with CC. Matthew Frederick's obituary appeared in the *Record-Herald*, "Matthew Frederick Succumbs, Father of Mrs. Crowding," June 25, 1946. The letter to "Dr. Dudley" from PF is dated April 22, 1939, and is in the possession of CC.

Frank's comments on "gavel-to-gavel" coverage: Frank, *Out of Thin Air*, 6–7.

The slight television coverage of the 1947 conventions: Bliss, *Now the News*, 208.

The cities located on the coaxial cable: Frank, *Out of Thin Air*, 9.

Letter writers' view of convention "shenanigans": See Herman Branschain, "Democratic Convention," *Broadcasting*, July 5, 1948, 60.

The role of the kinescope: Frank, *Out of Thin Air*, 9.

Murrow, Collingwood, and Smith shunning television: This was discussed by Mike Conway in "Before the Bloggers: The Upstart News Technology of Television at the 1948 Political Conventions," presented at the annual conference of the Association for Education in Journalism and Mass Communication, San Antonio TX, 2005. Frank also discussed it in *Out of Thin Air*, 11.

Emergence of the term *anchorman*: See Matusow, *Evening Stars*, 65.

Bulletin board posting for television reporters: PF talked about this in a speech to the American Women in Radio and Television (AWRT), New York, September 20, 1983, LAB.

PF "horrified" about being asked to cover the convention: AWRT speech, September 20, 1983.

Women's behind-the-scenes roles at the convention: Bliss, *Now the News*, 209.

Photo of PF surrounded by men at the Democratic convention: This appeared in the July 19, 1948, issue of *Broadcasting*, 23.

Media partnerships during the convention: See Conway, "Before the Bloggers: The Upstart News Technology of Television at the 1948 Political Conventions."

PF's recollection of what to wear and how to apply makeup for television: She talked about this in the AWRT speech.

PF getting advice about makeup: She discussed this during a speech on May 23, 1952 in Bay City MI, audience unknown, SSC, box 23, folder 3.

Vogue magazine's coverage of cosmetics' role in the convention: See "Television: New Eye on the Conventions," *Vogue*, August 1, 1948, 82–83, 85.

PF's manner of dressing: See Cohen, "In a Man's World."

Kintner and the bow on PF's dress: "Kintner Dies at 71; Headed ABC, NBC," *Broadcasting*, January 5, 1981, 90–92.

PF's first broadcast next to the elephant and her joint broadcast with Davis: Bay City speech.

PF on wearing eyeglasses and flat hair on the air: AWRT speech.

Horseshoe pin: PF mentioned this frequently in interviews. See, e.g., Katherine Harrington, "She Deflates Soviet 'Supermen,'" *Knickerbocker News*, February 2, 1959.

Cosmetics for color television: See Lawrence Laurent, "UN Is Pauline's Beat," *Washington Post Magazine*, March 12–18, 1961, H3.

Talese's profile: This story, "Perils of Pauline," appeared in the *Saturday Evening Post* on January 26, 1963, 20–22.

Viewer's letter to PF: Letter, Augustus T. Graydon of Columbia SC to PF on March 2, 1966. Her response to him is not dated. SSC, box 37, folder 3.

Times headline about the heat: "Convention Hall Is Rechristened as 'the Steam-heated Iron Lung,'" June 25, 1948.

Reporters with walkie-talkies: See Gail Crotts, "'A Spectacular Coup': Television and the 1948 Conventions," *Journalism History* 1, no. 3 (1974): 90–93.

Velotta's laudatory memo and regrets about her illness: Memo, Tom Velotta to PF, July 20, 1948, SSC, box 3, folder 4.

Kintner's memo about "splendid" job: Memo, RK to PF, July 28, 1948, SSC, box 3, folder 4.

PF's salary in 1948: This was taken from Tozier, "Pauline Frederick and the Rise of Network Television News." Tozier got the information from PF's law firm, Hall, Dickler, Kent, Friedman and Wood. The conversion to current dollars was taken from the Bureau of Labor Statistics website, www.bls.gov/data/ (accessed June 9, 2012).

Estimates on the number who watched and covered the conventions: *Broadcasting* offered its estimates of television and radio viewers in "Philly Coverage," *Broadcasting*, July 19, 1948, 62, 70. Conway gave his estimates in "Before the Bloggers: The Upstart News Technology of Television at the 1948 Political Conventions."

Radio audience and public reaction to the conventions: See Bliss, *Now the News*, 213.

Correspondents moving away from spot news: *Broadcasting*, July 19, 1948.

Videotape machines melting: Bliss, *Now the News*, 211.

Problems with floodlights and monitor: This was mentioned in *Broadcasting*, June 28, 1948, 13.

Frank on the reporting of serious news on television networks: Frank, *Out of Thin Air*, 27.

Correspondents learning to be "showmen": This was a quote by Burke Crotty, an ABC executive producer, as reported in *Broadcasting*, July 5, 1948, 60.

Kenneth Fry on the effect of television at the conventions: "TV Important: Coverage Effect Stressed at Democratic Session," *Broadcasting*, July 19, 1948, 34.

Broadcasting editorial about televised conventions: "TV Elected," *Broadcasting*, July 12, 1948, 52.

The 1952 political conventions: ABC listed its correspondents in a news release to affiliates headlined "Co-op Commentators to Attend Political Conventions, American Broadcasting Company Co-operative Radio Programs," May 28, 1953, SSC, box 3, folder 22. McBride made a career as "Martha Deane" on radio, where she focused on interviews and human interest stories. She is widely considered a pioneering woman journalist. See, e.g., Marzolf, *Up from the Footnote*, 125–26.

"Pauline Frederick's Feature Story" transcript: This transcript, dated February 9, 1949, is in SSC, box 3, folder 7.

"Vacation Time" description: This appeared in a news release from WJC Radio in New York dated March 1950 and is in SSC, box 3, folder 13.

Epigraph: James Reston, "Star Villain of TV: Jacob A. Malik," *NYT*, August 13, 1950.

ABC public relations for PF: These undated news releases to affiliates were found among her personal papers, in SCC, box 39, folder 10.

Number of television sets sold: "TV Sets," *Broadcasting*, July 5, 1948, 61.

Televisions in two-thirds of households: Daniel, *Harry Reasoner*, 60.

Summary of newly formed nightly news broadcasts: Bliss, *Now the News*, 222–23.

ABC as "laughing stock": Daniel, *Harry Reasoner*, 121.

Frugality and background of Edward Nobel: Kisseloff, *Box*, 538–39.

Differing time slots of *All-Star News* and its status as precursor to future shows: Bliss, *Now the News*, 223, 308; see also Kisseloff, *Box*, 350.

NYT interview: MacLennan, "Only One of Her Kind."

Number of women in broadcasting after World War II: Sanders and Rock, *Waiting for Prime Time*, 9.

Local women broadcasters: Hosley and Yamada, *Hard News*, 3–6.

Information about Glick and Jarvis: Hosley and Yamada, *Hard News*, 48, 76–77.

Women broadcasters in behind-the-scenes jobs: Sanders and Rock, *Waiting for Prime Time*, 11–13; and Marzolf, *Up from the Footnote*.

Summary of the amount of supplies delivered by the airlift: Bliss, *Now the News*, 216.

PF's recollections of planes filled with supplies rather than bombs: She said this in a Miami Heart Dinner speech to cardiologists on May 18, 1950, SSC, box 23, folder 1.

***Times* story about how correspondents covered the airlift:** "Radio and Television: Major Air Networks Will Cover the Lifting of Berlin Blockade Tomorrow Night," *NYT*, May 10, 1949.

PF's thank-you notes: Many of these notes can be found in SSC. The ones from this era, the early and mid-1950s, are in box 3, folder 19.

Hottelet's recollections of UN coverage: See the Yale–UN OHist interview by Jean Krasno with Richard Hottelet, May 6, 2005.

UN as "debating society": Telephone interview by the author with Marlene Sanders, December 23, 2011.

LeSueur's background: See his obituary, Richard Goldstein, "Larry Le Sueur, Pioneering War Correspondent, Dies at 93," *NYT*, February 7, 2003.

Background of the Korean invasion: See O'Sullivan, *United Nations*, 24–27. See also W. T. Stone, "Red China and the United Nations," in *Editorial Research Reports 1954*, vol. 2 (Washington DC: CQ Press, 1954), http://library.cqpress.com/cqresearcher /cqresrre1954091500 (accessed February 14, 2013).

PF's broadcast about the Security Council emergency meeting: She said this in a broadcast on June 20, 1950. A recording of it is available at SSC.

PF on the most important aspect of her job: "Pioneer on the Air," *Times of London*, February 17, 1958.

PF on building trust with sources: "Busy Redhead Reporting," *Newsweek*, August 11, 1948, 54.

The Korean invasion as part of the new Cold War: See O'Sullivan, *United Nations*, 24–27.

PF's daily schedule during the Korean crisis: She talked about this frequently in speeches and in interviews. See, e.g., Marzolf, *Up from the Footnote*, 160–61.

PF on diplomats "exposing their views": She said this in the Broadcast Pioneers OHist, LAB.

PF and having her "trials and tribulations" out of view: She said this during the speech to the Miami Heart Dinner, May 18, 1950, SSC, box 23, folder 1.

PF as proudest of Korean War coverage: She said this in the Broadcast Pioneers OHist, LAB.

PF's regular show schedule: MacLennan, "Only One of Her Kind."

Emergence of three events during the Korean War: See Frank's memoir, *Out of Thin Air*, 37.

Drama of the UN talks about Korea: "Television from Lake Success," *NYT*, August 13, 1950.

Reston on the villain of the UN talks: Reston, "Star Villain of TV: Jacob A. Malik."

Gould's assessment of Korea coverage: Jack Gould, "Men of Opinion," *NYT*, August 13, 1950.

Complimentary letter from ambassador Austin: Letter, Warren Austin to PF, September 1, 1950, SSC, box 36, folder 10.

Reuven Frank on Korean War images in living rooms: Frank, *Out of Thin Air*, 38–41.

Frank on the importance of words with pictures on television: Frank said this during an interview on C-SPAN 2's *Booknotes*, September 15, 1991, interviewed by Brian Lamb. It is available at www.booknotes.org/Watch/21239-1/Reuven+Frank .aspx (accessed January 21, 2013).

PF's broadcasts from and about the *Repose*: These were taken from scripts dated February 19 and 20, 1953, and airing beginning March 2, SSC, box 3, folder 2.

Overview of the leading names in broadcasting of the era: See Bliss, *Now the News*, 185–86.

Background on Murrow: Murrow's broadcasts about McCarthy are discussed in the Museum of Broadcast Communications website, www.museum.tv/eotvsection .php?entrycode=seeitnow (accessed February 19, 2013). For a fictionalized account, see the 2005 film *Good Night and Good Luck*, Warner Independent Pictures.

Details of Murrow's broadcast: Bliss, *Now the News*, 234–44.

PF's comments about the "true picture" of UN activities: Lois Fegan, "Miss Frederick: Former Harrisburger Follows History in the Making," *Harrisburg Patriot-News*, August 27, 1950.

PF's views on the responsibilities of a reporter: She said this during a speech to the American Women in Radio and Television, in Buffalo NY, on September 25, 1953, SSC, box 23, folder 4.

6. PERILS OF PAULINE

Epigraph: PF quoted Stevenson in an interview with Norman Ho, April-May 1984, UN OHist. She repeated this line occasionally in speeches and, in at least one case, in a 1980 news broadcast for NPR. Script available in SSC, box 18, folder 1.

PF's UN broadcast after the fighting ended: A transcript of this broadcast, dated August 17, 1953, is in SSC box 4, folder 2.

Broadcast near end of war: A transcript of this broadcast, dated June 15, 1953, is in SSC, box 4, folder 1.

Ending broadcasts wishing audience has a "courageous" day: A broadcast she did about the daily schedule of DH, which aired on August 30, 1956, also ended this way. This is available digitally in SSC, audiocassette in box 54.

Details about Theta Sigma Phi Award: This is in SSC, box 43, folder 1.

Salary and contract details: Contract outlined in letter from American Broadcasting Company, Inc., signed by Thomas Velotta, to PF in care of her attorney, Gerald Dickler, September 14, 1951, SSC, box 3, folder 20.

Apartment and new puppy: Several stories described PF's apartment, including Watson, "Woman Finds Man's World of Radio a Challenging Field." A story in the *Baton Rouge State Times* also described the apartment. See Clayton Cox, "Pauline Frederick Spends Busy Day in Baton Rouge as Farm Home Speaker," August 8, 1954. The poodle was discussed in the *Johnson City (TN) Press*, March 21, 1951.

PF giving up smoking: Letter, PF to Ann Cordell, May 11, 1954, SSC, box 37, folder 5.

PF ailment: Letter, PF to Ann Cordell, September 19, 1954, SSC, box 38, folder 13.

Number of social engagements: Letter, PF to Ann Cordell, August 22, 1954, SSC, box 38, folder 16.

PF's hectic schedule: Letter, PF to Ann Cordell, October 17, 1952, SSC, box 38, folder 13. PF told many interviewers about her morning routine before work. See, e.g., Watson, "Woman Finds Man's World of Radio a Challenging Field."

PF giving up her dog: Letter, PF to Ann Cordell, September 9, 1953, SSC, box 38, folder 13.

***Motorola Television Hour* program about the nuclear blast:** The episode, named "Atomic Attack," aired on season 1, episode 15. It was directed by Ralph Nelson. It can be seen at BTV Guide website, www.btvguide.net/The-Motorola-Television-Hour/Season-1/episode-15 (accessed June 12, 2014).

PF's reaction to McMahon's stance on nuclear power: Letter, PF to Brien McMahon, February 3, 1950, SSC, box 36, folder 10.

PF's broadcast about McMahon: Notes of a broadcast transcript of this topic, dated February 3, 1950, are in SSC, box 3, folder 25.

McMahon's response to PF: Letter, Brien McMahon to PF, February 20, 1950, SSC, box 36, folder 10.

Battle over the League of Nations: A. Scott Berg discussed this at length in his biography of Wilson, *Wilson*. See Lodge's obituary, "Senator Lodge Dies, Victim of Stroke in His 75th Year," NYT, November 10, 1924.

PF quoting Benét: This came during a talk she gave to the YWCA of New York City. She was quoted in YWCA *Magazine*, January 1960. The article in SSC, box 35, folder 9.

PF invoking what would be known as the "military-industrial complex": She talked about this in the speech to the YWCA. For information about Eisenhower's comments, see, e.g., "This Day in History," January 17, 1961, History.com website, www.history.com/this-day-in-history/eisenhower-warns-of-military-industrial-complex (accessed January 13, 2013).

PF on the fifteenth anniversary of the UN charter: This came from one of her scripts for NBC dated June 26, 1960, SSC, box 8, folder 1.

PF's hopes that the United States and the USSR could get together: See Cohen, "In a Man's World," 6.

PF on the fingerprinting of UN employees: UN OHist, July 11, 1986.

PF on investigation of news scripts: Letter, PF to Ann Cordell, August 22, 1954, SSC, box 38, folder 16.

Peace being "sold": PF said this at the speech she gave on April 26, 1957, SSC, box 23, folder 1.

PF's hours at NBC: She described them to Ann Cordell in a letter, April 21, 1953, SSC, box 37, folder 15.

Resignation letter: Letter, PF to RK, undated but believed to have been written in mid-April 1953, SSC, box 3, folder 6.

PF saying McAndrew had hired her: She said this in a speech at Ohio University while accepting the university's Carr Van Anda Award, May 7, 1971. A digitized version of the speech is available at SSC, box 56.

Kintner's acceptance of resignation: Letter, RK to PF, April 21, 1953, SSC, box 3, folder 6.

NBC news release about PF's hiring: NBC Radio News, "Pauline Frederick and Joseph C. Harsch, Noted Radio Commentators, Join NBC News Staff; New Assignment for Clifton Utley," SSC, box 14, folder 17.

Frank's comments about renewed interest in international news: Frank said this during an interview on C-SPAN 2's *Booknotes*, September 15, 1991, interviewed by Brian Lamb. It is available at www.booknotes.org/Watch/21239-1/Reuven+Frank .aspx.

PF grateful about ABC contract release: Letter, PF to Ann Cordell, April 21, 1953, SSC, box 3, folder 6.

Urquhart's first impressions of DH: He said this during an interview with UN officials published at the UN website: www.un.org/apps/news/newsmakers .asp?NewsID=42#.uw3nUneMqVI.email (accessed January 3, 2013).

PF on DH's spirituality: Broadcast Pioneers Library OHist, LAB.

What was found with DH's body: See Thorpe, *Dag Hammarskjöld*, 42.

Lipsey's biography: Lipsey, *Hammarskjöld*, xii.

PF's comments about the Meditation Room: UN OHist, June 20, 1986. PF's specific comments on the light shining on the altar were quoted in Olivia Skinner, "Pauline Frederick Hides Her Emotions," *St. Louis Post-Dispatch*, January 13, 1965. But PF spoke in interviews throughout her life about the Meditation Room.

Lie's tenure as secretary-general: For a summary, see, e.g., O'Sullivan, *United Nations*, 16–17.

DH and the captured flyers: PF talked about this at length in the UN OHist, June 20, 1986.

DH as a man of the people: PF talked about this in the UN OHist, July 11, 1986.

Broadcast about incoming secretary-general DH: This is dated August 30, 1953, and is available digitally at the Sophia Smith Collection. A disk version is stored in box 54.

PF denying romantic relationship with DH: She did this many times during her career. See, e.g., Jean Henniger's story in the *Oregonian*, May 10, 1969, headline unknown. A copy is in SSC, box 17, folder 9.

Rumors of DH's sexuality: Lipsey, Hammarskjöld, 93–103.

DH's daily routine: This is outlined in PF's NBC broadcast of August 30, 1956, available digitally in SSC. A disk of it is in box 54.

Comparison of DH to Norgay: NBC broadcast, August 30, 1956, available digitally at SSC.

PF's self-described political leanings: Letter, PF to Ann Cordell, January 24, 1952, SSC, box 38, folder 15.

PF's view of Stevenson: Letter, PF to Ann Cordell, June 26, 1952, SSC, box 38, folder 15.

Republicans having "nothing new to offer": Letter, PF to Ann Cordell, July 2, 1952, SSC, box 38, folder 15.

PF fearing an Eisenhower White House: Letter, PF to Ann Cordell, September 3, 1952, SSC, box 38, folder 15.

PF not changing her views on Eisenhower: Letter, PF to Ann Cordell, June 26, 1952, SSC, box 38, folder 15.

PF on Eisenhower's attitudes toward the "Fifth Estate": She said this in a broadcast dated January 12, 1953. Transcript is in SSC, box 4, folder 1.

Report on Dulles's foreign policy: Broadcast dated January 12, 1953. A transcript is in SSC, box 4, folder 1.

Story about first filmed news conference: "President's News Conference Filmed for TV and Newsreels for First Time," *NYT*, January 20, 1955.

***Channel Chuckle* and *Family Circle* cartoons:** PF apparently had the *Channel Chuckle* framed (the one about "convening the Security Council") and left it with her niece CC. It is now at the Newseum in Washington DC.

Reasons PF won the duPont Award: These are stated in a duPont document, stored in SSC, box 43, folder 2. For a list of duPont recipients, see the website: www.journalism.columbia.edu/page/412/9?printing=true (accessed February 1, 2013).

Congratulations from Pat Weaver: Letter, Sylvester "Pat" Weaver to PF, March 26, 1954, SSC, box 43, folder 5.

Congratulations from HRB: Letter, HRB to PF, April 1, 1954, SSC, box 43, folder 5.

Speech at the Peabody Awards dinner: This is undated but believed to be in late March 1955, SSC, box 43, folder 3.

Coverage of the Peabody Awards: "Gobel, Daly Win Peabody Awards," *Broadcasting*, April 11, 1955, 105.

Reasons PF received the Peabody: NBC listed these in a news release about the award: "Secretary-General Dag Hammarskjöld of the UN Extends Congratulations to NBC Radio's Pauline Frederick for Winning Peabody," NBC Radio Network News, April 21, 1955, SSC, box 43, folder 5.

Velotta's congratulations on the Peabody: Letter, Tom Velotta to PF, April 21, 1955, SSC, box 43, folder 5.

DH's congratulations on Peabody: Telegram, DH to PF, April 20, 1955, SSC, box 43, folder 5. His telegram was also featured in the news release sent out by NBC. PF's response to DH is dated April 27, 1955, SSC.

PF's speech at the Peabody Awards ceremony: She is quoted in NBC's news release about the award.

Reasons for winning *McCall's* Award: These are given in an NBC news release announcing the award, dated April 18, 1956, SSC, box 43, folder 10.

Congratulatory letter from Weaver: Letter, Sylvester "Pat" Weaver to PF, undated, SSC, box 43, folder 10.

Photo of PF with Molotov: This framed photo is now at the Newseum in Washington DC.

Details of the "scoop" with Molotov: This is described in a news release from NBC about the exclusive story. See the release from NBC's radio show *Monitor* dated June 2, 1955, SSC, box 43, folder 10.

Possibility of Overseas Press Club Award and get-together at her home: Letter, PF to Ann Cordell, undated other than "post-Thanksgiving" (1955), SSC, box 38, folder 16.

Urquhart's comments about DH: He was quoted in the UN's website, www.un.org. His book is titled *Hammarskjöld*.

Urquhart's comments about DH and PF: He said this in an email message to the author dated July 23, 2013.

DH as loner: Lipsey, *Hammarskjöld*, 32–33.

PF's note to DH: Note, PF to DH, November 18, 1956, SSC, box 16, folder 6.

DH note on plane: CC has this note in her possession.

DH's views against preferential treatment of the press: Urquhart, email message to the author.

7. THE GREAT ASSEMBLY HALL

Epigraph: Schlesinger was quoted in John Bartlow Martin's biography of Adlai Stevenson, *Adlai Stevenson and the World*, 668.

PF's broadcast of the Korean War armistice: This broadcast is dated August 17, 1953, SSC, box 4, folder 2.

"You and Article 71": A recording of this special feature is available at the UN website, www.unmultimedia.org/radio/library/classics/detail/758.html (accessed November 11, 2012).

PF's description of nuclear damage: She said this in Chicago at the Katherine Legge Memorial luncheon, May 11, 1955, SSC, box 23, folder 6.

Speech to Lynchburg graduates: This took place on June 3, 1956, SSC, box 23, folder 5. The NYT story, "Airborne H-bomb Exploded by U.S. over Pacific Isle," by William L. Laurence, was published on May 21, 1956.

Broadcast about McCarthy and the Greeks: A transcript of this broadcast is dated March 9, 1953, and is in SSC, box 3, folder 2.

Broadcast quoting newspaper commentary about McCarthy: This is dated March 15, 1954, SSC, box 4, folder 4.

Gallup Poll about McCarthy: See Fried, *Nightmare in Red*, 138.

Letter to Cordell about McCarthy and the army: Letter, PF to Ann Cordell, March 12, 1954, SSC, box 38, folder 16.

PF's recollection of DH's Mideast visit: UN OHist, June 20, 1986.

Background of the Suez crisis: See www.history.com/topics/cold-war/suez -crisis (accessed June 10, 2014).

PF "chained to the microphone": "Busy Redhead Reporting," *Newsweek*, August 11, 1958, 54.

DH's note on the plane: This undated note was apparently a prized possession of PF. She had it framed and kept it at her home. It was not sent with her papers to SSC but, instead, was included among a small cache of possessions in Florida recovered after she died, according to CC.

PF's retelling of DH as a target: UN OHist, June 20, 1986.

NBC officials angry that PF did not get an exclusive: See Talese, "Perils of Pauline," 21.

PF's romances: Talese, "Perils of Pauline," 22. CC mentioned this in an interview with the author, December 9, 2012.

PF saying she would not hinder negotiations: "Busy Redhead Reporting."

DH as loner: PF said this during a 1959 broadcast about the secretary-general (month and day unknown), SSC, box 35, folder 2.

DH's sexuality: Roger Lipsey discussed this in his biography of DH, *Hammarskjöld*, 95, 110.

NBC's news release about PF's show: This is dated June 1953, SSC, box 13, folder 5.

PF finding time to wash her hair: NBC Feature news release, July 27, 1960, SSC, box 14, folder 16.

Brokaw's tribute to PF: Brokaw said this on the May 10, 1990, edition of the *NBC Nightly News*. A recording is available at the Vanderbilt University Television News Archive, www.tvnews.vanderbilt.edu/.

Announcement of PF as "anchorman": This came in an NBC news release dated April 30, 1956, SSC, box 13, folder 5.

Women covering the conventions: A story in *Glamour* magazine, in July 1956, noted that some other women would cover the convention.

Coverage by television: See "Coverage Chronology," *Broadcasting*, August 6, 1956, 30.

Television's scope and improving technology: "Covering History and Making It," *Broadcasting*, August 6, 1956, 27, 29.

Politicians aware of the camera: "Conventions: Change on Tap?" *Broadcasting*, August 27, 1956, 28–29.

Fashion story in the *Herald Tribune*: Eugenia Sheppard, "Radio Reporter Picks Wardrobe for Conventions," *New York Herald Tribune*, June 27, 1956.

Column about PF's anchor appointment: Marie Torre, "No Frills on Pauline's Reports," *New York Herald Tribune*, May 31, 1956.

Walter Cronkite at the 1952 conventions: Matusow, *Evening Stars*, 65.

Hiring of Weaver and his opinion of Swayze: Frank, *Out of Thin Air*, 48.

Murrow's long shadow: Matusow, *Evening Stars*, 64–65, 69–70.

Summary of the beginnings of *Today*: Frank, *Out of Thin Air*, 47–48.

Communication forms merging and the power of television: Thomas Whiteside, "Profile: The Communicator," *New Yorker*, October 16, 1954, 42, 47–48. The second part of the Weaver profile appeared on October 23, 1954, 10–23, 42–44, 62, 64–70.

Background of the creation of the *Huntley-Brinkley Report*: *Out of Thin Air*, 110–25.

Description of Huntley and Brinkley: Bliss, *Now the News*, 303.

Chet and David as "Superstars": Matusow, *Evening Stars*, 70. The *New Yorker* story was written by William Whitworth and was published on August 3, 1968.

Huntley and Brinkley's legendary sign-off: Frank recalls this in *Out of Thin Air*, 113.

PF's acquaintance with Huntley and Brinkley: In "Perils of Pauline," Talese quoted Huntley about PF, 20. In an interview with Mary-Ann Bendel in USA *Today*, "Topic: Women on the Air," January 14, 1985, PF recalled her first view of Brinkley.

PF irked at network executives' reaction to her performance: Talese, "Perils of Pauline," 22.

PF covering 1956 general election: "Our Cover and Our Election Coverage," *San Francisco Call-Bulletin*, November 3, 1956.

Harrison's critique of coverage: Bernie Harrison, "On the Air," *Washington Evening Star*, November 9, 1956.

News release about *Monitor* UN series: A copy of this news release, dated November 1956, is in SSC, box 14, folder 13.

PF's response to *Monitor* series: Memo, PF to WM, November 28, 1956, SSC, box 14, folder 13.

PF "using her elbows": Telephone interview by the author with Robert Asman, December 17, 2012.

PF's comments about David Sarnoff: A transcript of this broadcast is dated June 1953, SSC, box 4, folder 1.

PF confirming Sarnoff's remarks: NBC Inter-Department Correspondence memo, PF to "General Sarnoff," June 17, 1957, SSC, box 14, folder 2.

PF's salary in 1956: This is evident from her employment contract, found in SSC, box 14, folder 11. Her income was converted to current dollars using the Bureau of Labor Statistics website, www.bls.gov/data/ (accessed January 30, 2013).

Critics' award: NBC sent out a news release on this dated January 15, 1957, SSC, box 44, folder 13.

Praise from Gould: Jack Gould, "Radio-TV: UN Debate Coverage," *NYT*, November 5, 1956.

Gift of panty hose: This was given to her by R. E. Kell. Letter, Kell to PF, February 1, 1954, SSC, box 36, folder 12.

PF as honorary colonel: This honor was described in an NBC news release dated June 10, 1954, SSC, box 14, folder 6.

PF's "encouraging" broadcasts: Letter, Alta M. and Charles Hancock to PF, July 22, 1958, SSC, box 36, folder 13.

Thanks for her coverage of Russians: Letter, Mrs. Robert Coody to PF, May 24, 1960, SSC, box 36, folder 14.

Thanks for interpreting the news: Letter, Myrtle Henderson to PF, May 26, 1960, SSC, box 36, folder 14.

Letter asking PF to hire his daughter: Letter, Alex Marcus to PF, May 17, 1960, SSC, box 36, folder 14. PF's response is dated June 14, 1960.

8. IF NOT MISS FREDERICK, WHO?

Epigraph: The president was unhappy with this report by PF, in which he claimed she had been "used" by the Soviets. Recording of telephone conversation between LBJ and Arthur Goldberg, April 22, 1966, 6:45 p.m., citation no. 11046, Recordings and Transcripts of Conversations and Meetings, LBJ Library. A tape of the conversation is available online at YouTube.com, www.youtube.com/watch?v=w7-hgLPAUDA&list =ple4ezrXJCEORIGndWG-3putubzIMPJAHN&index=4 (accessed March 3, 2013).

Russia's refusal to pay fees: PF talked about this in a speech to the Sixty-Ninth Annual Congress of American Industry, New York, December 3, 1964. A transcript of the speech was reprinted in *Vital Speeches of the Day*, February 15, 1965, 265–66.

Fedorenko's comments to PF: This was recounted in an NBC news release, April 22, 1963, "Soviet UN Delegate's Criticism of NBC's Pauline Frederick Gets Prompt Rebuttal," SSC, box 21, folder 15.

Gornicki's gift of vodka: PF wrote about this incident many years later in a letter to the NYT. See PF, letter to the editor, NYT, January 22, 1982.

PF's comments about the Fedorenko incident: Memo, PF to WM, April 16, 1963, SSC, box 21, folder 15. See also Donald Grant, "New Russian UN Ambassador Gives a Confusing Impression," *Baltimore Evening Sun*, April 19, 1963. The news release and the *Evening Sun* story mentioned that the Polish correspondent had given PF vodka "in sympathy" for the incident. PF talked about the vodka in the Broadcast Pioneers OHist, LAB.

PF "our favorite lady": John O'Connor, "Television and Radio," *Trenton Catholic Monitor*, May 3, 1963.

PF's later "friendship" with Fedorenko: See Eleanor Roberts, "Pauline Frederick Gives NBC a Jump at UN," *Boston Traveler*, June 16, 1967.

Khrushchev angry about call-in show: This is recounted in *Editor & Publisher*, June 15, 1954, 87.

PF's story about Vietnam ceasefire: The Soviets' rebuttal of the story came in a news release from the Soviet embassy dated April 25, 1966, SSC, box 14, folder 13.

PF's comments about the Vietnam cease-fire story: These were made in an interview. See Dick Crouch, *Jacksonville (FL) Times-Union*, April 26, 1966.

PF's comments about being "used" by sources: Broadcast Pioneers OHist, LAB.

Brinkley's "heads-up" to the White House: See memo, Bob Fleming to LBJ, April 22, 1966, filed in the PF Name File, SHCF, box 243, LBJ Library.

Johnson's phone conversation to Goldberg: Recording of telephone conversation between LBJ and Arthur Goldberg, April 22, 1966.

PF's call from Goldberg: She recalled this in the Broadcast Pioneers OH.

Johnson's call to Ball: Recording of telephone conversation between LBJ and George Ball, April 22, 1966, 7:15 p.m., citation no. 10047, Recordings and Transcripts of Conversations and Meetings, LBJ Library.

Huntley's comments about the three television sets: Transcript, Chet Huntley, OH interview, May 12, 1969, by Joe B. Frantz, Internet Copy, LBJ Library.

Bombeck column: This syndicated column appeared in most newspapers on December 18, 1969.

Review of PF's UN show: "Radio Reviews," *Variety*, September 18, 1957, 36.

Brokaw's note: Note, Brokaw to PF, January 20, 1964, SSC, box 14, folder 10.

Photo of Bush and PF: This is in SSC, box 48, folder 6.

Humphrey's complimentary letter: Letter, Hubert Humphrey to PF, March 9, 1962, SSC, box 36, folder 14.

PF's friendship with Carl Sandburg: This was noted by CC in an interview with the author, April 6, 2013, Evanston IL. The original poem and photos of PF and Sandburg are in Cole's possession. The July 1960 letter from Sandburg to PF is in SSC, box 37, folder 8.

Correspondents' tour: This was frequently written about and referred to in interviews with PF. See, e.g., "NBC Correspondents Gather from Afar," *Broadcasting,* January 9, 1967, 62. Two memos from press officers in the Johnson White House indicate that the correspondents sought to speak with LBJ. See memo, Bill Monroe to George Christian, January 2, 1968, filed in the PF Name File, WHCF, box 243, LBJ Library; and memo, Bob Fleming to LBJ, January 3, 1967, filed in the Pauline Frederick Name File, WHCF, Box 243, LBJ Library. No response was found to either memo.

PF's "celebrity" script: This was written about in "Pauline's Pen Is Mightier," *Radio-Television Daily*, May 10, 1962.

PF barely having time to wash her hair: This was included in a news release from NBC, July 27, 1960, SSC, box 14, folder 16. The anecdote about broadcasting after the basketball game was also recounted in an NBC news release dated February 18, 1958, SSC, box 14, folder 16.

PF in hair curlers: She told this story during an interview with Henry Mitchell of the *Memphis Commercial-Appeal.* See "Hair Curlers Pose Problem in Midst of World Crisis," April 17, 1963.

NBC News pulling ahead of CBS: See Matusow, *Evening Stars,* 78.

Cronkite as rising star: Matusow, *Evening Stars,* 110.

Response to Maxwell Taylor story: *Today* "Mail Report" for the week beginning February 6, 1967, SSC box 14, folder 3.

Viewers' comments in "Mail Report": These appeared in the "Mail Report" for the week beginning February 6, 1967. The writers "Just a Disgusted Listener" and Johnston wrote in response to an interview PF had with UN ambassador George H. W. Bush in July 1972. They are in SSC, box 14, folder 4. ·

PF keeping her emotions from her broadcasts: This was discussed in Bob Brock, "Pauline Frederick: Don't Fence Her In," *Dallas Times Herald,* April 17, 1963.

PF as person of "deep feelings": See Lucy Baggett, *National Business Woman,* June 1961.

Stevenson background: See his obituary, "Adlai Ewing Stevenson, an Urbane, Witty, Articulate Politician and Diplomat," *NYT,* July 15, 1965.

Stories about PF's naming as head of UNCA: The *Washington Post* story appeared on March 8, 1958; a story in the *Christian Science Monitor* appeared on April 6, 1959. Her appointment to the position also prompted other media interviews with her.

PF's access at the UN: See Jim Holton, "Pauline Frederick: Not for Today's Hucksters," *Reading (PA) Eagle,* May 19, 1990.

PF discussing formal UN dinners: See Hope Lawder Richie, "The Only Woman . . . ," *Greenfield (MA) Recorder-Gazette,* April 24, 1959. She described what she wore to her first formal UN dinner in a speech to the American Women in Radio and Television, September 20, 1983, LAB.

The "kissingest" scene: This appeared in "Ladies of the Press," *Connecticut Sunday Herald TV Channels,* July 10–16, 1960.

UN Correspondents article: John MacVane, "The Regulars Cover the United Nations," *Overseas Press Bulletin,* September 17, 1960, SSC, box 39, folder 11.

PF's introduction of DH: Transcript of the talk, September 10, 1959, SSC, box 21, folder 16.

Castro's speech: An audiotape of this speech, dated April 22, 1959, is in SSC, box 56 (no folder).

History of the Bay of Pigs: See information at the John F. Kennedy Library, www .jfklibrary.org/jfk/jfk-in-History/The-Bay-of-Pigs.aspx (accessed March 13, 2013).

Stevenson's role in the Bay of Pigs: www.historyofcuba.com/history/baypigs /pigs4.htm (accessed March 13, 2013).

Stevenson's thank-you note: Letter, Adlai Stevenson to PF, February 9, 1961, SSC, box 38, folder 10.

PF's comments about Stevenson's role in the Bay of Pigs: See the UN OHist, April and May 1984. She said in several interviews that she thought Stevenson should have resigned after the incident. See Broadcast Pioneers OHist, September 8, 1984; and Clarke Taylor, "The Perils of Pauline Frederick," *Los Angeles Times*, September 24, 1983. In that article PF questioned Kennedy's loyalty to the UN.

Van Horn's critique of PF's and Cronkite's coverage: This appeared in Van Horn's column in the *New York World-Telegram* on April 24, 1961.

Background of the Cuban Missile Crisis: John F. Kennedy Presidential Library and Museum website, www.jfklibrary.org/jfk/jfk-in-History/Cuban-Missile-Crisis .aspx (accessed March 13, 2013).

Debate about the Khrushchev shoe-banging incident: See, e.g., William Taubman, "Did He Bang It?" *NYT*, July 2, 2003. In an interview with former CBS correspondent Richard Hottelet for the UN OHist project, the interviewer, Jean Krasno, said the UN cameras, which usually videotaped General Assembly meetings, were not on when Khrushchev banged his shoe. The OH is dated May 6, 2005.

PF's comments about Khrushchev: "Surf Club" speech, December 6, 1960, to the Committee of One Hundred (city and state not noted but likely Miami), SSC, box 23, folder 14.

Talese's *Saturday Evening Post* story: "Perils of Pauline" appeared on January 26, 1963.

Offer to write a book: Morrie Helitzer to PF, undated. PF's handwritten response is undated, SSC, box 38, folder 13.

Talese's comments to PF: See letter, Gay Talese to PF, January 31, 1962, SSC, box 36, folder 1.

Letters in response to Talese's article: These are in SSC, box 37, folder 1; Voula Demas to Pauline PF, January 22, 1963; an unnamed fan from Florence SC, to PF, January 24, 1963; C. H. Fox to PF, January 24, 1963; Therese Howe to PF, January 29, 1963.

NBC news release about Purex special: This is dated September 1960 and is in SSC, box 13, folder 10.

PF's discussion of her doubts about participating in the Purex shows: She said this in "Gal in a Man's World," *Miami Herald*, December 11, 1960.

Review of "The Cold Woman": R.F.S., "TV: The Cold Woman," *NYT*, October 15, 1960.

PF's interview with *New York World-Telegram and Sun*: This *World-Telegram and Sun* is dated October 11, 1960; a copy of it, with no headline, is in SSC, box 13, folder 10.

Thank-you note from Gitlin: Irving Gitlin to PF, May 4, 1962, SSC, box 14, folder 11.

Background on Gitlin: Bliss, *Now the News*, 405.

9. DEATH OF THE PEACOCK

Epigraph: Telephone interview by the author with Robert Asman, December 12, 2012.

DH's travels: O Sullivan, *United Nations*, 17.

Fear of "foreigners": PF discussed this in the UN OHist, April–May 1984.

Differing problems of smaller and larger nations: PF talked about this in the Broadcast Pioneers OHist, LAB.

Problems of smaller countries in the UN: PF, *YWCA Magazine*, January 1960. A copy of it is in SSC, box 35, folder 9.

UN "used" by some nations: UN OHist interview with Hottelet, May 6, 2005.

PF's quote from Quaison-Sackey: She recounted this in the Broadcast Pioneers OHist, LAB.

DH as "casualty": PF said this many times over the years, including in the UN OHist, April–May 1984.

Reason for Khrushchev shoe pounding: This has been discussed many times, and Hottelet brought it up in his UN OHist interview.

NBC special broadcast: This special evening broadcast aired on September 17, 1961. Transcript is in SSC, box 11, folder 15.

PF's speculation about possible sabotage in DH's death: Transcript of her talk at the Rice University Associates dinner meeting, Houston, March 7, 1962, SSC, box 23, folder 13. The possibility of sabotage has been discussed at length by many others. See, e.g., documents at the UN website, "Special Report on the Fatal Flight of the Secretary-General's Aircraft," September 19, 1961, www.un.org/Depts/dhl/dag /docs/s4940ad5ef.pdf (accessed December 4, 2012); as well as a story in the *Guardian* newspaper by Julian Borger, "New Inquiry Set Up into Death of UN Secretary General Dag Hammarskjöld," July 18, 2012, www.guardian.co.uk/world/2012/jul/18 /inquiry-death-un-dag-hammarskjold-2 (accessed December 4, 2012); Lipsey, *Hammarskjöld*, 558–70; Williams, *Who Killed Hammarskjöld*, 3–15.

AP story about DH's funeral: A wire copy of this story by Elizabeth Kitson is in SSC, box 15, folder 8.

NBC broadcast after the plane crash: This thirty-minute broadcast, called "Death of a Statesman," aired on September 18, 1961. Chet Hagan was the producer and Bob Priaulx director. A transcript is in SSC, box 11, folder 15.

PF's comments about reaction to her "Death of a Statesman" broadcast: She said this in the Broadcast Pioneers OHist, LAB.

Notes about the week before DH's death: Typewritten and hand-edited copies of these are in SSC, box 35, folder 6.

PF's pessimistic comments: See "New UN Attitudes after Dag Hammarskjöld Tragedy," *Kansas City Star*, November 18, 1961.

PF's belief that both superpowers had blame for world problems: *Kansas City Star*, "New UN Attitudes after Dag Hammarskjöld Tragedy."

PF's broadcast a year after DH's death: She repeated those lines of the broadcast in the UN OHist interview, July 11, 1985.

Urquhart's comments: These are available in a digital interview with him on the UN website: www.un.org/apps/news/newsmakers.asp?NewsID=79 (accessed January 9, 2013).

Background of U Thant and the reasons he was selected: UN OHist interview with Nassif Ramses, March 9, 1998, interviewed by Jean Krasno, www.un.org.

U Thant's role in the Cuban Missile Crisis: This was noted by Hottelet in his UN OHist interview as well as by Brian Urquhart in the interview posted on the UN website.

New York newspaper strike: See Joseph Bernt and Marilyn Greenwald, "Well Worth the Dime: Reader Loyalty to the *New York Standard* When Television Was New," presented to the Association for Education in Journalism and Mass Communication annual conference, August 2007, Washington DC. Also, Barbara Matusow noted that 1963 marked the first year that more people said they got their news from television than from newspapers. See Matusow, *Evening Stars*, 126

CBS announcement of evening news expansion: Bliss, *Now the News*, 305.

"Glamour" of the news: See Matusow, *Evening Stars*, 95. Matusow also noted that the decision by CBS to do a thirty-minute newscast likely came because the network was behind NBC in the ratings.

Minow's speech: Minow gave this speech at a conference of the National Association of Broadcasters on May 9, 1961.

Frank's comments about the golden age of television news: He made these comments during an interview on C-SPAN 2's *Booknotes*, interviewed by Brian Lamb, September 15, 1991. A recording of it is available at www.booknotes.org /Watch/21239-1/Reuven+Frank.aspx (accessed March 7, 2013).

Frank's memo on the evening news expansion: Memo, Reuven Frank to WM, January 18, 1963, LOC, NBC History Files, folder 310.

Comments by Utley: Telephone interview by the author with Garrick Utley, November 16, 2012.

Comments by Coates: Telephone interview by the author with Charles Coates, November 24, 2012.

Details on the Pope's visit to the UN: These were spelled out in a news release from NBC dated October 5, 1965, SSC, box 13, folder 6.

PF's broadcast of the Pope's visit: A transcript of the October 4, 1965, broadcast is in SSC, box 13, folder 8.

Letters to PF about Pope Paul VI's visit: Mrs. Harvey K. Bleeker wrote to PF on October 9, 1965; Francis Regis's letter is dated October 7, 1965. They are in SSC, box 13, folder 7.

PF's broadcast about the UN and the moon: This is dated July 11, 1969. A transcript is in SSC, box 13, folder 14.

Laurent's criticism: This came in Laurent's column, "Excellent U-2 Coverage Stirs Ridiculous Beefs," *Washington Post and Times-Herald*, May 20, 1960.

Compliments on U-2 coverage: Both of these critiques were in the *New York Daily News*. See Kay Gardella's column, May 4, 1960; and Ben Gross's column, May 2, 1960.

PF's article about the U-2 incident and the Cold War: See PF, "Substitute for the Battlefield," *NEA Journal*, October 1960, 34-37.

PF on complaints from both sides: PF said this in the Broadcast Pioneers OHist, LAB.

Reaction to Golda Meir story: Edward Pearlstein to PF, September 30, 1969; Martin J. Segal to PF, September 30, 1969; Virginia Tanner to PF, September 30, 1969. Schulberg received a letter of thanks from Shaul Ben-Haim, October 9, 1969; see also letter from Margaret Mozzanini to PF, September 30, 1969. All are in SSC, box 14, folder 2.

Measuring the time devoted to the Riad and Meir stories: This is spelled out in a memo from Stuart Schulberg to Reuven Frank, Don Meaney, and PF, October 6, 1969, SSC, box 14, folder 2.

Critical memo about *Today* interview: Memo, Stuart Schulberg to PF, undated. PF's response is dated July 27, 1970; his response to her is undated. All are in SSC, box 14, folder 2.

Asman's comments about PF: Interview by the author with Robert Asman.

Network coverage of the Kennedy assassination: See Matusow, *Evening Stars*, 89; and Frank, *Out of Thin Air*, 189-90.

Kennedy assassination as a pivotal event in broadcasting: See Caro, *Years of Lyndon Johnson*, 386.

Praise to PF about Kennedy assassination coverage: Memo, RK to PF, November 27, 1963, SSC, box 14, folder 11.

U Thant's comments about the shooting of Robert Kennedy: See a transcript of PF's June 5, 1968, broadcast, SSC, box 11, folder 1.

PF's prediction that the People's Republic of China would gain UN admission: She said this in several broadcasts and also made the prediction in an interview. See Mary Lou Loper, "Newswomen Assess Nixon's 100 Days," *Los Angeles Times*, May 25, 1969.

PF's comments about Nixon and the UN: Loper, "Newswomen Assess Nixon's 100 Days."

Goodman's praise of PF's Mideast coverage: JG to PF, June 19, 1967, SSC, box 14, folder 2.

NBC news release about PF's speech: This was issued on May 8, 1969; PF gave the speech in Seattle on May 7. The news release is in SSC, box 17, folder 9.

10. LIBERATING THE AIRWAVES

Epigraph: See Lee Graham, "Women Don't Like to Look at Women," *NYT*, May 24, 1964.

Zelnick and treatment of correspondents: Telephone interview by the author with Bob Zelnick, November 14, 2012.

Selection of correspondents to travel to China: See Frank, *Out of Thin Air*, 330–33; and Matusow, *Evening Stars*, 202–4.

Barbara Walters and live coverage from Europe: She discusses this in her memoir, *Audition*, 145–46.

Congratulatory note from Goodman: Memo, JG to PF, undated, but believed to be in December 1971, SSC, box 14, folder 12.

Walters's trip to China: See her memoir, *Audition*, 217–28.

Effect of the trip on Walters's career: See Frank, *Out of Thin Air*, 330–31; see also Matusow, *Evening Stars*, 205.

Kintner's career: See his obituary, "Kintner Dies at 71; Headed ABC, NBC," *Broadcasting*, January 5, 1981, 90.

McAndrew's career: See his obituary, "William R. McAndrew, 53, Dies; Directed NBC News since 1951," *NYT*, May 31, 1968.

Walters's troubles with McGee: See Matusow, *Evening Stars*, 204.

Technology and the role of the UN: See "On the UN Beat," *Newsweek*, October 14, 1968, 58.

Johnson's, Fedorenko's, and U Thant's speeches: See *NYT* stories by Drew Middleton: "Johnson Appeals to UN to Press Reds on Vietnam," June 26, 1965; and "Soviet Denounces U.S. as Aggressors at UN Ceremony," June 27, 1965.

Hottelet's comments about Vietnam and the Russians: UN OHist interview with Jean Drasno, May 6, 2005. www.unmultimedia.org/oralhistory/2011/06/hottelet -richard/ (accessed December 17, 2012).

***Meet the Press* show after Johnson's speech:** A transcript of this June 27, 1965, broadcast is in SSC, box 12, folder 9.

The UN as a news beat: See "On the UN Beat," *Newsweek*.

Hottelet's comments about UN coverage: See his UN OHist interview.

The UN and the Mideast: This relationship is discussed in detail in O'Sullivan, *United Nations*, 53–80.

Sanders's recollections of the news environment in 1964: See her book with Marcia Rock, *Waiting for Prime Time*, 39–41. She discussed Howard and her death on 44–45 and 50; and in an article she did for *Television Quarterly*, "A Farewell to Some of the Firsts," *Television Quarterly* 30, no. 1 (1999): 12–14.

Lee Hall's background: See her obituary, Patricia Sullivan, "Lee Hall: Correspondent for NBC-TV and Radio," *Washington Post*, March 29, 2006.

TV Guide story on women in media: "They Refuse to Pitch Their Curves," *TV Guide*, June 16, 1962, 6–9.

PF not overtly sexual or threatening: Telephone interview by the author with Marlene Sanders, October 23, 2011.

PF's comment that women should listen and not talk: She said this during a speech in Miami on March 3, 1962, audience unknown.

Comparison of the civil rights and women's movements: Lilla Anderson, "Pauline Frederick, Reporter," *TV Radio Mirror*, January 1960, 62–64.

Elmer Lower quote about women's voices: This appeared in Lee Graham, "Women Don't Like to Look at Women," *NYT*, May 24, 1964.

PF's colleagues as "sweethearts": See Jerry Stein, *Cincinnati Post and Times Star*, September 22, 1967.

Sylvia Chase on women walking a narrow line: See Judith Hennessee, "Some News Is Good News," *Ms.*, July 1974, 25–29.

Marya Mannes's comment about women and experience: See Marya Mannes, "Should Women Be Seen and Not Heard?" *TV Guide*, November 23, 1968, 6–9.

ABC news release about Sanders: This is dated June 1968 and is in the Hedges Collection, LAB, box 5, file 18.

Quotes by Goodman and Salant: *TV Guide*, "They Refuse to Pitch Their Curves."

Nancy Dickerson's personal life: See her memoir, *Among Those Present*.

John Dickerson's comments about appearance and women journalists: See his book *On Her Trail*, 110.

Comparing appearance of PF and Dickerson: "Ladies of the Press," *(Bridgeport) Connecticut Sunday Herald*, *TV Channels*, July 10–16, 1960.

PF and Hall as "no-frills" reporters: See Marie Torre, television column, *New York Herald Tribune*, June 6, 1961.

John Dickerson's quote from PF: Dickerson, *On Her Trail*, 152.

Sanders on women being "competitive": Telephone interview with the author.

Thank-you note from Dickerson: Nancy Dickerson to PF, April 23 (no year given), SSC, box 14, folder 12.

Trotta on PF's advice: See C-SPAN 2's *Book Notes*, Brian Lamb interviewing Liz Trotta, August 18, 1991, www.booknotes.org/Watch/20663-1/Liz+Trotta.aspx (accessed April 21, 2013).

Sanders's comments about Lisa Howard: Sanders, *Waiting for Prime Time*, 44–45.

"Nylons in the Newsroom": Gloria Steinem, "Nylons in the Newsroom," *NYT*, November 7, 1965.

Problems with women in the newsroom: Lee Graham, "Women Don't Like to Look at Women," *NYT*, May 24, 1964.

PF commenting on competing with women: She said this in a speech to the American Women in Radio and Television, September 20, 1983, New York City, transcript, LAB.

Study about women in the newsroom in 1970: See Vernon Stone, "Attitudes toward Television Newswomen," *Journal of Broadcasting* 18, no. 1 (Winter 1973-74): 49-61. This study quoted another done by Irving R. Fang and Frank G. Gerval, "A Survey of Salaries and Hiring Preferences in Television News," *Journal of Broadcasting,* 15 (Fall 1971): 421-33.

Study of women in television in 1973: This was quoted in Georgia Dullea, "The Women in TV—A Changing Image, a Growing Impact," *NYT*, September 18, 1974.

Sanders on unequal job assignments: Sanders, *Waiting for Prime Time*, 51; and "A Farewell to Some of the Firsts," *Television Quarterly*.

Salaries for women in broadcasting: Gay Talese mentioned PF's salary in his profile "Perils of Pauline," 20; Dickerson's salary was mentioned in Hosley and Yamada, *Hard News*, 84. Sanders discussed salary in *Waiting for Prime Time*, 43. The salary survey done in 1960 was described in Don C. Smith and Kenneth Harwood, "Women in Broadcasting," *Journal of Broadcasting* (Fall 1966): 339-55. Contracts between PF and the Harry Walker, Inc., speakers' bureau outline her speech income (box 27, folder 10). A letter to PF from the law firm of Hall, Dickler and Howley indicated that she had earned six thousand for a speech to IBM in April 1972, SSC, box 31, folder 6.

News managers' views about women on the air: Vernon Stone, "Attitudes toward Television Newswomen," *Journal of Broadcasting*. *Ms.* quoted a study from the University of Wisconsin with similar results. See Hennessee's story, "Some News Is Good News," *Ms.*, 27.

Jessica Savitch's view about anchorwomen: See Savitch's memoir, *Anchorwoman*, 180.

Women as anchors outside of primetime: Hennessee, "Some News Is Good News," 29.

Goodman's comment that women's skills are "underutilized": JG gave this speech to the American Women in Radio and Television, May 18, 1973, Miami Beach. A transcript of it is in the NBC History files, LOC, folder 1251.

Lesley Stahl and election night 1974: This anecdote is recounted in Tina Pieraccini, "Women and Media," in Hakanen and Wells, *Mass Media and Society*, 547.

Goodman on the PF-Dickerson-Saarinen success: John Horn, "The Ladies Arrive in Force," *New York Herald Tribune*, June 20, 1965.

"No place for broads": Savitch, back cover, *Anchorwoman*.

PF on coming a long, long way: She said this in a speech at De Anza College, Cupertino CA, undated but believed to have been given in 1976, SSC, box 23, folder 1.

Anna Quindlen on Charlotte Curtis's advice: Quindlen, *Lots of Candles, Plenty of Cake*, 47–48.

***Open Mind* with PF and Friedan:** A transcript of the show dated 1963 (no month and year) is in SSC, box 13, folder 4.

Complacency of some women: PF discussed this during the YWCA awards dinner in Philadelphia, December 29, 1969, SSC, box 24, folder 6.

Women as different from men: Mannes, *TV Guide*, 10.

Special edition of *Today*: An audiotape of this show that aired on August 26, 1970, is in SSC, box 56 (no folder). A transcript of PF's commentary about women is in SSC, box 11, folder 3.

Words of James Stephens: PF often quoted the poet in speeches. See, e.g., a speech she gave at De Anza College, undated but delivered in 1976. SSC, box 23, folder 1.

Interview with Mrs. Khrushchev: A transcript of this August 1, 1963, interview is in SSC, box 10, folder 3.

Contract for *Ten First Ladies of the World*: This is in SSC, box 36, folder 6. The book was published by Meredith Press in New York in 1967.

Book reviews of *Ten First Ladies of the World*: See *Library Journal*, September 15, 1967, 3, 212; and *Library Journal*, April 15, 1967, 1, 615. See also "World's First Ladies," *Los Angeles Examiner*, September 3, 1967; Nancy Joy, "First Ladies: How They Fare," *Raleigh News and Observer*, July 24, 1967; Anne Yetter, "Wives of Famous Men," *Providence Journal*, July 19, 1967; and Lee Leavengood, *Tampa Tribune* (undated). Copies of these reviews, with the exception of the capsulized ones in *Library Journal*, are found in SSC, box 6, folder 36.

PF's interview with American University: A recording of the interview called "Alumni Alert" from American University, dated February 1970, is in SSC box 56 (no folder).

11. GOOD NEWS, BAD NEWS, AND AGNEWS

Epigraph: Letter, Howard McCauley to "the President, NBC," et al., June 9, 1972, SSC, box 31, folder 5.

Statistics about viewership: JG offered these figures during a speech of the eleventh annual KMTV Television Public Service Awards, Omaha, January 27, 1969. Transcript is in NBC History Files, LOC, folder 31.

Trotta on the shift triggered by Huntley's retirement: Trotta, *Fighting for Air*, 205.

NBC's task in replacing Huntley and ABC's rise with the hiring of Harry Reasoner: See Matusow, *Evening Stars*, 162–63.

CBS outpacing NBC with Cronkite and Kuralt: Brinkley, *Cronkite*, 364.

Reuven Frank on media and Vietnam: Interview with Frank by Brian Lamb on C-SPAN 2's *Booknotes*, September 15, 1991, www.booknotes.org/21239-1/Reuven+Frank.aspx.

Coverage of Vietnam by a new breed of reporter: Matusow, *Evening Stars*, 151-53.

Cronkite's historic broadcast about Vietnam: Matusow, *Evening Stars*, 152-53; and Brinkley, *Cronkite*, 377-79.

Reaction to broadcast "seismic" and Johnson acknowledging he lost the nation: Brinkley, *Cronkite*, 379.

Liz Trotta on "turning point" in broadcasting: Liz Trotta said in *Fighting for Air* that Cronkite "planted . . . seed" of partiality in broadcasting (65). During a 1991 interview she said he "nudged" the line of objectivity. See C-SPAN 2's *Book Notes*, August 18, 1991, www.booknotes.org/Watch/20663-1/Liz+Trotta.aspx.

Vietnam as the "living room war": Altschuler and Grossvogel discussed this in *Changing Channels*, 170.

Goodman's comments about blaming the messenger: He said this in the Omaha speech, January 27, 1969.

Details of the Fairness Doctrine: See, e.g., Edward Bliss's history of broadcasting, *Now the News*, 423-33.

Nixon's relationship with the press "radioactive": Brinkley, *Cronkite*, 441.

Nixon and CBS: In *Cronkite* Brinkley talked about the role of CBS in the Watergate story, 466.

Johnson's early affection toward Cronkite: Brinkley, *Cronkite*, 287.

Goodman's recollections of Johnson and the press: Interview appeared in *Television Digest and Consumer Electronics* 19, no. 2, May 14, 1979, 20.

Chancellor's comments about Johnson: Transcript, John Chancellor OHist Interview 1, April 25, 1969, by Dorothy Pierce McSweeny, Internet Copy, LBJ Library.

McGruder's plan: Kutler, *Wars of Watergate*, 182.

Conversation between Goodman and Johnson: Recording of telephone conversation between LBJ and JG, June 21, 1967, 9:50 a.m., citation no. 11910, Recordings and Transcripts of Conversations and Meetings, LBJ Library.

NYT coverage of the Johnson-Kosygin meeting: See Peter Grose, "Gromyko Meets with Rusk Here," *NYT*, June 22, 1967; and Max Frankel, "Halfway Point: Choice Is Compromise—School's President's Home to Be Site," *NYT*, June 23, 1967; and Max Frankel, "A Cordial Session: But There Is No Sign of Substantive Gains on Major Issues," *NYT*, June 24, 1967.

Goodman's complimentary memo: JG to PF, June 19, 1967, SSC, box 20, folder 12.

PF's afternoon at the White House: She wrote about this in detail in a memo to WM, January 27, 1964, SSC, box 14, folder 13.

Goodman's speeches: Transcripts of many of these are available in the NBC History Files, LOC; some NBC news releases summarizing those speeches are available in the Julian Goodman Collection at the University of Kentucky, box 1, folders 1, 6, 7, and 8.

PF on the UN and "mature nations": She said this in the speech at Ohio University, Athens, on July 26, 1965, SSC, box 24, folder 2.

PF's Town Hall speech: This event was held in Fresno CA on January 19, 1966, SSC, box 3, folder 24.

PF on the disregard for civilian deaths: She said this in her speech to the Assembly of Delphian Chapters.

Soldier who had body counts on his wall: PF discussed this during a speech at the Westchester Country Club, Rye NY, on April 22, 1970, SSC, box 24, folder 7.

Cost per person of the war: PF discussed this at a Savings Bond Luncheon, New York City, April 14, 1970, SSC, box 24, folder 7.

Kissinger zoo story: PF related this during a speech to the Iowa Veterinary Medical Association, Des Moines, January 24, 1978, SSC, box 26, folder 1.

Nixon's snub of the UN during the anniversary: PF related this anecdote during a speech at Barat College, Lake Forest IL, on February 17, 1971, SSC, box 24, folder 8.

"Good news and Agnews": PF told this anecdote during the Ohio University speech.

"Big Brother Spiro": PF gave the former vice president that nickname during a speech at the Haas Symposium, University of Washington, April 18, 1977, SSC, box 25, folder 7.

Address to AARP members: PF addressed the St. Louis chapter of the American Association for Retired Persons in 1973 (specific date unknown), SSC, box 25, folder 2.

PF's San Diego speech: She gave this on June 9, 1972. A transcript is in SSC, box 25, folder 7. The letter from Howard McCauley to the president of NBC, Ronald Reagan, and others is dated June 9, 1972, and is in SSC, box 31 folder 5. The letter from Stanley Price of Piedmont CA, is dated June 27, 1972; the letter from Beatrice Blinkhorn of China Lake CA, to PF is dated June 12, 1972; the letter from Mrs. Douglas Barker of La Mesa CA, is dated June 9, 1972. The letter from acting president Donald Holman to PF is dated June 21, 1972, and the letter from Dorothy Holman to PF is dated June 21, 1972. All are in box 31, folder 5.

Letter from NBC corporate official: Letter, Harold Queen to Howard McCauley, June 20, 1972, SSC, box 31, folder 5.

PF "simplistic": Interview by the author with CC, April 6, 2013, Evanston IL.

Television correspondents as stars: McGee said this in an interview with Peter Benchley, "He Never Carried a Pencil," *TV Guide*, June 25, 1966, 14–16.

***Dallas Morning News* article about opinion:** This appeared in the *Dallas Morning News* television tabloid, *TV Channels*, June 19–25, 1960.

Sanders and "skittish" network officials: Sanders and Rock, *Waiting for Prime Time*, 45.

Goodman on government interference in broadcasting: Some of this was quoted in an NBC news release dated February 19, 1966, in NBC History files, LOC, Washington DC, folder 1249.

Valeriani on the atmosphere at NBC: Interview by the author with Richard Valieriani, telephone, November 12, 2012.

Trotta on NBC's respect for correspondents and the atmosphere of the network: Trotta, *Fighting for Air*, 27, 44.

Utley on correspondents offering opinion: Telephone interview by the author with Garrick Utley, November 16, 2012.

McGee on networks being "responsible": Benchley, "He Never Carried a Pencil," *TV Guide*, 16.

Zelnick on correspondents offering opinion: Telephone interview by the author with Bob Zelnick, November 14, 2012.

Notes from PF to CR: She wrote the cordial note on August 12, 1968; the notes from her California trip were written on May 4 and May 6, 1969. All are in SSC, box 39, folder 5.

PF's calendar marking off Nixon's term: This was discussed in interviews with the author by Dick Robbins, July 9, 2012, and Ann Stevens, August 16, 2012, both by telephone.

Background of CR and details of the wedding: Details about attendees and ceremony were provided in interviews by the author with Dick Robbins and Ann Stevens. CC noted that wedding was not as simple as FF had hoped in an email message to the author on August 29, 2013. Robbins and Stevens also noted that PF and CR had a calendar marking off the days of Nixon's term.

PF's reports about the Mideast war and Nasser's death: Scripts of the Mideast war broadcast, August 25, 1970, and of the news of Nasser's death, September 28, 1970, are in SSC, box 14, folder 1.

PF's broadcast about U Thant retirement: This is dated September 20, 1971, and is in SSC, box 14, folder 1.

U Thant's interest in journalists: UN release about U Thant's pleas for the release and safety of captured journalists dated September 3, 1979, SSC, box 15, folder 5.

U Thant on an increasingly dangerous world: U Thant said this often in speeches. PF quoted him during his last address to the General Assembly in the September 20, 1971, broadcast about his retirement.

Details of the Westport house: Interviews by the author with Robbins, Stevens, and Cole. CR described it in a letter to his son, Dick, and daughter-in-law, Ann, and to Helen and Fred Brabook in letters sent to them on June 2, 1971, SSC, box 39, folder 1.

Congratulatory cards and telegrams: The note from Kalber is dated April 29, 1969; from "Barbara Walters Guber," April 7, 1969. Both are in SSC, box 39, folder 3.

PF on how meeting Robbins was worth the "heartbreak": She said this in an interview broadcast for American University alumni, "Alumni Alert," which aired in February 1970. An audio copy is available in SSC, box 58.

PF "angry" that the UN had not lived up to its goals: Interview by the author with CC, December 9, 2012.

Details about PF's accident: NBC issued a news release on this on December 5, 1971, SSC, box 39, folder 5.

12. FULL CIRCLE

Epigraph: Newman wrote this message in a congratulatory note to PF after she received a top award from the American Women in Radio and Television. It is dated May 25, 1977, and is in SSC, box 44, folder 5.

George Bush get-well note: George H. W. Bush to PF, December 7, 1971. This note is in the possession of CC.

Note from Walters: Barbara Walters to PF, undated, SSC, box 39, folder 5.

Note from Munn: Bruce Munn to PF, December 7, 1971, SSC, box 39, folder 5.

Get-well wishes from Wald and Goodman: These are undated and are in SSC, box 39, folder 5.

Pennsylvania award: This was given to PF in 1967. Programs from these award ceremonies are in SSC, box 44, folder 13.

Well-known women and the White House invitation: David Gergen to Dave Parker, May 3, 1972, Prominent Female File, box 163, Nixon Presidential Library, www.nixonlibrary.gov (accessed November 1, 2012).

PF having it all: She said this in an interview with Jean Sprain Wilson, "A Low-Keyed Voice for Peace," *Detroit Free Press*, September 10, 1969.

CR as avid sailor and the Robbinses' daily life: This was discussed in an interview by the author with Ann Stevens, August 16, 2012, and in an interview by the author with CC, April 6, 2013, Evanston IL.

Note about Trotta's views about flying: Note PF to CR, May 6, 1969, SSC, box 39, folder 5.

The home in Westport and PF's dogs: Interviews by the author with Stevens and CC.

Lesley Stahl on turning forty-two: Stahl's memoir, *Reporting Live*, 71.

Holton on PF's role at NBC: Holton wrote this shortly after PF's death. See Jim Holton, "Not for Today's Hucksters," *Reading (PA) Eagle*, May 19, 1990.

PF asked to serve as an American University trustee: Letter, George H. Williams to PF, September 28, 1973, SSC, box 20, folder 12.

PF as "refined": Holton, "Not for Today's Hucksters."

PF learning she was retiring: James Brown, "Pauline Frederick: Back on the Beat," *Los Angeles Times*, April 7, 1979.

NYT item about PF's retirement: Les Brown, "FCC Rules Give Networks More Program Time," *NYT*, January 26, 1974.

Congratulatory note from Ziegler: Ron Ziegler to PF, January 31, 1974, SSC, box 38, folder 13. PF criticized the spelling of the note in a speech to the Mortar Board Society (city unknown), March 29, 1980, SSC, box 26, folder 2.

PF on Stanton's retirement: Brown, "Pauline Frederick: Back on the Beat."

Retirement as "low point": See, e.g., Claudia Waterloo, "Pauline Frederick Fought Sex Bias, Avoided Retirement," *Des Moines Register*, January 25, 1978.

Malaise at NBC: Matusow, *Evening Stars*, 243–45.

Background of Scali's remarks: See Scali's obituary, Lawrence Van Gelder, "John A. Scali, 77, ABC Reporter Who Helped Ease Missile Crisis," *NYT*, October 10, 1995.

Declaration of Interdependence: PF first mentioned this during a speech at Wayne State University in Detroit on December 10, 1974, SSC, box 39, folder 5. See also letter, CR to President Gerald Ford, October 17, 1974, SSC, box 38, folder 5.

Letters to senators: See PF's letter to Stuart Symington, December 11, 1974; her letter to Charles Percy, December 10, 1974; and her letter to Lowell Weicker, December 10, 1974. Weicker responded to PF in a letter dated January 8, 1975; Abraham Ribicoff responded in a letter to PF on December 19, 1974. All letters are in SSC, box 38, folder 5.

Weaver on getting all the awards: See memo, Sylvester "Pat" Weaver to PF, undated, SSC, box 43, folder 10.

Details about the 1975 Deadline Club award: *Quill*, June 1975, 35.

United Nations Association Award: The program for this award is in SSC, box 21, folder 13.

NPR as an "upstart": PF talked about her being hired there in James Brown, "Pauline Frederick Back on the Beat," *Los Angeles Times*, April 8, 1979.

Birth of NPR: See, e.g., "Public Radio Perks Up," *Newsweek*, March 12, 1979, 84–85; and NPR, "Overview and History," www.npr.org/about-npr/192827079/overview-and-history (accessed June 7, 2013).

PF fearing "sitting around": Brown, "Pauline Frederick Back on the Beat."

NPR seeking experienced newscaster: Interview by the author with Bob Zelnick, November 14, 2012.

NPR contract: A copy of this contract, from C. Robert Zelnick to PF, is dated September 11, 1975, and is in SSC, box 20, folder 9.

PF's duties at NPR: See memo, Josh Darsa to PF, undated, SSC, box 20, folder 10.

PF as a seasoned professional: Interview by the author with Bob Zelnick.

PF's physical fortitude: Holton, "Not for Today's Hucksters."

Praise from Russell: See memo, Jim Russell to PF, July 1975, SSC, box 18, folder 6.

PF acknowledging that she earned less than men: See, e.g., Brown, "Pauline Frederick Back on the Beat."

PF asking for a raise: Memo, PF to James Russell, May 26, 1976, SSC, box 20, folder 9. A note from Russell giving her the raise is in the same folder.

PF as being available for *Meet the Press*: See letter, PF to Lawrence Spivak, September 12, 1975. Spivak's response is dated September 18, 1975. Both are in SSC, box 13, folder 1.

PF's 1977 NPR contract: The contract, dated January 1977, is in SSC, box 20, folder 9.

PF's panel participation: Nora Taylor, "Off Camera There's a Tense Countdown," *Christian Science Monitor*, August 5, 1977. The Kennedy Center panel took place on November 19, 1978.

PF's scoops for NPR: NPR issued news releases about several of these stories. The release about the interview with Chaim Herzog is dated March 28, 1978, SSC, box 18, folder 6; an Associated Press story by Barry Schweid dated November 4, 1977, described the interview she did with Donald B. Sole, SSC, box 18, folder 6.

PF's apprehension about the debates: See Marcia Norman, "A First-Hand Report on the Great Debate," *Westport (CT) News*, October 13, 1976.

Congratulatory notes and telegrams about the debate: These are in SSC, box 20, folder 1.

PF as self-described "traffic cop": She said this in a speech, "The Influence of Women on Foreign Affairs," 1977 (specific date and location unknown). Transcript is in SSC, box 25, folder 7.

PF's debate outfit: Anthony Mancini, "Daily Close-Up: the Lady in the Debate," *New York Post*, October 6, 1976.

Ford-Carter debate: Audio of the debate is available at the Paley Center for Media, New York City: www.paleycenter.org/collection/item/?q=Ford-carter+debate&p=1&item=t78:0800 (accessed at the museum on May 10, 2013).

Telling the president to shut up: PF spoke of this in her speech "The Influence of Women in Foreign Affairs" on January 24, 1945, at De Anza College in Cupertino CA. Transcript of this is in SSC, box 35, folder 3.

Frankel's reaction to Ford's gaffe: Max Frankel described this in his memoir, *Max Frankel*, 228–29.

Newspaper coverage of Ford's erroneous comment: These stories were published on October 7, 1976. See Jack Germond, "Debate Bolsters Carter as Ford Slips on Soviets," *Washington Star*; Bernard Gwertzman, "Ford Denies Moscow Dominates East Europe; Carter Rebuts Him," NYT; and Clyde Haberman, "Carter Won in Most Polls," *New York Post*.

Congratulatory messages: Memos, Bob Zelnick to PF and James Russell to PF, both dated October 7, 1976, both in SSC, box 18, folder 6. Helen Cowles's note is dated October 4, 1976, and is in SSC, box 20, folder 2.

News of the debate postmortem: This was described in "News Beat," *Washington Star*, October 9, 1976.

Success of the debates: "Just How Great Were Those 'Great Debates?'" *Broadcasting*, January 3, 1977, 54–58.

"Hollywoodization" of news: PF spoke of this often after she retired, in speeches and to personal friends and relatives. See, e.g., her speech "The Influence of Women in Foreign Affairs"; and a talk she gave to B'nai B'rith Women of Columbus OH, November 16, 1976, SSC, box 23, folder 14.

Connecticut Public Radio press release: This is dated September 29, 1978, and is in SSC, box 44, folder 8.

Seventieth birthday party: The guest list, cards, notes, and poems are in SSC, box 41, folder 5. The note from Waldheim is dated October 10, 1978.

Carter's policy contradictions: PF often pointed them out. See, e.g., transcripts of speeches she made at the University of Alabama, June 13, 1979, SSC, box 26, folder 3; and at Claremont Men's College, May 21, 1978, box 26, folder 1.

Congratulatory notes on the AWRT award: These notes from JG, Richard Wald, David C. Adams, Reuven Frank, David Adams, Edwin Newman, and Jane Barton, and the note from Jody Powell to AWRT, are in SSC, box 44, folder 5.

13. OUT OF THE BOX

Epigraph: Joe Dembo, "Pauline Frederick: Breaking the Sex Barrier," *Long Beach (CA) Independent*, May 24, 1990.

PF's reduced workload at NPR: There is evidence of this in her NPR contract dated November 25, 1980, SSC, box 20, folder 12.

PF's letter to American University president: Letter, PF to Richard Berendzen, December 12, 1981, SSC, box 20, folder 12.

PF's reaction to being named trustee emerita: She noted how pleased she was in a letter to James K. Matthews, April 26, 1982, SSC, box 20, folder 12.

CR's op-ed piece: Robbins, "Atoms for Peace—30 Years Later," *Christian Science Monitor*, March 1, 1984. For background on the Atoms for Peace speech, see Eisenhower Presidential Library and Archive website, www.eisenhowerarchives .gov/research/online_documents/atoms_for_peace.html (accessed June 2, 2013).

PF on *Firing Line*: A transcript of the *Firing Line* show, taped in New York City on September 4, 1974, and broadcast four days later, is available at the Hoover Institution Library, Stanford University, www.hoover.org/library- and-archives (accessed June 19, 2013).

PF on the meaning of a "free press": She was quoted in "SDX Marks Anniversary with Essays on Free Press," *Broadcasting*, February 4, 1985, 67.

NBC *Nightly News* on Paul White Award: This was broadcast on July 6, 1980. A recording of it is available at the Vanderbilt TV News Archive.

CR's letter about PF's award and health: Letter, CR to Phyllis and Howard Nason, August 20, 1980, SSC, box 39, folder 1.

Details of Radio Television News Directors Association (RTNDA) gala in Florida: *Broadcasting*, July 7, 1980, 70.

PF's speech at RTNDA ceremony: Most of this was taken from the RTNDA newsletter, December 18, 1980, in SSC box 44, folder 9. Some was taken from a partial transcript of the speech in SSC, box 44, folder 7.

PF's osteoporosis: Interview by the author with Ann Stevens, August 16, 2012.

PF and CR's problems taking care of their home: Interview by the author with CC, December 9, 2012.

PF's discussions of world events in social situations: Interviews by the author with Stevens; Cole; and Dick Robbins, July 9, 2012, by telephone.

PF's last days: Interviews by the author with CC and Stevens.

PF's burial service: Interview by the author with CC.

PF as no "movement leader": Shirley-Anne Owden, "Pauline Frederick Recalls Life in a Man's Field," *Palo Alto Times*, January 27, 1975.

PF acknowledging she could not "have it all": Mary-Ann Bendel, "'I Was Told a Woman's Voice Had No Authority,'" *USA Today*, January 14, 1985.

PF on helping other women: American University "Alumni Alert," conducted by Leonore Sylvan, February 1970. An audio recording of this is available at SSC.

Woodruff's comments: See "Woodruff Says One Barrier Women Still Have to Overcome Is Age," *Broadcasting*, June 14, 1984, 43.

Amanpour similar to PF: Dusty Saunders, "Amanpour Follows Frederick as a Trailblazer," *Rocky Mountain News*, July 2, 1996.

PF no huckster: See Jim Holton, "Pauline Frederick: Not for Today's Hucksters," *Reading (PA) Eagle*, May 19, 1990.

PF's opinion of the presidents: Kennedy: She often mentioned what she thought was Kennedy's shabby treatment of Adlai Stevenson. See, e.g., Judy Flander, "Pauline: Still Dean of the Newsroom," *Washington Star*, April 29 1977. Eisenhower: See James Brown, "Pauline Frederick: Back on the Beat," *Los Angeles Times*, April 7, 1979. Nixon: Mary Lou Loper, "Newswomen Assess Nixon's 100 Days," *Los Angeles Times*,

May 25, 1969. Johnson: email message CC to the author, August 29, 2013. Carter: See Waterloo, "Pauline Frederick Fought Sex Bias."

PF's opinion of UN ambassadors: She summarized her views of several diplomats in Bendel, "'I Was Told a Woman's Voice Had No Authority.'" She talked about Cyrus Vance in Waterloo, "Pauline Frederick Fought Sex Bias."

The UN as a "human" institution: " Hottelet is quoted in James Brooke, "UN Notes: Switching Sides: Reporter Joins UN Mission," *NYT*, October 3, 1985.

PF addressing UN Day in Chicago: Her speech, titled "The Heresy of Independence in an Interdependent World," was given on October 24, 1974. A transcript is in SSC, box 25, folder 3.

SELECTED BIBLIOGRAPHY

Altschuler, Glenn C., and David I. Grossvogel. *Changing Channels: America in TV Guide*. Urbana: University of Illinois Press, 1992.

Beasley, Maurine. *Women of the Washington Press: Politics, Prejudice, and Persistence*. Evanston IL: Northwestern University Press, 2012.

Beasley, Maurine H., and Sheila J. Gibbons. *Taking Their Place: A Documentary History of Women in Journalism*. 2nd ed. State College PA: Strata Publishing, 2003.

Berg, A. Scott. *Wilson*. New York: Penguin Group, 2013.

Bliss, Edward, Jr. *Now the News: The Story of Broadcast Journalism*. New York: Columbia University Press, 1991.

———, ed. *In Search of Light: The Broadcasts of Edward R. Murrow, 1938–1961*. New York: Knopf, 1967.

Brinkley, Douglas. *Cronkite*. New York: HarperCollins, 2012.

Caro, Robert. *The Years of Lyndon Johnson: The Passage of Power*. New York: Knopf, 2012.

Creedon, Pamela J., and Judith Cramer. *Women in Mass Communication*. 3rd ed. Thousand Oaks CA: Sage Publications, 2007.

Curtin, Michael. *Redeeming the Wasteland: Television Documentary and Cold War Politics*. New Brunswick NJ: Rutgers University Press, 1995.

Daniel, Douglass K. *Harry Reasoner: A Life in the News*. Austin: University of Texas Press, 2007.

Dickerson, John. *On Her Trail: My Mother, Nancy Dickerson TV News' First Woman Star*. New York: Simon & Schuster, 2006.

Dickerson, Nancy. *Among Those Present*. New York: Random House, 1976.

Edwards, Julia. *Women of the World: The Great Foreign Correspondents*. Boston: Houghton Mifflin, 1973.

Fang, Irving E. *Those Radio Commentators!* Ames: Iowa State University Press, 1977.

Frank, Reuven. *Out of Thin Air: The Brief Wonderful World of Network News*. New York: Simon & Schuster, 1991.

Frankel, Max. *Times of My Life and My Life with the Times*. New York: Delta Publishing, 1999.

Frederick, Pauline. *Ten First Ladies of the World*. New York: Meredith Press, 1967.

Fried, Richard. *Nightmare in Red: The McCarthy Era in Perspective*. New York: Oxford University Press, 1990.

Gellhorn, Martha. *The Face of War*. New York: Atlantic Monthly Press, 1988.

Graham, Katharine. *Personal History*. New York: Vintage Books, 1998.

Hakanen Ernest A., and Alan Wells, eds. *Mass Media and Society*. Greenwich CT: Ablex Publishing Corp., 1997.

Halberstam, David. *The Fifties*. New York: Fawcett Columbine, 1993.

———. *The Powers That Be*. New York: Knopf, 1979.

Hallock, Steve. *The Press March to War*. New York: Peter Lang, 2012.

Hartmann, Susan M. *Not June Cleaver: Women and Gender in Postwar America, 1945-1960*. Philadelphia: Temple University Press, 1994.

Horowitz, Daniel. *Betty Friedan and the Making of the Feminine Mystique: The American Left, the Cold War, and Modern Feminism*. Amherst: University of Massachusetts Press, 1998.

Hosley, David H., and Gayle K. Yamada. *Hard News: Women in Broadcast Journalism*. New York: Greenwood Press, 1987.

Kisseloff, Jeff. *The Box: An Oral History of Television, 1920-1961*. New York: Viking, 1995.

Kutler, Stanley. *Wars of Watergate*. New York: Knopf, 1990.

Lipsey, Roger, *Hammarskjöld: A Life*. Ann Arbor: University of Michigan Press, 2013.

Marlane, Judith. *Women in Television News Revisited*. Austin: University of Texas Press, 1999.

Martin, John Bartlow. *Adlai Stevenson and the World: The Life of Adlai E. Stevenson*. Garden City NY: Doubleday, 1977.

Marzolf, Marion. *Up from the Footnote*. New York: Hastings House, 1977.

Mascaro, Tom. *Into the Fray: How NBC's Washington Documentary Unit Reinvented the News*. Washington DC: Potomac Press, 2012.

Matusow, Barbara. *The Evening Stars: The Making of the Network News Anchor*. Boston: Houghton Mifflin, 1983.

Mills, Kay. *A Place in the News: From the Women's Pages to the Front Page*. New York: Dodd, Mead, 1988.

Mires, Charlene. *Capital of the World*. New York: New York University Press, 2013.

Mudd, Roger. *The Place to Be: Washington, CBS, and the Glory Days of Television News*. New York: PublicAffairs, 2008.

Nicholson June O., Pamela J. Creedon, Wanda S. Lloyd, and Pamela J. Johnson.

The Edge of Change: Women in the 21st Century Press. Urbana: University of Illinois Press, 2009.

O'Dell Cary. *Women Pioneers in Television*. London: McFarland & Co., 1997.

O'Sullivan Christopher D. *The United Nations: A Concise History*. Malabar FL: Krieger Publishing Co., 2005.

Quindlen Anna. *Lots of Candles, Plenty of Cake*. New York: Random House, 2012.

Quinn, Sally. *We're Going to Make You a Star*. New York: Simon & Schuster, 1975.

Robertson, Nan. *The Girls in the Balcony: Men, Women, and the New York Times*. New York: Random House, 1992.

Ross, Ishbel. *Ladies of the Press: The Story of Women in Journalism by an Insider*. New York: Harper & Bros., 1936.

Sanders, Marion K. *Dorothy Thompson: A Legend in Her Time*. Boston: Houghton Mifflin, 1973.

Sanders Marlene, and Marcia Rock. *Waiting for Prime Time: The Women of Television News*. Urbana: University of Illinois Press, 1994.

Savitch, Jessica. *Anchorwoman*. New York: Putnam, 1982.

Sloan, William David, and James Glen Stovall, eds. *The Media in America: A History*. 6th ed. Northport AL: Vision Press, 2005.

Stahl, Lesley. *Reporting Live*. New York: Simon & Schuster, 1999.

Thorpe, Deryck. *Dag Hammarskjöld: Man of Peace*. Devon, Ilfracombe UK: Arthur H. Stockwell, 1969.

Tozier, Carolyn. "Pauline Frederick and the Rise of Network Television News, 1948–1960." Ph.D. diss., University of Maryland, 1995.

Trotta, Liz. *Fighting for Air: In the Trenches with Television News*. New York: Simon & Schuster, 1991.

Urquhart, Brian. *Hammarskjöld*. New York: Knopf, 1972.

Wagner, Lilya. *Women War Correspondents of World War II*. New York: Greenwood Press, 1989.

Walters, Barbara. *Audition*. New York: Knopf, 2008.

Ware, Susan. *It's One O'Clock and Here Is Mary Margaret McBride: A Radio Biography*. New York: New York University Press, 2005.

Whitt, Jan. *Women in American Journalism*. Urbana: University of Illinois Press, 2008.

Williams, Susan. *Who Killed Hammarskjöld? The UN, the Cold War and White Supremacy in Africa*. New York: Oxford University Press, 2012.

INDEX

appearance: Frederick's self-consciousness of, 9, 10, 11; importance of, in television, 5, 76–80, 82, 139, 168, 199, 203, 204–5, 206, 255; of politicians, 82; *vs.* credibility, 204; women judged by, 76, 79, 199, 203, 204–5, 206, 265

Arab-Israel War, 201, 225

arms race, 107, 181, 256–57; RCA's involvement in, 145; Vietnam War and, 193

As He Saw It (Roosevelt), 51–52

Ashton, Ruth, 88

Asman, Robert, 144, 191

Aswan High Dam, 134

atabrine poisoning, 49

"Atomic Attack" (*Motorola Television Hour*), 106, 289n

Atomic Industrial Forum, 219

"Atoms for Peace" speech (Eisenhower), 261

Audience Research Institute, 85–86

audiences: and gender of broadcaster, 211–12; responsibility of, 124–25

Auschwitz, Pope John Paul II's visit to, 257

Austin, Warren, 96, 97, 110

authority and voice, 6, 24, 25, 57, 63, 203–4, 209–10, 265

Ball, George, 153–54

Bandaranaike, Sirimavo, 216

Barat College, speech to, 232

Barton, Jane, 258–59

Baukhage, Hilmar Robert (H. R.), 23, 24–25, 31, 39, 51, 124; career of, 24; critiquing Frederick's broadcasting style, 45; and formation of UN, 32; hiring Frederick as editorial assistant, 25; on *News and Views*, 86; paternalism of, 33

Bay of Pigs, 164–66, 182, 267, 298n

Belgium, Congo threatened by, 2, 175

Benchley, Peter, 235–36

Benét, Stephen Vincent, 108

Benson, Lucy Wilson, 215

Berlin Airlift, 88–90

Bernstein, Kenneth, 155, 156

Berreta, Tomás, 58

Bevin, Ernest, 60

Bidault, Georges, 60

Big Four conference, 60

Bliss, Edward, Jr., 142; *And Now the News*, 53, 57

blogging, 75–76

body counts, victory measured by, 228

Boland, Frederick, 182

Bombeck, Erma, 154

Brabrook, Helen, 23

Brad Crandall Show (radio show), 151

Breckinridge, Mary Marvin, 63

Bricker, John W., 110

Bricker amendment, 110

Brinkley, David, 140, 142, 152, 220

Brinkley, Douglas, 221

broadcasting: long work hours of, 1, 105, 111–12, 197; in New York City, 50; and power of broadcaster, 101; speaking style and, 63; as a specialty, 24, 30; technological advances and, 53, 138, 140, 199

Broadcasting (magazine), 74

broadcasting, women in, 64–65, 87–88, 203–5, 243, 257, 258, 265; achieving parity with men, 65, 213–14; assigned "women's" stories, 210–11; behind the scenes, 88; competing with men, 208–9; competition between, 207, 209; Frederick praised by, 265; held back by executives, 56, 208, 210–12, 213; increase in, 195, 210; need for more, 29, 202; networks ambivalent about, 54–55; as newsworthy, 202–3; pay inequities

of, 211; and physical appearance, 76,
79, 199, 203, 204–5, 206, 265; public
response to, 8, 209, 210; in radio
industry, 28, 29, 45; relationships
among, 207–8; as unfeminine, 210;
views of, on war, 50
Brokaw, Tom, on Frederick, 5, 137, 155
Brooks, Angie, 216
Buckley, William F., 261–62
Bush, George H. W., 155, 158, 192, 240;
Frederick on, 268
byline, addictive quality of, 15
Byrnes, James, 60

Cambodia, U.S. invasion of, 189–91
capitalism, 120
career and marriage, as dichotomy, 11,
12, 168, 169, 170, 264
Caro, Robert, 191
Carpenter, Liz, 226
Carr Van Anda journalism award, 229
Carter, Jimmy, 251, 252–54, 256–57;
Frederick on, 267
Castro, Fidel, 162–64
censors, 48
Chancellor, John, 220, 223
Charles Pearson Lecture Management
Agency, 65–66
Chase, Sylvia, 204
Chester, Giraud, 210
Chiang Kai-shek, 35, 192
China: Frederick broadcasting from,
35–36. See also People's Republic of
China (PRC)
Chou En-lai, 116
Churchill, Randolph, 51–52
Churchill, Winston: in As He Saw It,
51–52; meeting with Franklin Delano
Roosevelt, 31–32
civilian casualties, 227–28
Coates, Charles, 185
Cohn, Roy, 133

Cold War: driven by fear, 109, 110, 133,
174, 176, 188; economic dependence
on, 109; end of colonialism and, 135,
174, 175–76; fought in UN, 177; Frederick as calming presence in, 147;
media's role in, 151–52, 225; origins
of, 88–90; and threat of nuclear war,
106, 227; UN weakened by, xix, 2–3,
67–68, 173, 182, 195, 268–69
Cole, Catharine Crowding, 4, 10, 70,
232, 256, 270, 271
Cole, Dan, 4, 232, 256
Columbia Broadcasting System (CBS),
28, 53, 220; Edward Murrow and, 55,
56; nightly newscasts on, 86, 183,
300n; as "producer's network," 235
Committee on Atomic Energy, 107
communism, spread of, 92, 133, 190. See
also Cold War
Congo, Republic of the: desirability of,
to larger nations, 178; threatened by
Belgium, 2, 175, 176, 177, 182
Conway, Mike, 75–76, 81
Cook, Joseph, 210
Le Corbusier, 123
Cordell, Ann, 44, 104–5; Frederick
discussing politics with, 119–20, 121,
133–34
Cordier, Andrew, 114, 180
Cowles, Helen, 254
"Crisis Pauline," 123
Cronkite, Walter, 140, 142, 157, 166, 191,
197, 220; influencing public opinion
on Vietnam, 221–22, 226; and Lyndon
Johnson, 223
Crotty, Burke, 82
Crowding, Catharine "Kitty," 9, 10,
11, 35, 237, 256, 270; and Frederick,
close relationship with, 69; letters
to Frederick from, 39–40; Frederick
recuperating at home of, 49; sending
care packages to Frederick, 40

Fuldheim, Dorothy, 87–88

Gallup, George, 86
Gandhi, Indira, 216
Gardella, Kay, 187
Garroway, Dave, 144
gender: appearance and, 76, 79, 199, 203, 204–5, 206, 265; barriers, 23, 55, 58, 211–12, 213–14; and news, 18, 21, 22, 28–29, 55, 64, 75, 137, 139–40, 171, 172 (*See also* "women's news")
gender-neutral byline, 23
Gergen, David, 241–42
Germany: attitudes toward, 41; division of, into two states, 90; and fraternization stories, 46–48, 280–81n; and reeducation of German youth, 41–42; and suffering of German people, 40, 41. *See also* Nuremburg trials
Gibbons, Jim, 86
GIs fraternizing with German women, 46–48, 280–81n
Gitlin, Irving, 171, 172
"glamour code," 79, 168
Glick, Marion, 88
Goering, Hermann, 45, 46, 280n
Goldberg, Arthur, 153, 267–68
Goodman, Julian, 100, 193, 197, 198, 205, 222, 241, 245, 257–58; and First Amendment rights, 222–23, 226; Lyndon Johnson and, 224–25; on need for interpretation in reporting, 224; pledging to hire more women, 213
Good Night and Good Luck (film), 100
Gornicki, Wieslaw, 150
Gould, Jack, 96–97, 100, 146
Grady, Lucretia, 29
Graham, Lee: "Women Don't Like to Look at Women," 209
Great Britain, Suez Canal and, 134, 135
Gromyko, Andrei, 187
Gross, Ben, 187

Hagy, Ruth Geri, 137
Hall, Lee, 202, 206
Hallock, Steve, 50
Hamilton, Tom, 160
Hammarskjöld, Dag: appointed UN secretary-general, 111, 113, 122; captured American pilots and, 116; and Frederick, relationship between, 125, 128–29, 136–37, 161, 181–82, 266, 274n, 293n; Frederick's private interview of, 135–36; funeral for, 179; idealism inspired by, 67; life of, 114, 115; Mideast conflicts mediated by, 134–35; *Monitor* special on, 144; mountain climbing and, 119; NBC special on, 3, 6–7, 8, 177–78, 179–80; Nobel Prize awarded to, 113; personality and leadership style of, 113–14, 115, 116–17, 119, 173–74; plane crash of, 1–2, 3, 6–7, 178–79, 269; read at Frederick's funeral, 271; relationship status of, 118; resignation demanded by USSR, 2; "sacrifice" of, 2, 177; Soviet disapproval of, 167, 176, 177; spirituality of, 114–15
Hammarskjöld: A Life (Lipsey), 114, 118, 127
Hanna, Lee, 197
Hard News (Hosley and Yamada), 1
Harrelson, Max, 160
Harrison, Bernie, 143
Harsch, Joseph, 112, 144
Hasker, Edward, 90
Headline Edition, 71
Helitzer, Morrie, 170
Helsinki Accords, 253
Herzog, Chaim, 251
Hewitt, Don, 74
Holman, Dorothy, 231–32
Holton, Jim, 161, 243, 249, 266
Hosley, David H.: *Hard News*, 1

Suez crisis, 128, 131, 134–35
Swayze, John Cameron, 74, 140–41, 142

Taft, Martha Bowers, 28–29
Talese, Gay, 62, 79, 135, 143, 167; "Perils
of Pauline," 167–71, 211
Tansill, Charles Callan, 18, 27, 51
Taylor, Maxwell D.: *Responsibility and
Response,* 158
technology: and advances in broadcasting, 53, 138, 140, 199, 219; and desire
for provocative video, 201; negative
effects of, on reporting, 264; poverty
and, 269; problems with, 81; and
resistance to change, 73–74
television, 53, 82; cost of access to, 86;
cost of production of, 72–73; cultural
importance of, 82, 219; and emphasis on appearance, 5, 76–80, 82, 139,
168, 199, 203, 204–5, 206, 255; programming interrupted for "special
reports," 95; and public opinion, 95,
133; technological advances in, 53,
138, 140, 199, 219; viewership of, 81,
85–86, 138, 139, 222, 300n
television news: and 1948 political
conventions, 71–78, 79–82, 85;
appearance of bias on, 234; blogging
compared to, 75–76; contributing to
government transparency, 100–101;
corporate sponsorship of, 138; golden
years of, 184; hiring boom of, 183;
and hour-long show, 54; immediacy
of, 96, 184–85, 222; live reporting of,
72, 73, 74, 157, 187, 191, 199; makeup
for, 76–77; more popular than newspapers, 183, 300n; nightly broadcasts
of, 86, 183, 300n; radio broadcasters
and, 74, 82; UN as, 91, 94, 96; *vs.*
radio news, 81, 141, 234
Ten First Ladies of the World (Frederick),
217–18

Tet offensive, 192
Thant, U, 182, 191, 192, 199–200;
praying with Pope Paul VI, 186;
retirement of, 238
Theta Sigma Phi, 103
Thompson, Dorothy, 21–22; as negative
role model, 21–22
"Tide of World Affairs" (column), 23
Today (TV show), 141, 157–59, 198; Bar-
bara Walters on, 196, 198, 202, 215;
Frederick on, 78, 142, 157–58, 188–91,
215–16, 241, 243; special broadcast on
women's voting, 215–16
Torre, Marie, 139, 206–7
Tozier, Carolyn, 278n
traveling, inconvenience of, 34, 38, 39
Trewhitt, Henry, 252
Trotta, Liz, 202, 207, 220, 221–22, 242;
hired by NBC, 213; on NBC culture,
235
Truman, Harry, 73, 109; Korean War
and, 92
Truman, Margaret, 52

U-2 spy plane incident, 186–87, 188
Uncle Sam's Diary (magazine), 17, 22, 23
Union of Soviet Socialist Republics
(USSR): behind on UN dues, 149–50;
Berlin Airlift and, 88–90; and Cuban
Missile Crisis, 166; Eastern Europe
dominated by, 253–54; and Helsinki
Accords, 253; Hungary attacked
by, 146; media portrayals of, 151;
obstructionism of, in UN, 150–51,
167, 200; and pledge of neutrality,
23; and vilification of Russians, 106
United Nations (UN), 59, 146, 227,
267–68; American attitudes toward,
201; beat, 91, 113, 154, 160, 201; and
Berlin Airlift, 89; charter, 130–31,
150–51, 175, 192, 199–200; declining
power of, 199, 200–201, 219, 245–46;

and decolonized countries, 174, 175, 181; dinners for visiting dignitaries, 161–62; faults in, 67, 99, 268; fingerprinting of American employees of, 110; formation of, 31, 32, 33, 98–99; Frederick assigned to cover, 60; Frederick's belief in, xix, 68, 99, 101, 107–8, 109, 261, 268; human rights championed by, 268, 269; Korean War and, 91–94; Meditation Room, 114–15, 186; move to Manhattan, 106, 123; networks' relationship to, 90–91; Nixon's disdain toward, 229; peacekeeping forces of, 175; People's Republic of China (PRC) and, 186, 192–93, 197; perceived as anti-Israel, 201; perceived as communist, 159; representing US interests, 176; Soviet obstructionism in, 150–51, 167, 200; television and, 91, 94, 96; US hostility to, 93; visited by Pope Paul VI, 185–86; voting procedures of, 246; weakened by Cold War, xix, 2–3, 67–68, 173, 182, 195, 268–69; women in, 216; world government and, 101. *See also* Hammarskjöld, Dag; Security Council (UN)

United Nations Association, 247
United Nations Children's Fund (UNICEF), 156
United Nations Correspondents Association (UNCA), 122, 160–62, 240; Castro invited to address, 162–64; Frederick as president of, 121, 149, 159–60, 161–64; Hammarskjöld invited to address, 162
United Nations Emergency Force (UNEF), 134–35
United Nations in Action (TV show), 91
"The United Nations in a World of Conflict" (Frederick), 227

United States: China and, 92, 93, 116, 192–93; criticism of, 165–66, 176, 181; and fingerprinting of UN employees, 110; government interfering in media, 110, 222–23, 226; interest of, in international relations, 113; international responsibilities of, 109–10; and media distrust of government, 221; tension with UN, 93; and UN, 110–11
United States News (magazine), 23
Urquhart, Brian, 113, 127, 128
USS Repose, 98–99
Utley, Clifton, 112
Utley, Garrick, 112, 185, 235

Vacation Time (radio show), 84
Valeriani, Richard, 234–35, 252
Vance, Cyrus, 268
Van Horn, Harriet, 166
Vanocur, Sander, 156
Velotta, Tom, 54, 75; Frederick praised by, 80–81, 125
Vietnam War, 68, 152–53, 158, 193–94, 229; American attitudes toward, 158–59; body counts as measure of victory in, 228; civilian casualties in, 227–28; cost of, in dollars, 228; culture of violence created by, 192; Frederick on, 152–53, 193, 226–29, 230–32, 239; international opinion on, 199–200; Johnson and, 152–54, 199, 200, 222; as "living-room war," 222; media and, 221–22, 226; as retaliation for Soviet aggression, 153; UN and, 68, 182–83, 195, 199, 200
Vogue (magazine) on 1948 conventions, 77
voice, female, 6, 24, 25, 57, 63, 203–4, 209–10, 265

Waiting for Primetime (Sanders), 202
Wald, Richard, 241, 258

Waldheim, Kurt, 256

Walters, Barbara, 196, 198, 202, 208; in China, 196–97; Frederick and, 237, 240; as "personality," 205–6, 212–13

war: aftermath of, 35, 36, 37, 38, 40, 41–42, 45–48, 49–50, 102–3, 227; as common enemy, 2, 108–9; imagery on television, 97–98, 100; journalists' safety in, 238; negotiation as alternative to, 101; sacrifices to prevent, 37; senselessness of, 40, 99; UN as preventive of, 31, 92, 108, 227

War Department, 34; banning women war correspondents, 33

Warren, Earl, 73

Washington Star: Frederick published in, 12, 20, 22; and "Women and Diplomacy" column, 20, 22

Watergate, 221, 223

Weaver, Sylvester "Pat," 124, 141–42, 247

Weicker, Lowell, Jr., 246

Western Newspaper Union (WNU), 32–36

Westmoreland, William, 222

Wheeler, John, 52

White House Conference on Youth, 242

Wile, Frederic William, 20

Wilson, Woodrow, 108

wives of diplomats, interviews with, 18–19, 20, 22, 216–17; radio show on, 26–27. See also *Ten First Ladies of the World* (Frederick)

Wogan, Robert, 195, 210

women: appearance and, 79, 203–5, 265; barred from being war correspondents, 33; family perceived as essential to, 169; filing lawsuits for equal treatment, 264; heads of state, 216; negotiating skills of, 216–17; as peacemakers, 215, 216–17; rights of, 204, 215, 264; sexism of, against other women, 209, 210; in top professional jobs, 27–28; voting, 28–29, 215–16. *See also* broadcasting, women in

"Women and Diplomacy" (column), 20

"Women Don't Like to Look at Women" (Graham), 209

"women's news": all news as, 25–26, 64; as domestic in orientation, 21, 24, 210–11; as society and fashion news, 21, 57, 211

Woodruff, Judy, 265

World War II: and American attitudes following, 13, 37, 38; beginning of, 30; in China, aftermath of, 35; destruction by Allies in, 40; in Europe, aftermath of, 36, 37, 38, 40, 41–42, 45–48, 49–50; Frederick covering aftermath of, xix, 5–6, 17; rebuilding after, 46; starvation following, 41; and women's hairstyles, 52

Yamada, Gayle K.: *Hard News,* 1

Zelnick, Bob, 196, 248, 249, 254

Ziegler, Ron, 244